Humanitarians
and Reformers

MACMILLAN
PROFILES

Humanitarians and Reformers

MACMILLAN LIBRARY REFERENCE USA
New York

Cover design by Berrian Design

Macmillan Library Reference USA
1633 Broadway, 7th Floor
New York, NY 10019

Manufactured in the United States of America

Printing number
1 2 3 4 5 6 7 8 9 10

ISBN: 0-02-865377-7

Library of Congress Cataloging-in-Publication Data

Humanitarians and reformers.
     p.   cm. — (Macmillan profiles ; 9)
   Includes bibliographical references (p.) and index.
   ISBN 0-02-865377-7 (hardcover : alk. paper)
   1. Social reformers Biography Dictionaries.   2. Philanthropists
Biography Dictionaries.   3. Nobel Prizes Biography Dictionaries.
4. Civil rights workers Biography Dictionaries.   5. Political
activists Biography Dictionaries.   I. Series.
HV27.H34   1999
361.7′092′2—dc21
   [B]   99-38793
                                                            CIP

Front cover clockwise from top: Paul Newman (Corbis); Susan B. Anthony (Corbis/Bettmann); Nelson Mandela (Paul Velasco; ABPL/Corbis); Martin Luther King (Corbis/Bettmann)

This paper meets the requirements of ANSI/NISO Z39.48-1992 (Permanence of Paper).

Contents

Preface

Macmillan Profiles: *Humanitarians and Reformers* is a unique reference featuring over one hundred and twenty-five articles describing international civil rights activists, antislavery reformers, human rights advocates, Nobel Peace Prize winners, and philanthropists. Macmillan Library Reference recognizes the need for reliable, accurate, and accessible reference works covering important aspects of the social studies and history curriculum. The Macmillan Profiles series can help meet that need by providing new collections of articles that were carefully written and edited for a young adult audience. Macmillan Library Reference has published a wide array of award-winning reference materials for libraries across the world. It is likely that several of the encyclopedias on the shelves in this library were published by Macmillan Reference or Charles Scribner's Sons. Twenty articles were newly written for *Humanitarians and Reformers*. Other articles were drawn from Macmillan's *Encyclopedia of African-American Culture and History*, the *Encyclopedia of the American West*, the *Encyclopedia of Latin American History and Culture*, and *The Nobel Laureates*. All extracted articles were recast and tailored for a younger audience by a team of experienced writers and editors.

In today's social studies and history curriculum, we study the wrenching social upheavals of the nineteenth and twentieth centuries. Social reformers led the way as governments were forced to face inequities and societal prejudice. The reformers profiled in this volume represent a selection of international figures, many of whom have faced severe hardship in their campaign for equality. The contributions of the humanitarians described in *Humanitarians and Reformers* have also made our world a better place. Their generous spirit and courage inspire us, professionals and students alike, to take action and make a difference. As we selected the articles for this volume, we were forced to make some difficult choices but we feel that these biographies represent a broad cross section of international humanitarians and social reformers. After long discussion and debate, we decided against career soldiers and thus did not include Menachem Begin, Mohamed Anwar El Sadat, Yitzak Rabin, Yasir Arafat, or George Marshall. The article list was refined and expanded in response to advice from a lively and generous team of librarians from school and public libraries across the United States.

Features

Humanitarians and Reformers is the ninth volume in Macmillan's Profiles Series. To add visual appeal and enhance the usefulness of the volume, the page format and backmatter were designed to include the following helpful features:

- **Time Lines:** Found throughout the text in the margins, time lines provide a quick reference source for dates and important events in the history of these humanitarians and reformers.

- **Definitions and Glossary:** Brief definitions of important terms in the main text can be found in the margins. A glossary at the end of the book provides students with an even broader list of definitions.

- **Sidebars:** Appearing in shaded boxes throughout the volume, these provocative asides relate to and amplify topics.

- **Pull Quotes:** Found throughout the text in the margins, pull quotes highlight essential facts.

- **Primary Source Documents:** A selection of primary source documents provides historical context for the biographies in the main text.

- **Ways to Help:** A list of volunteer opportunities.

- **Suggested Reading:** An extensive list of books, articles, and Web sites about the humanitarians and reformers covered in the volume will help students who want to do further research.

- **Index:** A thorough index provides thousands of additional points of entry into the work.

 # Acknowledgments

We thank our colleagues who publish the Merriam Webster Collegiate Dictionary. Definitions used in the margins and many of the glossary terms come from the distinguished Webster's Collegiate Dictionary, Tenth Edition, 1996.

The biographies herein were written by leading authorities at work in the fields of social reform, human rights, and American history. *Humanitarians and Reformers* contains over fifty-five photographs. Acknowledgments of sources for the illustrations can be found on page 409.

This work would not have been possible without the hard work and creativity of our staff. We offer our sincere thanks to all who helped create this marvelous work.

Macmillan Library Reference

Abernathy, Ralph David

MARCH 11, 1926–APRIL 17, 1990 ● CLERGYMAN AND CIVIL RIGHTS LEADER

Born in Linden, Alabama, initially among family members he was called only "David"; later, through the inspiration a teacher gave one of his sisters, the appellation "Ralph" was added. After serving in the U.S. Army during World War II, Abernathy seized the opportunity offered by the G.I. Bill of Rights and earned a B.S. degree in 1950 from Alabama State College (now Alabama State University). In 1951 he earned an M.A. in sociology from Atlanta University.

In his formative years Abernathy was deeply influenced by his hardworking father, William L. Abernathy, who was a Baptist deacon and a farmer who owned 500 acres of choice real estate. The son's admiration for his father was a major factor in his work in public life.

In 1948 Abernathy was ordained a Baptist minister. He served as pastor of the following congregations: Eastern Star Baptist Church, Demopolis, Alabama, 1950–51; First Baptist Church, Montgomery, Alabama, 1951–61; West Hunter Street Baptist Church, Atlanta, Georgia, 1961–90.

While a student at Alabama State, Abernathy had two experiences that would prepare him for his later role as a civil rights leader: he was urged to contribute to the

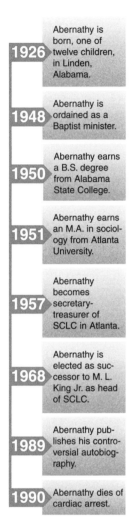

1926 — Abernathy is born, one of twelve children, in Linden, Alabama.

1948 — Abernathy is ordained as a Baptist minister.

1950 — Abernathy earns a B.S. degree from Alabama State College.

1951 — Abernathy earns an M.A. in sociology from Atlanta University.

1957 — Abernathy becomes secretary-treasurer of SCLC in Atlanta.

1968 — Abernathy is elected as successor to M. L. King Jr. as head of SCLC.

1989 — Abernathy publishes his controversial autobiography.

1990 — Abernathy dies of cardiac arrest.

boycott: to refuse to deal with a person, store, or organization.

freedom struggle of African Americans by such professors as J. E. Pierce and Emma Payne Howard, and, as president of the student council, he led two campus protests, for improved cafeteria services and dormitory conditions. Due to his dignified protests, Abernathy won the respect of the institution's administration. As a result, in 1951 he returned to his alma mater to become dean of men.

While pastor of First Baptist, he became a close friend of Dexter Avenue Baptist Church's courageous pastor Vernon Johns. Johns, as an older, seasoned pulpiteer, displayed extraordinary boldness in his personal defiance of Montgomery's oppressive Jim Crow climate.

When Johns's ties with Dexter were severed, Abernathy developed an even closer friendship with his successor, Martin Luther King Jr. The two young pastors' families became intertwined in a fast friendship that prompted alternating dinners between the two households. At these social meetings numerous conversations were held that frequently centered around civil rights.

In 1955 the two friends' ideas were propelled into action by the arrest of Rosa Parks, a black seamstress. After a long day of toil, Parks refused to yield her seat on a public bus for a white passenger who boarded after her. This refusal by Parks was in violation of the city's segregationist laws. Her action was not the first of its kind by African Americans in Montgomery. However, when Parks was arrested, her quiet, admirable demeanor coupled with her service as secretary of the local NAACP branch helped to stir the black community to protest.

King and Abernathy became leaders of what came to be known as the Montgomery Improvement Association (MIA). Through meetings in churches, the two men spearheaded a mass **boycott** of Montgomery's buses. While King served as head of the MIA, Abernathy functioned as program chief. Nonviolence was the method with which the protest was implemented. Despite having been a soldier, Abernathy, like King, was convinced that nonviolence was the only acceptable means of dissent. Both had read and accepted the philosophies of Henry David Thoreau and Mahatma Gandhi.

The boycott persisted for more than a year. Despite the inordinate length of the struggle, the black community was consolidated in its refusal to ride segregated buses. Finally, in June 1956 a federal court upheld an injunction against the bus company's Jim Crow policy.

This successful boycott inspired the two young clergymen to expand their efforts to win civil rights for American's black citizens. As a result, in January 1957 the Southern Christian Leadership Conference (SCLC) was born in Atlanta. King was elected president of the new organization, and Abernathy became its secretary-treasurer. While he attended this meeting, Abernathy's home and church in Montgomery were bombed. Although it was a close call, Abernathy's family was spared any physical harm.

King moved to Atlanta in 1960, and a year later persuaded Abernathy to follow him and take on the pastorate of West Hunter Street Baptist Church. In the years that followed, the two men, under the auspices of SCLC, led nonviolent protests in cities such as Birmingham and Selma, Alabama; Albany, Georgia; Greensboro, North Carolina; and St. Augustine, Florida. As a consequence, both were arrested many times, and experienced violence and threats of violence. In 1965 Abernathy became vice president at large of SCLC. When King was assassinated in Memphis, Tennessee, in 1968, Abernathy was unanimously elected his successor. Soon after, Abernathy launched King's planned Poor People's Campaign. He led other protests until he resigned as head of SCLC in 1977.

After Abernathy assumed the leadership of SCLC, many compared him to King. Unfortunately, he was often perceived as lacking the charisma and poise of his friend. Some even accused Abernathy of being gross or crude in his leadership style. Perhaps the best historical defense of Abernathy's reputation came from his autobiography, *And the Walls Came Tumbling Down* (1989). However, its content and literary style were unappreciated by many because of the book's revelations about King's extramarital affairs. The critics accused Abernathy of betraying his long-deceased friend. ◆

> *"Bring on your tear gas, bring on your grenades, your new supplies of mace, your state troopers and even your national guards. But let the record show we ain't going to be turned around."*
> Ralph David Abernathy, 1989

Addams, Jane

1860–1935 ● SOCIAL REFORMER

Jane Addams was a social worker and humanitarian. She founded Hull House, a settlement community in Chicago. In recognition for her life of social reform and **advocacy,** she received the Nobel Peace Prize in 1931.

advocacy: the act of supporting a cause or individual.

Jane Addams graduated from Rockford College, Illinois, in 1881, and began studies at the Woman's Medical College in Philadelphia, hoping to become a physician. However, her own health failed and she spent two years as an invalid. After she recovered, Addams spent several years traveling and studying in Europe. In England she visited the Toynbee Hall settlement house, which helped poor and needy people in many ways. She resolved to create a similar institution in the United States.

Upon her return in 1889, Addams settled in a working-class neighborhood in Chicago. There she rented a portion of the old Hull mansion and with Ellen Gates Starr founded Hull House, one of the first settlement communities in the United States. The mission of Hull House was to aid needy immigrants in the Halsted Street area around the settlement. Originally a kindergarten for needy children, Hull House soon expanded to include a day nursery and an infant care clinic. Addams invited neighborhood residents into the house to study their problems and to provide them with adult guidance, good companionship, and recreational activities. The settlement expanded to include secondary and college-level classes. As buildings were added from year to year, Hull House became a complex containing a gymnasium, social and cooperative clubs, shops, a bookbindery, and a music studio.

Addams had a special affinity for the mothers and children of the neighborhood. Her impulse to help and her revulsion for all forms of injustice and cruelty led to a lifetime devoted to social reform. She recruited a large group of capable women of widely different gifts and interests to settle at Hull House, which became a centerpiece for social reform. In 1910 Addams published *Twenty Years at Hull-House*, a lively look back at her career as well as a handbook for potential settlement workers.

In addition to her work at Hull House, Jane Addams became a strong advocate for peace. She and an international group of women attempted to talk the governments of Europe into a peaceful settlement of World War I, but failed. Following the war, Addams helped send food and clothing to women and children in many countries of Europe, including former enemies. She worked to support national organizations of women

Settlement Houses

Settlement houses were neighborhood centers founded to help immigrant families adjust their styles of housekeeping, child rearing, and health care to the realities of urban living. The settlement house movement, which mobilized tens of thousands of educated women in the late 19th century to serve immigrant workers in urban areas, was a powerful expression of social feminism and social justice progressivism. The movement began in London in 1884 with the founding of Toynbee Hall by Oxford University students. Inspired by this example, Jane Addams and Ellen Gates Starr established Hull House amid the slums of Chicago in 1889. By 1910 there were more than 400 settlement houses in the United States managed by thousands of middle-class missionaries to the poor, 60 percent of them women.

Initially the movement's pioneers had sentimental notions about "civilizing" the immigrant poor; for example, in the early days of Hull House, Jane Addams and her colleagues treated their neighbors to literary evenings, art classes, and tea parties. Soon, however, settlement workers developed more practical services: kindergartens, day-care facilities, boardinghouses for working girls, and classes in sewing, nutrition, and health care. Eventually, settlement workers realized that no amount of private voluntarism could cope with the problems of the urban poor. Reluctantly concluding that many kinds of essential services could be provided only by municipal governments, settlement leaders learned to get their hands dirty in urban politics.

Settlement workers labored not to eliminate class exploitation and class conflict but to heal the wounds they inflicted. Moreover, the professionalism of social work after 1900 blunted their idealism and reformism, and eventually replaced those qualities with a common-sense emphasis on solutions.

in various countries and as president of the Women's International League for Peace and Freedom, she advocated international meetings of women. For her life of social reform and advocacy for peace she received many awards, and in 1931 Addams and Nicholas Murray Butler jointly received the Nobel Peace Prize. ◆

Anthony, Susan Brownell

FEBRUARY 15, 1820–MARCH 13, 1906 ●
SUFFRAGIST AND WOMEN'S RIGHTS ACTIVIST

Born in Adams, Massachusetts, Susan B. Anthony was raised in a progressive household in which her father respected his daughters' intelligence and gave them a

good education. As one of eight children, Anthony saw her quiet, worn-out mother as a symbol of married life and it made her eager to improve the condition of married women in the United States.

Growing up in a Quaker household, Anthony heard women speaking freely and participating equally in church affairs. She was sent to a boarding school in Philadelphia and received an education superior to that usual for girls at that time.

In 1838 Anthony experienced discrimination firsthand after a brush with what she considered unfair property laws in Rochester, New York. Rochester was considered a center of reform, and many abolitionist and temperance workers became friends of the family; Anthony became known for her honesty, sense of humor, and sympathetic view of people. While working as a schoolteacher in nearby Canajoharie Academy she joined the local chapter of the Daughters of Temperance, soon becoming an officer of the organization.

Anthony became bored with teaching and returned home to Rochester, where she directed her father's farm for two years and became increasingly involved in reform circles. In 1852 she organized the first women's state temperance society in the United States, and soon became active in the antislavery movement.

After attending several reformers' conventions at which women were not allowed to participate fully, Anthony heeded the advice of her friend Elizabeth Cady Stanton and began to work full-time for the women's rights movement, becoming secretary of the National Woman's Rights Convention. As she toured the country with Stanton, she was the main organizing force behind the tours, though Stanton gave the speeches. In March 1860 she and Stanton were successful in lobbying to change a New York state property law to give women the right to keep their own earnings, enter into contracts, or use their earnings as they saw fit. Widows now had the same property rights as widowers.

Anthony soon turned her attention to suffrage for women, helping to found the National Woman Suffrage Association in

1869 Anthony cofounds the National Woman Suffrage Association.

1872 Anthony casts a ballot in the presidential election and is arrested.

1873 Anthony is brought to trial and fined for voting.

1920 Women in the United States are granted the right to vote.

1979 U.S. Treasury mints the Susan B. Anthony silver dollar, the first U.S. coin to honor a woman.

1869, for which she served as the vice president at large until 1892, when she became the president. From 1868 to 1870 she was the proprietor of a weekly newspaper, *The Revolution,* whose motto was "The true republic—men, their rights and nothing more; women, their rights and nothing less." With Stanton, Anthony helped to bring previously **taboo** subjects, such as divorce, into public debate.

taboo: banned on the grounds of morality or taste.

In 1872 Anthony cast a ballot in the presidential election, as she felt she was entitled to do according to the Fourteenth Amendment of the Constitution. She was arrested and fined $100 but never paid the fine. As the debate over women's suffrage heated up, Anthony continued fighting for her cause. "Abraham Lincoln said, 'No man is good enough to govern another man without his consent.' Now I say to you, 'No man is good enough to govern any woman without her consent,'" she said in 1895. Her pioneering led to women's suffrage in the United States in 1920.

She organized the International Council of Women, and along with Stanton, Matilda Joslyn Gage, and Ida Husted Harper, published a four-volume history of their cause, called *The History of Women's Suffrage* (1902). In the last years of her life, though she suffered from a serious heart condition, she continued to work for women's rights, attending her last convention two months before her death at the age of eighty-six. Anthony's last public words were said at her eighty-sixth birthday celebration: "Failure is impossible." ◆

Arias Sánchez, Oscar

SEPTEMBER 13, 1941– ● PEACE ACTIVIST AND PRESIDENT OF COSTA RICA

Oscar Arias Sánchez was president of Costa Rica (1986–90) and winner of the Nobel Peace Prize in 1987 for designing a plan for peace in Central America. Arias Sánchez's father was an early follower of José Figures Ferrer and an active member of the National Liberation Party (PLN). His mother's family was part of the Costa Rican coffee elite that emerged during the nineteenth-century coffee boom. Arias Sánchez came to international prominence shortly after his inauguration in 1986 when he took bold initiatives to propel Central America into a peace process. His proposals

"When hope is born, it is necessary to unite courage with wisdom. Only then is it possible to avoid violence."

Oscar Arias Sánchez, 1987

for peace and stability in the region led to an agreement, signed in 1987, between Honduras, Guatemala, Nicaragua, El Salvador, and Costa Rica.

The Arias plan, or Esquipulas II, established the framework for the pacification and democratization of Central America. It provided for the restoration of civil liberties, for amnesty for political prisoners, for free elections, and for genuine dialogue between governments and opposition forces. The plan contributed to the process that brought peace and free elections to Nicaragua and new hope for the eventual **demilitarization** of the region.

demilitarization: to declare a zone or region free from military control.

Even though Arias came to the international scene at a relatively young age, he had served a long apprenticeship in the highly competitive arena of Costa Rican party politics and in the rigorous intellectual environment of the University of Costa Rica (UCR). He received his law and economics degrees from the UCR, was awarded a master of arts degree in political science and economics from the London School of Economics (1967), and earned a doctor of philosophy degree from the University of Essex, England (1974). He joined the faculty of UCR in 1969 and served as a member of the ad hoc Commission of the National University (1972–75). He was a director of the Costa Rican Technological Institute from 1974 to 1977.

Arias began his political career in the PLN and held high elected and appointed positions in the national government and in the party. He served as secretary to the president (1970–72) during the last José Figueres Ferrer administration. From 1972 to 1977 he held a cabinet-level position as minister of national planning and economic policy. While serving as a member of the National Assembly (1978–82), he also held other leadership positions. He was secretary of international affairs (1975–79) and he was elected secretary general in 1979 on a reformist platform that brought a new generation of leaders to the fore. Arias ascended to the presidency in 1986, chiefly by serving in positions of party leadership and in the administration of President Luis Alberto Monge Álvarez. He won the PLN primary and then defeated Rafael Angel Calderón Fournier in the general election.

The Arias plan brought peace and free elections to Nicaragua and new hope for the eventual demilitarization of the region.

Arias has received many awards and honorary degrees from universities in Europe, Central America, and the United States. Since his presidency he has lectured widely on the related questions of world peace and the environment, donating the proceeds from the lectures to the Arias Foundation, which was established to support research on these issues. He has also continued to be active in politics. ◆

Aung San Suu Kyi

JUNE 19, 1945– ● HUMAN RIGHTS ACTIVIST

Aung San Suu Kyi is a Burmese human rights activist and the head of Burma's popular opposition party, the National League for Democracy (NLD). She won the 1991 Nobel Peace Prize for her nonviolent struggle to bring democracy to Burma. In 1989 she was placed under house arrest by the country's military regime and was detained through much of the 1990s.

"I've always thought that the best solution for those who feel helpless is for them to help others."

Aung San Suu Kyi, 1996

Aung San Suu Kyi was born on June 19, 1945, in Rangoon (also spelled Yangon), the capital of Burma, which is now called Myanmar. Her mother, Khin Kyi, became a prominent Burmese diplomat, and her father, Aung San, was a nationalist leader who helped bring about Burma's independence in 1948 after more than fifty years of British colonial rule and three years of Japanese occupation during World War II. He was chosen to become the first prime minister of independent Burma in 1947, but was assassinated on July 19, 1947, when Suu Kyi was two. Aung San Suu Kyi eventually came to emulate her father in his struggle against oppression, but only after living much of her life abroad.

As a child Aung San Suu Kyi attended schools in Burma until 1960. That year she moved to India with her mother, who became Burma's ambassador to India. Aung San Suu Kyi led a privileged existence in India and attended good schools there. While in India she became familiar with the teachings of Mohandas K. Gandhi, the Indian spiritual and political leader known for his use of nonviolent civil disobedience against British colonial rule.

devout: devoted to religion.

In 1964 Aung San Suu Kyi began studies at St. Hugh's College at Oxford University in England, where she majored in politics, philosophy, and economics. Her friends remembered her as a **devout** Buddhist who was always eager to learn. She received her B.A. in 1967. Following graduation Aung San Suu Kyi worked in England as a teacher and research assistant and later in New York City at the United Nations.

While at Oxford, Aung San Suu Kyi met Michael Aris, a scholar of Tibetan culture. The couple married in 1972, and Suu Kyi followed her husband to the kingdom of Bhutan, where he worked as a tutor for the royal family. In Bhutan she held a job in the Foreign Ministry as a research officer on United Nations issues. In 1973 the couple returned to England, where Suu Kyi gave birth to two sons, Alexander and Kim. Aung San Sue Kyi lived comfortably as a mother and homemaker while her husband worked as a scholar at Oxford. During this period, her interest in her father intensified, and she began to research his life. Through her research, Aung San Suu Kyi found that she shared many attitudes with the father she had never known, and like Aung San she developed a sense of duty toward serving Burma in its time of need.

In 1985 Aung San Suu Kyi traveled to Japan to continue scholarly work on her father at the University of Kyoto in Japan, bringing her youngest son, Kim, with her. She then spent a year in Simla in northern India with her husband and sons. In 1987, she enrolled in a doctorate program in Burmese literature at the School of Oriental and African Studies at London University. Her studies were interrupted in April 1988, when she returned to Burma to care for her dying mother.

At the time of her arrival in Burma, the country was seething with hostility toward the socialist government. After years of political **repression**, limited civil freedoms, and continued economic decline, people took to the streets in revolt. In mid-1988 student demonstrations calling for an end to the country's one-party rule led to violent clashes with riot police and hundreds of demonstrators were killed. The protests spread, and tens of thousands of people took to the streets. The army responded to demonstrations by firing into the crowds, killing thousands.

Unable to remain a silent bystander while the Burmese government massacred unarmed citizens, Aung San Suu Kyi joined in the protest movement. She made her first major public appearance before 500,000 people at the Shwe Dagon

1945 Suu Kyi is born in Rangoon, Burma.

1947 Suu Kyi's father, prime minister of Burma, is assassinated.

1988 Suu Kyi helps found the National League for Demcracy (NLD).

1989 The Burmese government places Suu Kyi under house arrest.

1991 Suu Kyi wins the Nobel Peace Prize.

1995 Suu Kyi is released from house arrest.

1996 The Burmese government increases pressure on the NLD.

repression: to discourage by force.

Pagoda in Rangoon on August 26, marking the beginning of her nonviolent struggle for democracy and human rights. In September the army overthrew the government and replaced it with the State Law and Order Restoration Council (SLORC), which scheduled elections for 1990. At the same time, however, the military cracked down on civil rights. It immediately banned political demonstrations and political gatherings of more than four people. Once again, thousands of people took to the streets in protest, and soldiers fired upon them, killing hundreds.

In September 1988 Aung San Suu Kyi helped found the National League for Democracy (NLD), the leading opposition party. She campaigned all around the country for the NLD and spoke openly against the military in command. On July 20, 1989, the government placed Aung San Suu Kyi under house arrest. In January the following year she was denied the right to have visits from family members and in July all written communication with her was severed. In the May 1990 elections the NLD won about 80 percent of the seats in parliament, but the government refused to step down. Many NLD candidates were subsequently arrested.

Aung San Suu Kyi spent her time under house arrest meditating and reading literature and works on politics, philosophy, and Buddhism. On several occasions the government offered to let her go free on the condition that she leave Burma, but Aung San Suu Kyi refused to go unless the country was returned to a civilian government and political prisoners were released. She also rejected all suggestions to move to an armed struggle, believing that such a move would perpetuate a cycle of violence. In 1991 Aung San Suu Kyi was awarded the Nobel Peace Prize for her nonviolent struggle for democracy and human rights. Her son Alexander traveled to Oslo, Norway, to accept the award on her behalf.

In 1995 the government suddenly released Aung San Suu Kyi from house arrest, but she remained in Burma to continue her work for democracy. From her front gate she gave weekly speeches on democracy, human rights, and ethnic **tolerance** to thousands who gathered there to listen. Her words were heard around the world and a number of nations began to withhold economic aid to Burma because of SLORC's human rights violations. In late 1996 and early 1997 repression against Aung San Suu Kyi and other members of the NLD mounted. The government banned the gatherings at her house, arrested hundreds of

"The people of my country want the two freedoms that spell security: freedom from want and freedom from fear."
Aung San Suu Kyi, 1995

tolerance: allowing something.

NLD party members, prevented journalists and diplomats from speaking with her, and put her under house arrest once more. Despite her isolation from the world, Aung San Suu Kyi has remained a potent symbol of the nonviolent struggle for democracy and human rights. ◆

Baker, Ella J.

DECEMBER 13, 1903–DECEMBER 13, 1986 ● ACTIVIST

Ella J. Baker was a leading figure in the struggle of African Americans for equality. In the 1960s she was regarded as the godmother of the civil rights movement, or, as one activist put it, "a Shining Black Beacon." Though she was not accorded recognition by the media, Baker was affiliated with all the major civil rights organizations of her time, and she worked closely with all the better-known leaders of the movement.

Ella Baker was the daughter of a waiter on the Norfolk–Washington ferry, and was a grade school teacher and the granddaughter of slaves. From the extended family of aunts, uncles, and cousins who lived on land her grandfather had purchased from owners of the plantation on which they had worked as slaves, Baker acquired a sense of community, a profound sense of the need for sharing, and a sense of history and of the continuity of struggle. She also gained a fierce sense of independence and a belief in the necessity of rebellion, which guided her work for the rest of her life.

After leaving Shaw University in Raleigh, North Carolina, from which she graduated as valedictorian, Baker immersed herself in the cause of social justice. She moved to New York, where she continued her education on the streets of the city, attending all kinds of political meetings to absorb the intellectual atmosphere. In the 1930s, while earning her living working in restaurants and as a correspondent for several black newspapers, Baker helped to found the Young Negroes Cooperative League, of which she became executive director.

> *"Men didn't do the things that had to be done and you had a large number of women who were involved in the bus boycott. They were the people who kept the spirit going."*
> Ella J. Baker, 1974

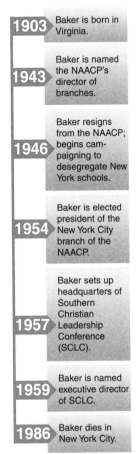

1903 Baker is born in Virginia.

1943 Baker is named the NAACP's director of branches.

1946 Baker resigns from the NAACP; begins campaigning to desegregate New York schools.

1954 Baker is elected president of the New York City branch of the NAACP.

1957 Baker sets up headquarters of Southern Christian Leadership Conference (SCLC).

1959 Baker is named executive director of SCLC.

1986 Baker dies in New York City.

She worked for the Works Project (originally Works Progress) Administration (WPA), teaching consumer and labor education. During the depression, Baker learned that, in her words, "a society could break down, a social order could break down, and the individual is the victim of the breakdown, rather than the cause of it."

In 1940 Baker accepted a position as field secretary at the National Association for the Advancement of Colored People (NAACP). She soon established regional leadership-training conferences with the slogan "Give light and the people will find a way." While a national officer, Baker traveled for several months a year throughout the country (concentrating on the segregated South), building NAACP membership and working with the local people who would become the sustaining forces of the civil rights movement. Her organizing strategy was to stress local issues rather than national ones and to take the NAACP to people, wherever they were. She ventured into beer gardens and nightclubs where she would address crowds and secure memberships and campaign workers. Baker was named director of branches in 1943, but frustrated by the top-down approach of the NAACP leadership, she resigned in 1946. In this period she married a former classmate, Thomas Roberts, and took on the responsibility of raising her sister's daughter, Jacqueline.

From 1946 to 1957, while working in New York City for the New York Cancer Society and the New York Urban League, Baker participated in campaigns to desegregate New York City schools. She was a founder of In Friendship, a group organized to support school desegregation in the South; a member of the zoning subcommittee of the New York City Board of Education's committee on integration; and president and later education director of the New York City branch of the NAACP.

In 1957 Bayard Rustin and Stanley Levison, advisers to the Rev. Dr. Martin Luther King Jr., asked her to return south to set up the office of the newly organized Southern Christian Leadership Conference (SCLC), headed by King, and to organize the Crusade for Citizenship, a voter-registration drive. Intending to stay six weeks, she remained with SCLC for two years, serving variously as acting director, associate director, and executive director.

In 1960 Baker mobilized SCLC support for a meeting to bring together the student **sit-in** protest groups that had sprung up across the South. A battle for control of the sit-in movement ensued. Older civil rights organizations, particularly SCLC,

sit-in: the act of sitting in seats or on the floor as a means of organized protest.

sought to make the new movement a youth arm of their own operations. Baker, however, advocated an independent role for the student activists.

Baker resigned from SCLC in 1960 to accept a part-time position as human-relations consultant to the Young Women's Christian Association (YWCA), working with colleges across the South to further integration. In 1963 she joined the staff of the Southern Conference Educational Fund (SCEF), a region-wide interracial organization that put special emphasis on developing white support for racial justice. While affiliated with the YWCA and SCEF, Baker devoted much of her time to the fledgling Student Nonviolent Coordinating Committee (SNCC), in which she found the **embodiment** of her belief in a "group-centered leadership, rather than a leadership-centered group."

embodiment: the representation of something.

SNCC was for Baker the "new community" she had sought. Her work was an inspiration for other activist movements of the 1960s and '70s: the anti-Vietnam War movement and the feminist movement. But Baker's greatest contribution was her counseling of SNCC. During one crisis she pointed out that both direct action and voter registration would lead to the same result—confrontation and resolution. Her support of confrontation was at variance with the Kennedy administration's policy, which advocated a "cooling-off" period. Baker also counseled the young mavericks of SNCC to work with the more conservative southern ministers, who, she advised, had resources that could help them.

In 1964 SNCC was instrumental in organizing the Mississippi Freedom Democratic Party (MFDP), which sent its own delegation to Atlantic City to challenge the seating of the segregationist Mississippi delegation at the Democratic National Convention. Baker, in the new party's Washington headquarters and later in Atlantic City, orchestrated the MFDP's fight for the support of other state delegations in its claim to Mississippi's seats. This challenge eventually resulted in the adoption of new Democratic party rules that guaranteed the inclusion of blacks and women in future delegations.

After the convention, Baker moved back to New York, where she remained active in human-rights affairs. Throughout her life she had been a speaker at hundreds of Women's Day church meetings across the country, a participant in tenants' associations, a consultant to the wartime Office of Price Administration, an adviser to the Harlem Youth Council, a

Baker believed that SNCC was the embodiment of "group-centered leadership, rather than a leadership-centered group."

founder and administrator of the Fund for Education and Legal Defense. In her later years she worked with such varied groups as the Puerto Rican Solidarity Committee, the Episcopal Church Center, and the Third World Women's Coordinating Committee.

ideology: a vision, theory, or belief.

While never professing a political **ideology**, Baker consistently held views far to the left of the established civil rights leadership. She was never a member of a political party, but she did run for the New York City Council on the Liberal party ticket in 1951. She acted within the constraints of a radical critique of society and was drawn toward "radical" rather than "safe" solutions to societal problems. Her credo was "a life that is important is a life of service." ◆

Baldwin, James

AUGUST 2, 1924–NOVEMBER 30, 1987 ● AUTHOR AND CIVIL RIGHTS ACTIVIST

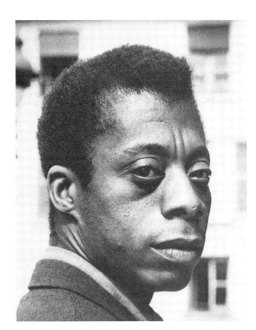

Born in New York City's Harlem in 1924, James Baldwin, who started out as a writer during the late 1940s, rose to international fame after the publication of his most famous essay, "The Fire Next Time," in 1963. However, nearly two decades before its publication, he had already captured the attention of an assortment of writers, literary critics, and intellectuals in the United States and abroad. Writing to Langston Hughes in 1948, Arna Bontemps commented on Baldwin's "The Harlem Ghetto," which was published in the February 1948 issue of *Commentary* magazine. Referring to "that remarkable piece by that 24-year-old colored kid," Bontemps wrote, "What a kid! He has zoomed high among our writers with his first effort." Thus, from the beginning of his professional career, Baldwin was highly regarded and began publishing in magazines and journals such as the *Nation,* the *New Leader, Commentary,* and *Partisan Review.*

Much of Baldwin's writing, both fiction and nonfiction, has been autobiographical. The story of John Grimes, the traumatized son of a tyrannical, fundamentalist father in *Go Tell It on the Mountain*, closely resembles Baldwin's own childhood. His celebrated essay "Notes of a Native Son" describes the writer's painful relationship with his stepfather. Born out of wedlock before his mother met and married David Baldwin, young Jimmy never fully gained his stern patriarch's approval. Raised in a strict Pentecostal household, Jimmy became a preacher at age fourteen, and his sermons drew larger crowds than his father's. When Jimmy left the church three years later, the tension with his father was exacerbated, and as "Notes of a Native Son" reveals, even the impending death of David Baldwin in 1943 did not reconcile their mutual disaffection. In various forms, the problems of father–son conflict, with all of its Old Testament connotations, became a central preoccupation of Baldwin's writing.

Baldwin's career, which can be divided into two phases— up to "The Fire Next Time" (1963) and after—gained momentum after the publication of what were to become two of his more controversial essays. In 1948 and 1949, respectively, he wrote "Everybody's Protest Novel" and "Many Thousands Gone," which were published in *Partisan Review*. These two essays served as a forum from which he made pronouncements about the limitations of the protest tradition in American literature. He scathingly criticized Harriet Beecher Stowe's *Uncle Tom's Cabin* and Richard Wright's *Native Son* for being firmly rooted in the protest tradition. Each writer failed, in Baldwin's judgment, because the "power of revelation . . . is the business of the novelist, that journey toward a more vast reality which must take precedence over all other claims." He abhorred the idea of the writer as a kind of "congressman," embracing Jamesian ideas about the art of fiction. The writer, as Baldwin envisioned himself during this early period, should self-consciously seek a distance between himself and his subject.

Baldwin's criticisms of *Native Son* and the protest novel tradition precipitated a rift with his mentor, Richard Wright. Ironically, Wright had supported Baldwin's candidacy for the Rosenwald Fellowship in 1948, which allowed Baldwin to move to Paris, where he completed his first novel, *Go Tell It on the Mountain* (1953). Baldwin explored his conflicted relationship with Wright in a series of moving essays, including "Alas, Poor Richard," published in *Nobody Knows My Name*.

Baldwin left Harlem for Paris when he was twenty-four. Although he spoke little French at the time, he purchased a

1924 Baldwin is born, the eldest of eight children, in Harlem, New York City.

1948 Baldwin receives a Rosenwald Fellowship, which allows him to move to Paris.

1953 Baldwin completes his first novel, *Go Tell It on the Mountain*.

1961 Baldwin's second collection of essays, *Nobody Knows My Name: More Notes of A Native Son*, becomes a best-seller.

1963 *The Fire Next Time*, another volume of essays is published, raising Baldwin's profile as a prophet of his race.

1963 Baldwin's presence at the historical March on Washington is considered important.

1987 Baldwin dies of cancer in southern France.

one-way ticket and later achieved success and fame as an expatriate. Writing about race and sexuality (including homosexuality), he published twenty-two books, among them six novels, a collection of short stories, two plays, several collections of essays, a children's book, a movie scenario, and *Jimmy's Blues* (1985), a chapbook of poems. Starting with his controversial *Another Country* (1962), many of his books, including *The Fire Next Time* (1963), *If Beale Street Could Talk* (1974), and *Just Above My Head* (1979), were best-sellers. His play *Blues for Mr. Charlie* (1964) was produced on Broadway. And his scenario *One Day When I Was Lost: A Scenario Based on Alex Haley's "The Autobiography of Malcolm X"* was used by the movie director Spike Lee in the production of his feature film on Malcolm X.

Baldwin credits Bessie Smith as the source of inspiration for the completion of his first novel, *Go Tell It on the Mountain* (1953). In "The Discovery of What It Means to Be an American," he writes about his experience of living and writing in Switzerland: "There, in that alabaster landscape, armed with two Bessie Smith records and a typewriter, I began to re-create the life that I had first known as a child and from which I had spent so many years in flight . . . . Bessie Smith, through her tone and cadence . . . helped me dig back to the way I myself must have spoken when I was a pickaninny, and to remember the things I had heard and seen and felt. I had buried them very deep."

Go Tell It on the Mountain recaptures in some definitive ways the spirit and circumstances of Baldwin's own boyhood and adolescence. John Grimes, the shy and intelligent protagonist of the novel, is remarkably reminiscent of Baldwin. Moreover, Baldwin succeeds at creating a web of relationships that reveals how a particular character has arrived at his or her situation. He had, after all, harshly criticized Stowe and Wright for what he considered their rather stereotypical depiction of characters and their circumstances. His belief that "revelation" was the novelist's ultimate goal persisted throughout his career. In his second and third novels—*Giovanni's Room* (1956) and *Another Country* (1962)—he explores the theme of a varying, if consistent, American search for identity.

In *Giovanni's Room* the theme is complicated by international and sexual dimensions. The main character is forced to learn a harsh lesson about another culture and country as he wrestles with his ambivalent sexuality. Similarly, in *Another Country* Baldwin sensationally calls into question many American taboos about race, sexuality, marriage, and infidelity. By presenting a stunning series of relationships—heterosexual,

"Words like 'freedom,' 'justice,' 'democracy' are not common concepts; on the contrary, they are rare. People are not born knowing what these are. It takes enormous and, above all, individual effort to arrive at the respect for other people that these words imply."

James Baldwin, 1956

homosexual, interracial, bisexual—he creates a *tableau vivant* of American mores. In his remaining novels, *Tell Me How Long the Train's Been Gone* (1968), *If Beale Street Could Talk* (1974), and *Just Above My Head* (1979), he also focuses on issues related to race and sexuality. Furthermore, he tries to reveal how racism and sexism are inextricably linked to deep-seated American assumptions. In Baldwin's view, race and sex are hopelessly entangled in America's collective psyche.

Around the time of "The Fire Next Time"'s publication and after the Broadway production of *Blues for Mr. Charlie,* Baldwin became known as a spokesperson for civil rights and a celebrity noted for championing the cause of black Americans. He was a prominent participant in the March on Washington at which the Rev. Dr. Martin Luther King Jr. gave his famous "I Have a Dream" speech. He frequently appeared on television and delivered speeches on college campuses. Baldwin actually published two excellent collections of essays—*Notes of a Native Son* (1955) and *Nobody Knows My Name* (1961)—before "The Fire Next Time." In fact, various critics and reviewers already considered him in a class of his own. However, it was his **exhortative** rhetoric in the latter essay, published on the one hundredth anniversary of the Emancipation Proclamation, an essay that anticipated the urban riots of the 1960s, that landed him on the cover of *Time* magazine. He concluded: "If we—and now I mean the relatively conscious whites and the relatively conscious blacks who must, like lovers, insist on or create the consciousness of the others—do not falter in our duty now, we may be able . . . to end the racial nightmare, and achieve our country, and change the history of the world."

After the publication of "The Fire Next Time," several black nationalists criticized Baldwin for his conciliatory attitude. They questioned whether his message of love and understanding would do much to change race relations in America. Eldridge Cleaver, in his book *Soul on Ice,* was one of Baldwin's more outspoken critics. But Baldwin continued writing, becoming increasingly more dependent on his early life as a source of inspiration, accepting eagerly the role of the writer as "poet" whose "assignment" was to accept the "energy" of the folk and transform it into art. It is as though he was following the wisdom of his own words in his story "Sonny's Blues." Like Sonny and his band, Baldwin saw clearly as he matured that he was telling a tale based on the blues of his own life as a writer and a man in America and abroad: "Creole began to tell us what the blues were all about. They were not about anything very new.

Baldwin became known as a spokesperson for civil rights and a celebrity noted for championing the case of black Americans.

exhortative: serving to urge strongly by argument or advice.

He and his boys up there were keeping it new at the risk of ruin, destruction, madness, and death, in order to find new ways to make us listen. For, while the tale of how we suffer, and how we are delighted, and how we may triumph is never new, it always must be heard. There isn't any other tale to tell, it's the only light we've got in all this darkness."

Several of his essays and interviews of the 1980s discuss homosexuality and homophobia with fervor and forthrightness, most notably "Here Be Dragons." Thus, just as he had been the leading literary voice of the civil rights movement, he became an inspirational figure for the emerging gay rights movement. Baldwin's nonfiction was collected in *The Price of the Ticket* (1985).

During the final decade of his life, Baldwin taught at a number of American colleges and universities—including the University of Massachusetts at Amherst and Hampshire College—frequently commuting back and forth between the United States and his home in St. Paul de Vence in the south of France. After his death in France on November 30, 1987, the *New York Times* reported on its front page for the following day: "James Baldwin, Eloquent Essayist in Behalf of Civil Rights, Is Dead." ◆

> *"While the tale of how we suffer, and how we are delighted, and how we may triumph is never new, it always must be heard."*
>
> James Baldwin in "Sonny's Blues"

Belo, Carlos Ximenes

FEBRUARY 3, 1948– ● ROMAN CATHOLIC BISHOP

Ramos-Horta, José

DECEMBER 26, 1949– ● JOURNALIST AND POLITICAL ACTIVIST

In 1996 the Norwegian Nobel Committee paid heed to a little-known corner of the world when it awarded the Nobel Peace Prize jointly to Carlos Ximenes Belo, Bishop of Dili, East Timor, and José Ramos-Horta, the Australia-based leader of East Timor's government-in-exile since 1975, for "their work towards a just and peaceful solution to the conflict in East Timor."

East Timor is one half of Timor, a remote island located at the southeastern end of the Indonesian archipelago, closer to northern Australia than to the center of Indonesia. During the nineteenth century, the Dutch took control of West Timor, and the Portuguese colonized East Timor. After World War II, Indonesia took control of West Timor and Portugal continued to rule East Timor.

Indonesia invaded and annexed East Timor in December 1975, after the collapse of Portugal's colonial rule plunged East Timor into a civil war. International human rights groups have long accused the Indonesian military of a campaign of killing and torture to enforce the annexation of East Timor. Human rights groups estimate that as many as 200,000 East Timorese have lost their lives since 1975 as a result of human rights abuses or fighting with government forces. The United Nations has refused to recognize Indonesian sovereignty over East Timor. In May 1999 Indonesia and Portugal signed a UN-brokered agreement to allow the people of East Timor to choose between independence and enhanced **autonomy** within Indonesia.

As a boy Carlos Belo herded water buffalo in an East Timor village before settling down to his studies in Timorese missionary schools and later in Portugal and Rome. Becoming a monk of the Salesian Order, he studied philosophy and theology before being ordained in 1980. Returning to East Timor in 1981, he first taught and administered at the Salesian College at Fatumaca, then was appointed Apostolic Administrator of the diocese of Dili, East Timor's capital.

In 1988 Father Belo was consecrated a bishop. Within a short time, Bishop Belo began regularly protesting the brutalities of the Indonesian military regime and earning its disfavor. He called for a United Nations referendum on the future of East Timor. In 1989, 1991, and 1996 he was the target of assassination attempts.

The Nobel Committee said of Bishop Belo, "At the risk of his own life, he has tried to protect his people from infringements by those in power. In his efforts to create a just settlement based on his people's right to self-determination, he has been a constant spokesman for non-violence and dialogue with the Indonesian authorities."

José Ramos-Horta was born in Dili to a Timorese mother and a Portuguese father whom the Salazar government of Portugal had exiled to East Timor for his outspoken views. José was educated both at Catholic schools and at the government secondary school in Dili. In 1974 Ramos-Horta helped found

1948 Belo is born in East Timor.

1949 Ramos-Horta is born in Dili, East Timor.

1974 Ramos-Horta helps found the Timorese Association of Social Democrats.

1975 Indonesia invades and annexes East Timor.

1975 Ramos-Horta leaves East Timor for Australia.

1988 Father Belo is consecrated a bishop; he begins regularly protesting the Indonesian military regime.

1996 Ramos-Horta shares the Nobel Peace Prize with Bishop Belo.

1999 Indonesia agrees to allow East Timor to choose between independence and greater autonomy within Indonesia.

autonomy: the right of self-government.

Nobel Peace Prize

The Nobel Peace Prize was established by the will of Alfred Nobel, the Swedish inventor of dynamite, who died in 1896. Winners of the endowed award were to be persons "who shall have done the most . . . work for fraternity between nations, for the abolition or reduction of standing armies, and for holding and promotion of peace conferences." After Nobel's death, provisions were modified to permit awarding the Peace Prize to organizations. Recipients are chosen by the Nobel Committee, which is selected by the Norwegian parliament. Those eligible to nominate candidates include members of national assemblies and governments; university professors of law, political science, history, and philosophy; members and former members of the Nobel Committee; and Peace Prize holders. The prize is awarded annually on December 10, in Oslo, Norway, except when the Nobel Committee cannot agree on a winner. The first Nobel Peace Prize, granted in 1901, was shared by Henri Dunant and Frederic Passy. More recent recipients include Martin Luther King Jr. (1964), Amnesty International (1977), Lech Walesa (1983), Nelson Mandela and Frederik W. de Klerk (1993), and Carlos Belo and José Ramos-Horta (1996). By the late 1990s the value of the prize had risen to over $1 million.

> *"Let us banish anger and hostility, vengeance and other dark emotions, and transform ourselves into humble instruments of peace."*
>
> Carlos Ximenes Belo, 1996

the Timorese Association of Social Democrats, known by its Portuguese acronym as Fretilin, and began a lifetime of lobbying for an independent East Timor. On December 4, 1975, three days before the Indonesian invasion, Ramos-Horta left East Timor for Australia and a permanent life in exile. Of his ten brothers and sisters, four were killed by the Indonesian military in the ensuing violence.

Throughout the 1980s Ramos-Horta single-handedly represented East Timor at the United Nations in New York, and he helped draw up a peace plan for the pullback of Indonesian troops from East Timor and the UN-sponsored referendum on self-rule. He continued through the 1990s, traveling ceaselessly throughout the world to promote the cause of self-determination for the East Timorese people. ◆

Bethune, Mary McLeod

JULY 10, 1875–MAY 18, 1955 ● CIVIL RIGHTS ACTIVIST

"I f I have a legacy to leave my people, it is my philosophy of living and serving. As I face tomorrow, I am content, for I think I have spent my life well. I pray now that my philosophy may be helpful to those who share my vision of a world of peace, progress, brotherhood, and love." With these words, Mary McLeod Bethune concluded her last will and testament outlining her legacy to African Americans. Bethune lived up to her stated philosophy throughout her long career as a gifted institution builder who focused on securing rights and opportunities for African-American women and youth. Her stunning successes as a leader made her one of the most influential women of her day and, for many years, a premier African-American leader.

Mary McLeod was born in 1875, the thirteenth of fifteen children of Sam and Patsy (McIntosh) McLeod. The McLeod family, many of whom had been slaves before the Civil War, owned a farm near Mayesville, South Carolina, when Mary was growing up. Mary McLeod attended the Trinity Presbyterian Mission School near her home from 1885 until 1888, and with the help of her mentor, Emma Jane Wilson, moved on to Scotia Seminary (later Barber-Scotia College), a Presbyterian school in Concord, North Carolina.

McLeod set her sights on serving as a missionary in Africa and so entered the Bible Institute for Home and Foreign Missions (later known as the Moody Bible Institute) in Chicago. She was devastated when she was informed that the Presbyterian church would not support African-American missionaries to Africa. Instead, McLeod turned her attentions and talents to the field of education at home.

From 1896 through 1897 McLeod taught at the Haines Institute, a Presbyterian-sponsored school in Augusta, Georgia, an experience that proved meaningful for her future. At Haines, McLeod worked with Lucy Craft Laney, the school's founder and a pioneering African-American educator. McLeod took away examples and skills she would put into action throughout her life.

From Haines, McLeod moved on to another Presbyterian school, the Kendall Institute in Sumter, South Carolina, where she met and married Albertus Bethune in 1898. The couple moved to Savannah, Georgia, and in 1899 their only child, Albert Bethune, was born. Although Albertus and Mary McLeod Bethune remained married until Albertus's death in 1918, they were no longer together by 1907. In 1900 Bethune

"I am actually dying on my feet because I am giving every moment, almost night and day – every little crevice I can get into, every opportunity I can get to whisper into the ear of an upper official, I am trying to breathe my soul, a spiritual something, into the needs of our people."

Mary McLeod Bethune, 1938

1875 McLeod is born in South Carolina.

1896 McLeod begins teaching at the Haines Institute in Augusta, Georgia.

1904 Bethune founds the Daytona Educational and Industrial Institute.

1923 Daytona Educational and Industrial Institute merges with Cookman Institute to later become Bethune-Cookman College.

1924 Bethune becomes president of the National Association of Colored Women.

1935 Bethune founds the National Council of Negro Women.

1936 Bethune organizes the Federal Council on Negro Affairs.

1955 Bethune dies in Daytona Beach, Florida.

accredited: to have credentials.

moved to Palatka, Florida, where she founded a Presbyterian school and later an independent school that also offered social services to the community.

In 1904 Bethune settled in Daytona, Florida, in order to establish a school for African-American girls. She opened her Daytona Educational and Industrial Institute in a rented house with little furniture and a tiny group of students. Students at the school learned basic academic subjects, worked on homemaking skills, engaged in religious activities, and worked with Bethune in the fields of a farm she bought in 1910. Through the farm, Bethune and her students were able to feed the members of the school community, as well as sell the surplus to benefit the school. The Daytona Institute also emphasized connections with the community, offering summer school, a playground for children, and other activities. All of this made Bethune an important voice in her local community.

The school's reputation began to grow at the national level through a visit by Booker T. Washington in 1912 and the addition of Frances Reynolds Keyser to the staff in the same year. Keyser had served as superintendent of the White Rose Mission in New York and was a well-known activist. After World War I, the school grew to include a high school and a nurses' training division. In 1923 the school merged with the failing Cookman Institute of Jacksonville, Florida, and embarked on a coeducational program. In 1929 it took the name Bethune-Cookman College. By 1935 Bethune's school, founded on a tiny budget, had become an **accredited** junior college and, by 1943, a fully accredited college, awarding bachelor's degrees. This success gained Bethune a national reputation and won her the NAACP's prestigious Spingarn Medal in 1935.

In addition to her success as an educator, Bethune also made a major mark on the black women's club movement in America. In 1917 she was elected president of the Florida Association of Colored Women, a post she retained until 1924. Under her leadership, the organization established a home for young women in Ocala. In 1920 Bethune organized the Southeastern Federation of Colored Women and guided this group through 1925. From 1924 to 1928 she served as president of the National Association of Colored Women (NACW), the most powerful organization of African-American women's clubs in the country. During this period, she toured Europe as the NACW's president and established the organization's headquarters in Washington, D.C., in 1928. Bethune's crowning achievement in the club movement was the 1935 founding of the National Council of Negro Women (NCNW). This organization served to coordinate and streamline the cooperative work of a wide variety of black women's organizations. During Bethune's fourteen years as president, the NCNW achieved this goal, began to work closely with the federal government on issues facing African Americans, and developed an international perspective on women's lives.

Bethune's influence with the Franklin D. Roosevelt administration led her to activities that made her an even greater public figure on behalf of African Americans. In 1936 she organized the Federal Council on Negro Affairs, popularly known as the Black Cabinet, a group of black advisers who helped coordinate government programs for African Americans. In this same period, she became deeply involved in the work of the National Youth Administration (NYA), serving on the advisory committee from its founding in 1935. In 1936 Bethune began functioning as director of the NYA's Division of Negro Affairs, a position that became official in 1939 and that she held until 1943. This appointment made her the highest ranking black woman in government up to that point. Bethune's goals in the NYA were to increase the representation of qualified African Americans in leadership in local and state programs and to ensure that NYA benefits distributed to whites and to blacks achieved parity.

In addition to Bethune's many other achievements, she served as the president of the Association for the Study of Negro Life and History from 1936 to 1951, established the Mary McLeod Bethune Foundation, and wrote a column for the *Pittsburgh Courier*. Bethune's career is testimony to her leadership skills, her commitment to justice and equality for African Americans, her unfailing dedication to the ideals of American democracy, and her philosophy of service. ◆

> Bethune's career is testimony to her leadership skills, her commitment to justice and equality for African Americans, her unfailing dedication to the ideals of American democracy, and her philosophy of service.

Bidwell, Annie Ellicott Kennedy

JUNE 30, 1839–MARCH 9, 1918 ● WOMAN SUFFRAGIST AND NATIVE AMERICAN RIGHTS ACTIVIST

Born in Washington, D.C., to a prominent middle-class family, Annie Ellicott Kennedy Bidwell became a devoted reformer, a member of the Native American National Woman Suffrage Association, and a follower of the Women's Christian Temperance Union. In 1868 she married

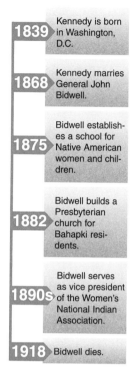

1839 Kennedy is born in Washington, D.C.

1868 Kennedy marries General John Bidwell.

1875 Bidwell establishes a school for Native American women and children.

1882 Bidwell builds a Presbyterian church for Bahapki residents.

1890s Bidwell serves as vice president of the Women's National Indian Association.

1918 Bidwell dies.

dispossessed: deprived of possessions, homes, security.

General John Bidwell, an early settler in northern California and a U.S. congressman from 1864 to 1868.

Joining her husband in 1868 on Rancho Chico, in present-day Chico, California, Annie Bidwell became fascinated with the Native Americans, mostly Maidu Indians, who, in exchange for working for the general, lived in a village on his land. Known as "Bahapki" by its residents, the village became a refuge for **dispossessed** northern California Native Americans fleeing from Euro-American violence.

As other women reformers of the late nineteenth century had done, Annie Bidwell decided to convert the Bahapki residents to Christianity and to promote their adoption of Euro-American clothes, homes, and values. She established a school for Native American women and children in 1875 and built a Presbyterian church for the Bahapki residents in 1882. In the 1890s she served as vice president of the Women's National Indian Association, a reform organization of middle-class white women who worked to assimilate Native Americans into mainstream Euro-American society. In her efforts to promote Christianity and Euro-American lifestyles, Bidwell also discouraged Bahapki burial practices and ceremonial dances. Despite her efforts to stifle them, however, the Native Americans at Bahapki secretly maintained many of their own traditions. Some historians view Bidwell as a humanitarian while others criticize her for pressuring Native Americans to abandon their culture. ◆

Biko, Stephen

DECEMBER 18, 1946–SEPTEMBER 12, 1977 ● LEADER OF THE BLACK CONSCIOUSNESS MOVEMENT IN SOUTH AFRICA

"The power of a movement lies in the fact that it can indeed change the habits of people. This change is not the result of force but of dedication, of moral persuasion."
Stephen Biko, 1976

Stephen Biko was born in Kingwilliamstown, in eastern Cape Province, South Africa. After graduating from Marianhill in Natal, he attended the University of Natal, where he studied medicine from 1966 to 1972.

Throughout the late 1960s and early 1970s Biko was the chief proponent of black consciousness, a movement influenced by black liberation movements in the United States. The movement was based on two main principles. First, as Biko wrote in "White Racism and Black Consciousness," the institutional divisions between blacks and whites in South Africa were so great that blacks could not rely on whites, not even reform-minded liberal whites, to end apartheid: "Total identification with an oppressed group in a system that forces one group to enjoy privilege and to live on the sweat of another, is impossible." Second, Biko insisted that blacks must form separate political structures and change the way they understood their own identities. This included awareness of and renewed pride in black culture, religion, and ethical systems.

To this end, Biko helped establish several all-black associations, such as the South African Students Organisation (1969) and the Black People's Convention (1972), a coalition of black organizations. In 1973, as a result of his political activities, the government restricted Biko's movements and forbade him to speak or write publicly. Thereafter he was repeatedly detained by the police. In August 1977 police arrested him for violating his travel ban and held him without trial. In early September, soon after being tortured by the police, he died of a brain hemorrhage. Biko's death became a rallying cry for opponents of apartheid, and he has been commemorated around the world in popular music, drama, and cinema. ◆

1972 Biko helps establish the Black People's Convention, a coalition of black organizations.

1973 The South African government restricts Biko's movements and speaking.

1977 Biko dies of a brain hemorrhage after being tortured by police.

Bond, Julian

JANUARY 14, 1940– ● ACTIVIST AND ELECTED OFFICIAL

Julian Bond was born in Nashville, Tennessee, of a prominent family of educators and authors. He grew up in the town of Lincoln University, Pennsylvania, where his father, Horace Mann Bond, was then president of the university, and later in Atlanta, when his father became president of Atlanta University. While attending Morehouse College in the early 1960s, Julian Bond helped found the Committee on Appeal for Human Rights. He dropped out of Morehouse to join the Student Nonviolent Coordinating Committee (SNCC), of which he became communications director in 1962. In 1964 he traveled to Africa and upon his return became a feature writer for the *Atlanta Inquirer*. Later he was named its managing editor. He eventually received his B.A. from Morehouse in 1981.

Bond won election to the Georgia House of Representatives in 1965, triggering controversy. On January 10, 1966, fellow legislators voted to prevent him from taking his seat in the house

"I tell my students, the civil rights movement didn't begin in Montgomery [Ala.] and it didn't end in the 1960s. It continues on to this very moment."

Julian Bond, 1996

when he refused to retract his widely publicized support of draft evasion and anti-Vietnam War activism. Protest in defense of Bond's right to expression was strong and widespread. Both SNCC and the Southern Christian Leadership Conference (SCLC) sought mass support for Bond through community meetings, where discussion and ferment strengthened African-American awareness of the relationship between peace activism and the civil rights struggle. The Rev. Dr. Martin Luther King Jr. rallied to Bond's defense, Vice President Hubert Humphrey publicly supported Bond, and noted cultural figures took out ads for pro-Bond campaigns.

After nearly a year of litigation, the U.S. Supreme Court ruled that Bond's disqualification was unconstitutional. The Georgia House was forced to seat Bond, and he remained there until 1975. In 1968 Bond was presented as a possible vice presidential candidate by opposition Democrats at the Democratic Convention in Chicago. He was too young, however, to qualify for the office, and his name was withdrawn. In 1972 he published *A Time to Speak, a Time to Act: The Movement in Politics*, in which he discussed ways of channeling civil rights activism into the electoral system. In 1975 Bond was elected to the Georgia State Senate, where he served for twelve years. His activities during this period included the presidency of the Atlanta NAACP, where he served until 1989, and service as the narrator of both parts of the popular PBS documentary series about the civil rights movement, "Eyes on the Prize" (1985–86, 1988–89).

In 1986 Bond ran for the U.S. Congress from Georgia and narrowly lost in a bitter contest with John Lewis, his former civil rights colleague. In the early 1990s Bond served as visiting professor and fellow at various colleges, including the University of Pennsylvania, Drexel University, Harvard University, and the University of Virginia, and was a frequent essayist and commentator on political issues. He also was, in the early 1990s, the host of a syndicated television program, *TV's Black Forum*. In February 1998 Bond was elected chair of the board of the National Association for the Advancement of Colored People. ◆

1940 Bond is born in Nashville, Tennessee.

1962 Bond becomes community affairs director of Student Nonviolent Coordinating Committee (SNCC).

1965 Bond is elected to the Georgia House of Representatives.

1975 Bond is elected to the Georgia State Senate.

1981 Bond receives his B.A. from Morehouse College.

1998 Bond is elected chairman of the board of the NAACP.

Bonilla, Tony

MARCH 2, 1936– ● MEXICAN–AMERICAN ATTORNEY AND ACTIVIST

Tony Bonilla is a prominent civil rights attorney based in Corpus Christi, Texas, a city on the Gulf Coast, who has made an impressive career out of his commitment to bringing people together, Hispanics and blacks and Anglos all, in the cause of social justice and equal rights. In his position as national executive director of the League of United Latin American Citizens (LULAC) in the early 1970s, and as president of LULAC in the early 1980s, and today as chairman of the National Hispanic Leadership Conference, Bonilla has always reached out to join Hispanic interests with other groups to build stronger coalitions for the common good.

Tony Bonilla was born in Calvert, a rural town in central Texas, on March 2, 1936, of Mexican immigrant parents. He went to Del Mar College in Corpus Christi on a football scholarship in 1953, where he received his two-year associate's degree, then in 1955 transferred to Baylor University in Waco. At Baylor he studied education, minored in government and Spanish, and received his bachelor of arts degree in 1958. He studied law at the University of Houston and received his degree in 1960.

In that year, Bonilla joined one of his brothers and formed the law firm of Bonilla, Thomas, DePena, and Bonilla (which eventually became the firm of Bonilla and Chapa), specializing in personal injury litigation. In addition to his law practice, Bonilla has served in many political and administrative positions in public advocacy groups, and was a representative in the Texas state legislature from 1964 to 1967. He has also been appointed to special positions in state government, including the Texas Constitutional Revision Committee, the Coordinating Board for Texas Colleges and Universities, and the Governor's Select Committee on Public Education.

A powerful influence in the development of Bonilla's political philosophy and career was Corpus Christi's widely respected Dr. Hector Garcia, a physician who was immensely influential in Texas politics—particularly regarding the Hispanic population of south Texas. Dr. Garcia was known as an expert negotiator who excelled at bringing people together to resolve issues, rather than playing one side against the other. He also

> Bonilla has always reached out to join Hispanic interests with other groups to build stronger coalitions for the common good.

1936 Bonilla is born in Calvert, Texas.

Bonilla graduates from Houston Law School; **1960** becomes national chairman of the Viva Kennedy Club.

Bonilla is elected **1964** a representative in the state legislature.

Bonilla is made national executive director of **1972** the League of United Latin American Citizens (LULAC).

Bonilla helps found the National Hispanic **1983** Leadership Conference (NHLC).

Bonilla leads an effort to found the organization **1997** Leadership, Education, Awareness, Prevention (LEAP).

made a practice of encouraging others to become politically involved in issues and causes.

When Tony Bonilla graduated from the University of Houston Law School in 1960, Garcia took on the young lawyer as a protégé and groomed him for a future in Corpus Christi politics. In 1960 Garcia was national chairman of the Viva Kennedy Club, a Hispanic organization affiliated with the Democratic party campaigning on behalf of then Senator John F. Kennedy (D-Mass.). Garcia appointed Bonilla south Texas chairman of Viva Kennedy, and the two traveled all over south Texas campaigning for JFK and Kennedy's running mate, their fellow Texan Lyndon B. Johnson. In making these rounds, Bonilla learned the dos and don'ts of campaigning, and forged relationships that would later help him win election as a state legislator in 1964. "I literally learned at his footsteps," Bonilla says of Garcia. "Just as Dr. Martin Luther King taught many aspiring blacks to take positions of leadership, Dr. Hector taught many would-be Hispanic leaders."

In 1968, just days after the assassination of Martin Luther King (on April 4), Bonilla joined with local black and Jewish leaders to organize a citywide memorial service held on April 7 in Corpus Christi. Bonilla explains that the intention was to do something affirmative to commemorate King's life and work. "We had so much turmoil around cities in the country," Bonilla recalls, "so our citizens here wanted to make certain that did not happen. There were some meetings held in order to mark his death with something significant as opposed to rioting and looting." Bonilla, the Rev. Harold Branch (later elected as Corpus Christi's first black councilman), and Rabbi Sidney Wolf were among the leaders intent on holding the city together in "tri-ethnic" peace among blacks, Hispanics, and whites. In addition to the King commemoration, the coalition builders organized other events to bring people together and cultivate bonds of familiarity and trust.

Bonilla was national executive director of the League of United Latin American Citizens (LULAC) from 1972 to 1975. Founded in 1929, LULAC is dedicated to seeking social, political, economic, and educational rights for Hispanic Americans, and has over 100,000 members in twelve regional and forty-three state groups.

As national executive director and later as president (1981–83), Tony Bonilla led efforts to meet with members of the news media and film industry to press for more positive representation and employment of Hispanics, and lobbied corporation executives to persuade them to be more responsive to the Hispanic community. He fostered national coalitions with black leadership, particularly with his friend the Rev. Jesse L. Jackson, and with Mrs. Coretta Scott King and the Martin Luther King Jr. Center in Atlanta.

Bonilla expected some skepticism and criticism for his eagerness to forge ties with the black community—skepticism he was quite ready to dispel by arguing that for him, personally, he has always considered himself to be "on the same side of the tracks" as African Americans, so in that sense he was not going "outside" his own neighborhood at all. Bonilla's most impressive memory from his youth was growing up on the "dark-skinned side of town," as Calvert, Texas, was divided by a highway and railroad tracks. Onstage beside the Rev. Jackson at a ceremony in Chicago during Harold Washington's mayoral campaign in 1983, Bonilla recounted to a black and Hispanic audience, "All the blacks and Hispanics lived on one side of the track. And all the whites lived on the other side of the track. So I was raised with the black people."

A sense of community with African Americans has long been a driving force in Bonilla's career as a bridge builder and a reconciling agent in civil rights work. Bonilla has long sought to find ways in which people of different backgrounds can work together to fulfill their common interests. Bonilla's philosophy is a natural fit with the Rainbow Coalition idea of strength in numbers as advocated by Jesse Jackson. Indeed, in 1983, early in Jackson's first presidential campaign, he presented Bonilla with an award for building good relations between LULAC (of which Bonilla was then president) and Jackson's own Operation PUSH (People United to Serve Humanity), an organization formed to promote social and economic improvement and political representation for the poor.

In 1983 Bonilla and other activists founded the National Hispanic Leadership Conference (NHLC), a think tank (or research group) that brings together prominent Hispanics and promotes political and economic involvement in the mainstream of American society. Delegations of NHLC members have traveled to Latin America to speak with political and business leaders about the conference's efforts in establishing drug education and awareness programs in the United States. The conference has also worked with Jesse Jackson and Operation PUSH to forge agreements with several major corporations to ensure that blacks and Hispanics receive a fair share of jobs and opportunities from those firms.

> *"All the blacks and Hispanics lived on one side of the tracks. And all the whites lived on the other side of the tracks. So I was raised with the black people."*
> Tony Bonilla

> A sense of community with African Americans has long been a driving force in Bonilla's career as a bridge builder and a reconciling agent in civil rights work.

hate crime: assault on a person or defacement of property motivated by hostility toward a creed, color, gender, or sexual orientation.

epidemic violence: a rapid growth of violence.

In November 1997, as chairman of the National Hispanic Leadership Conference, Bonilla was invited to attend President Clinton's National Conference on **Hate Crimes**, and came back to Corpus Christi inspired to put into practice some of the good ideas generated in Washington. In December 1997 he led an effort to create a coalition organization called Leadership, Education, Awareness and Prevention—commonly called by its acronym, LEAP—to bring together civic groups, churches, public agencies, and local businesses to publicize the problem of hate crimes.

LEAP was founded not so much in reaction to **epidemic violence** or intolerance in Corpus Christi—according to city police there were six such crimes in 1997—but in an effort to make sure that such a problem would not get started. "We're not trying to be alarmists and create problems where none exist," Bonilla explains, but "the minority community is always subject to being the victims of some form of hate." LEAP meets monthly and invites guest speakers to discuss hate crimes and suggest ways to cultivate tolerance and goodwill among communities. The organization has formed a "pool" of volunteer speakers who visit local schools to address the topic, and has devised ways to work with local police. One cooperative effort with the police involved the creation of a standardized hate crimes reporting policy.

In his widespread, all-embracing work for social justice, Tony Bonilla passes on the lessons learned from Dr. Hector Garcia and other good influences, and continues to show the practical and social benefits of working *together* for the things that matter most. ◆

Bonnin, Gertrude Simmons (Zitkala-Sa)

1876–1938 ● NATIVE AMERICAN RIGHTS ACTIVIST

Gertrude Simmons Bonnin, whose Indian name was Zitkala-Sa, was a well-known Indian reformer, writer, and musician. Through her writings and lectures, she demanded better treatment of Indians and supported giving Indians more control over decisions that affected their lives.

Zitkala-Sa was born at the Tankton Sioux Reservation in South Dakota. At the age of eight, she left the reservation to attend a Quaker missionary school in Indiana. From 1895 to 1897 she attended Earlham College (Indiana), where she excelled in oratory. In 1899 she studied violin at the Boston Conservatory of Music, and in late 1900 she performed at the Paris Exposition and toured Europe.

Returning to the United States, she embarked on a literary career. Her articles were published in the *Atlantic Monthly* and *Harper's Monthly* and in two books, *Old Indian Legends* (1901) and *American Indian Stories* (1921). Her writings dealt with needed Indian reforms, Indian stories, and her experiences.

She taught at the Carlisle Indian School in Pennsylvania from 1897 to 1899. In 1902 she served as issue clerk at Standing Rock reservation in North Dakota, where she married Raymond Bonnin, another Sioux employee. She then worked as a teacher, issue clerk, and band organizer at the Uintah and Ouray reservation in Utah from 1902 to 1916. In 1916 Bonnin moved to Washington, D.C., to become secretary of the Society of American Indians, a **pan-Indian** organization, and to assume the editorship of its journal, the *American Indian Magazine*. She called for educational and social reforms on reservations and denounced the use of peyote by Indians.

During the 1920s Bonnin accomplished some of her most effective work through the General Federation of Women's Clubs, an organization that had as one of its main interests the improvement of Indian conditions. She called for better educational opportunities and improved health care for Indians and worked with a research team to investigate corruption and graft in Oklahoma against the Five Civilized Tribes. In 1926 Bonnin and her husband established the National Council of American Indians, an organization that lobbied for Indian reform legislation in Washington, D.C. She headed the council until its demise in the mid-1930s. ◆

> *"I prefer my excursions into the natural gardens where the voice of the Great Spirit is heard in the twittering of birds, the rippling of mighty waters, and the sweet breathing of flowers. If this is Paganism, then at present, at least, I am a Pagan."*
> Zitkala-Sa, 1902

pan-Indian: involving all American Indians.

Brown, Hubert G. (H. Rap)

OCTOBER 4, 1943– ● WRITER AND ACTIVIST

H Rap Brown was born in Baton Rouge, Louisiana. He became involved in the civil rights movement while a student at Southern High School. He attended

Southern University in Baton Rouge, but in 1962 he left school and devoted his time to the civil rights movement. He spent summers in Washington, D.C., with his older brother, Ed, and became a member of the Nonviolent Action Group (NAG). In 1964, Brown was elected chairman of NAG. Simultaneously, he became involved with the Student Nonviolent Coordinating Committee (SNCC).

In May 1966 he was appointed director of the SNCC voter registration drive in Alabama. Brown increased his involvement with SNCC, and in June 1967 he became Stokely Carmichael's successor as National Chairman of SNCC, where he continued its militant stance. In 1968 Brown also served as minister of justice for the Black Panther Party during a brief working alliance between the two black power organizations.

As urban rebellions expressing black discontent spread across the United States, Brown's militant advocacy of black power made him a popular public speaker; his advocacy of black self-defense and condemnations of American racism—perhaps most memorably in his oft-quoted aphorism that "violence is as American as cherry pie"—made him a symbol of resistance and black pride within the Black Power movement. His rhetorical and vituperative talents—the source of his adopted name, "Rap"—were displayed in his one book, *Die Nigger Die!* (1969), a semiautobiographical account of his experiences with white racism. Brown embraced the term "nigger" as an embodiment of black resistance against racism.

Brown was consistently harassed by the police, and was targeted by the FBI's Counter Intelligence Program (COINTELPRO) because his speeches supposedly triggered volatile situations and violent outbreaks. On July 24, 1967, he was accused of "counseling to arson" in Cambridge, Maryland, because a city school that had been set on fire twice before was burned a third time after one of his speeches.

On August 19, 1967, Brown was arrested for transporting weapons across state lines while under indictment, despite the fact that he had never been formally notified that he was under

1943 ▶ Brown is born in Baton Rouge, Louisiana.

1962 ▶ Brown leaves Southern University to devote time to the civil rights movement.

1967 ▶ Brown becomes national chairman of SNCC.

1972 ▶ Brown is apprehended and imprisoned on federal weapons charges.

indictment. In May 1968 Brown resigned as SNCC chairman. Later that year, he was found guilty of the federal weapons charges and sentenced to five years in prison. He was released on bond in order to stand trial on the Cambridge, Maryland, charges. Brown never appeared at the Maryland trial; two of his friends had recently been killed in a suspicious automobile explosion, and his defense attorney claimed that Brown would be endangered if he appeared. Brown went into hiding, and in 1970 he was placed on the FBI's Ten Most Wanted List. He was apprehended in 1972, and was released four years later.

Brown converted to Islam while in prison and took the name Jamil (beautiful) Abdullah (servant of Allah) Al-Amin (the trustworthy). Upon his release from jail, he moved to Atlanta, Georgia. Al-Amin continues to reside in Atlanta as the proprietor of a grocery called the Community Store and as the imam (leader) of the Community Mosque. He is the spiritual leader of hundreds of Muslim families in Atlanta and in thirty other cities, including Chicago, New York, and Detroit. Al-Amin practices a strict Sunni interpretation of the Koran, and his followers maintain a spiritual distance from the larger society. His mosque operates its own 300-student school, and his followers make aggressive outreach efforts to college campuses, malls, and surrounding housing projects. ◆

> *"Revolutionaries are not necessarily born poor or in the ghetto. There is a role for every person in the revolution."*
> H. Rap Brown, 1969

Brown, John

MAY 9, 1800–DECEMBER 2, 1859 ● ABOLITIONIST

Tanner, surveyor, sheepherder, farmer, wool merchant, and land speculator, John Brown was best known as a preacher and abolitionist who led the Pottawatomie Creek Massacre and the raid on Harpers Ferry. Born in Torrington, Connecticut, the son of an ardent abolitionist, Brown spent most of his adult life speaking and acting against slavery in America. Although he has often been described as a failure in business, he was sometimes quite successful, particularly in the tanning and wool businesses, but he tended to move into other areas of endeavor whenever an operation of his collapsed.

The father of twenty children (only twelve of whom reached maturity) by two wives, he lived in Ohio, Pennsylvania,

Massachusetts, and New York and traveled to England and the European continent.

While he shelved his desire to become a minister after developing eye problems, religion remained the driving force behind his political feelings. He detested slavery from his earliest years and was an active participant in the antislavery movement beginning in the 1850s.

With the creation of the Kansas Territory, the doctrine of popular sovereignty went into effect. As a result, that region became a jousting field between proslave and abolitionist forces, each determined to secure Kansas as a state. As settlers from both philosophies poured into the region, five of Brown's sons pioneered near Osawatomie as "free-staters." In October 1855 their father joined them.

Confrontations between proslavers and free-staters accelerated in late 1854 and culminated in the bloodless Wakarusa War, which ended in December 1855 with the dispersal of armed forces at the order of the territorial governor. At the time Brown, as captain of a militia company, proposed continued armed resistance rather than cooperation.

"Now, if it is deemed necessary that I should forfeit my life for the furtherance of the ends of justice, I say let it be done."

John Brown's Final Address to the Court upon his being sentenced to death, November 2, 1859

Tensions increased in early 1856. In retaliation for the partial destruction of Lawrence, Kansas, by a proslave "posse" on May 21, Brown and a small band of men, including four of his sons, killed five proslavery men on Pottawatomie Creek in Franklin County three days later. The first serious reprisal against proslave violence, the killings were later hailed by abolitionists as the single most important act to make Kansas a free state.

During the ensuing months, Brown defeated proslave forces at the Battle of Black Jack, three miles east of Baldwin. He helped defend Osawatomie when it was sacked on August 29, and wrote numerous letters to newspapers and individuals condemning slavery. His fanaticism and acts of violence brought him national recognition.

In 1857 the armed clashes between proslavers and free-staters moved to east-central Kansas. Eventually, free-staters assumed the ascendancy, and the fight in Kansas turned from violence to politics with proslavers and free-staters calling themselves Democrats and Republicans. It had become obvious that Kansas would ultimately be admitted to the Union as a free state. Brown continued to battle against slavery in the west, however. In December 1858 he led a raid from Kansas into Missouri, where he destroyed considerable property, killed a slaveholder, and freed nearly a dozen slaves whom he took northward. He never returned to Kansas.

Years before the fight in Kansas, Brown had determined to invade the South to free the slaves. After years of self-admitted procrastination, he finally developed a plan that he hoped would cause slaves to rise up in revolt. To accomplish his plan, he needed arms and a daring coup to rouse public sentiment and the slaves' cooperation.

The act was the attack on the United States arsenal at Harpers Ferry. As early as 1857 he had begun training troops in Iowa, but when his intentions leaked out, he shelved the plan for two years. In June 1859 he was ready to start over; he rented a farm near Harpers Ferry and began gathering supporters.

On Sunday evening, October 16, 1859, he and a small force, including two of his sons, attacked and took possession of the **arsenal**. A group of marines, under the command of U.S. Army colonel Robert E. Lee, arrived from Washington, D.C., the next evening and trapped Brown and his band in the engine house. After his sons were killed, Brown surrendered to the federal authorities.

Two weeks later, he was tried for treason and found guilty. He was hanged on December 2, 1859. ◆

arsenal: a collection of weapons.

1800 Brown is born.

1856 Brown leads a small band of men who kill five men who support slavery at Pottawatomie Creek in Kansas.

1858 Brown leads a raid from Kansas to Missouri, freeing nearly a dozen slaves.

1859 Brown leads an attack on the U.S. arsenal at Harpers Ferry; he is captured, tried for treason, and hanged.

Bunche, Ralph Johnson

AUGUST 7, 1904–DECEMBER 9, 1971 ● DIPLOMAT AND CIVIL RIGHTS LEADER

Ralph Bunche was born in Detroit, Michigan, to Fred and Olive Johnson Bunch. His father, a barber, abandoned the family when his son was young. Bunche moved with his mother to Albuquerque, New Mexico, where she died in 1917. He then went to Los Angeles to be raised by his mater-

valedictory address: a speech given by the highest ranking student in the class.

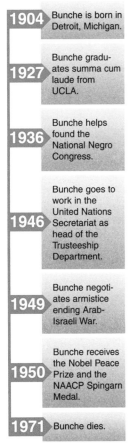

1904 Bunche is born in Detroit, Michigan.

1927 Bunche graduates summa cum laude from UCLA.

1936 Bunche helps found the National Negro Congress.

1946 Bunche goes to work in the United Nations Secretariat as head of the Trusteeship Department.

1949 Bunche negotiates armistice ending Arab-Israeli War.

1950 Bunche receives the Nobel Peace Prize and the NAACP Spingarn Medal.

1971 Bunche dies.

nal grandmother, Lucy Taylor Jackson. During his teen years, he added a final "e" to his name to make it more distinguished. Bunche lived in a neighborhood with relatively few blacks, and he was one of only two blacks in his class at Jefferson High School, where he graduated first in his class, although Los Angeles school authorities barred him from the all-city honor roll because of his race. Bunche's **valedictory address** was his first public speech. Bunche entered the University of California at Los Angeles (UCLA) on scholarship, majoring in political science and philosophy. He was active on the debating team, wrestled, played football and baseball, and was a standout basketball player. In 1927, he graduated summa cum laude and again, first in his class.

Assisted by a tuition fellowship and a $1,000 scholarship provided by a group of African-American women in Los Angeles, Bunche enrolled at Harvard University in 1927 to pursue graduate study in political science. He received a master's degree in 1928, and then accepted an invitation to join the faculty of Howard University. Bunche was only twenty-five when he created and chaired Howard's political science department. His association with Howard continued until 1941, although he pursued graduate work at Harvard during leaves.

Bunche's graduate work combined his interest in government with a developing interest in Africa. He conducted field research in western Africa in 1932 and 1933, and wrote a dissertation on the contrast between European colonial and mandatory governments in Africa. The dissertation, completed in 1934, won a Harvard award as the best political science dissertation of the year, and Bunche was awarded the first Ph.D. in political science ever granted an African American by an American university. Bunche undertook postdoctoral studies in 1936 and 1937, first at Northwestern University, then at the London School of Economics and at South Africa's University of Cape Town. In 1936 he published a pamphlet, *A World View of Race*. His notes, taken during fieldwork in South Africa and detailing the political and racial situation were published in 1992 under the title *An African American in South Africa*.

During Bunche's time at Howard in the 1930s, he was deeply involved in civil rights questions. He believed that black people's principal concerns were economic, and that race, though significant, was secondary. While he participated in civil rights actions—notably a protest he organized against segregation in Washington's National Theater in 1931—Bunche, a principled integrationist, warned that civil rights efforts founded on race would collapse over economic issues. He felt that the best hope for black progress lay in interracial working-class economic improvement, and he criticized Franklin Roosevelt both for his inattention to the needs of black people and for the New Deal's failure to attack existing political and economic structures. In 1936 Bunche and others founded the National Negro Congress, a broad-based coalition he later termed "the first sincere effort to bring together on an equal plane Negro leaders [and] professional and white-collar workers with the Negro manual workers and their leaders and organizers." The Congress was eventually taken over by Communist Party workers. Bunche, disillusioned, resigned in 1938.

In 1939 Bunche was hired by the Swedish sociologist Gunnar Myrdal to work on what would become the classic study of race relations in the United States, *An American Dilemma: The Negro Problem and Modern Democracy* (1944). Over the next two years Bunche wrote four long research memos for the project (one was published in 1973, after Bunche's death, as *The Negro in the Age of FDR*). The final report incorporated much of Bunche's research and thought. The unpublished memos, written for the Carnegie Corporation, have remained an important scholarly resource for researchers on black America, both for their exhaustive data and for Bunche's incisive conclusions.

In 1941, after the United States entered World War II, Bunche left Howard to work for the Office of the Coordinator of Information for the Armed Service, and later joined the newly formed Office of Strategic Services, the chief American intelligence organization during World War II, precursor of the Central Intelligence Agency. Bunche headed the Africa section of the Research and Analysis Branch. In 1944 Bunche joined the U.S. Department of State's Postwar Planning Unit to deal with the future of colonial territories.

From this point forward, Bunche operated in the arena of international political affairs with an ever-increasing degree of policymaking power. In 1945 he was appointed to the Division of Dependent Area Affairs in the Office of Special Political Affairs, becoming in the process the first African American to head a **State Department "desk."**

In 1944, Bunche was a member of the U.S. delegation at the Dumbarton Oaks Conference in Washington, D.C., which laid the foundation for the United Nations. Appointed to the

> *"We must adhere strongly to the basic principle that anything less than full equality is not enough. If we compromise on that principle our soul is dead."*
> Ralph Bunche, 1935

State Department "desk": an office in the State Department.

U.S. delegation in San Francisco in 1945 and in London in 1946, Bunche helped set up the UN Trusteeship system to prepare colonies for independence. His draft declaration of principles governing all dependent territories was the basis of Chapter XI, "Declaration Regarding Non-Self-Governing Territories," of the United Nations Charter.

Bunche went to work in the United Nations Secretariat in 1946 as head of the Trusteeship Department. In 1947 he was assigned to the UN Special Commission on Palestine, which was a United Nations Trusteeship. The outbreak of the First Arab-Israeli War in 1948, and the assassination of UN mediator Folke Bernadotte by Jewish militants, propelled Bunche, Bernadotte's assistant, into the position of acting mediator. Bunche brought the two sides together, negotiating with each in turn, and succeeded in arranging an armistice. Bunche's actions earned him the 1950 Nobel Prize Peace. He was the first United Nations figure, as well as the first African American, to win a Nobel Prize. Bunche also won the NAACP's Spingarn Medal (1950), and other honors. In 1953 the American Political Science Association elected him its president, the first time an African American was so honored. In 1950 President Truman offered him the post of Assistant Secretary of State. Bunche declined it, and in a rare personal statement on racism, explained that he did not wish to raise his family in Washington, a segregated city.

Bunch was the first United Nations figure, as well as the first African American to win a Nobel prize.

Bunche remained at the United Nations until shortly before his death in 1971. In 1954 he was appointed United Nations Undersecretary General for Special Political Affairs, and served as a roving specialist in UN work. Bunche's most significant contribution at the United Nations was his role in designing and setting up UN peacekeeping forces, which supervise and enforce truces and armistices and have arguably been the UN's most important contribution to global peace. Building on the truce supervising operation he put into place after the 1949 Middle East **armistice**, Bunche created a United Nations Emergency Force in 1956, after the Suez crisis. UN peacekeepers played a major role in Lebanon and Yemen, later in Congo, in India and Pakistan, and in Cyprus. Sir Brian Urquhart, Bunche's assistant and successor as UN Undersecretary General for Special Political Affairs, said: "Bunche was unquestionably the original principal architect of [what] is now called peacekeeping . . . and he remained the principal architect, coordinator, and director of

armistice: a temporary suspension of hostilities between two opponents.

United Nations peacekeeping operations until the end of his career at the UN."

While Bunche remained primarily involved as an international civil servant with the United Nations, promoting international peace and aiding developing countries, he also remained interested in the civil rights struggle in America. Indeed, Bunche demanded and received special dispensation from the United Nations to speak out on racial issues in the United States. Bunche served on the board of the NAACP for many years, and served as an informal adviser to civil rights leaders. In 1963 he attended the March on Washington, and two years later, despite poor health, he traveled to Alabama and walked with the Rev. Dr. Martin Luther King Jr. in the front row of the Selma-to-Montgomery Voting Rights March. ◆

Carmichael, Stokely

JULY 29, 1941–NOVEMBER 15, 1998 ● CIVIL RIGHTS LEADER

Born in Port of Spain, Trinidad, Stokely Carmichael graduated from the Bronx High School of Science in 1960 and Howard University in 1964. During his college years, he participated in a variety of civil rights demonstrations sponsored by the Congress of Racial Equality (CORE), the Nonviolent Action Group (NAG), and the Student Nonviolent Coordinating Committee (SNCC). As a freedom rider, he was arrested in 1961 for violating Mississippi segregation laws and spent seven weeks in Parchman Penitentiary. After college, he worked with the Mississippi Summer Project, directed SNCC voter-registration efforts in Lowndes County, Alabama, and helped organize black voters through the Lowndes County Freedom Organization.

Elected SNCC chairman in 1966, he proffered an outspoken, militant stance that helped distance SNCC from the moderate leadership of competing civil rights organizations. A chief architect and spokesperson for the new Black Power ideology, Carmichael coauthored (with Charles V. Hamilton) *Black Power* (1967) and published a collection of his essays and addresses, *Stokely Speaks* (1971). He left his SNCC post in 1967. The next year he was made

Student Nonviolent Coordinating Committee

The Student Nonviolent Coordinating Committee (SNCC, or "Snick") was formed in 1961 by a group of student leaders who believed that existing civil rights organizations were overly cautious. From the fall of 1961 through the spring of 1966, SNCC shifted its focus from nonviolent desegregation protests to long-term voting rights campaigns in the Deep South. Veterans of the Mississippi Freedom Rides gradually displaced representatives of local protest groups as principal policymakers. Initially dominated by Christian followers of Mahatma Gandhi, SNCC began to focus on black leaders in local communities.

During 1965 and 1966 SNCC members became increasingly dissatisfied with the tactics of civil rights groups like the Southern Christian Leadership Conference (SCLC). Militant members of the SNCC, under the leadership of Stokely Carmichael, established the Black Panther Party. In May 1966 SNCC workers' growing willingness to support racial separatism and radical social change led to a shift in the group's leadership, electing Carmichael as chairman. The national controversy surrounding Carmichael's Black Power speeches distanced SNCC from the NAACP, SCLC, and other elements of the more mainstream coalition that had supported civil rights reform. After a period of external opposition, police repression, and internal conflict, SNCC alienated many former supporters. In addition, its leaders' emphasis on ideological issues detracted from long-term community-organizing efforts. SNCC did not have much impact on African-American politics after 1967.

prime minister of the Black Panther Party; in 1969 he quit the Black Panthers and became an organizer for Kwame Nkrumah's All-African People's Revolutionary Party. Studies with Nkrumah of Ghana and Sékou Touré of Guinea confirmed his Pan-Africanism and in 1978 moved him to change his name to Kwame Toure. For the last thirty years of his life he made Conakry, Guinea, his home, and he continued his work in political education, condemning Western imperialism and promoting the goal of a unified socialist Africa. He died of prostate cancer in 1998. ◆

Carnegie, Andrew

NOVEMBER 25, 1835–AUGUST 11, 1919 ● INDUSTRIALIST AND PHILANTHROPIST

Andrew Carnegie, who became one of the wealthiest men in American history, was born in Dunfermline, Scotland, on November 25, 1835. He arrived in the United States as a penniless Scottish immigrant. He was thirteen when his parents brought him to America. He began work almost at once, in a textile factory. His second job, as messenger boy for a Pittsburgh telegraph company, led to a rapid rise. Carnegie was a quick learner, and became an expert telegraph operator. As a result, he came to the attention of Thomas Scott, then superintendent of the Pennsylvania Railroad, who made the bright young Carnegie his secretary and his personal telegrapher.

At the start of the Civil War, Carnegie helped work out a signal system for use in handling military shipments. He soon discovered that the wartime needs of the country offered great business opportunities. He left the railroad, and began a career of organizing and reorganizing iron and steel companies, beginning with a bridge company that he reorganized in 1862. Recognizing the great need for steel in the United States, he turned all his talent for work and organization to the business of making steel. His mills became the most important and best managed in the United States, at the time when the nation was moving ahead to lead the world in steel production.

Carnegie was a hard-driving manager and an expert at selecting aides and assistants. He never organized his companies as corporations, but kept them as partnerships, which he controlled himself. His chief associates were rewarded with shares of the ownership of companies, and were placed in positions where their talents were able to produce very successfully. Carnegie was also a clever judge of business trends and used this skill to help improve his companies. During times of depression or slow business, he often bought the newest equipment available at relatively low prices. When business improved, his factories were able to produce better steel, faster and cheaper, than his competitors'. Carnegie's policies were very strongly anti-labor unions. His steel mills were involved in several long, bitter strikes, and the Carnegie Company was never successfully unionized.

In 1901 Carnegie decided that he had made enough money and had spent enough of his time in business. He sold out all his interests to the new United States Steel Corporation, acquiring a quarter of a billion dollars. Carnegie planned to use his money as a means of improving the lives of others. He began with the

"A man who dies rich, dies disgraced."
Andrew Carnegie, 1889

1835 Carnegie is born in Dunfermline, Scotland.

1901 Carnegie sells his steel company to the U.S. Steel Corporation.

1911 Carnegie founds the Carnegie Corporation to "promote the advancement and diffusion of knowledge."

1919 Carnegie dies in Lenox, Massachusetts.

men who had worked for him and set up a five-million-dollar pension fund for the employees of the Carnegie Company. During the rest of his life, he spent a great deal of his time and effort supervising ways to put his enormous wealth to work for general public good. Among his special gifts were funds to build "Carnegie Libraries" to be operated as public libraries in many parts of the United States and the world. His gifts were largely responsible for starting public libraries in many American cities. He also created funds to improve school teaching, to support scientific research, and to advance international peace. Many of his funds were used for organizations in Great Britain as well as for United States groups. Carnegie provided funds for building the "Peace Palace" at The Hague.

He died in Lenox, Massachusetts, in August 1919. ◆

Carter, Jimmy

OCTOBER 1, 1924– ● HUMANITARIAN AND FORMER U. S. PRESIDENT

James Earl Carter Jr. rose to office from a background that though somewhat varied, was, compared with that of most presidents, quite narrow. The most obvious limitation was lack of previous experience in Washington.

Carter was a southerner, the first one since before the Civil War who had come to the presidency by election. He came from the small-town South—from Plains, Georgia, where he was born on October 1, 1924—the first of four children of Earl and Lillian Carter. A native southerner, Earl was a successful farmer-businessman active in public affairs.

Prior to the presidency, the United States Navy gave Carter his only extended experience outside the South. Following graduation from a segregated public school in Plains and two years at Georgia Southwestern and Georgia Tech, he entered the United States Naval Academy in 1943, an institution that stresses discipline and engineering. A strong student, he graduated in 1946 in the top 10 percent of his class. After marrying Rosalynn Smith of Plains on July 7, he served as a naval officer until October 1953, mostly in the submarine service, including the nuclear program headed by Hyman Rickover, a man Carter admired greatly.

Following his father's death, Carter returned home to look after the family farm and business, which specialized in peanuts. The business prospered but did not dominate his attention. He became active in public affairs, serving, for example, on the Sumter County Board of Education from 1956 to 1962. In the last year, he was elected to the state senate, where he served successfully for four years, devoting much attention to education. Civil rights was the most prominent issue at the time, but he continued to support segregation and largely avoided the controversy.

In 1966 Carter suffered his first serious failure, and it affected him significantly. He failed in a bid for the Democratic nomination for governor. In 1970, in his second bid for the governorship, Carter succeeded, and for the next four years, he presided over the state's affairs. He embraced a quite **eclectic** philosophy with a strong conservative bent, especially on fiscal matters, though he liked to present himself as a populist, the representative of the common people against the establishment and the special interests. Proposing a large agenda of welfare reform, educational advance, budget reform, and other matters, he emphasized government reorganization in hopes of making government operate more efficiently and effectively, and he achieved some success. Also eager to promote economic growth, he cooperated with business leaders. And he demonstrated a new, though cautious, interest in reforming race relations.

Ambitious and self-confident, Carter decided well before his term as governor ended to run for the presidency in 1976. Not a man of national prominence and power, the Georgian surprised the nation by gaining the nomination on the first ballot at the Democratic National Convention in New York. Behind this victory lay strenuous and successful participation in the now numerous primaries throughout the nation. His campaign, which began early in 1975, stressed Washington's defects and his own virtues, not specific issues or a clearly defined ideology. He sensed a widespread yearning for change in leadership and great distrust of and skepticism about established leaders. He tried to persuade the disenchanted that he had the personality

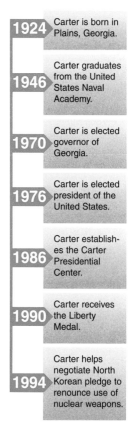

1924 Carter is born in Plains, Georgia.

1946 Carter graduates from the United States Naval Academy.

1970 Carter is elected governor of Georgia.

1976 Carter is elected president of the United States.

1986 Carter establishes the Carter Presidential Center.

1990 Carter receives the Liberty Medal.

1994 Carter helps negotiate North Korean pledge to renounce use of nuclear weapons.

eclectic: composed of elements drawn from various sources.

and values the situation demanded. He was moral and intelligent, tough yet compassionate.

In midsummer, Carter and his vice-presidential candidate, Walter Mondale of Minnesota, seemed likely to win the election by a wide margin, but President Gerald Ford gained ground rapidly. He took advantage of his incumbency, spending much of the campaign period in the White House "being president." He attacked his foe as inexperienced, inconsistent, unclear, misguided, and liberal, and charged that the big-spending Democratic Congress was the major source of inflation. He pointed with pride to his record, arguing that no Americans were fighting a war, tension between the United States and the Soviet Union had been reduced, employment was increasing, and inflation was declining.

Carter defeated Ford by just 1.7 million popular votes in November 1996.

As president, Carter adopted an informal style of dress and speech in order to reinforce his image as a man of the people. He hoped to restore confidence in government as well as to establish confidence in him. He relied heavily on both television and direct contacts to accomplish these objectives. And he seemed quite successful. At the same time, Carter had campaigned as an outsider, a critic of America's leadership of the recent past, and he proved unsuccessful in converting his ideas into legislative realities.

As his popularity rose and fell, Carter pushed forward along several lines of policy. Foreign affairs commanded much of his time, and though he had grown up in the 1930s and early 1940s and had served in the navy during World War II and during the years that saw the establishment of the Truman policy of the containment of communism, he had been affected by the mood of withdrawal from world affairs that had been gaining strength in the United States for a decade. In addition, even though they had served in the Kennedy and Johnson administrations and had supported their policies in Vietnam, many of the men Carter appointed to the top spots in international and military affairs had been influenced by the American failure in Vietnam and by détente. Secretary of Defense Harold Brown indicated just before taking office that he had learned from Vietnam that "we must become more cautious about . . . interventions." Carter, according to observers, had by then "made it abundantly clear that the United States ought not to go plunging militarily into underdeveloped countries." Soon after taking

President Carter adopted an informal style of dress and speech in order to reinforce his image as a man of the people.

office, he praised the nation for having overcome its "inordinate fear of Communism," and Andrew Young suggested that the administration rejected "military activism."

Carter did embark upon an international campaign for human rights. In part, he did so to distinguish himself from Nixon, Ford, and Kissinger, although the campaign made use of the 1975 Helsinki treaty that the Ford administration had helped to develop. In addition to affirming the boundaries established after World War II in Eastern Europe, the treaty contained promises to respect human rights. Carter hoped the campaign would enable the United States to "regain the moral stature we once had." He explained, "We've been through some sordid and embarrassing years recently, and I felt like it was time for our country to hold a beacon light . . . that would rally our citizens to a cause." But was this policy a response to criticism of past practices as much as it was a basis for renewed activism? "In a nation supposedly instructed in its limitations by its recent failures," a critic charged, "Jimmy Carter . . . has demonstrated how little America has learned"; Carter expressed "that traditional American delusion that, if only America can devise the right . . . formula, then the world will stop being what it is, and become what we wish it to be."

In any event, Carter had difficulty maintaining a firm course on **human rights**. He regarded this crusade as the centerpiece—the "fundamental tenet"—of his foreign policy. He criticized many countries, not just the Soviet Union, for violating human rights. But many people—inside as well as outside the United States, State Department officials as well as journalists, allies as well as opponents—charged that the campaign was meddling, harmful to international relations, destructive of détente, and a return to the Cold War. The administration often retreated under pressure.

The campaign had mixed results. To the distress of European leaders, it infuriated the Soviet Union, contributing to the emergence of what some called a New Cold War. On the other hand, it pressured authoritarian regimes in Latin America and sub-Saharan Africa and encouraged democratic forces in those parts of the world.

In 1978 Carter brought Egyptian president Anwar el-Sadat and Israeli prime minister Menachem Begin together at Camp David, Maryland. There, the three men talked for thirteen days in September 1978 and the president achieved a great success: a "framework for peace" that ended the state of war that had

"We've been through some sordid and embarrassing years and I felt like it was time for our country to hold a beacon light that would rally our citizens to a cause."

President Jimmy Carter

human rights: the rights belonging to all persons.

existed between the two countries since Israel's founding in 1948. The accords provided for the establishment of full diplomatic and economic relations between them on condition that Israel withdraw from the Sinai Peninsula.

These achievements in foreign policy were eclipsed by a serious crisis in Iran. On November 4, 1979, several thousand Iranian youths seized the American embassy in Teheran and took most members of the staff hostage. Their actions were sanctioned by Iran's revolutionary government, and a standoff developed between the United States and Iran. Carter relied on diplomatic and economic pressures to free the hostages. After six months of mounting public dissatisfaction and personal soul searching, a frustrated president broke with past policy and authorized a military rescue operation. The mission failed when a helicopter collided with a transport plane, killing eight men and injuring others. Carter's inability to obtain the hostages' release had become a major political liability for him.

In 1980 Carter ran for reelection but public confidence in his ability to govern had fallen to an all-time low. In the November general election Carter was soundly defeated by the Republican presidential nominee, Ronald W. Reagan. The fifty-two remaining hostages in Iran were not released until January 20, 1981, Carter's last day in office.

Out of office and free of the political pressures that had limited his accomplishments as president, Carter became an unusually active and widely admired former president. He found new ways of expressing his humanitarianism: monitoring elections in other countries, mediating international disputes, bringing experts together to develop solutions to pressing problems, and building low-priced housing with the Habitat for Humanity organization. ◆

> The Camp David accords provided for the establishment of full diplomatic and economic relations between Egypt and Israel.

Cassin, René-Samuel

OCTOBER 5, 1887–FEBRUARY 20, 1976 ● NOBEL PEACE PRIZE WINNER AND CHAMPION OF UNIVERSAL HUMAN RIGHTS

I n 1968, twenty years to the day after the approval by the UN General Assembly of the Declaration of Human Rights on December 10, 1948, the Nobel Committee gave the Nobel Peace Prize to René-Samuel Cassin for his contribution to that landmark international development and for his continuing efforts for the protection of human rights. Cassin took a leading role in the collective effort that produced the declaration and subsequently contributed to its implementation in the Council of Europe, the one regional organization in the world where the principles of the declaration became the basis of an international judicial institution, the European Court of Human Rights.

Cassin was born in Bayonne in southern France, the son of a Jewish merchant. As a schoolboy he showed great academic promise, and made a brilliant record at the University of Aix-en-Provence and the Faculty of Law at Paris, where in 1914, at age of twenty-seven, he received his doctorate in juridical, political, and economic sciences.

He began to practice law in Paris, but with the coming of the war in August 1914, Cassin had to leave his law books for the army. In 1916 he was severely wounded when a piece of shrapnel pierced his abdomen. He was taken to the ward of hopeless cases in the hospital. By an extraordinary coincidence, his mother was serving as a nurse in that hospital, and she persuaded a surgeon to attempt the operation that saved her son's life.

Invalided home, Cassin married and became professor of law at his old University of Aix. His career in the law was distinguished. From Aix he moved to Lille in 1920, and then in 1929 he was appointed to the chair of fiscal and civil law at the University of Paris, where he taught until retirement in 1960 at the age of seventy-three. Through his writings and lectures in France and abroad, he enjoyed an international reputation among legal scholars.

The impact of Cassin's war experiences turned him toward international and humanitarian activities. Almost immediately after the Armistice, he took up the cause of victims of the war—disabled soldiers, war orphans, war widows—working for legislation that would provide adequate government care for them. In 1918 he founded the French Federation of Disabled War Veterans, serving as president and then honorary president until 1940. Beginning in 1921 he arranged conferences with war veterans of other nations, including former enemy countries, and in 1926 he established an international organization of disabled veterans. These associations of former combatants were strong supporters of peace and disarmament, and Cassin himself worked for disarmament as a delegate of France to the Assembly of the League of Nations and its conference on disarmament.

1887 Cassin is born in Bayonne, France.

1914 Cassin receives his doctorate in juridical, political, and economic sciences from the Faculty of Law in Paris.

1918 Cassin founds the French Federation of Disabled War Veterans.

1946 Cassin plays a key role in the writing of the Declaration of the Rights of Man with the United Nations.

1968 Cassin receives the Nobel Peace Prize.

1976 Cassin dies in Paris.

invalid: suffering from a disease or disability that prevents mobility.

"The exploitation of women, mass hunger, disregard for freedom of conscience and for freedom of speech, widespread racial discrimination— all these evils are far too prevalent to be overlooked."

René Cassin, 1968

When Germany invaded France in 1940, Cassin was one of the first prominent civilians to join General Charles de Gaulle in London in the effort to free France from its German invaders and their French collaborators of Vichy. Cassin became minister of justice in the government-in-exile, and he drew up the agreement with Winston Churchill according to which the French forces were to be independent and not under British orders. He next became commissioner of public instruction and represented France in the wartime meetings of the Allied ministers of education. He was also in a position to make sure that the principle of human rights was included in the Atlantic Charter. For his services to the Free French, Cassin was deprived of his French citizenship by the Vichy government and sentenced to death in absentia.

After the war Cassin was given high positions in educational administration and in the judiciary of France, and he made his international contribution as delegate to the UN General Assembly and as a founding delegate to UNESCO and one of the authors of its charter. It was, however, in the UN Commission on Human Rights that Cassin made his most important contribution. The UN Charter had declared one of the purposes of the organization to be the respect for and promotion of human rights. This marked a new development in international relations, since up to this time a state's treatment of its nationals was considered its own business and any interference an encroachment upon its sovereignty. The war against Hitlerism, however, was not only to resist German armed aggression but to free the world from Nazi atrocities and brutal violations of human rights. Especially after the facts of the Holocaust became known, it was only natural that the international organization that emerged from this war would create a Commission on Human Rights. Thus when the UN General Assembly met in 1946, it asked the commission to prepare a Declaration of Human Rights and an international convention by which states would be obliged to respect these rights.

Eleanor Roosevelt was the first chair of the commission and Cassin was the vice chairman. Mrs. Aase Lionaes, who made the presentation on behalf of the Nobel Committee, had been a Norwegian delegate to the UN General Assembly when it discussed the document proposed by the commission, and she told how Cassin had held a key position in formulating the concepts of the declaration. She said he had served as **mediator** between the Western emphasis upon civil and political rights

mediator: someone who helps bring about agreement between opposing parties.

and the Eastern European concern for economic, social, and cultural rights. She felt that the bridging of "many minds, many religions, many ideologies, and many hearts . . . was primarily the engineering feat of René Cassin."

Cassin is often spoken of as "the principal author" of the declaration, but historians are not agreed that he deserves top billing since so many others made important contributions. There is no denying the fact, however, that he had been one of the world's most tireless and authoritative champions of human rights, and the Nobel Committee could not have found a more appropriate recipient of the prize in International Human Rights Year. After his term as vice chairman of the UN Commission on Human Rights expired, Cassin served as vice president and then president of the European Court of Human Rights.

Cassin used the prize money to establish the International Institute of Human Rights at Strasbourg. It was with this objective in mind that he had actively promoted his own candidacy for the prize. He died in 1976 in Paris at the age of eighty-nine. ◆

> René Cassin was one of the most tireless and authoritative champions of human rights.

Catt, Carrie Chapman

JANUARY 9, 1859–MARCH 9, 1947 ● SUFFRAGIST

Carrie Chapman Catt was one of the most active and effective leaders of the movement to gain political equality for American women during the early years of the twentieth century. After graduating from Iowa State College, Catt became the principal of Mason City High School. Her success as principal led to superintendency of the Mason City schools in 1883. After marrying Leo Chapman, she became assistant editor of her husband's newspaper, the *Mason City Republican*.

After Leo Chapman died in 1886, Carrie Chapman resolved to devote her life to the cause of emancipation of women. She helped organize the Iowa Women's Suffrage Association in the late 1800s. In 1890 she married George William Catt, who not only approved of his wife's dedication to reform but supported it by legally stipulating that Catt could spend four months each year in suffrage work. At his death in 1905 he left her financially independent and able to devote her life to the cause.

Susan B. Anthony chose Carrie Chapman Catt to succeed her as president of the National American Women Suffrage Association (NAWSA) in 1900. Catt shifted the group's emphasis toward political reform during her presidency, encouraging action and social reform. After William Catt's death, Catt became active in international women's suffrage, touring the world and organizing feminists in Europe, Scandinavia, Asia, and Africa. In 1915 she returned to the presidency of NAWSA, presiding over the effort to ratify the Nineteenth Amendment to the U.S. Constitution, which granted women the right to vote. A great deal of the political background for that Amendment was developed by Catt, and ratification of the Amendment (1920) was the crowning achievement of her career.

Carrie Chapman Catt founded the League of Women Voters in 1919, to encourage women to be active in political affairs and to encourage a wise and honest influence by women on political decision making. She was honorary president of the League from 1920 until her death. During the latter part of her life, Catt was actively interested in the cause of international disarmament and in promoting the means of preserving world peace, founding the National Committee on the Cause and Cure of War in 1925. Catt died at her home in New Rochelle, New York, at the age of eighty-eight. ◆

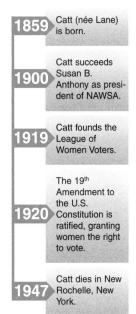

1859 Catt (née Lane) is born.

1900 Catt succeeds Susan B. Anthony as president of NAWSA.

1919 Catt founds the League of Women Voters.

1920 The 19th Amendment to the U.S. Constitution is ratified, granting women the right to vote.

1947 Catt dies in New Rochelle, New York.

Chaney, James Earl

MAY 30, 1943–JUNE 21, 1964 ● CIVIL RIGHTS MARTYR

James Chaney was born in Meridian, Mississippi, to Ben Chaney and Fannie Lee Chaney. His parents instilled a strong sense of racial pride in him, and in 1959 he, along with a group of his friends, was suspended from high school for wearing a button meant to criticize the local NAACP chapter for its unresponsiveness to racial issues. One year later he was expelled from school and began to work alongside his father as a plasterer. Chaney's experiences traveling to different job sites throughout Mississippi on segregated buses, at the same time that Freedom Rides mounted by civil rights organizations aimed at challenging segregated interstate transportation were occurring throughout the South, further spurred his activism. In 1963 he became directly involved in civil rights activities and joined the Congress of Racial Equality (CORE). One year later CORE joined forces with the Mississippi branches of the Student Nonviolent Coordinating Committee (SNCC), and the National Association for the Advancement of Colored People (NAACP) to form the Council of Federated Organizations (COFO) to spearhead a massive voter registration and desegregation campaign in Mississippi called the Freedom Summer.

During Chaney's work with COFO, he met Michael Schwerner, a white Jewish liberal who had been a New York City social worker before he joined CORE in 1963 and relocated to become a field worker in Mississippi, and Andrew Goodman, a young Jewish college student who had volunteered for the Mississippi Freedom Summer project. Assigned to work together in Meridian, on June 21, 1964, the three men went to Longdale—a black community in Neshoba County, Mississippi—to investigate the burning of a church that had been a potential site for a Freedom School teaching literacy and voter education. The Ku Klux Klan was firmly entrenched in large areas of Mississippi, and it was widely suspected that the Klan had burned the church down to prevent civil rights activities. As the three men were driving back to Meridian, they were detained by the police in Philadelphia, Mississippi. Chaney was arrested for speeding and Schwerner and Goodman were arrested as suspects in the church bombing. None of the men was allowed to make a phone call or pay the fine that would have **facilitated** his release from the Neshoba County jail.

The arrest of Chaney, Schwerner, and Goodman was no accident. Civil rights workers were constantly harassed by white night riders and local policemen who were often Klan members more committed to maintaining the racial status quo than to upholding justice. Schwerner was the first white civil rights worker to be stationed outside of Jackson, Mississippi. His activities and presence had made him well known to Meridian whites and his success in initiating civil rights programs and his Jewish background had made him a target of the Klan, who had

facilitated: helped to cause.

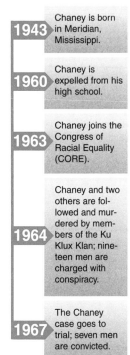

1943 Chaney is born in Meridian, Mississippi.

1960 Chaney is expelled from his high school.

1963 Chaney joins the Congress of Racial Equality (CORE).

1964 Chaney and two others are followed and murdered by members of the Ku Klux Klan; nineteen men are charged with conspiracy.

1967 The Chaney case goes to trial; seven men are convicted.

"*These three men gave their lives for all of us to become participants in the democratic process. They died right here in America. Their deaths should never be forgotten. They put their bodies on the line for the cause of freedom.*"
U.S. congressman
John Lewis, 1999

The murders of Chaney, Schwerner, and Goodman became a milestone in the civil rights movement.

nicknamed him "Goatee" because he wore a beard. After Neshoba County Deputy Sheriff Cecil Ray Price confirmed the fact that the car Chaney had been driving was registered to CORE, he alerted local Klan leader Edgar Ray Killen. Killen quickly organized a posse of Klansmen and formulated a plan of action with as many as twenty conspirators. Later that same night, Price released the three men from jail after Chaney paid the fine. They were followed out of town by a Klan posse, forcibly removed from their cars, driven to an isolated wooded area a few miles away and killed. Their bodies were buried in an earthen dam in the immediate vicinity of Philadelphia, a burial site that had been chosen beforehand.

Attempts to locate Chaney, Schwerner, and Goodman had been initiated by COFO when the trio had not called or reached their destination at the allotted time. As it became increasingly apparent that harm had befallen them, COFO renewed its long-standing request for assistance from the Justice Department, and mobilized a campaign among its membership to put pressure on governmental officials. Social violence against black people in Mississippi was commonplace, and despite the high proportion of lynchings that took place in Mississippi, no white person had ever been convicted of murdering a black person in the history of the state. The heightened interest in civil rights, and the likely involvement and disappearance of two white men commanded national attention, and federal response. President John F. Kennedy and Attorney General Robert Kennedy met with the families of the missing men, and FBI agents were dispatched to the scene to mount an extensive investigation. When the charred remains of Chaney's car were found a few days after the incident, Neshoba county was flooded with journalists who reported to the shocked nation the hostility of Mississippi whites who seemed to epitomize southern racism.

The FBI recovered the bodies of the three civil rights workers from the earthen dam on August 4, 1964, and four months later nineteen men were charged with the conspiracy. The federal government was forced to use a Reconstruction era statute to charge the men with conspiring to deprive Chaney, Schwerner, and Goodman of their civil rights because the social consensus behind the lynch mob's actions made state prosecution for murder unlikely.

Recalcitrant judges, defense delays, and problems with jury selection hampered the due process of law for three years. In 1966 the U.S. Supreme Court stepped in to reinstate the original indictments after the case had been thrown out of court, and in February 1967 the long delayed trial finally began. Despite various confessions and eyewitness accounts, only seven defendants, one of whom was Deputy Sheriff Price, were convicted nine months later. Only two men were convicted of the maximum sentence of ten years under the law. Two of the other men received sentences of six years, and three received three-year sentences. The conspirators were all paroled before serving full jail terms and most had returned to the Mississippi area by the mid-1970s.

The murders of Chaney, Schwerner, and Goodman became a milestone in the civil rights movement. Although an important precedent for federal intervention on behalf of civil rights workers was set, this incident was memorialized by many in the civil rights movement, not only as an instance of southern injustice but as the result of many years of federal indifference to the plight of African Americans. ◆

> *"What has happened is over. We can feel sorry for ourselves and be downtrodden, or we can take the goodness of these three men and use it to help people."*
> Ben Chaney,
> James Chaney's
> brother, 1999

Chávez, César

MARCH 31, 1927–APRIL 23, 1993 ● LABOR ACTIVIST

César Estrada Chávez was a Mexican-American labor activist. He is known for his years of tireless work to improve the lives of migrant farm workers through nonviolent action. In the mid-1900s he led one of the most successful agricultural boycotts in American history. Chávez founded what is now the United Farm Workers of America (UFW), the first successful union of agricultural workers in the United States.

At the time Chávez founded his union in the 1960s farmworkers in California earned an average of $1.50 per hour and had no benefits or rights to challenge abuses by employers. Unionization eventually helped bring about wage increases, medical benefits, pensions, and other benefits to farm workers.

Chávez was born on March 31, 1927, near Yuma, Arizona, to Juana and Librado

Migrant Labor

Migrant workers are a labor force employed for a short time in places to which they must travel. Most migrant workers are employed as farm labor that moves into an area temporarily to help harvest and process crops. Historically, these jobs have been low-status; workers have been segregated, isolated from community involvement, and subject to discrimination. Living and working conditions have been consistently below standard, migrants' work is intermittent and insecure, their wages are artificially deflated by the attraction of an oversupply of workers at job sites, and, failing to meet residency requirements, migrants have been denied adequate health, welfare, education, and medical services.

It is very difficult to determine how many migrants work in the United States. Estimates range from 125,000 to over a million. Many migrant workers have trouble finding other kinds of work because they lack education and training. Migrant children tend to fall behind on their education because they change schools so often. Children also work to help support their family, further interrupting their classwork.

In the 1960s Edward R. Murrow's television documentary "Harvest of Shame" reminded Americans of the price being paid for their inexpensive food. Congress responded with health and education programs specifically for migrants. Also in the early 1960s migrant workers began to organize. Utilizing nonviolent, direct-action tactics learned from the civil rights movement, Cesar Chavez's United Farm Workers union won significant concessions from growers. In the 1970s, as educational and job-training programs, legal and employment services, and more accessible welfare increased their options, the number of impoverished families employed in migratory farm work declined proportionately. Illegal aliens from Mexico, Puerto Rico, and Guatemala have taken their places in the fields.

"Once social change begins, it cannot be reversed. You cannot uneducate the person who has learned to read. You cannot humiliate the person who feels pride. You cannot oppress the people who are not afraid anymore."

César Chávez, 1984

Chávez. He lived on the family's 160-acre farm in Arizona until he was ten, when the family lost the farm due to the effects of the Depression. His family then moved to California to become migrant farmworkers. They lived in poverty and resided in tents or shacks in various migrant labor camps. Chávez attended dozens of different schools during his youth because his family was always on the move. He finally graduated from eighth grade at the age of fifteen, when he quit school to work full-time in the fields and help support his family. At the age of seventeen, Chávez joined the U.S. Navy and served two years during World War II. He then returned to migrant work and married Helen Fabela in 1948. They had eight children.

Chávez first became involved in organizing workers in 1952, when he joined the Community Service Organization (CSO). He spent the next ten years helping to register Mexican-

American voters and aiding them on immigration, welfare, and other issues. He quit the CSO in 1962 after the organization refused to support his proposal of a union movement for farmworkers. He then formed the National Farm Workers Association (NFWA).

To build membership for his union, Chávez spent several months in the fields and towns of California, convincing workers to join the union. Building membership and getting dues from a migratory population was difficult, but by 1965 the association had 1,700 members. By that time he had also succeeded in persuading two crop growers to raise worker wages. In 1965 NFWA joined forces with the Agricultural Workers Organizing Committee (AWOC), part of the AFL-CIO, and embarked on one of the longest and most successful strikes in labor history. The strike was against California grape growers and it stemmed from protests over wage inequities.

In 1966 the two unions merged and formed the United Farm Workers Organizing Committee (UFWOC). After the merger, California's wine grape growers agreed to accept the UFWOC as the collective bargaining agent for the grape pickers. However, the table-grape growers refused to negotiate with the UFWOC. Chávez reacted to their opposition by organizing a nationwide boycott against all California table grapes. The boycott was a tremendous success. An estimated 17 million Americans stopped buying grapes because of it. Finally, after losing millions of dollars, the growers agreed to sign a contract with the union in 1970 and the strike came to an end.

Over the years Chávez continued his efforts to organize farm laborers and obtain union contracts for them, and he remained committed to obtaining results through nonviolent means. He often urged consumers to boycott farm products produced by nonunion workers and sometimes used fasting as a nonviolent means of protest. In one instance after some Mexican-American strikers became tired with a drawn-out strike and threatened to use force against crop growers, Chávez went on a **hunger strike**, vowing not to eat until union members pledged themselves to nonviolence once more. Twenty-five days later, when he felt he had gotten his message across the ranks, he ended his fast.

Chávez was known for his gentle manner, his sincerity, and his religious devotion, and he won the admiration of many respected civil rights advocates of his time. Chávez died in his sleep on April 23, 1993, while on union business in Arizona. ◆

1927	Chávez is born in Arizona.
1952	Chávez joins the Community Service Organization (CSO).
1962	Chávez founds the National Farm Workers Association (NFWA).
1965	Chávez leads a strike against California grape growers .
1970	Strike ends with union contract being signed by grape growers.
1993	Chávez dies in his sleep while on union business in Arizona.

hunger strike: refusal to eat as an act of protest.

Chavis, Benjamin Franklin, Jr. (Muhammad)

January 22, 1948– ● Civil Rights Leader

1948 Chavis is born in Oxford, North Carolina.

1967 Chavis joins Southern Christian Leadership Conference (SCLC).

1972 Chavis and nine others wrongfully convicted of arson and conspiracy to assault.

1975 The Wilmington Ten enter prison.

1978 Amnesty International designates Chavis and the others as political prisoners.

1980 Chavis is released from prison.

1995 Chavis helps organize the Million Man March.

conspiracy: the act of plotting together to carry out an unlawful act.

Born and raised in Oxford, North Carolina, the Rev. Dr. Benjamin F. Chavis Jr. came from a long line of preachers. His great-great-grandfather, the Rev. John Chavis, was the first African American to be ordained a Presbyterian minister in the United States. Chavis first became involved in the struggle for civil rights at the age of twelve, when his persistence in seeking privileges at a whites-only library in Oxford started a chain of events that led to its integration. In 1967, while a student at the University of North Carolina (UNC) at Charlotte, Chavis became a civil rights organizer with the Southern Christian Leadership Conference (SCLC); he remained active with the organization until he graduated from UNC in 1969 with a B.A. in chemistry. After a year spent as a labor organizer with the American Federation of State, County, and Municipal Employees (AFSCME), Chavis joined the Washington field office of the United Church of Christ's Commission for Racial Justice (UCCCRJ).

On February 1, 1971, Chavis was sent to Wilmington, North Carolina, in response to a request from Wilmington ministers for a community and civil rights organizer. The racial climate in Wilmington had become explosive when court-ordered desegregation began in 1969. In January 1971 black students began a boycott of Wilmington High School; Chavis was sent to help organize this student group. Within two weeks of his arrival, Wilmington erupted in a week long riot.

In March 1972, fourteen months after the riot ended, Chavis and fifteen former students were arrested for setting fire to a white-owned grocery store and shooting at firemen and policemen who answered the call. Chavis, eight other black men, and a white woman were convicted for arson and **conspiracy** to assault emergency personnel. Chavis and the nine other defendants became known as the Wilmington Ten. In 1975, after his appeals were exhausted, Chavis entered prison. Because of the weak nature of the evidence against them, they were designated political prisoners by Amnesty International in 1978, the first time the organization had done so for any U.S. convicts. Their case received national and international support.

In 1977 all three witnesses who testified against the Wilmington Ten admitted they had given false testimony and had been either pressured or bribed by the Wilmington police. Despite this new evidence, the defendants were denied the right to a new trial. Chavis, the last of them to be paroled, was released in 1980, having served more than four years of his thirty-four-year sentence at Caledonia State Prison. On December 4, 1980, a federal appeals court overturned the convictions, citing the coercion of prosecution witnesses.

While in prison, Chavis taught himself Greek, translated the New Testament, wrote two books (*An American Political Prisoner Appeals for Human Rights*, 1979, and *Psalms from Prison*, 1983) and earned a master of divinity degree magna cum laude from Duke University. After his release, he earned a doctor of ministry degree from the Divinity School of Howard University. In 1986 Chavis became the executive director of the UCCCRJ. In this capacity, he focused on combating both what he calls "environmental racism"—the government and industry's practice of burdening poor and **predominantly** black neighborhoods with toxic waste dumps—and gang violence. In 1993 Chavis became the seventh executive director of the National Association for the Advancement of Colored People; his election at age forty-five made him the youngest person ever to lead the organization. He pledged to revitalize the organization, whose aging membership has been a source of concern, and to sharpen its focus; he also cited the longer-term goal of expanding membership to include other minorities.

Chavis's policies during his tenure as executive director proved extremely controversial. In an attempt to reorient the NAACP toward young urban blacks, he held dialogues with militant black leaders, including Louis Farrakhan. In the summer of 1994 he acknowledged that he had used NAACP funds in an out-of-court settlement with a female NAACP staff member who accused Chavis of sexual harassment. Amid these and other charges of financial impropriety, the board of directors relieved Chavis of his position as executive director on August 20, 1994.

Following his resignation from the NAACP, Chavis joined the Nation of Islam as an organizer and close adviser of Minister Louis Farrakhan. In 1995, Chavis was the principal organizer of the Million Man March. In February 1997 he

predominantly: for the most part.

announced his conversion to Islam, and he took the name Benjamin Chavis Muhammad. He was subsequently defrocked by the United Church of Christ. He was named by Farrakhan to lead Malcolm X's old mosque in Harlem. ◆

Clark, Septima Poinsette

MAY 3, 1898–DECEMBER 15, 1987 ● EDUCATOR AND CIVIL RIGHTS ACTIVIST

> "We know we are citizens because it is written in an amendment to the Constitution."
>
> Septima Clark, 1964

inequities: unfair disparities.

Septima Poinsette was born and reared in Charleston, South Carolina. Her mother, Victoria Warren Anderson, was of Haitian descent and worked as a laundress, and her father, Peter Porcher Poinsette, was a former slave who worked as a cook and a caterer. Her parents deeply influenced Poinsette and instilled in her a willingness to share one's gifts and a belief that there was something redeeming about everyone. In addition, Poinsette's early education, which brought her into contact with demanding black teachers who insisted that students have pride and work hard, left a positive and lasting impression on her. Partly as a result of these influences, Poinsette pursued a career in education. In 1916 she received her teaching certificate from Avery Normal Institute, a private school for black teachers founded after the end of the Civil War by the American Missionary Association in Charleston.

Poinsette's first teaching position was on Johns Island, South Carolina, from 1916 to 1919, because African Americans were barred from teaching in the Charleston public schools. She tried to address the vast educational, political, and economical **inequities** that faced Johns Island blacks by instituting adult literacy classes and health education and by working with the NAACP. In 1919 she returned to Charleston to work at Avery and spearheaded a campaign against Charleston's exclusionary education system that resulted, one year later, in the overturning of the law barring black teachers from teaching in public schools. In May 1920 Poinsette married Nerie Clark, a black navy cook. She had two children, one of whom died at birth. After her husband died in 1924, Clark sent her other child, Nerie Jr., to live with his paternal grandmother because she could not support him financially.

Shortly thereafter, Clark returned to Columbia, South Carolina, became active in various civic organizations, and continued her education, receiving a B.A. from Benedict College (1942) and an M.A. from Hampton Institute (1945). She led the fight for equal pay for black teachers in South Carolina. Her efforts attracted the attention of the NAACP, which initiated litigation and won a 1945 ruling mandating equal pay for black teachers in South Carolina. In 1947 Clark returned to Charleston to teach in public schools and continued her civic activities until she was fired in 1956 because of her membership in the NAACP. Unable to find another position in South Carolina, Clark moved to the Highlander Folk School, in Monteagle, Tennessee, an interracial adult education center founded by Myles Horton in 1932 to foster social activism and promote racial equality. There Clark became director of education. Together with Horton and South Carolina black activists such as Esau Jenkins from Johns Island, she devised educational strategies to challenge black illiteracy and encourage black voter registration. Clark, guided by the belief that literacy was integral to black equality, instituted the citizenship school program, an adult literacy program that focused on promoting voter registration and empowering people to solve their own problems through social activism.

The first **citizenship** school, founded on John's Island in 1957, was a success, and Clark traveled throughout the Deep South, trying to make links with other local activists to foster the expansion of the schools. In 1961 the citizenship school program was transferred to the Southern Christian Leadership Conference (SCLC) after the Tennessee legislature's persistent efforts to disrupt Highlander activities resulted in the school's charter being revoked and its property being confiscated. Clark joined SCLC to oversee the newly renamed Citizen Education Project, and by 1970 over 800 Citizenship schools had been formed that graduated over 100,000 African Americans who served as a key grassroots base for the civil rights movement throughout the Deep South. In 1971, however, she retired from SCLC because long-term commitment to the schools had faded.

Clark remained an outspoken spokesperson for racial, as well as gender, equality. She chronicled her life of activism in her autobiography, *Echo in My Soul*, in 1962. In 1966 she spoke at the first national meeting of the National Organization of Women (NOW) about the necessity of women challenging male dominance. In 1976 she was elected to the Charleston, South Carolina, school board. Three years later she was awarded the Living Legacy award from President Jimmy Carter in

1898 Clark is born in Charleston, South Carolina.

1942 Clark receives a B.A. from Benedict College.

1962 Clark publishes her autobiography, *Echo in My Soul*.

1966 Clark speaks at the first national meeting of National Organization for Women (NOW).

1976 Clark is elected to the Charleston, South Carolina, school board.

1979 Clark is awarded the Living Legacy Award by President Jimmy Carter.

1987 Clark dies in Charleston, South Carolina.

citizenship: status as a citizen, entitled to the rights and privileges of society.

honor of her continuing dedication to black empowerment through education. In 1987 she received an American Book Award for her second autobiography, *Ready from Within: Septima Clark and the Civil Rights Movement*. Later that year, Septima Clark died in Charleston, South Carolina. ◆

Cleaver, Eldridge Leroy

AUGUST 31, 1935–MAY 1, 1998 ● WRITER AND CIVIL RIGHTS ACTIVIST

> *"You don't have to teach people how to be human. You have to teach them how not to be inhumane."*
>
> Eldridge Cleaver, 1976

Eldridge Cleaver was born in Wabbaseka, Arkansas, where he attended a junior college. From 1954 to 1957 and again from 1958 to 1966 he was incarcerated on drug and rape charges, and furthered his education while in prison. In 1965 Cleaver became the most prominent "Black Muslim" prisoner to break with Elijah Muhammad's Nation of Islam after Malcolm X's assassination. Just as FBI director J. Edgar Hoover had begun to target the Black Panthers as the nation's "greatest threat," Cleaver became the party's minister of information in 1966, calling for an armed insurrection to overthrow the United States government and replace it with a black socialist government. During the late 1960s and early '70s he also was an assistant editor and contributing writer to *Ramparts* magazine.

In 1968 Cleaver published *Soul on Ice*, which remains his primary claim to literary fame. A collection of autobiographical and political essays in the form of letters and meditations, *Soul on Ice* articulated the sense of alienation felt by many black nationalists who refused to work within an inherently corrupt system. Cleaver viewed his own crimes as political acts and spelled out how racism and oppression had forged his revolutionary consciousness.

Later that year, while on parole, Cleaver was involved in a shootout with Oakland police during which a seventeen-year-old Black Panther, Bobby Hutton, was killed; Cleaver and a police officer were wounded. Cleaver's parole was revoked and he was charged with assault and attempted murder. Although he received worldwide support and was chosen to run as the presidential candidate for the Peace and Freedom Party, Cleaver feared for his safety if he surrendered to the authorities. He fled the country, jumping a $50,000 bail, and lived for the next seven years in Cuba, France, and Algiers. He also visited the Soviet Union, China, North Vietnam, and North Korea during these years of exile. But in 1975 he returned to the United States and struck a deal with the FBI. Although he faced up to seventy-two years in prison, he was sentenced instead to 1,200 hours of community service.

In 1978 Cleaver published *Soul on Fire,* a collection of essays on his newly acquired conservative politics, and in 1979 he founded the Eldridge Cleaver Crusades, an evangelical organization. In 1984 he ran as an independent candidate for Congress in the eighth Congressional District in California. In the 1980s he lectured on religion and politics, and published his own poetry and polemical writings. In March 1994 his struggle with drugs came to national attention when he underwent brain surgery after he had been arrested in Berkeley, California, late at night with a serious head injury, in a state of drunkenness and disorientation.

Cleaver had been a prolific writer and speaker and was seen by some in the late 1960s as a black leader capable of organizing and leading a mass movement. *Soul on Ice* won the Martin Luther King Memorial Prize in 1970. Most of his work consists of nonfiction writing: *Eldridge Cleaver: Post-Prison Writings and Speeches* (1969), *Eldridge Cleaver's Black Papers* (1969), the introduction to Jerry Rubin's *Do It!* (1970), and contributions to *The Black Panther Leaders Speak: Huey P. Newton, Bobby Seale, Eldridge Cleaver, and Company Speak Out Through the Black Panther Party's Official Newspaper* (1976) and to *War Within: Violence or Nonviolence in Black Revolution* (1971). He has also authored and coauthored numerous pamphlets for the Black Panther party and the People's Communication Network. Some of his work has also appeared in anthologies such as the *Prize Stories of 1971: The O. Henry Awards*.

Cleaver has had both his critics and his followers. There are those who felt that his commitment to violence and his use of rape as a political weapon in the 1960s had no place within society. Others have questioned the sincerity and credibility of

1935 Cleaver is born in Wabbaseka, Arkansas.

1966 Cleaver becomes minister of information for the Black Panthers.

1968 Cleaver is involved in a shoot-out, violating his parole, and flees the country.

1970 *Soul on Ice* receives the Martin Luther King Memorial Prize.

1975 Cleaver returns to the United States.

1978 Cleaver publishes *Soul on Fire.*

1979 Cleaver founds the Eldridge Cleaver Crusades.

1994 Cleaver undergoes brain surgery.

1998 Cleaver dies.

his later *volte face* to right-wing politics and fundamentalist Christianity, and Cleaver often felt compelled to explain and defend himself. According to him, combined with his growing disenchantment with communism and radical politics was a mystical vision resulting in his conversion to Christianity. When accused of having mellowed with age, Cleaver replied, "That implies that your ideas have changed because of age. I've changed because of new conclusions." Cleaver died on May 1, 1998. ◆

Corrigan, Mairead

JANUARY 27, 1944– ● COFOUNDER OF THE COMMUNITY OF THE PEACE PEOPLE IN NORTHERN IRELAND

Williams, Betty

MAY 22, 1943– ● COFOUNDER OF THE COMMUNITY OF THE PEACE PEOPLE IN NORTHERN IRELAND

"I couldn't really say that Betty Williams started the peace movement in Ireland because that would be a lie. The death of three children started the peace movement in Ireland."

Betty Williams,
1995

In 1976 the Nobel Peace Prize was shared by Mairead Corrigan and Betty Williams for their "courageous acts of peace" in founding a movement "to put an end to the violence that has characterized the unfortunate division in Northern Ireland and taken so many innocent lives."

Their actions had been inspired by a tragic incident that occurred during the summer of 1976 in Belfast, capital of the province ruled by the British. The city, divided between the Protestant majority and the Catholic minority, for seven years had been the scene of unbridled violence. The Provisional Irish Republican Army (IRA) wanted to drive out the British and unite with the Republic of Ireland to the south. Their bombings, murders, and other acts of violence were directed not only against British soldiers but against Protestant and Catholic civilians. On the other side were Protestant extremists, who had formed their own paramilitary units and returned violence for violence.

On a sunny day in August of 1976 a mother was going for a stroll with her three children, the eldest pushing her six-week-old baby brother in his carriage. Suddenly they heard a shot, and a car came careening into them, killing two of the children outright, mortally injuring the third, and leaving the mother in critical condition. Following a shoot-out, British soldiers pursuing IRA gunmen had shot dead the driver of the car, which had gone out of control and smashed the little family against an iron railing. This senseless killing of innocent children evoked a wave of revulsion against the violence that had held the city so long in its grip, and a spontaneous movement for peace began that brought together Protestants and Catholics. It was led by two young women, Mairead Corrigan and Betty Williams.

Both had been born in Catholic sectors of Belfast, but Betty Smyth was the first child of a mixed marriage between a Catholic mother and a Protestant father, something that Belfast Catholics decried, and her maternal grandfather, whom she dearly loved as a child, was a Polish Jew whose relatives had been killed in World War II. She attended Catholic schools, but her father, a butcher, tried to keep her free of the religious prejudices she found all around her. It was not surprising that she herself married a non-Catholic, Ralph Williams, an engineer in the merchant marine. She saw something of the world with her seaman husband, but they came back to Belfast, where she continued working after they had their two children. In 1976, when she was thirty-four, she held a secretarial job in a casualty firm and also worked as a waitress.

She had originally sympathized with the Northern Irish revolutionaries, but she had come to realize that violence only breeds violence and makes victims of the innocent. In 1972 she had joined a movement started by a Protestant clergyman to try to end the violence. In 1973, when a young British soldier was shot before her eyes and lay dying on the sidewalk, she tried to comfort him, only to meet with insults from Catholic women who watched. "I learned that people had obviously lost their sense of value of human life," she said when relating this story in later years.

Mairead Corrigan was the second of seven children of a working-class family. Her father, who worked as a window cleaner, could not pay for her high school tuition, so after completing the primary grades, she left school at fourteen and earned money as a baby-sitter in order to enroll in business courses. At sixteen she was an assistant bookkeeper in a textile factory, and at twenty-one she was hired as secretary in a brewery.

1943 Williams (née Smyth) is born in Belfast, Northern Ireland.

1973 Williams attempts to comfort a young British soldier who is shot before her eyes.

1976 Williams witnesses a runaway car, caught in a shoot-out between the IRA and British soldiers, kill three children.

1976 Williams and Mairead Corrigan lead a peace march to the graves of the Maguire children.

1976 Williams and Corrigan found the Community of the Peace People.

1977 Willaims and Corrigan receive the 1976 Nobel Peace Prize.

"We have really got to create a culture in our world today where we recognize that every human life is sacred and precious and we have no right to take another human life."

Mairead Corrigan, 1995

paramilitary: a force formed in a military pattern.

riffraff: disreputable people.

She stayed with the firm, and by 1976, when she was thirty-three, she had become private secretary to one of the directors.

Her religion always meant much to her. After leaving her Catholic school, she joined the Legion of Mary, a Catholic lay welfare organization, in which she worked with children and adolescents and organized recreational activities for the disadvantaged. The legion sent her as a youth leader to a meeting of the World Council of Churches in Thailand when she was twenty-eight, and the next year to the Soviet Union, to help make a film on the life of religious believers. On her return she showed the film and lectured at Catholic centers.

Mairead Corrigan grew up hating the British soldiers and fearing the Irish Revolutionary Army, but she never felt herself to be a revolutionary and she watched the increasing violence with dismay. She sympathized with the British-held political prisoners of both sides, whom she visited in her work with the legion, but she felt that the acts of violence of which they were accused were not consistent with the way of Christ, and she told them so.

The tragedy on the Belfast street changed her life. It was her sister, Anne Maguire, whose children had been killed by the car. The next evening Mairead Corrigan was interviewed on a television program. She burst out sobbing: "It's not violence that people want. Only one percent of the people of this province want this slaughter." With courage, she condemned those who encouraged young people to join the **paramilitary** groups.

Betty Williams had actually witnessed the accident, and she had immediately set about walking the streets of her neighborhood, collecting signatures to a petition demanding peace and a stop to the violence. In two days she announced over television that she had six thousand signatures. She asked all women, both Catholic and Protestant, to help "rid our community of this **riffraff**." She admitted, "I've always been afraid of the IRA. I am afraid of it at this very moment. But after such a tragedy, we must and will have peace."

Corrigan joined Williams in leading a peace march of ten thousand women to the new graves of the Maguire children. Protestants marched with Catholics and persisted when IRA supporters physically assaulted them. The next week thirty-five thousand marched from a Catholic to a Protestant area of Belfast.

The two women were joined by Ciaran McKeown, a newspaper reporter, who helped them give more lasting direction to the movement. He suggested that an organization be established to be called "Community of the Peace People" rather than "Women for Peace," since men should be included as well. He wrote a "Declaration of Peace," a simple statement of aims, and gave the movement its nonviolent ideology, founding its journal, *Peace by Peace*. It was also McKeown who planned the strategy of the marches that were staged during the following months in cities both in Northern Ireland and in Great Britain.

The IRA claimed that the Peace People were **dupes** of the British and wanted "peace at any price" instead of "peace with justice." They continued to harass the marchers, but the thousands who joined these occasions testified to a deep yearning for peace in the land.

dupes: those deceived by underhanded means.

The movement captured the imagination of the world and was given wide publicity. In Norway, where it was too late for a nomination for the Nobel Peace Prize, a campaign organized by newspapers and civic organizations raised $340,000, which was presented to Corrigan and Williams at a mass meeting at Oslo's city hall. The two visited other countries in Europe and across the seas to raise more funds. In October 1976 they came to the United States to appeal to Irish Americans to stop sending the money that was buying the guns and bombs for IRA terrorism.

The Peace People used the contributions to arrange non-sectarian activities, to repair damaged factories and schools, and to make loans for small businesses. It was clear that poverty and unemployment were giving rise to violence, and on their trips abroad Williams and Corrigan tried to generate foreign investments in Northern Ireland.

The Nobel Committee considered fifty nominations for the 1976 prize and then reserved it, presumably feeling that none of the candidates was as well qualified as the two Irish peace leaders. In 1977 Williams and Corrigan were properly nominated and duly presented with the 1976 prize at the same ceremony at which Amnesty International was given the prize for 1977.

The enduring quality of the service to peace of Mairead Corrigan and Betty Williams was highlighted in the words of Egil Aarvik, vice chairman of the Nobel Committee, in his presentation speech:

> Love of one's neighbor is one of the foundation stones of the humanism on which our western civilization is built. But it is vital that we should have the courage to sustain this love of our neighbor in the very circumstances when the pressure to abandon it is at its greatest—otherwise it is of little worth. This is why it should shine forth when hatred and revenge threaten to dominate. . . .
>
> Betty Williams and Mairead Corrigan have shown us what ordinary people can do to promote the cause of peace.

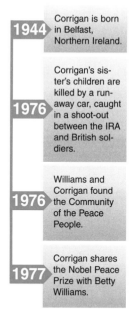

1944 Corrigan is born in Belfast, Northern Ireland.

1976 Corrigan's sister's children are killed by a runaway car, caught in a shoot-out between the IRA and British soldiers.

1976 Williams and Corrigan found the Community of the Peace People.

1977 Corrigan shares the Nobel Peace Prize with Betty Williams.

Until recently, the hope for peace in Northern Ireland remained unrealized. The Peace People declined in numbers and influence. Betty Williams emigrated to the United States, where she teaches in a university and has become an inspirational lecturer on peace. Mairead Corrigan Maguire has continued to work with the Peace People in Belfast and has also effectively carried her message of nonviolence into other countries. In 1998 peace talks in Northern Ireland resulted in an agreement that includes a commitment to using peaceful means to resolve political differences. The agreement was put to vote in a referendum that was approved in both Ireland and Northern Ireland. The fragile peace continues. ◆

Cosby, William Henry, Jr. (Bill)

JULY 12, 1937– ● COMEDIAN AND PHILANTHROPIST

Bill Cosby was born in Germantown, Pennsylvania, to William and Annie Pearle Cosby. After a stint in the navy (1956–60), Cosby studied at Temple University in Philadelphia, but dropped out to pursue a career as a stand-up comic.

During the 1960s Cosby worked in network television as a comedian featured on late-night talk shows. In 1965 he became the first African-American network television star in a dramatic series when producers named him to costar with Robert Culp in *I Spy* (1965–68). Cosby's character, Alexander Scott, did not usually address his blackness or another character's whiteness. As with other forms of popular entertainment with black characters at the time, Cosby's character was portrayed in a manner in which being black merely meant having slightly darker skin. He won Emmy Awards for the role in 1966 and 1967.

From 1969 through 1971 Cosby appeared as Chet Kincaid, a bachelor high school coach, on the situation comedy series *The Bill Cosby Show*. Cosby portrayed

Kincaid as a proud but not militant black man. The series was moderately successful. A few years later, Cosby and CBS joined forces in a television experiment, *Fat Albert and the Cosby Kids* (1972–77), a cartoon series for children. The series set the course for television in the vital new area of ethics, values, judgment, and personal responsibility. By the end of its three-year run, *Fat Albert* had inspired a number of new directions in children's television.

In 1972 and 1973 Cosby starred in *The New Bill Cosby Show,* a comedy-variety series. Cosby's Jemmin Company, which he had recently established, produced the shows, allowing him to have more control over the productions. As he did in all his television series, Cosby made great use of other black artists who had had few opportunities to practice their craft elsewhere.

For a few months in late 1976, largely because of his success as a regular guest on the PBS educational series *The Electric Company,* where he demonstrated great skill at working with and entertaining youngsters, ABC hired Cosby to host a prime time hour-long variety series oriented toward children, *Cos.* It did not catch on with viewers, however, and was canceled after a few months.

In the fall of 1984 *The Cosby Show* began on NBC, featuring Cosby as Cliff Huxtable, an obstetrician living with his wife and four children in a New York City brownstone. Their fifth child, away at college most of the time, appeared sporadically in featured parts. The show put black images on the screen that many people admired. The characters on *The Cosby Show* represented a real African-American upper-middle-class family, rarely seen on American television. Cosby sought black artists who had not been seen on network television in years for cameo roles (Dizzy Gillespie and Judith Jamison, for example). He also included black writers among his creative staff, and by the third year, he insisted on using a black director for some of the episodes. In its first year *The Cosby Show* finished third in the ratings; from the second season through the fourth season, it was the number-one-rated show in the United States.

Conscious of the need to lead the networks toward more equitable treatment of African Americans, Cosby used his position to require that more doors be opened. He had a presence in almost every area of television programming: he was a mass volume spokesman and star presenter for advertisements and public relations image campaigns that included Jello, Coca-Cola,

"We cannot afford to settle for being just average; we must learn as much as we can to be the best that we can. The key word is education – education with maximum effort. Without it, we cannot be in charge of ourselves or anyone else."
Bill Cosby, 1990

Conscious of the need to lead the [television] networks toward more equitable treatment of African Americans, Cosby used his position to require that more doors be opened.

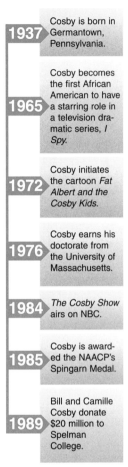

1937 Cosby is born in Germantown, Pennsylvania.

1965 Cosby becomes the first African American to have a starring role in a television dramatic series, *I Spy.*

1972 Cosby initiates the cartoon *Fat Albert and the Cosby Kids.*

1976 Cosby earns his doctorate from the University of Massachusetts.

1984 *The Cosby Show* airs on NBC.

1985 Cosby is awarded the NAACP's Spingarn Medal.

1989 Bill and Camille Cosby donate $20 million to Spelman College.

Delmonte, Kodak, and E. F. Hutton. He appeared in dramas, action-adventure stories, comedies, and children's programs. In 1992 he also entered into prime time syndication with Carsey-Werner Productions with a remake of the old Groucho Marx game series, *You Bet Your Life.* The show lasted only one season. That same year, however, Cosby made public his bid to purchase the National Broadcasting Corporation (NBC-TV), a television network worth $9 billion. Cosby was determined to call attention to the proliferation of negative images of black people and the titillation of viewers with sex and violence. All television viewers, he argued, were diminished by the spate of "drive-by images" that reinforced shallow stereotypes. In 1995 Cosby produced another unsuccessful syndicated series, *The Cosby Mysteries.* In 1996 he began a new hit series, *Cosby,* in which he played a working-class man from Queens, New York.

Throughout his career Cosby appeared at highly popular concert performances across the United States. His comedy focused on his own life as a reflection of universal human needs. He also produced more than twenty comedy/musical record albums, many of which have won Grammy awards, including *Bill Cosby Is a Very Funny Fellow* (1963), *I Started Out as a Child* (1964), *Why Is There Air?* (1965), *Wonderfulness* (1966), *Revenge* (1967), *To Russell, My Brother, Whom I Slept With* (1968), *Bill Cosby,* (1969), *Bill Cosby Talks to Children About Drugs* (1971), and *Children, You'll Understand* (1986). Cosby has written many best-selling books, including *The Wit and Wisdom of Fat Albert* (1973), *You Are Somebody Special* (1978), *Fatherhood* (1986), *Time Flies* (1987), and *Love and Marriage* (1989). He has served on numerous boards, including the NAACP, Operation PUSH, the United Negro College Fund, and the National Sickle Cell Foundation.

Cosby, who in 1993 was listed in *Forbes* magazine as one of the 400 richest people in the world with a net worth of more than $315 million, has been one of the most important benefactors to African-American institutions. In 1986 he and his wife gave $1.3 million to Fisk University; the following year they gave another $1.3 million to be divided equally among four black universities—Central State, Howard, Florida A & M, and Shaw; in 1988 they divided $1.5 million between Meharry Medical College and Bethune Cookman College. In 1989 Bill and Camille Cosby announced that they were giving $20 million to Spelman College, the largest personal gift ever made to any of the historically black colleges and universities.

In 1994 the couple donated a historic landmark building in downtown Washington, D.C., to the National Council of Negro Women to help them establish a National Center for African-American Women. Cosby himself has been the recipient of numerous awards, including the NAACP's Spingarn Medal (1985). He holds an M.A. (1972) and a doctorate (1976) in education from the University of Massachusetts at Amherst. In 1976 he also finally received a B.A. from Temple University. Cosby, who married Camille Hanks in 1964, has lived in rural Massachusetts since the early 1970s.

In 1997 Cosby's life was shattered when his son, Ennis, was robbed and murdered in Los Angeles. (Mikail Markhasev, a Russian immigrant, was convicted of the murder in 1998.) In the fall of 1997 Cosby was the target of an **extortion** plot by Autumn Jackson, an African-American woman who threatened to reveal that Cosby was her father unless he paid her. At Jackson's extortion trial, Cosby was forced to admit to an extramarital affair with Jackson's mother, but he denied he was Jackson's father. In 1998 he began a new television series, *Kids Say the Darnedest Things*. ◆

"I don't know the key to success, but the key to failure is trying to please everybody."
Bill Cosby, 1985

extortion: the act of obtaining money by threat or intimidation.

Dalai Lama

JUNE 6, 1935– ● TIBETAN RELIGIOUS LEADER AND PEACE ACTIVIST

The Dalai Lama is the religious and political leader of the Tibetan people. He is a renowned Buddhist scholar and a man of peace who is widely respected for his humanity, his compassion, and his qualities of leadership. Since 1959 he has led a campaign to end China's domination of Tibet through nonviolent means, and for this effort he won the 1989 Nobel Peace Prize.

On July 6, 1935, the Dalai Lama was born to a humble farming family in the small village of Taktser in northeastern Tibet. He was named Lhamo Thondup. In 1938 a delegation of monks recognized him as the **reincarnated** Dalai Lama, who is the leader of the Yellow Hat order, the chief Buddhist sect of Tibet. The monks then brought him to Lhasa to raise him according to the monastic tradition. He began his monastic education at the age of six and completed his Doctorate of Buddhist Philosophy when he was twenty-five.

reincarnated: to be reborn in a new body or form of life.

In 1950 Communist Chinese troops poured over the Tibetan border with the intention of "liberating" Tibet from imperialist rule. The Chinese invasion frightened the Tibetan people and they turned to their spiritual leader for guidance. In response to their appeals for political leadership, the Dalai Lama was made head of the state of Tibet at the age of fifteen, three years short of the typical ascension to political power.

In order to avoid a confrontation with the advancing army, the Tibetan government sent a delegation to the Chinese capital of Peking to negotiate with the Communist authorities and make it clear that Tibet did not require liberation. The result of the negotiations was a document called the Seventeen Point

"True happiness comes from a sense of brotherhood and sisterhood. We need to cultivate a universal responsibility for one another and the planet we share."

His Holiness the Dalai Lama, 1989

1935 The Dalai Lama is born Lhamo Thondup in Takster, Tibet.

1938 A group of Buddhist monks recognizes him as the reincarnated Dalai Lama.

1940 The Dalai Llama is enthroned as Dalai Llama XIII.

1950 Chinese Communist troops invade Tibet.

1959 The Dalai Lama flees to India to escape threats to his life.

1989 The Dalai Lama wins the Nobel Peace Prize for his opposition to the use of violence in his struggle for human rights in Tibet.

entourage: attendees or associates.

Agreement, which provided that the Tibetan people would become a part of the People's Republic of China and that the Chinese would assume control of foreign affairs and military responsibilities in Tibet. In return the Tibetans would be assured religious and political freedom. The young Dalai Lama was alarmed by the terms of the agreement that surrendered the sovereignty of Tibet to the Chinese government and he felt it must have been coerced out of the delegates. But rather than face the massive Chinese army with force, which seemed futile and was also against his Buddhist nature, the Dalai Lama decided to maintain further negotiations with the Chinese.

In 1954 the Dalai Lama traveled to China, where he met with Mao Zedong, China's ruler, and Zhou Enlai, the premier of China. He found the Chinese leaders cordial but oblivious to the importance of Buddhism to himself and the Tibetan people. While traveling, he eagerly learned about the Chinese advances made in industry and science. He felt that Tibet was in dire need of reform in certain areas—including education, communications, the judicial system—and he was open-minded to the Chinese approaches in these areas.

Through the mid-1950s tension between the Chinese authorities and Tibetans increased and resistance to Communist authority was met with beatings and executions. In early 1959 thousands gathered on the streets of Lhasa in protest of Chinese rule and out of concern for what they perceived as a threat to the life of the Dalai Lama. In a show of authority, the Chinese sent armed troops to crush the demonstration. At the urging of his family and ministers, who were convinced that the loss of his life would mean the end of Tibetan life, the Dalai Lama fled with an **entourage** across the Himalaya to seek political assistance for his country in India. Several hours after his departure, the Chinese began an attack on the Tibetan demonstrators. The crackdown continued into 1960, and by 1961 more than 80,000 Tibetans had been killed.

Once in India, the Dalai Lama was granted political asylum. In 1960 he established a government-in-exile in Dharamsala in northern India with military protection from the Indian government. From Dharamsala he devoted himself to supporting the increasing numbers of Tibetan refugees seeking exile in India and to preserving Tibetan culture against adverse odds. He also worked tirelessly on building international support for Tibetan autonomy. Throughout these campaigns he continued to conduct his life as a monk, meditating four hours a day and spending several hours more daily studying and writing on Buddhist texts.

In the meantime China continued to increase its control over Tibet and repress Tibetan culture. It placed restrictions on religious practice and the economy and installed Chinese as local government administrators and teachers. It began agricultural reforms that required peasants to sell a fixed amount of grain to the government and forced them to grow wheat rather than barley, their traditional crop. Aggressive farming methods also rapidly eroded the thin layer of topsoil on the Tibetan plains, and led to crop failure and years of famine. Communications and road systems were built, but China remained in control of the local media and travel for Tibetans was restricted in the early years. During the Cultural Revolution of the 1960s, formal religion was banned, and Chinese soldiers looted and destroyed all but about ten of Tibet's 6,000 monasteries. Many thousands of Tibetans were killed and many others were thrown in prison to face starvation. Though the Chinese government began to relax some restrictions on the Tibetan economy, religious practice, and culture in the 1980s, restrictions were renewed after a riot in Lhasa against the slow pace of reform and the continued discrimination in Tibet.

In an effort to aid his people the Dalai Lama traveled around the world to talk about the disregard for human rights in Tibet and the destruction of the indigenous culture there. He met political, religious, and human rights leaders around the world, and formed large groups in support of his cause. And despite criticisms from some exiled Tibetans for his insistence on nonviolence, the Dalai Lama has continued to advocate peaceful solutions to the Tibetan problem based upon tolerance and mutual respect with the Chinese people.

For his leadership in the pursuit of freedom and peace and for his distinguished writings in Buddhist philosophy the Dalai Lama has received numerous honors around the world. In 1989 he won the Nobel Peace Prize for his consistent opposition to the use of violence in his struggle for human rights in Tibet.

The Dalai Lama describes himself as a simple monk who spends at least four hours daily in meditation and much of the rest of his day tending Tibetan affairs of state and studying Buddhist texts. In the 1990s he began to speak out on the need for better understanding and respect among the different faiths of the world. ◆

In an effort to aid his people the Dalai Lama traveled around the world to talk about the disregard for human rights in Tibet and the destruction of indigenous culture there.

"I believe all suffering is caused by ignorance. People inflict pain on others in the selfish pursuit of their happiness or satisfaction."
The Dalai Lama, 1989

Davis, Angela Yvonne

JANUARY 26, 1944– • POLITICAL ACTIVIST

> *"It is important not only to have the awareness and to feel impelled to become involved, it's important that there be a forum out there to which one can relate, an organization, a movement."*
>
> Angela Davis

Angela Davis lived in a section of Birmingham, Alabama, known as "Dynamite Hill" because of the violent attacks by white night riders intent on maintaining the residential demarcation line between blacks and whites. Both of her parents were educators, worked actively for the NAACP, and taught their children not to accept the socially segregated society that existed at the time. She attended Brandeis University, where she was influenced by the teachings of Marxist philosopher Herbert Marcuse. After graduating in 1961, she spent two years in Europe, where she was exposed to student political radicals. Her own radicalism, however, came into focus with the murder in 1963 of four young black Sunday school children in a Birmingham, Alabama, church bombing. In California, where she went to pursue graduate study with Marcuse (who was now at the University of California, San Diego), Davis began working with the Student Nonviolent Coordinating Committee (SNCC), the Black Panthers, and the Communist party, which she joined in 1968.

Hired in 1969 by UCLA to teach philosophy, Davis not long after was fired by the Board of Regents and then-governor Ronald Reagan because of her Communist party affiliation. Ultimately, her case went to the Supreme Court, which overturned the dismissal. By that time, however, Davis herself was in hiding as a result of an incident at the Soledad state prison. In August 1970 George Jackson, a prisoner and member of the Black Panthers, assisted by his brother Jonathan, attempted to escape using smuggled guns. Both brothers were killed, and some of the guns were traced to Davis. Fearful for her safety and distrustful of the judicial system, Davis went underground. For two months she was on the FBI's Ten Most Wanted list before being apprehended and incarcerated. She remained in jail for sixteen months before being tried for murder and conspiracy. In

June 1972 she was acquitted of all charges against her. Davis resumed her academic career at San Francisco State University and again became politically active, running as the Communist party candidate for vice president in 1980 and 1984. In 1991 she joined the faculty of the University of California, Santa Cruz, as professor of the history of consciousness. She is the author of several books, including *If They Come in the Morning* (1971), *Women, Race, and Class* (1983), and *Women, Culture, and Politics* (1989). Her autobiography, *Angela Davis: An Autobiography*, originally published in 1974, was reissued in 1988. In 1998 Davis published *Blues Legacies and Black Feminism: Gertrude 'Ma' Rainey, Bessie Smith, Billie Holiday.* ◆

de Klerk, Frederik Willem

MARCH 18, 1936– ● FORMER PRESIDENT OF SOUTH AFRICA

F. W. de Klerk was born in Johannesburg on March 18, 1936. His father, Jan de Klerk, had been a cabinet minister and president of the Senate. De Klerk graduated with a B.A. and L.L.B. (cum laude) from Potchefstroom University for Christian Higher Education in 1958. He was an attorney at Vereeniging (1961–72), where he was active in the National Party (NP). He was elected member of parliament for Vereeniging in the by-election of 1972, and was returned, unopposed, in the general election of 1974. From April 1978 de Klerk held cabinet portfolios that included Posts and Telecommunications; Mining, Environmental Planning, and Energy; Home Affairs; and National Education. He became head of the NP in February 1989 and was elected president of South Africa in September 1989, serving until April 1994. De Klerk was corecipient, with Nelson Mandela, of the Nobel Peace Prize in 1993.

"Today we have closed the book on apartheid."
F. W. de Klerk, 1992

Prior to becoming president in 1989, de Klerk was something of an unknown quantity. Over the years, he underwent a gradual political conversion from an overcautious approach to politics to fearless entrepreneurship, from ultraconservatism to outspoken enlightenment (*verligtheid*), from ideological correctness to open, critical **pragmatism** and realism. He came of age, politically, in an era in which he felt himself neither shackled to the baggage of the past nor historically bound to continue

pragmatism: a practical approach to problems.

Athol Fugard

Athol Fugard is an internationally acclaimed South African playwright whose best-known work deals with the political and social upheaval of the apartheid system in South Africa. An actor and director as well as a playwright vehemently opposed to apartheid, Fugard has written of the suffering and common humanity of blacks, coloreds, and poor whites in his country in such powerful plays as *The Blood Knot* (1961), *Boesman and Lena* (1969), *A Lesson from Aloes* (1978), *Master Harold . . . and the Boys* (1982), *The Road to Mecca* (1984), *My Children! My Africa!* (1991*), Playland* (1993), *Valley Song* (1995), and his latest, *The Captain's Tiger* (1998). Fugard's collaboration with black actors Winston Ntshona and John Kani produced *Sizwe Banzi Is Dead* (1971).

    Boesman and Lena, which featured whites playing black roles when it was first presented in South Africa in the early 1960s, is widely regarded as one of Fugard's greatest works, as well as one of the most eloquent artistic statements against apartheid. The story follows the play's namesake characters, two itinerants who take stock of their lives by a riverbank. *Boesman and Lena* (1999) was made into a feature film starring Danny Glover and Angela Bassett.

1936 De Klerk is born in Johannesburg, South Africa.

1972 De Klerk is elected a member of the parliament of South Africa.

1989 De Klerk becomes head of the National Party and is elected president of South Africa.

1990 De Klerk releases Nelson Mandela from prison and begins to dismantle apartheid.

1993 De Klerk shares the Nobel Peace Prize with Nelson Mandela.

subsquently: following in time.

what became outdated policies. De Klerk brought a different style of government; he sought advice from civilians rather than the military, which for South Africa at the time was a sea change. Faced by issues that went to the heart of the status quo, issues that would change the face of South Africa, he embarked on the most radical period of political reform the nation had experienced.

No other NP leader had broken so fundamentally with party orthodoxy. De Klerk permitted peaceful mass demonstrations by extraparliamentary groups; in October 1989 he released eight long-term prisoners belonging to the African National Congress (ANC); on February 2, 1990, he started negotiations on South Africa's future with the ANC, the Pan-Africanist Congress, the South African Communist Party, and allied organizations. On February 11, 1990, de Klerk released Nelson Mandela from prison; **subsequently,** he initiated several meetings between the government and the ANC on the transitional process that led to the Groote Schuur Minute (May 1990) and the Pretoria Minute (August 1990). He also headed the government delegation to the Convention for a Democratic South Africa (December 1991–December 1993). In May 1994 he became second executive-deputy president in the government of national unity, from which he resigned in June 1996 to reposition the NP (which he still led) for the next election in 1999.

Within a relatively short time span, the South African state self-consciously dismantled apartheid, thereby effecting socio-economic reconstruction and **reconciliation**, and devising a new political order in which race has no role in determining life chances of citizens. De Klerk realized from the start that these actions would reform himself and the NP out of exclusive political power; he pursued this course knowingly and from a position of relative strength. ◆

reconciliation: the act of restoring harmony.

Dewey, John

OCTOBER 20, 1859–JUNE 1, 1952 ● EDUCATOR AND REFORMER

John Dewey was an American educator renowned for his educational philosophy of "instrumentalism," emphasizing "learning by doing" rather than by memorization of material. Dewey was born on a farm in Burlington, Vermont, and initially studied at the University of Vermont, receiving his bachelor's degree in 1879. For the next three years he taught school in Vermont and in Pennsylvania. From 1882 he did graduate work at Johns Hopkins University, receiving his Ph.D. in 1884. He became an assistant professor of philosophy at the University of Michigan and in 1890 he was appointed chairman of the philosophy department, where he served until 1894, when he assumed the chairmanship of the department of philosophy, psychology, and pedagogy at the University of Chicago, which he held until 1904.

In 1902 he published *The Child and the Curriculum,* presenting his philosophy of education. He believed that the educational process must begin with and build upon the interests of the child, opportunity must be provided in the classroom experience for the interplay of the child's thinking and doing, for which purpose the school should be organized as a miniature community, and the teacher should be a guide and coworker with the child rather than a mere taskmaster.

> *"I believe that the community's duty to education is its paramount moral duty."*
> John Dewey, 1897

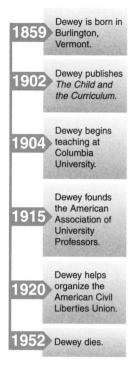

1859 ▸ Dewey is born in Burlington, Vermont.

1902 ▸ Dewey publishes *The Child and the Curriculum.*

1904 ▸ Dewey begins teaching at Columbia University.

1915 ▸ Dewey founds the American Association of University Professors.

1920 ▸ Dewey helps organize the American Civil Liberties Union.

1952 ▸ Dewey dies.

inevitable: unavoidable.

From 1904 until his retirement in 1930 he taught as professor of philosophy and education at Columbia University in New York City and remained an emeritus professor there until 1951. In 1919 and again in 1931 he was a lecturer in philosophy and education at the University of Peking in China. In the course of his extensive career, he even found time to serve on national organizations. He was president of the American Psychological Association and later president of the American Philosophical Association. In 1915 he was a founder and first president of the American Association of University Professors and helped organize the American Civil Liberties Union in 1920. The latter activity was related to his philosophy of legal realism, which is based on the belief that inasmuch as the judge plays such an active role in the making of the law, he should be aware of the **inevitable** social consequence of the decisions he makes. This was in keeping with Dewey's feeling that the true function of philosophy was to solve human problems.

His extensive publications included *The School and Society* (1899), *How We Think* (1909), *The Influence of Darwin on Philosophy and Other Essays in Contemporary Thought* (1910), *Essays in Experimental Logic* (1916), *Human Nature and Conduct* (1922), his classic work *Experience and Nature* (1925), *The Quest for Certainty* (1929), *Philosophy and Civilization* (1931), *Art as Experience* (1934), *Experience and Education* (1938), *Freedom and Culture* (1939), and *Problems of Men* (1946).

As a philosopher he favored the pragmatism of William James, from which his theory of "instrumentalism" was derived. Dewey favored progressive education and did much to foster its development through the years. His views were adopted by the progressive movement in education, stressing that education should be student-centered rather than subject-centered, that is, education through doing. ◆

Diana, Princess of Wales

JULY 1, 1961–AUGUST 31, 1997 ● HUMANITARIAN

During her eleven-year marriage to Charles, Prince of Wales, Princess Diana lent her celebrity to numerous charities and humanitarian causes, including the abolition of land mines and support for AIDS patients. Following their divorce, she continued to work for her favorite causes and to introduce her son William, England's future king, to meaningful philanthropy and social activism. Her death, after an automobile crash, was met with an outpouring of grief and worldwide mourning.

The third daughter of the Earl of Spencer, Diana grew up in the aristocratic comfort of Althorp House in Northamptonshire, England. Educated first at home by a succession of nannies with her younger brother, Charles, and later at Riddlesworth Hall and the West Heath School in Kent. Her parents' divorce, following a tumultuous breakup, was a continuous source of heartache for the sensitive Diana and her siblings, whose school holidays were divided between the households of the two parents. Diana's response was to become something of a substitute mother to her brother and to take satisfaction from community service, paying visits to convalescent and retirement homes and to the psychiatric institute near her preparatory school.

When she turned eighteen, she was permitted to move to London to share an apartment with three girlfriends. There she held jobs cleaning and baby-sitting, before becoming a kindergarten teacher. During their growing-up years, the Spencer children had shared Christmas parties with Queen Elizabeth and her family. Now a single girl in London, Diana renewed her acquaintance with Prince Charles, the heir apparent. Following a brief courtship, Charles proposed marriage.

The wedding of Charles and Diana in St. Paul's Cathedral in July 1981 was witnessed by an international television audience of millions, with some half million more lining the streets to view the wedding party parade to the church. The following June, William was born.

The marriage, however, was not happy. Diana was miserable, struggling with depression, an eating disorder, and strong suspicions of her husband's infidelity. Her distress continued for several years although she took great delight in the birth of her second son, Harry, whom she described as "a complete joy." After formally separating in 1992, Diana and Charles were divorced in August of 1996.

Following her divorce, Princess Diana continued to work for her favorite causes and to introduce her son William, England's future king, to meaningful philanthropy and social activism.

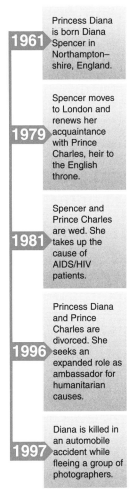

rapport: relationship marked by harmony and affinity.

Shrewd organizers of charitable events understood early on that the glamorous presence of the Princess of Wales meant money and attention to their causes. She became the most sought after speaker, guest, and honorary chairperson in England. Her popularity caused a further tension in her marriage, as her husband became aware that he was traveling in her shadow. When she began selecting her own issues and causes she caused further consternation in the royal family. Seeking affirmation, she threw herself into service work with a fervor uncharacteristic of royalty.

During her marriage she took up the cause of AIDS/HIV patients and their caregivers, becoming a patron of the National AIDS Trust and a frequent visitor at hospices, clinics, and nursing homes. Working with the Leprosy Mission, she brought world attention to leprosy and its sufferers. As the honorary president of Royal Marsden Hospital and the Hospital for Sick Children, perhaps her most remarkable contribution was her willingness to hug and hold patients and their caregivers and to establish **rapport** with ailing people, to chat, to laugh, to go beyond the obligatory rounds that are the expected duties of the royals. She became a passionate campaigner for a ban on the manufacture and use of antipersonnel land mines, traveling to Angola and Bosnia, successfully calling for a global focus on the issue of disarmament. She was acclaimed for her extraordinary empathy with the infirm, with battered women, and with the terminally ill.

After her divorce, she continued her charitable work with unexpected zeal, taking particular care to introduce her sons to her work for homeless shelters, for the disabled, and for the Red Cross.

Among the contradictions of Diana's short life was her love-hate relationship with the press. She sometimes courted reporters and photographers, in efforts to reach the public with good news stories. On the night of August 30, 1997, she was killed in an automobile accident along with her companion, Dodi al-Fayed, as they attempted to elude pursuing photographers by driving at high speed.

Diana's death and funeral received unprecedented worldwide attention. Flowers carpeted the sidewalks outside Kensington Palace, her last home; notes and letters of condolence poured in to her sisters, her brother, and her two sons. At first, the royal family reacted with chilly civility, but in the face of the frenzied mourning, Queen Elizabeth gave a brief public address, with some warm words about her former daughter-in-law. At the funeral service at Westminster Abbey, Diana's brother offered a stirring eulogy that paid tribute to her devotion to her sons and her dedication to humanitarian causes.

Mother Teresa, who had been a particular heroine for the princess, died in the same week. The two funerals threw a brilliant spotlight on AIDS/HIV, a cause cherished by both women. ◆

Douglass, Frederick

FEBRUARY 1818–FEBRUARY 20, 1895 ● ABOLITIONIST, JOURNALIST, ORATOR, AND SOCIAL REFORMER

Born Frederick Augustus Washington Bailey to Harriet Bailey, a slave, and an unacknowledged father (perhaps his master Aaron Anthony) in Tuckahoe, Maryland, Frederick Douglass—he assumed this name in 1838 when he escaped north to freedom—soon became the most famous African American of the nineteenth century. Separated from his family while young, he was a personal slave to several whites during his formative years. Consequently, he early learned self-reliance and began honing the arts of survival. At the same time, he found a sense of belonging through his relationships with various families and individuals, white and black, who liked and encouraged the bright and precocious youth. Ultimately, the lure of freedom and equality proved irresistible and propelled him on an extraordinary journey of both individual achievement and service to his people and his nation.

Taken in 1826 to Baltimore—where, as an urban slave, he could expand his horizons greatly—he taught himself how to read and write with the witting and unwitting assistance of many around him. Similarly, this more open urban environment, with its large and expanding free African-American population, further whetted his desire to learn as much as possible about freedom, including runaway slaves and the abolitionist movement.

Around the age of thirteen, he converted to Christianity, but over time he became increasingly disillusioned with a religious establishment that compromised with and supported evil and injustice, especially slavery and racial prejudice and

> *"Those who profess to favor freedom and yet depreciate agitation, are people who want crops without ploughing the ground; they want rain without thunder and lightning; they want the ocean without the roar of its many waters."*
>
> Frederick Douglass, 1857

1818 Frederick Augustus Washington Bailey is born in Tuckahoe, Maryland.

1838 Bailey assumes the name Frederick Douglass when he escapes to freedom in the north.

1841 Douglass joins other abolitionists allied with William Lloyd Garrison as a lecturer against slavery.

1848 Douglass attends the first Women's Rights Convention in Seneca Falls, New York.

1887 Douglass is appointed U.S. marshal for the District of Columbia.

1895 Douglass attends a meeting of the National Council of Women. Later that day, he dies.

disunion: termination of union.

discrimination. Also around that age, he purchased his first book, *The Columbian Orator*, which deepened not only his understanding of liberty and equality but also the enormous power of rhetoric, as well as literacy. Indeed, throughout his life he firmly believed in the power of the written and spoken word to capture and to change reality.

As a rapidly maturing eighteen-year-old, developing spiritually and intellectually as well as physically, he revealed an intensifying longing to be free that led him to plan an unsuccessful runaway scheme with several fellow slaves. Several months previously he had fought Covey, the "Negro breaker"— one versed in subduing unruly slaves—another sign of the depth of that longing. He later portrayed his triumph over Covey as a turning point in his struggle to become a free man. With the aid of Anna Murray, a free African-American woman in Baltimore with whom he had fallen in love, he escaped to freedom. They moved to New Bedford, Massachusetts (1838); Lynn, Massachusetts (1841); Rochester, New York (1847); and Washington, D.C. (1872).

In the North, Douglass found it very hard to make a living as a caulker because of racial discrimination and often had to resort to menial jobs. Anna worked hard as well, creating a comfortable domestic niche for a family that eventually included five children: Rosetta, Lewis Henry, Frederick Jr., Charles Remond, and Annie. Frederick's speeches within the local black communities brought him to the attention of the mostly white abolitionists allied with William Lloyd Garrison, and in 1841 they asked him to join them as a lecturer. An increasingly powerful lecturer and draw for the Garrisonian Massachusetts Anti-Slavery Society, Douglass learned a great deal from his work with such people as Garrison and Wendell Phillips. Most important, he adopted their pacifism and moral suasionist approach to ending slavery and was deeply influenced by their interrelated perfectionism and social reformism. As a good Garrisonian, he argued for **disunion** and rejected the political approach to ending slavery as a compromise with a proslavery Constitution.

Douglass also began to come into his own as an activist and a thinker. Drawing upon his experiences as a slave, he lambasted slavery and its notorious effects, most notably antiblack prejudice and discrimination in both North and South. As the living embodiment of a small measure of success in the enormous struggle against slavery, he spoke eloquently with uncommon authority. In 1845 his *Narrative of the Life of Frederick Douglass*, *an American Slave* was published and its huge success, followed by a successful speaking tour of Great Britain, heightened his celebrity immeasurably. Ever conscious of his public persona and his historical image, he carefully crafted both. *My Bondage and My Freedom* (1855) and *Life and Times of Frederick Douglass* (1881; revised 1892), fuller autobiographies, were likewise crucial in this regard.

His stirring narrative and equally stirring oratory derived much of their power and authenticity from Douglass's deep-seated engagement with the plethora of issues confronting blacks north and south, free and slave. His strong involvement in the national Negro convention movement, as well as with various state and local black conferences, furthered his impact and by 1850 made him the principal spokesman for his race. His fierce commitment to egalitarianism, freedom, and justice similarly led him to embrace the women's rights movement, notably women's suffrage, and to become one of the most important male feminists of the nineteenth century. He attended the first Women's Rights Convention, in Seneca Falls, New York, in 1848; on the day of his death, February 20, 1895, he had earlier attended a meeting of the National Council of Women.

Shortly after his return from Great Britain in 1847, Douglass embarked upon a distinguished career in journalism. He edited the *North Star* (1847–51), *Frederick Douglass' Paper* (1851–1860), *Douglass' Monthly* (1859–63), and, for a time, the *New National Era* (1870–74). Complementing the other aspects of his varied public voice and extending its reach and influence, Douglass's work as a journalist furthered his use of the printed word as a tool for agitation and change. Stressing self-reliance, hard work, **perseverance**, education, and morality, Douglass exemplified the embrace by many African Americans of middle-class values and the American success ethic. Likewise, invoking America's revolutionary tradition, he emphasized the imperative of full black liberation within the confines of the American nation. After 1851, when he formally broke with the Garrisonians and accepted political action against slavery as viable and necessary, he became more politically engaged. By the outbreak of the Civil War, he supported the Republican party.

The **tumultuous** events of the 1850s convinced Douglass, like untold numbers of his compatriots, that war was unavoidable, the Union cause just, and slave emancipation inevitable. He urged his audience, most notably President Abraham

Douglass's involvement in the national Negro convention movement furthered his impact and by 1850 made him the principal spokesman for his race.

perseverance: the act of persisting in the face of discouragement or opposition.

tumultuous: marked by a turbulent uprising or upheaval.

"The struggle may be a moral one, or it may be a physical one, or it may be both. But it must be a struggle. Power concedes nothing without a demand; it never has and it never will."

Frederick
Douglass, 1857

In his fiery condemnation of the alarming growth of lynchings of black men in the 1880s and 1890s, it was clear that Douglass's commitment to justice never wavered.

Lincoln, to further ennoble the Union cause by accepting black troops into the Union army and treating them fairly. He exhorted his people to support fully the Union cause and to struggle ceaselessly to ensure that Union victory would mean emancipation and the necessary conditions for black progress. His often arduous efforts to recruit black Union troops, who braved strong white hostility and mistreatment, showed him grappling intensely with the central and complex issue of African-American identity. African Americans, he cogently argued, honored their group as well as national heritage and mission through vigorous support of an abolitionist Union cause.

Douglass emerged from the war even more widely known and respected. He continued to urge his nation to deal justly and fairly with his people, even after the nation reneged on its insufficient and short-lived efforts to do so during Reconstruction. While many blacks questioned his continuing allegiance to the Republican party, Douglass valiantly—albeit unsuccessfully—endeavored to help the party rediscover its humanistic and moral moorings. Appointed to serve as the United States marshal for the District of Columbia (1877–81), recorder of deeds for the District of Columbia (1881–86), and chargé d'affaires for Santo Domingo and minister to Haiti (1889–91), he remained a stalwart Republican.

Over the years, Douglass's status as a comfortable middle-class elder statesman tended on occasion to blind him to the harsh conditions confronting rural, impoverished, and migrant blacks. Still, as in his fiery condemnation of the alarming growth in the number of lynchings of black men in the 1880s and 1890s (often upon the false accusation of an attack on a white woman), it was clear that his commitment to justice never wavered. Likewise, while many women's rights advocates criticized him for supporting the Fifteenth Amendment, which failed to enfranchise women as it enfranchised black men, Douglass contended that the greater urgency of the black male need for the vote and its greater likelihood of passage made support imperative. After its passage, he continued his efforts on behalf of women's rights and sought to heal the rift within the movement.

When Douglass married Helen Pitts, his white secretary, in January 1884, a year and a half after the death of his first wife, they endured much criticism from many blacks and whites, including close family members. Nonetheless, Douglass, the quintessential humanist, steadfastly articulated his commitment to a composite American nationality, transcending race, as an integral component of his vision of a democratic and egalitarian country. When others criticized him for a lack of race spirit, Douglass, refusing to be imprisoned within a **racialist** universe, claimed ultimate allegiance to the human race.

racialist: racist.

Yet he also fully understood and vividly personified his people's struggle from slavery to freedom, from obscurity and poverty to recognition and respectability. His enduring legacy to his people and all Americans is best captured in his lifelong and profound dedication to the imperative of agitation and concerted action: "If there is no struggle," he declared, "there is no progress." ◆

Du Bois, William Edward Burghardt

FEBRUARY 23, 1869–AUGUST 27, 1963 ● INTELLECTUAL AND NEGRO ACTIVIST

W E. B. Du Bois was born in Great Barrington, Massachusetts. His mother, Mary Burghardt Du Bois, belonged to a tiny community of African Americans who had been settled in the area since before the Revolution; his father, Alfred Du Bois, was a visitor to the region who deserted the family in his son's infancy. In the predominantly white local schools and Congregational church, Du Bois absorbed ideas and values that left him "quite thoroughly New England."

From 1885 to 1888 he attended Fisk University in Nashville, where he first encountered the harsher forms of racism. After earning a B.A. (1888) at Fisk, he attended Harvard University, where he took another B.A. (1890) and a doctorate in history (1895). Among his teachers were the psychologist William James, the philosophers Josiah Royce and George Santayana, and the historian A. B. Hart. Between 1892 and 1894 he studied history and sociology at the University of Berlin. His dissertation, *The Suppression of the African Slave-Trade to the United States,* was published in 1896 as the first volume of the Harvard Historical Studies.

"Would America have been America without her Negro people?"
W. E. B. Du Bois

Between 1894 and 1896 Du Bois taught at Wilberforce University, Ohio, where he met and married Nina Gomer, a student, in 1896. The couple had two children, Burghardt and Yolande. In 1896 he accepted a position at the University of Pennsylvania to gather data for a commissioned study of blacks in Philadelphia. This work resulted in *The Philadelphia Negro* (1899), an acclaimed early example of empirical sociology. In 1897 he joined the faculty at Atlanta University and took over the annual Atlanta University Conference for the Study of the Negro Problems. From 1897 to 1914 he edited an annual study of one aspect or another of black life, such as education or the church.

Appalled by the conditions facing blacks nationally, Du Bois sought ways other than scholarship to effect change. The death of his young son from dysentery in 1899 also deeply affected him, as did the widely publicized lynching of a black man, Sam Hose, in Georgia the same year. In 1900, in London, he boldly asserted that "the problem of the Twentieth Century is the problem of the color line." He repeated this statement in *The Souls of Black Folk* (1903), mainly a collection of essays on African-American history, sociology, religion, and music, in which Du Bois wrote of an essential black double consciousness: the existence of twin souls ("an American, a Negro") warring in each black body. The book also attacked Booker T. Washington, the most powerful black American of the age, for advising blacks to surrender the right to vote and to a liberal education in return for white friendship and support. Du Bois was established as probably the premier intellectual in black America, and Washington's main rival.

His growing radicalism also led him to organize the Niagara Movement, a group of blacks who met in 1905 and 1906 to agitate for "manhood rights" for African Americans. He founded two journals, *Moon* (1905–06) and *Horizon* (1907–10). In 1909 he published *John Brown*, a sympathetic biography of the white abolitionist martyr. Then, in 1910, he resigned his professorship to join the new National Association for the Advancement of Colored People (NAACP) in New York, which had been formed in response to growing concern about the treatment of blacks. As its director of research, Du Bois founded a monthly magazine, *The Crisis*. In 1911 he published his first novel, *The Quest of the Silver Fleece*, a study of the cotton industry seen through the fate of a young black couple struggling for a life of dignity and meaning.

The Crisis became a powerful forum for Du Bois's views on race and politics. Meanwhile, his developing interest in Africa led him to write *The Negro* (1915), a study offering historical and demographic information on peoples of African descent around the world. Hoping to affect colonialism in Africa after World War I, he also organized Pan-African Congresses in Europe in 1919, 1921, and 1923, and in New York in 1927. However, he clashed with the most popular black leader of the era, Marcus Garvey of the Universal Negro Improvement Association. Du Bois regarded Garvey's "back to Africa" scheme as ill-considered, and Garvey as impractical and disorganized.

Du Bois's second prose collection, *Darkwater: Voices from Within the Veil* (1920), did not repeat the success of *The Souls of Black Folk* but captured his increased militancy. In the 1920s *The Crisis* played a major role in the Harlem Renaissance by publishing early work by Langston Hughes, Countee Cullen, and other writers. Eventually, Du Bois found some writers politically irresponsible; his essay "Criteria of Negro Art" (1926) insisted that all art is essentially propaganda. He pressed this point with a novel, *Dark Princess* (1928), about a plot by the darker races to overthrow European colonialism. In 1926 he visited the Soviet Union, then nine years old. Favorably impressed by what he saw, he boldly declared himself "a Bolshevik."

The Great Depression increased his interest in socialism but also cut the circulation of *The Crisis* and weakened Du Bois's position with the leadership of the NAACP, with which he had fought from the beginning. In 1934 he resigned as editor and returned to teach at Atlanta University. His interest in Marxism, which had started with his student days in Berlin, dominated his next book, *Black Reconstruction in America* (1934), a massive and controversial revaluation of the role of the freedmen in the South after the Civil War. In 1936, Du Bois commenced a weekly column of opinion in various black newspapers, starting with the *Pittsburgh Courier*. He emphasized his continuing concern for Africa with *Black Folk: Then and Now* (1939), an expanded and updated revision of *The Negro*.

In 1940 Du Bois published his first full-length autobiography, *Dusk of Dawn: An Essay Toward an Autobiography of a Race Concept*, in which he examined modern racial theory against the major events and intellectual currents in his lifetime. In 1944 his life took another dramatic turn when he was suddenly

In *The Souls of Black Folk,* Du Bois wrote of an essential back double consciousness: the existence of twin souls (an American and a Negro) in each black body.

"One never feels his two-ness—an American, a Negro; two souls, two thoughts, two unreconciled strivings; two warring ideals in one dark body, whose dogged strength alone keeps it from being torn asunder."
W. E. B Du Bois,
The Souls of Black Folk, 1903

Du Bois joined
Paul Robeson at
the Council on
African Affairs,
which had been
officially declared
a "subversive"
organization.

subversive: a systematic
attempt to overthrow a
government or political
system.

retired by Atlanta University after growing tension between himself and certain administrators. When the NAACP rehired him that year, he returned to New York as director of special research. In 1945 he was honored at the Fifth Pan-African Congress in Manchester, England, and published a bristling polemic, *Color and Democracy: Colonies and Peace*. A year later, he produced a controversial pamphlet, "An Appeal to the World," submitted by the NAACP on behalf of black Americans to the United Nations Commission on Civil Rights. In 1947 came his *The World and Africa*, an examination of Africa's future following World War II.

By this time Du Bois had moved to the left, well beyond the interests of the NAACP, which generally supported the Democratic party. In 1948, when he endorsed the Progressive party and its presidential candidate, Henry Wallace, he was fired. He then joined Paul Robeson, who was by this time firmly identified with radical socialism, at the Council on African Affairs, which had been officially declared a **"subversive"** organization. In 1950 Du Bois ran unsuccessfully for the U.S. Senate from New York on the American Labor party ticket. Also that year, in another move applauded by communists, he accepted the chairmanship of the Peace Information Center, which circulated the Stockholm Peace Appeal against nuclear weapons.

Early in 1951 Du Bois and four colleagues from the Peace Information Center were indicted on the charge of violating the law that required agents of a foreign power to register. On bail and awaiting trial, he married Shirley Lola Graham, a fellow socialist and writer (his first wife had died in 1950). At the trial in November 1951, the judge heard testimony, then unexpectedly granted a motion by the defense for a directed acquittal. Du Bois was undeterred by his ordeal. In 1953 he recited the Twenty-third Psalm at the grave of Julius and Ethel Rosenberg, executed as spies for the Soviet Union. For such involvements, he found himself ostracized by some black leaders and organizations. "The colored children," he wrote, "ceased to hear my name."

Returning to fiction, he composed a trilogy, *The Black Flame*, about the life and times of a black educator seen against the backdrop of generations of black and white lives and national and international events (the trilogy comprised *The Ordeal of Mansart*, 1957; *Mansart Builds a School*, 1959; and *Worlds of Color*, 1961). After the government lifted its ban on his foreign travel in 1958, Du Bois visited various countries, including the Soviet Union and China. In Moscow on May 1, 1959, he received the Lenin Peace Prize.

In 1960 Du Bois visited Ghana for the inauguration of Kwame Nkrumah as its first president. He then accepted an invitation from Nkrumah to return to Ghana and start work on an *Encyclopedia Africana,* a project in which he had long been interested. In October 1961, after applying (successfully) for membership in the Communist party, he left the United States. He began work on the project in Ghana, but illness the following year caused him to go for treatment to Romania. Afterward, he visited Peking and Moscow. In February 1963, he **renounced** his American citizenship and officially became a citizen of Ghana. He died in Accra, Ghana, and was buried there. ◆

renounce: to refuse to follow, obey, or recognize any longer.

Duniway, Abigail Scott

OCTOBER 22, 1834–OCTOBER 11, 1915 ● WOMAN SUFFRAGIST

The undisputed leader of the Women's Suffrage movement in Oregon, Abigail Scott Duniway fought for women's right to vote with, as she said, "jawbone and pen" for more than four decades. Called by historian Eleanor Flexnor "the hardest and most tireless suffrage worker the western states produced," Duniway established the state's first suffrage association, founded and edited its first suffrage newspaper, and spearheaded six statewide campaigns to amend Oregon's constitution to include the female franchise.

Born on a farm south of Peoria, Illinois, Abigail Jane Scott traveled the Oregon Trail with her family in 1852 and less than a year later married Ben C. Duniway, a Clackamas County farmer. During the next ten years, her feminist sensibilities were awakened as she bore four children, washed, scrubbed, cooked hundreds of free meals for bachelor farmers, churned thousands of

1834 Duniway is born in Peoria, Illinois.

1852 Duniway travels the Oregon Trail with her family.

1870 Duniway helps found the Oregon State Equal Suffrage Association.

1871 Duniway begins publishing the first suffrage newspaper in the Pacific northwest.

1912 The equal suffrage amendment is passed in Oregon.

1913 Duniway becomes Oregon's first registered female voter.

pounds of butter, and, in her words, became "a servant without wages" and "a general pioneer drudge."

In the early 1860s her husband lost their farm and soon thereafter became permanently disabled. Duniway became the family's sole financial supporter. She taught school briefly and operated a millinery and notions shop before moving the family to Portland, where, at age thirty-six, she began her life's work for suffrage.

In 1870 Duniway and two other Oregon women founded the Oregon State Equal Suffrage Association. Several months later she began the first suffrage newspaper in the Pacific northwest, *The New Northwest* (published from 1871 to 1887), a weekly she single-handedly edited and wrote for the next sixteen years. At the same time, she took to the lecture circuit and traveled thousands of miles by horseback, stagecoach, riverboat, and railroad throughout the northwest to speak on equal rights. Broadening her efforts, she lobbied the state legislature to place before Oregon voters a constitutional amendment to enfranchise women.

In 1884 the legislature finally placed the amendment on the ballot, but it was easily defeated. Duniway, however, was not. She continued the fight and led the state movement for most of the next three decades. But Oregon voters defeated the equal suffrage amendment in 1900, 1906, 1908, and 1910. In 1912, when the amendment finally passed, Duniway, still the movement's titular leader at the age of seventy-eight, was confined to a wheelchair with rheumatism. A year later, she became Oregon's first registered female voter. ◆

Eastman, Charles Alexander (Ohiyesa)

1858–1939 ● Physician and Native American Rights Activist

Charles Alexander Eastman, whose Indian name was Ohiyesa, was recognized in 1900 as the most educated Indian living in the United States. He devoted his career to helping Indian people through his writings, lectures, and criticism of federal Indian policies.

Born near Redwood Falls, Minnesota, Ohiyesa was raised in the traditional ways of a Santee Sioux hunter and warrior. At the age of fifteen, he reluctantly abandoned that life and agreed to his recently Christianized father's request that he attend a white school. Over the next seventeen years, Eastman attended a number of schools. He earned a B.S. degree from Dartmouth in 1887 and a medical degree from Boston University School of Medicine in 1890.

Eastman held several government appointments. As government physician at the Pine Ridge Reservation in South Dakota from 1890 to 1893, he witnessed the Wounded Knee tragedy in 1890. He later held positions at the Carlisle Indian School in Pennsylvania in 1899 and the Crow Creek Reservation in South Dakota from 1900 to 1903. From 1903 to 1909 he was head of the revision of the Sioux allotment rolls. Then from 1923 to 1925 he was Indian inspector of reservations.

His nongovernment employment included a brief medical practice in St. Paul, Minnesota, in 1893, Indian secretary of the International Committee of the YMCA from 1894 to 1898, and

1890 Eastman becomes government physician to the Pine Ridge Reservation.

1890 Eastman witnesses the Wounded Knee tragedy.

1911 Eastman helps organize the Society of American Indians.

1933 Eastman receives the first Indian Council Fire's award recognizing his work in helping Indians and non-Indians to understand each other.

a representative of a Santee Sioux claims case in Washington, D.C., for a number of years.

Eastman was a prolific writer. With the aid of his non-Indian wife, Elaine Goodale Eastman, he published numerous books and articles. Two of his books were autobiographies: *Indian Boyhood* (1902) and *From the Deep Woods to Civilization* (1916). Others, such as *The Soul of the Indian* (1911) and *The Indian Today* (1915), dealt with Indian–white relations and Indian culture and society. He even wrote a guidebook entitled *Indian Scout Talks* (1914) for Boy Scouts and Camp Fire Girls. He presented lectures throughout the United States and in England.

As an Indian reformer, Eastman helped organize and later served as president of the Society of American Indians, a pan-Indian organization established in 1911. He lobbied for Indian citizenship, condemned deplorable reservation conditions, and opposed the use of peyote by Indians. In 1933, he received the first Indian Council Fire's annual award in recognition of his work to help Indian and non-Indian people understand each other.

Eastman supported an acculturation policy in which Indians selected which non-Indian ways to adopt instead of an assimilation policy that often forced Indians to abandon their culture. He believed Indians could remain Indians and still operate successfully in the dominant culture. ◆

> " 'Ohiyesa (or Winner) shall be thy name henceforth. Be brave, be patient and thou shalt always win! Thy name is Ohiyesa.' "
>
> Charles Alexander Eastman (Ohiyesa), *Indian Boyhood*, 1902

Edelman, Marian Wright

<small>June 6, 1939– ● Attorney and Founder of the Children's Defense Fund</small>

The daughter of Arthur Jerome Wright, minister of Shiloh Baptist Church, and Maggie Leola Wright, a community activist, Marian Edelman was born and raised in Bennettsville, South Carolina. She attended Spelman College, from which she graduated as valedictorian in 1960. During her senior year, Edelman participated in a sit-in at City Hall in Atlanta. Responding to the need for civil rights lawyers, Edelman entered Yale Law School as a John Hay Whitney Fellow in 1960. After graduating from law school in 1963, she became the first black woman to pass the bar in Mississippi. From 1964 to 1968 she headed the NAACP Legal Defense and

> *"Education is a precondition to survival in America today."*
>
> Marian Wright Edelman

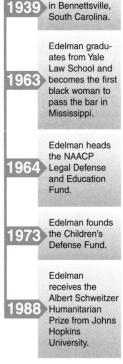

1939 ▸ Edelman is born in Bennettsville, South Carolina.

1963 ▸ Edelman graduates from Yale Law School and becomes the first black woman to pass the bar in Mississippi.

1964 ▸ Edelman heads the NAACP Legal Defense and Education Fund.

1973 ▸ Edelman founds the Children's Defense Fund.

1988 ▸ Edelman receives the Albert Schweitzer Humanitarian Prize from Johns Hopkins University.

Education Fund in Mississippi, where she met her husband, Peter Edelman, a Harvard Law School graduate and political activist. In 1971 she became director of the Harvard University Center for Law and Education. She was also the first black woman elected to the Yale University Corporation, where she served from 1971 to 1977.

Edelman is best known for her work with the Children's Defense Fund (CDF), a nonprofit child advocacy organization that she founded in 1973. The CDF offers programs to prevent adolescent pregnancy, to provide health care, education, and employment for youth, and to promote family planning. In 1980 Edelman became the first black and the second woman to chair the Board of Trustees of Spelman College. She has been the recipient of numerous honors and awards for her contributions to child advocacy, women's rights, and civil rights, including the MacArthur Foundation Prize Fellowship (1985) and the Albert Schweitzer Humanitarian Prize from Johns Hopkins University (1988). Edelman has published numerous books and articles on the condition of black and white children in America, including *Children Out of School in America* (1974), *School Suspensions: Are They Helping Children?* (1975), *Portrait of Inequality: Black and White Children in America* (1980), *Families in Peril: An Agenda for Social Change* (1987), and *The Measure of Our Success: A Letter to My Children and Yours* (1992). ◆

"Speak truth to power."
Marian Wright
Edelman

Farmer, James

JANUARY 12, 1920–JULY 9, 1999 ● CIVIL RIGHTS LEADER AND EDUCATOR

James Farmer was born in Holly Springs, Mississippi, where his father was a minister and professor at Rust College. The family moved when Farmer's father took a post at Wiley College in Marshall, Texas. Farmer grew up in Marshall and was educated at Wiley College and at Howard University, where he received a bachelor of divinity degree in 1941. During this time, he became interested in the philosophy of nonviolence espoused by Mahatma Gandhi in his movement for India's independence. Farmer refused to become ordained to serve a segregated Methodist congregation (he was committed to interracial forums), and his pacifist ideas and opposition to army segregation led him to oppose the wartime draft. Exempted from service by his ministerial background, Farmer dedicated himself to pacifist and civil rights causes.

Shortly after graduating from Howard in 1941, Farmer took a job as race-relations secretary of the pacifist group Fellowship of Reconciliation (FOR). In 1942, while living in Chicago, he drew up plans for a civil rights group operating on Gandhian principles, and set up an organization with aid from some University of Chicago students. Farmer became the first executive director of the Chicago-based organization named the Congress of Racial Equality (CORE). Farmer was a committed **integrationist**, and CORE's early leadership was predominantly white. The Congress remained small, and in 1946 Farmer tired of bureaucratic struggles with FOR and gave up his leadership role to work as a labor organizer for trade unions, and later as a civil rights campaigner for the NAACP. He remained involved with CORE as a field worker.

> *"Ultimately, Dr. King's dream still has a fascination for me. I shall keep as the ideal an open society where men are brothers—color-blind if you will—for eventually humanity must transcend color."*
> James Farmer, 1968

integrationist: a person who believes that all people should be treated as equals in a group or society.

1920 Farmer is born in Holly Springs, Mississippi.

1941 Farmer graduates from Howard University.

1961 Farmer organizes the first "freedom rides."

1965 Farmer publishes *Freedom, When?*

1969 Farmer accepts the post of assistant secretary of HEW in the Nixon administration.

1982 Farmer begins teaching at Mary Washington College in Fredericksburg, Virginia.

1985 Farmer publishes his memoirs, *Lay Bare the Heart.*

affirmative action: an active effort to improve educational or job opportunities for a minority group.

In 1960, after the Montgomery bus boycott and the sit-ins had made nonviolent protest a widespread civil rights tool, Farmer returned to leadership of CORE, by now based in New York City. In spring of 1961 he organized the first Freedom Rides, which were designed to desegregate buses and terminals in the South and publicize denials of civil rights. During the effort Farmer was jailed for forty days—the first of many such imprisonments during the days of the civil rights movement as CORE contingents participated in strikes, sit-ins, voter education programs, and demonstrations, both in the South and in the North. As CORE's national director, Farmer was one of the foremost leaders of the civil rights movement and participated in its major campaigns. His eloquent speaking voice and manner made him a popular lecturer and debater. He wrote many articles and essays, and in 1965 published *Freedom, When?*, a book dealing with the problem of institutionalized inequality and the debate over nonviolence as a protest tactic.

One of Farmer's significant efforts during his years in CORE was his ongoing attempt to improve the position of blacks in the job market and in labor unions. Realizing that African Americans faced disadvantages in schooling and training, Farmer pushed the idea of "compensatory" action by employers and government, including programs for the hiring of proportionate numbers of black workers within a labor pool, and their training in job skills, when necessary. These ideas were a major ingredient in the formation of **affirmative action** policies.

By 1966, as CORE turned away from its original integrationist goals and nonviolent tactics in civil rights action, Farmer decided to leave the organization. For two years, he taught social welfare at Lincoln University in Pennsylvania. In 1968, Farmer, who had long been active in New York's Liberal party, ran for Congress in Brooklyn on the Liberal and Republican tickets, but was defeated by African-American Democrat Shirley Chisholm.

The following year, Farmer faced a storm of criticism when he accepted the post of assistant secretary of Health, Education, and Welfare (HEW) in Richard Nixon's Republican administration. Farmer, who felt blacks should reach out to all political parties, was given the job of increasing minority participation in government. He soon grew dissatisfied with his role in HEW, however, and resigned in 1971.

In 1972 Farmer set up the Council on Minority Planning and Strategy, a black think tank, but was unable to secure sufficient funding. In 1975, he became active with the Fund for an Open Society, and from 1977 through 1982 served as executive director of the Coalition of American Public Employees. Starting in 1982 and continuing through the early 1990s, he taught at Mary Washington College in Fredericksburg, Virginia. He continued to be a strong speaker for black equality, although he remained out of the political arena. In his later years, Farmer developed retinal vascular occlusion, a rare eye disease, and lost all vision in one eye and some vision in the other. Still, he managed to complete a volume of memoirs, *Lay Bare the Heart,* in 1985. Farmer's forceful leadership and eloquence combined with his dedication to nonviolent principles made him one of the central figures of the civil rights movement in the 1960s. ◆

> Farmer's forceful leadership and eloquence combined with his dedication to nonviolent principles made him one of the central figures of the civil rights movement.

Farrakhan, Louis Abdul

MAY 17, 1933– ● AFRICAN-AMERICAN ACTIVIST

Louis Walcott was born in New York, but raised in Boston by his West Indian mother. Deeply religious, Walcott faithfully attended the Episcopalian church in his neighborhood and became an altar boy. With the rigorous discipline provided by his mother and his church, he did fairly well academically and graduated with honors from the prestigious Boston English High School, where he also participated on the track team and played the violin in the school orchestra. In 1953, after two years at the Winston-Salem Teachers College in North Carolina, he dropped out to pursue his favorite avocation of music and made it his first career. An accomplished violinist, pianist, and vocalist, Walcott performed professionally on the Boston nightclub circuit as a singer of calypso and country songs. In 1955, at the age of twenty-two, Louis Walcott was recruited by Malcolm X for the Nation of Islam. Following its custom, he dropped his surname and took an X, which meant "undetermined." However,

1933 Farrakhan is born in the Bronx, New York.

1955 Farrakhan is recruited by Malcolm X for the Nation of Islam.

1964 Farrakhan is appointed National Spokesman of the Nation of Islam after the departure of Malcolm X.

1978 Farrakhan forms a new organization, also called the Nation of Islam.

1995 Farrakhan delivers the keynote speech at the Million Man March.

Like Malcolm X, Farrakhan is a dynamic and charismatic leader and a powerful speaker with the ability to appeal to masses of black people.

it was not until he had met Elijah Muhammad, the supreme leader of the Nation of Islam, on a visit to the Chicago headquarters that Louis X converted and dedicated his life to building the Nation. After proving himself for ten years, Elijah Muhammad gave Louis his Muslim name, "Abdul Farrakhan," in May 1965. As a rising star within the Nation, Farrakhan also wrote the only song, the popular "A White Man's Heaven Is a Black Man's Hell," and the only dramatic play, *Orgena* ("A Negro" spelled backward), endorsed by Elijah Muhammad.

After a nine-month apprenticeship with Malcolm X at Temple No. 7 in Harlem, Minister Louis X was appointed as the head minister of the Boston Temple No. 11, which Malcolm founded. Later, after Malcolm X had split with the Nation, Farrakhan was awarded Malcolm's Temple No. 7, the most important pastorate in the Nation after the Chicago headquarters. He was also appointed National Spokesman or National Representative after Malcolm left the Nation in 1964 and began to introduce Elijah Muhammad at Savior Day rallies, a task that had once belonged to Malcolm. Like his predecessor, Farrakhan is a dynamic and charismatic leader and a powerful speaker with an ability to appeal to masses of black people.

In February 1975, when Elijah Muhammad died, the Nation of Islam experienced its largest schism. Wallace Dean Muhammad, the fifth of Elijah's six sons, was surprisingly chosen as supreme minister by the leadership hierarchy. In April 1975 Wallace, who later took the Muslim title and name of Imam Warith Deen Muhammad, made radical changes in the Nation of Islam, gradually moving the group toward orthodox Sunni Islam. In 1975 Farrakhan left the New York Mosque. Until 1978 Farrakhan, who had expected to be chosen as Elijah's successor, kept silent in public and traveled extensively in Muslim countries, where he found a need to recover the focus upon race and black nationalism that the Nation had emphasized. Other disaffected leaders and followers had already formed splinter Nation of Islam groups—Silas Muhammad in Atlanta, John Muhammad in Detroit, and Caliph in Baltimore. In 1978 Farrakhan formed a new organization, also called the Nation of Islam, resurrecting the teachings, ideology, and organizational structure of Elijah Muhammad, and he began to rebuild his base of followers by making extensive speaking tours in black communities. Farrakhan claimed it was his organization, not that of Wallace Muhammad, that was the legitimate successor to the old Nation of Islam.

In 1979 Farrakhan began printing editions of *The Final Call*, a name he resurrected from early copies of a newspaper that Elijah Muhammad had put out in Chicago in 1934. The "final call" was a call to black people to return to Allah as incarnated in Master Fard Muhammad or Master Fard and witnessed by his apostle Elijah Muhammad. For Farrakhan, the final call has an eschatological dimension; it is the last call, the last chance for black people to achieve their liberation.

Farrakhan became known to the American public via a series of controversies which were stirred when he first supported the Rev. Jesse Jackson's 1984 presidential campaign. His Fruit of Islam guards provided security for Jackson. After Jackson's offhand, anti-Semitic remarks about New York City as "Hymietown" became a campaign issue, Farrakhan threatened to ostracize *Washington Post* reporter Milton Coleman, who had released the story in the black community. Farrakhan has also become embroiled in a continuing controversy with the American Jewish community by making **anti-Semitic** statements. Farrakhan has argued that his statements were misconstrued. Furthermore, he contends that a distorted media focus on this issue has not adequately covered the achievements of his movement.

Farrakhan's Nation of Islam has been successful in getting rid of drug dealers in a number of public housing projects and private apartment buildings; a national private security agency for hire, manned by the Fruit of Islam, has been established. The Nation has been at the forefront of organizing a peace pact between gang members in Los Angeles and several other cities. They have established a clinic for the treatment of AIDS patients in Washington, D.C. A cosmetics company, Clean and Fresh, has marketed its products in the black community. Moreover, they have continued to reach out to reform black people with the Nation's traditional dual emphases: self-identity, to know yourself; and economic independence, to do for yourself. Under Farrakhan's leadership, the Nation has allowed its members to participate in electoral politics and to run for office, actions that were forbidden under Elijah Muhammad. He has also allowed women to become ministers and public leaders in the Nation, which places his group ahead of all the orthodox Muslim groups in giving women equality. Although the core of Farrakhan's Nation of Islam continues to be about 20,000 members, his influence is much greater, attracting crowds of 40,000 or more in speeches across the

"If you are a champion of liberation for Black people and you're successful in freeing your people to a measure, you cannot stop until oppression and tyranny are rooted from the face of the earth."
Louis Farrakhan, 1985

anti-Semitic: hostile toward Jews as a religious, ethnic, or racial group.

In October 1995 Farrakhan delivered the keynote speech at the Million Man March where he called for black men to repent for their treatment of their wives and to organize in their community.

country. His group is the fastest growing of the various Muslim movements, largely through the influence of rap groups like Public Enemy and Prince Akeem. International branches have been formed in Ghana, London, and the Caribbean. In the United States throughout the 1990s, however, Farrakhan remained an immensely controversial figure. In January 1995 newspapers revealed that Qubilah Shabazz, daughter of Malcolm X, had plotted with a gunman to assassinate Farrakhan. He responded by expressing sympathy for Shabazz, and he helped persuade federal officials to allow Shabazz to plea-bargain. Later that year, Farrakhan's plans for a Million Man March on Washington drew national attention. In October 1995 he delivered the keynote speech at the march, and he called for black men to repent for their treatment of their wives and to organize in their communities. In March 1996 Farrakhan drew widespread condemnation following a trip to the Middle East that included stops in Iran, Libya, Syria, and Nigeria, and for his announcement that Libyan dictator Mohamar Khadaffi had contributed $1,000,000 to the Nation of Islam. ◆

Fisher, Mary

APRIL 6, 1948– ● AIDS ACTIVIST

"We measure our lives by the depth, not the length."
Mary Fisher, 1999

Mary Fisher came to prominence in August 1992 when she spoke at the Republican National Convention in Houston, Texas, as an advocate for increased awareness of AIDS. She had learned the year before that she was herself HIV infected. In a passionate speech in which she addressed her two-year-old son from the stage of the convention center, she said, "I will not rest, Max, until I have done all I can to make your world safe. I will seek a place where intimacy is not the prelude to suffering." The *New York Times* called the speech "exceptional for its deep emotion and sharp message."

Born in Louisville, Kentucky, on April 6, 1948, Fisher is the daughter of Marjorie and Max Fisher, a successful businessman, Republican party patron, and philanthropist. She began her education at the Cranbrook Academy, a private school in Bloomfield Hills, Michigan, and attended Wayne State

University and the University of Michigan. She tried her hand at television production and then joined the Gerald Ford administration, becoming the first woman to serve as a presidential advance worker. She married, gave birth to two sons, and divorced before learning she had contracted the HIV virus from her ex-husband.

After appearing before the Republican Presidential Platform Committee in the spring of 1992, Fisher was designated a prime-time convention speaker. She proclaimed a grim message to the convention and television audiences: "The epidemic is winning." Bringing the usually clamorous convention to a hush, she told the delegates, "The AIDS virus . . . does not ask whether you are black or white, male or female, gay or straight, young or old." Addressing the shame felt by those afflicted with AIDS, a sexually transmitted disease, she admonished her fellow Republicans, "We have killed each other with our ignorance, our prejudice, and our silence." Her audience responded to the speech with tears and an ovation.

After seizing the attention of her political party, Fisher established the Family AIDS Network and became a full-time advocate for AIDS patients and their caregivers as well as a spokesperson for people living with AIDS and HIV, especially women and children. From the convention podium she had offered "to the millions of you who are grieving, who are frightened, who have suffered the ravages of AIDS first hand: have courage and you will find comfort." Following her moving speech, she was sought by women's groups, political forums, churches, children's and gay advocacy organizations, and the media. She embarked on an energetic travel and public speaking schedule, averaging at least two appearances a week, reiterating her words about the AIDS plague: "If you do not see this killer, stalking your children, look again."

In forming the Family AIDS Network, she recruited celebrities including all-star pitcher Rod Beck of the Chicago Cubs and Al Roker of NBC's *Today Show* for its board, and signed openly gay former congressman Steve Gunderson, a Republican from western Wisconsin, as managing trustee. The network launched a campaign to raise awareness that AIDS is a malady that is not limited to needle-sharing drug users and to the homosexual population, but is increasingly a young people's disease affecting adolescents, women, and children.

Campaigning for AIDS education, Fisher explains that people under the age of twenty-five represent 50 percent of all

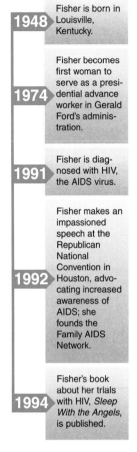

1948 Fisher is born in Louisville, Kentucky.

1974 Fisher becomes first woman to serve as a presidential advance worker in Gerald Ford's administration.

1991 Fisher is diagnosed with HIV, the AIDS virus.

1992 Fisher makes an impassioned speech at the Republican National Convention in Houston, advocating increased awareness of AIDS; she founds the Family AIDS Network.

1994 Fisher's book about her trials with HIV, *Sleep With the Angels*, is published.

"We have killed each other with our ignorance, our prejudice, and our silence." Her audience responded to Fisher's speech with tears and an ovation.

AIDS Research

AIDS is the final, life-threatening stage of infection with human immunodeficiency virus (HIV). The Community Research Initiative on AIDS (CRIA) was incorporated in December 1991 by a group of physicians, activists, and people living with AIDS (PLWAs) who were discouraged by the restraints and red tape that were slowing government and academic AIDS research efforts. Under the leadership of the medical community's foremost AIDS researchers and physicians, the group set out to create an agency that would bring activism to the ever-urgent task of studying AIDS-related illness and treatment. CRIA's status as an independent, not-for-profit clinical research and education organization has uniquely qualified it to evaluate drugs and treatments that for-profit groups lack the financial incentive to explore. Also, as the latest information becomes available, CRIA is able quickly to adapt its research initiatives at a much faster pace than do large academic or government groups. As a result, CRIA has consistently completed preliminary studies of new drugs within months rather than years.

Since its founding, CRIA's research agenda has been broad based. This agenda has included clinical trials resulting in the FDA approval of seven critical and commonly prescribed AIDS drugs, including Ritonavir, a member of a promising new class of anti-HIV treatments called protease inhibitors; Sustiva, Nevaripine, and Delavirdine (all an antiviral drug called a non-nucleoside reverse transcriptase inhibitor); and Rifabutin, which prevents MAC (Mycobacterium avium complex), a deadly disease that is a primary cause of AIDS-related wasting away. Also, CRIA has initiated national clinical studies comparing the impact of different types of nutritional supplements, examining the effects of testosterone injections, and other methods of combating deterioration, as well as studies to examine the potential relationship between new antiviral therapies and an array of metabolic side effects (and treatments to counter the side effects). CRIA has collaborated in efforts with leading pharmaceutical companies to investigate promising HIV/AIDS-related treatments and interventions, and is also a leading provider of HIV treatment education in New York City. Each year CRIA informs thousands of PLWAs of the latest advances in HIV health care through group treatment workshops, individual treatment education sessions, and CRIA's monthly series of large community treatment forums at St. Vincent's Hospital in Manhattan. Over 85 well-established AIDS service organizations (ASOs) citywide have partnered with CRIA's treatment educators to bring information on the newest HIV health-care advances to their PLWA clients within multiple communities in all five boroughs of the city. CRIA also provides treatment education to a national audience through the agency's quarterly newsletter, *CRIA Update*, which has an estimated annual circulation of approximately 50,000 individuals.

new HIV infection. She draws a sharp difference between AIDS and other illnesses, saying, "Adolescents don't give each other cancer or heart disease because they believe they are in love." Fisher is not reluctant to speak about AIDS and HIV issues on a personal level. Protease inhibitor drugs are currently recommended for preventing HIV infection from developing into full-blown AIDS, but because of the severe side effects, Fisher is on record as declining them.

Mary Fisher and sons, Zachary and Max, live in the suburbs of New York City. She continues to oversee her Family Aids Network, crisscrossing the country as an AIDS educator and spokesperson, visiting hospices, hospitals, nurseries, and schools. She continues to write and to work as a photographer, weaver, and artist. She pursues the mission she outlined for the Republican Convention. In her words, "I want my children to know that their mother was not a victim. She was a messenger." ◆

Fletcher, Alice Cunningham

MARCH 15, 1838–APRIL 6, 1923 ● ANTHROPOLOGIST AND NATIVE
AMERICAN REFORMER

A lice Cunningham Fletcher was born in Havana, Cuba, while her parents were on vacation. In the 1870s she studied archaeology and ethnology at the Peabody Museum of Harvard University. In 1881 she moved to Nebraska to live with the Omaha tribe, where she studied all aspects of tribal life. In her time with the Omaha people, she developed both a passionate concern for their well-being and decidedly paternalistic ideas about improving the conditions under which reservation Indians lived.

In 1882 she journeyed to Washington, D.C., drafted a bill apportioning Omaha tribal lands into individual holdings, and shepherded the bill through the U.S. Congress. President Chester A. Arthur appointed her to implement the program, which was completed in 1884. Two years later she went to Alaska and the Aleutian Islands to study the educational needs of the native peoples. She continued to agitate for better treatment of Native Americans from the federal government. Her efforts were rewarded in 1887 by the passage of the Dawes Act. This law directed that tribal lands be disbursed as the Omaha lands had been. Although reformers of the day considered the Dawes Act a major victory for Indian welfare, it fostered white exploitation and the dispossession of Native American lands.

Fletcher supervised the application of the Dawes Act provisions to the lands of the Winnebago and Nez Percé Indians.

1838 Fletcher is born in Havana, Cuba.

1881 Fletcher moves to Nebraska to live with the Omaha tribe.

1882 Fletcher travels to Washington, D.C., where she drafts the Dawes Act, a bill apportioning Omaha tribal lands into individual holdings, and shepherds the bill through the U.S. Congress.

1887 The Dawes Act is passed.

1923 Fletcher dies at the age of 85.

Later in her life, she wrote *Indian Story and Song from North America* (1900), *The Hako: A Pawnee Ceremony* (1904), and her major anthropological study, *The Omaha Tribe* (1911). The latter she produced with Francis LaFlesche, son of an Omaha chief, whom she treated as her adopted son. Fletcher died in Washington, D.C., at the age of eighty-five. ◆

Forman, James

OCTOBER 4, 1928– ● CIVIL RIGHTS ACTIVIST AND AUTHOR

Due to his tenacity, commitment, and organizational skills, the Student Nonviolent Coordinating Committee (SNCC) developed into a viable and durable civil rights organization.

Born in Chicago, James Forman spent his early childhood with his grandmother in Marshall County, Mississippi. He eventually returned to Chicago with his parents, attended Wilson Junior College in Chicago, and served in the Air Force from 1947 to 1951. In 1953, Forman returned to Chicago and attended Roosevelt University, earning a degree in public administration in four years. He began to teach and also worked as a reporter for the *Chicago Defender*, a leading African-American newspaper.

In 1960, Forman became active in the Emergency Relief Committee—an affiliate of the Congress of Racial Equality (CORE) that gave assistance to black farmers in Tennessee who were evicted for registering to vote. Later that same year, he traveled to Monroe, North Carolina, in an interracial "freedom ride." He was arrested and beaten because of his civil rights activities. These experiences with racial injustice solidified his commitment to the cause of black civil rights, and in September 1961, he joined the Student Nonviolent Coordinating Committee (SNCC) in Atlanta.

SNCC was a young organization with a weak operational apparatus when Forman joined. Older and more experienced than most SNCC activists, he was appointed executive secretary almost immediately. He assumed full-time responsibility for fund-raising and hired and directed a support staff for SNCC activists. Due to his tenacity, commitment, and organizational skills, SNCC developed into a viable and durable civil rights organization.

Along with his administrative responsibilities, Forman participated in mass protests. He was active in the Albany movement—a coalition of civil rights groups in Albany, Georgia—in

1961, and in 1963 he was one of the leaders of a march in Greenwood, Mississippi, aimed at precipitating federal intervention. He gave many speeches on the subject of racial justice and was an outspoken critic of U.S. involvement in Vietnam.

As SNCC fell prey to divisive debates about tactics, strategies and goals in the mid-1960s, Forman was at the center of factional conflict. His often heavy-handed attempts to shape SNCC into a tightly structured organization were criticized by those who, like Robert Moses, believed that SNCC's role was to serve as a catalyst for mass organization. By 1966 these pressures, coupled with ailing health, forced Forman to resign as executive secretary. He remained active within the organization, and played an integral role in promoting an alliance between SNCC and the Black Panther Party in 1967. When SNCC opted for a more collective leadership structure in 1968, Forman was elected as one of nine deputy chairmen. A year later, disheartened and exhausted by the years of factional infighting, he left the fragmenting organization.

He turned his energies toward black economic development. In 1969 he organized the National Black Development Conference (NBDC) in Detroit which produced the Black Manifesto, demanding that $500 million in reparations for slavery be given to African Americans by white churches and synagogues. Forman's bold and unannounced disruption of services at the Riverside Church in New York City to read the manifesto thrust him in the center of national publicity. The NBDC received over $1 million in donations from various white organizations. The money was used to establish Black Star Publications, a press controlled by Forman that published posters, pamphlets, and one book entitled *The Political Thought of James Forman* (1970). Funding was also given to the League of Revolutionary Black Workers, a Detroit-based militant organization made up of black industrial workers and others who **adhered** to a socialist ideology. Forman was active in the League and was the guiding force behind the creation of the Black Workers Congress, a vehicle that was used to try to develop organizations similar to the League in other cities.

In 1972 Forman published the first edition of his autobiography, *The Making of Black Revolutionaries.* (A revised edition appeared in 1985.) In the mid-1970s he served as president of the Unemployment and Poverty Action council. From 1977 to 1980 he pursued a masters degree in African and African-American studies at Cornell University in Ithaca, New York. In

adhere: a faithful attachment.

1928 Forman is born in Chicago, Illinois.

1957 Forman earns his degree in public administration from Roosevelt University.

1960 Forman becomes active in the Emergency Relief Committee of the Congress of Racial Equality (CORE).

1969 Forman organizes the National Black Development Conference in Detroit.

1972 Forman publishes the first edition of his autobiography, *The Making of a Black Revolutionary.*

1990 Forman receives the National Coalition of Mayors' Fannie Lou Hamer Freedom Award.

1982, he received a Ph.D. from the Union of Experimental Colleges and Universities (in corporation with the Institute for Policy Studies) in Washington, D.C. Out of his studies came a theoretical book, *Self Determination: An Examination of the Question and Its Application to the African-American People* (1984). Forman has continued to write and speak about issues of black empowerment and against **oppression** and discrimination. In 1990 he received the National Coalition of Black Mayors' Fannie Lou Hamer Freedom Award. ◆

oppression: an unjust exercise of authority or power.

Forten, James

SEPTEMBER 2, 1766–MARCH 15, 1842 ● BUSINESSMAN AND ABOLITIONIST

"It seems almost incredible that the advocates of liberty should conceive of the idea of selling a fellow creature to slavery."
James Forten, 1813

B orn free in Philadelphia in 1766, James Forten attended a Quaker school in Philadelphia headed by abolitionist Anthony Benezet. At the age of fourteen he went to sea and became a powder boy on the *Royal Louis*, a colonial privateer under the command of Captain Stephen Decatur, father of the nineteenth-century naval hero of the same name. After one successful sortie against the British, the *Royal Louis* was captured by a group of British ships; Forten and the rest of the crew were taken prisoner. Had he not befriended the son of the British captain, Forten, like many African Americans in his situation, might have been sent into slavery in the West Indies. Instead the British captain ensured that Forten would be transferred to the *Jersey*, a prison hulk in New York harbor; after seven months, Forten was released. On the prison hulk, many succumbed to rampant disease; Forten luckily avoided serious illness.

Shortly after his release, Forten began to work under the **tutelage** of Robert Bridges, a Philadelphia sail maker. Forten's skill and aptitude guaranteed his success in the industry: by the age of twenty he was the foreman of Bridges's shop. Upon Bridges's retirement in 1798, Forten became the undisputed master of the shop and developed a reputation for excellent service and innovative sail handling techniques. His business grew; some estimates suggest that he had a fortune of over $100,000 by the early 1830s.

tutelage: instruction.

Forten used both his fortune and his fame to forward his agenda for the destruction of slavery. One of the most prominent and vocal Philadelphians on the issue, Forten was a life-long advocate of immediate abolition. In 1800 he was a petitioner to the U.S. Congress to change the terms of the 1793 Fugitive Slave Law, which permitted suspected runaways to be seized and arrested without a warrant and access to due process. Forten refused to rig sails for ships that had participated in or were suspected of participating in the slave trade. In 1812, along with well-known Philadelphians Richard Allen and Absalom Jones, he helped raise a volunteer regiment of African Americans to help defend Philadelphia were the city to be threatened by the British.

In September 1830 Forten was a participant in the first National Negro Convention in Philadelphia. Its goal was to "consider the plight of the free Negro" and to "plan his social redemption." At the next annual convention, Forten used his influence to oppose funding for the American Colonization Society, which supported black emigration to Liberia; at other times, however, Philadelphia's black elite, including Forten, had advocated emigration to Haiti and Canada.

In 1832 Forten and several other African Americans forwarded another petition to the Pennsylvania legislature asking it not to restrict the immigration of free blacks into the state nor to begin more rigorous enforcement of the 1793 federal Fugitive Slave Law. Much of their argument was based on two main principles: a moral argument based on the evils of slavery and an economic argument—that free blacks were extremely productive members of the Philadelphia and Pennsylvania communities. As one of the organizers of the American Anti-Slavery Society in 1833, Forten provided support, especially economic, to abolitionist activities. Forten's generous support greatly aided the continuing publication of William Lloyd Garrison's abolitionist *Liberator*. Around 1838 he also went to court in a vain attempt to secure the right to vote.

Forten was a founder and presiding officer of the American Moral Reform Society. The society stressed temperance, peace, and other Garrisonian ideals, which included the full and equal participation of women in antislavery activism and society in general. Forten's reputation for good works was well known: he received an award from the city of Philadelphia for saving at least four, and perhaps as many as twelve, people from drowning in the river near his shop. When he died in 1842, thousands of people, many of whom were white, reportedly attended his funeral.

1766 Forten is born in Philadelphia, Pennsylvania.

1798 Forten becomes master sailmaker at Robert Bridges's sail shop, developing a reputation for excellent service and innovative sail handling techniques.

1800 Forten petitions the U.S. Congress to change the terms of the 1793 Fugitive Slave Law.

1830 Forten is a participant in the first National Negro Convention in Philadelphia.

1833 Forten is one of the organizers and main financial supporters of the American Anti-Slavery Society.

1842 Forten dies.

As one of the organizers of the American Anti-Slavery Society in 1833, Forten provided economic support to abolitionist activities.

Even before his death in 1842, the legacy of Forten's deep belief in abolition was carried on by his family. Forten's children, and later his grandchildren, would figure as prominent abolitionists and civil rights activists throughout the nineteenth century. Forten's son, James Jr., and his son-in-law Robert Purvis were very active in the abolitionist movement from the 1830s onwards, and often **collaborated** with the elder Forten in his various activities. All of Forten's daughters were involved in antislavery affairs, and Charlotte Forten Grimké, Forten's granddaughter, became a well-known author, educator, and activist for civil rights. ◆

collaborated: worked with.

Fortune, Timothy Thomas

OCTOBER 3, 1856–JUNE 2, 1928 ● JOURNALIST AND CIVIL RIGHTS ACTIVIST

"The moral, mental and material condition of the race must be properly looked after before we can hope to establish any sort of status in the country."

T. Thomas Fortune, 1886

Thomas Fortune was born a slave in Marianna, Florida, in 1856, to Emanuel and Sarah Jane Fortune. After Emancipation his father, active in Republican politics, was forced by white violence to flee to Jacksonville, where young Fortune became a compositor at a local newspaper. In the winter of 1874 Fortune enrolled at Howard University with fewer than three years of formal education behind him. But financial troubles compelled him to drop out, and he began working for a black weekly paper. Fortune married Carrie C. Smiley in the late 1870s and returned to Florida, where he worked on several newspapers. Chafing under southern racism, Fortune gladly moved to New York City in 1881 to accept a position with a white-owned weekly publication.

In New York Fortune joined with other African Americans who had founded a tabloid called *Rumor* (soon known as the New York *Globe*), and he became managing editor. Fortune set the *Globe*'s militant tone in his editorial advocacy of black civil rights and self-defense; he also shared Henry George's critique of monopoly and endorsed his land distribution program. Moreover, at a time when most black newspapers backed the Republican party, Fortune favored political independence. He expanded on these radical themes in his book, *Black and White: Land, Labor, and Politics in the South*, published in 1884.

The *Globe* folded in early November 1884. Just two weeks later, however, Fortune was producing the *Freeman* (soon called the *New York Freeman*), a four-page weekly whose circulation stood at 5,000 by the end of its first year. In October 1887 Fortune left the *Freeman*, which became the *New York Age*, and began to court Republican support. (Fortune had supported Democratic presidential candidate Grover Cleveland in 1888.) He returned as editor in February 1889, renouncing his past alliance with the Democrats but continuing to criticize the Republicans' inaction on racial issues. He supplemented his income by writing for the *New York Sun*, a leading newspaper.

Fortune was also a key figure in the Afro-American League (AAL), an early and important vehicle for civil rights agitation. In May 1887 Fortune proposed the formation of a nonpartisan organization to challenge lynch law in the South and to demand equal opportunities in voting, education, and public accommodations.

He also issued the call for the AAL's first national convention; at the January 1890 meeting, he was elected secretary. The AAL planned to fight Jim Crow through legal means; after Fortune himself was refused service at a New York hotel bar, the AAL sued the proprietor and won. But without adequate resources to mount regular legal challenges, and lacking support from prominent black Republicans, by 1893 the organization had sunk into decline.

Fortune continued to expose racist abuses, particularly in the South. After Ida B. Wells's Memphis newspaper office was destroyed by a mob, he offered her work on the *Age* and published her stunning exposé of lynching. In 1894–95 Fortune himself toured the South and reported on worsening conditions there. Despite the revival in 1898 of the old AAL as the Afro-American Council (AAC), Fortune had by then grown deeply pessimistic about the possibilities for securing racial justice.

During this period of disaffection, Fortune solidified his relationship with Booker T. Washington. The two had first come into contact in the early 1880s and despite their differences, Fortune helped launch the accommodationist Washington as a national figure. He not only publicized Tuskegee Institute in the *Age*, but also employed his literary talents to polish and promote Washington's views; he wrote a long introduction to *Black-Belt Diamonds* (1898), a collection of Washington's speeches, and he edited and revised Washington's *The Future of the American Negro* (1898). Because Fortune's only

1856 — Fortune is born in Marianne, Florida.

1881 — Fortune moves to New York City to accept a position at a white-owned newspaper.

1884 — Fortune's book *Black and White: Land, Labor, and Politics in the South* is published.

1900 — Fortune serves as chair of the National Negro Business League.

1902 — Fortune secures a six-month post as special immigrant agent of the U.S. Treasury Department.

1923 — Fortune becomes editor of *Negro World*.

1928 — Fortune dies.

Fortune employed his literary talents to polish and promote Booker T. Washington's views.

income came from journalism, the remuneration he received for these efforts, as well as emergency loans from Washington, helped tide him over through hard times.

As Washington rose in national stature, he relied increasingly on Fortune—his closest ally in the North—to advance his political agenda. Fortune, aware that Washington occasionally backed legal challenges to **Jim Crow** behind the scenes, tried to make Washington's views more palatable to a northern black audience. Fortune served as chair of the executive committee of the National Negro Business League (NNBL), formed by Washington in 1900. As AAC president in the early 1900s, Fortune helped squelch anti-Washington sentiment spearheaded by William Monroe Trotter of the *Boston Guardian*.

Jim Crow: ethnic discrimination against blacks by legal enforcement or traditional sanctions.

One reason for Fortune's efforts on Washington's behalf was that he hoped for a political appointment to resolve his financial difficulties. He did manage, in late 1902, to secure a six-month post as special immigrant agent of the U.S. Treasury Department, investigating racial conditions in Hawaii and the Philippine Islands. Evidence suggests, however, that Washington thwarted Fortune's future aspirations, possibly because he realized a government position would increase Fortune's economic independence.

Washington's heavy-handed management of the *Age* contributed to Fortune's nervous breakdown in 1907.

Fortune's greatest usefulness to Washington had been as an "independent" journalist, and observers had grown skeptical of his independence; as early as 1902 the *Guardian* had written scathingly that "much of the fat that now greases the way for the *Age*, comes out of the Tuskegee larder." Moreover, Fortune continued to take militant political stances that were not in line with Washington's own positions.

In February 1907 Washington secretly acquired direct control of the *Age*, and his heavy-handed management contributed to Fortune's nervous breakdown later that year. Believing he had been called by God to preach to the race, Fortune sold his shares in the *Age* to Fred R. Moore (1857–1943), a Washington loyalist, who claimed a "white friend" had backed the transaction. Unknown to Fortune, it was Washington's money that had clinched the deal.

Fortune left for Chicago and sought unsuccessfully to reestablish himself. With little to lose, he disclosed Washington's financial interest in the *Age* and was lauded by Washington's rivals. But this did nothing to resolve his deepening financial crisis. His marriage had collapsed by 1906; now he lost his home. Suffering from alcoholism and unable to obtain steady work, he scraped by for years on whatever intermittent journalistic employment he could find.

The *Age*, meanwhile, deteriorated dramatically in quality, and Washington lured Fortune back in the fall of 1914. While the compensation was poor and Fortune's editorial independence limited, he remained with the *Age* for three years. Thereafter he worked for papers in Philadelphia, Indianapolis, Washington, D.C., and elsewhere.

The early 1920s ushered in new political possibilities for African Americans and brought Fortune back from the edge of destitution and despair. In 1923 he became editor of the *Negro World*, the organ of Marcus Garvey's Universal Negro Improvement Association. While Fortune never embraced the Garvey movement, he had become deeply disillusioned by black people's failure to attain equality and justice by means of the political process. Through his work for the *Negro World*, he was able to regain his self-respect. In the late 1920s Fortune's colleagues in the National Negro Press Association (over which he himself had presided some thirty years before) lauded him as the "dean" of Negro journalists. He edited the *World* until his death on June 2, 1928, at the home of his son Fred in the Philadelphia area.

Fortune's erratic career has somewhat obscured his own historical importance. Before Booker T. Washington's ascent as a national figure began in 1895, Fortune himself was acknowledged as the major spokesperson for black America. His leadership role in the late nineteenth-century civil rights movement was instrumental in shaping the debate over how African Americans would respond to their legal and social oppression in the decades to come. ◆

Before Booker T. Washington's ascent as a national figure began in 1895, Fortune himself was acknowledged as the major spokesperson for black America.

Friedan, Betty

FEBRUARY 4, 1921– ● WOMEN'S RIGHTS ACTIVIST

One of the founders of the women's liberation movement in the 1960s, Betty Friedan is best known for her influential book *The Feminine Mystique*, which explored the sense of emptiness and dissatisfaction many women felt in lives exclusively devoted to child rearing and housework. Friedan's exhortation to women to seek fulfillment

Betty Friedan

1921 Friedan is born in Peoria, Illinois.

1963 *The Feminine Mystique* is published.

1966 Friedan cofounds and becomes president of NOW.

1970 Friedan leads the Women's Strike for Equality.

1972 The ERA is passed by the U.S. Senate, but fails to win ratification by a majority of state legislatures.

in work that utilized their full potential helped launch a movement that has transformed American society.

In writing *The Feminine Mystique*, Friedan drew on her own struggles as a highly educated woman who had given up a prestigious graduate fellowship and the possibility of a career to focus on marriage and family. Born in Peoria, Illinois, in 1921, the daughter of Miriam (Horowitz) and Harry Goldstein, a jeweler, Friedan graduated from Smith College with highest honors in 1942 and entered a Ph.D. program in psychology at the University of California at Berkeley. Friedan dropped out of graduate school after a year and moved to New York City, where she worked as a reporter before marrying Carl Friedan in 1947. She wrote articles on child rearing and other traditional women's subjects for such magazines as *Ladies' Home Journal* and *Redbook* while raising her own three children in the suburbs of Rockland County in New York.

In 1957, while she was conducting a questionnaire for her fellow Smith classmates fifteen years after their graduation, Friedan discovered that she was not alone in her frustrations as

Title IX

The women's movement made important legal gains during the 1970s and 1980s, including the enactment of Title IX of the Education Amendments in 1972. Title IX broadened the provisions of the Civil Rights Act of 1964 and barred gender bias in federally assisted education programs. The legislation stimulated colleges to admit more women to professional schools and also changed the nature of intercollegiate athletics by mandating that more money be spent on women's sports. Though complete equity remains a distant goal, fully 37 percent of the participants in intercollegiate athletics in 1995 were women, compared with 15 percent before Title IX had become law.

To comply with Title IX and qualify for federal subsidies, a university must have roughly the same percentage of female athletes as it has female undergraduates. The institution must also demonstrate a "continuing history" of expanding athletic opportunities for the underrepresented gender. In 1997 the National Collegiate Athletic Association (NCAA) reported that women's collegiate athletic programs are at least 10 years away from reaching equity with men's programs.

a suburban housewife who felt trapped in the 1950s American dream of female domesticity. "There was a strange discrepancy between the reality of our lives as women and the image to which we were trying to conform, the image that I came to call the feminine mystique," wrote Friedan. She devoted five years of research to the writing of *The Feminine Mystique*, which was published in 1963.

The Feminine Mystique called on women to find their identity in work that uses their full capacities. Friedan's message, aimed at an audience of middle-class, educated women, drew millions of women into feminism. Women went back to school, and they went to work, struggling for equal pay and equal access to promotion with men in the workplace.

In 1966 Friedan and other feminist leaders grew angry at the refusal of the federal Equal Employment Opportunity Commission to consider the problems of working women. In that year Friedan cofounded and became the first president of the National Organization for Women (NOW), an organization whose major goal was to combat discrimination against women in the workplace.

In its Statement of Purpose, NOW declared, "The purpose of NOW is to take action to bring women into full participation in the mainstream of American society now, exercising all the privileges and responsibilites thereof in truly equal partnership with men."

> *"We, men and women, who hereby constitute ourselves as the National Organization for Women, believe that the time has come for a new movement toward true equality for all women in America."*
>
> From the Statement of Purpose of the National Organization for Women (NOW), 1966

Friedan and other NOW activists were experienced lobbyists. They filed a complaint against the *New York Times* for its sex-segregated job ads and successfully lobbied airlines that forced stewardesses to retire at thirty-two or when they married. They supported the establishment of childcare centers and paid maternity leave for working mothers.

Friedan served as president of NOW until 1970. In that year she helped organize and lead a nationwide protest called the Women's Strike for Equality, commemorating the fiftieth anniversary of the passage of the Nineteenth Amendment, which gave women the right to vote. In 1971 she worked to form the National Women's Political Caucus, which encourages women to run for political office. She was also an active campaigner for the proposed Equal Rights Amendment (ERA) to the Constitution, which was written to protect women from sex discrimination. The ERA was passed by the Congress in 1972 but failed to win ratification by a majority of state legislatures and fell in 1982.

In addition to giving lectures at campuses and organizations across the country in the decades following her resignation from the presidency of NOW, Friedan continued to write on women's issues. In the fall of 1990 *Life* magazine included Friedan among "The 100 Most Important Americans of the 20th Century," calling her "The Housewife Who Liberated Everywoman." ◆

The ERA was passed by the Congress in 1972 but failed to win ratification by a majority of state legislatures.

Gandhi, Mohandas Karamchand (Mahatma)

OCTOBER 2, 1869–JANUARY 30, 1948 ● INDIAN ACTIVIST
AND SPIRITUAL LEADER

Born in Porbandar, the capital of a small principality in Gujarat, western India, where his father was chief minister, Mohandas Karamchand Gandhi grew up in a pious Hindu household. Gandhi took the doctrine of *ahimsa*—refraining from harming any living being—for granted; it was later to constitute an integral part of his personal philosophy of social and political action.

Married at thirteen, Gandhi overcame his mother's anxiety and ultraorthodox Hindu condemnation to sail to London to study law in 1888. Separated from his wife and family, the lonely youth was forced to question and justify such personal practices as his vegetarianism; becoming a member of the London Vegetarian Society's executive committee, he came into contact with such radical figures as Edward Carpenter, George Bernard Shaw, and Annie Besant. He was also exposed for the first time to the Hindu spiritual classic the *Bhagavadgita*, which was to have a profound and lasting effect upon him.

Unable to make a satisfactory living as a lawyer in India, Gandhi remained there for only two years, sailing to South Africa in 1893 to accept a position with an Indian firm. Journeying by train from Durban to Pretoria, Gandhi, despite his elegant Western dress and manner, was expelled from his first-class carriage at the insistence of a white passenger who objected to sharing it with an Indian. In later years, he was consistently to designate this as the single most important formative

> *"Nonviolence is the greatest force at the disposal of mankind. It is mightier than the mightiest weapon of destruction devised by the ingenuity of man."*
> Mohandas Gandhi

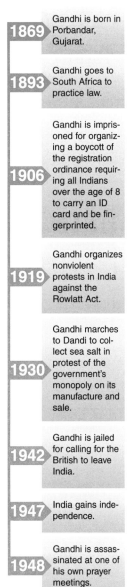

1869 Gandhi is born in Porbandar, Gujarat.

1893 Gandhi goes to South Africa to practice law.

1906 Gandhi is imprizoned for organizing a boycott of the registration ordinance requiring all Indians over the age of 8 to carry an ID card and be fingerprinted.

1919 Gandhi organizes nonviolent protests in India against the Rowlatt Act.

1930 Gandhi marches to Dandi to collect sea salt in protest of the government's monopoly on its manufacture and sale.

1942 Gandhi is jailed for calling for the British to leave India.

1947 India gains independence.

1948 Gandhi is assassinated at one of his own prayer meetings.

ordinance: authoritative decree or direction.

experience of his life; it moved him to determine to assert his dignity as an Indian and a man in a country where apartheid laws rendered him and his fellow Indians second-class citizens.

Gandhi soon became recognized as a leader of the South African Indian community, staying on to fight for its interests even after his original work was completed. His trip was to have lasted a few months; he remained in South Africa for a quarter of a century.

Founding the Natal Indian Congress, Gandhi organized demands for improved civil rights for the thousands of Indians living in the then-crown colony, most of whom were indentured laborers. In 1899, stressing duties as well as rights, he argued that as citizens of the British Empire, Indians should help defend Natal during the Boer War and formed an eleven-hundred-man Indian volunteer ambulance corps.

Gandhi's life constituted a continuous spiritual quest and in 1904, after reading *Unto This Last,* John Ruskin's avowal of the nobility of manual labor, he gave up his £5,000-a-year legal practice and with some of his growing band of followers, renounced material possessions and strove to satisfy human needs in the simplest manner, with all labor considered equally valuable and all goods shared. Tolstoy Farm (named after Leo Tolstoy, whose *The Kingdom of God Is Within You* profoundly impressed Gandhi, and with whom he corresponded briefly) near Johannesburg became Gandhi's home and a center for communal living. Throughout his life he was to continue such "experiments with truth," which led him to simplify his diet, renounce sex, spend an hour each morning in careful study of the *Bhagavadgita* (which he came to regard as his "spiritual dictionary"), profess the unity of all religions, dress in the garb of a simple Indian peasant, and even extol the virtues of a daily salt water enema.

The opposition to the Transvaal government's 1906 registration **ordinance**, which required all Indians over the age of eight to be fingerprinted and carry an identity card, marked the first use of strategies based on the principle of *satyagraha* (literally "truth-firmness," passive resistance), which Gandhi had formulated. His religious convictions had led him to a complete disavowal of violence, but he still received a jail sentence for organizing a boycott of the registration process and peaceful picketing of registration centers.

While in prison, he read Henry Thoreau's *On Civil Disobedience,* which asserted the individual's right to ignore unjust laws and refuse allegiance to a government whose tyranny had become unbearable; the book acted as a catalyst for his ideas and motivated his strategy for opposing the 1913 decision by the Transvaal government to close its borders to Indians. Thousands of floggings and hundreds of jailings could not break the nonviolent movement, and in the face of international condemnation of its heavy-handed retaliatory measures, Jan Smuts's government engineered a compromise agreement with Gandhi. "The saint has left our shores, I hope for ever," observed Smuts when Gandhi sailed for India in 1914.

Hailed as "Mahatma" (great-souled) by Rabindranath Tagore, Gandhi played little active role in Indian politics until 1919, when he organized nonviolent protests against the Rowlatt Act, which sought to repress agitation for Indian freedom. The British authorities' response was nowhere more brutal than in the city of Amritsar, Punjab, where some fifteen hundred unarmed and nonviolent protesters were gunned down by troops. Indians reacted with shock and horror and calls for independence from British rule became even stronger.

> Quickly recognized as the undisputed leader of the Indian nationalist movement, Gandhi launched a campaign of nonviolent noncooperation against British rule.

Quickly recognized as the undisputed leader of the Indian nationalist movement, Gandhi succeeded in transforming the Indian National Congress from a superannuated body of anglicized Indian gentlemen into a genuinely representative mass organization, using it as the launching pad for a campaign of nonviolent noncooperation against British rule. To the dismay of many of his colleagues, he called off the hugely successful campaign in 1922, when outbreaks of violence convinced him that his followers did not fully understand the importance of the principle of nonviolence. He was arrested shortly thereafter, but was released due to ill health after serving three years in jail.

Convinced that self-sufficiency was an essential prerequisite for successful Indian self-government, he called for a boycott of British goods, a return to the wearing of rough **homespun** cotton clothing; he himself spent an hour each day at a spinning wheel and homespun soon became the unofficial uniform of nationalist political leaders. In 1930 he marched to Dandi on the Gujarat coast and collected sea salt in defiance of the government monopoly on its manufacture and sale. The wave of civil disobedience this action triggered resulted in 60,000 arrests, including that of Gandhi himself, but the British government was eventually forced to acknowledge Indian nationalist aspirations. The man Winston Churchill derided as a "half-naked fakir" traveled to London to negotiate with the British

homespun: loosely woven wool cloth, obviously homemade.

government, but negotiations did not yield the timetable for a British withdrawal from India for which he had hoped.

After his return to India, he was increasingly occupied with projects such as the uplift of India's tens of millions of untouchables (economically and socially the lowest of the low, whom he renamed *Harijans,* or Children of God) and the promotion of village-based economics as opposed to the economics of industrialization and urbanization, which he considered inappropriate to Indian needs. Nevertheless, even after leaving the Indian National Congress in 1934, he remained the spiritual leader of the nationalist movement and the Indian people, exerting a considerable practical and moral influence.

> *"You assist an evil system most effectively by obeying its orders and decrees. A good person will resist an evil system with his or her whole soul."*
> Mahatma Gandhi, 1930

Gandhi's principles led him to staunchly refuse to approve Indian support for the British war effort, despite his acknowledgment that Nazi persecution of Jews meant that "if ever there could be justifiable war in the name of and for humanity, war against Germany to prevent the wanton persecution of a whole race would be completely justified." Meanwhile his 1942 call for the British to "Quit India" led to his imprisonment and that of the entire Congress leadership, but the writing was on the wall for British rule. Five years later, in August 1947, India became an independent state.

subcontinent: a large subdivision or subset of a continent.

Gandhi had consistently struggled against separating the **subcontinent** into a Hindu India and a Muslim Pakistan, and the sectarian bloodbath that followed partition and claimed a million lives was a realization of his worst fears. He spent the night of the independence celebrations in Calcutta, where his presence successfully prevented the communal violence that had flared elsewhere. When violence did finally erupt there, Gandhi, seventy-seven years old and in poor health, expressed his intention of fasting until the fighting had completely stopped. He had fasted before to achieve spiritual or political ends, but never before had his life been so obviously at risk; within seventy-two hours hostilities in the city ceased.

In early January of the following year Gandhi arranged a truce in the riot-torn capital, Delhi; at the end of that same month he was assassinated by a Hindu fanatic at one of his own prayer meetings. He died with the words "*He, Ram*" ("O! God") on his lips. Among the thousands of tributes to him, none was more moving or heartfelt than Jawaharlal Nehru's representation of him as "that light that represented the living, the eternal truths, reminding us of the right path, drawing us from error, taking this ancient country to freedom."

The initiator of the twentieth century's struggles against colonialism, racism, and violence, Gandhi has also been an influential symbol of the moral and spiritual resources of the developing world, while his theory and practice of nonviolent direct action influenced many, including the African-American civil rights leader, Martin Luther King Jr. ◆

García Robles, Alfonso

MARCH 20, 1911–SEPTEMBER 2, 1991 ● NOBEL PEACE PRIZE WINNER AND CHAMPION OF DISARMAMENT

In naming García Robles as cowinner of the 1982 Nobel Peace Prize the Nobel committee declared that he had "played a crucial role in launching and implementing the agreement on a denuclearized zone in Latin America," and also cited his central role in the United Nations' work to promote general **disarmament**.

García Robles spent his active life in the foreign service of his country, except for a period when he was a top UN official. He was born in Zamora, Mexico, the capital of Michoacán State. He first thought of becoming a priest, but then decided on the law. After his studies in Mexico City, he went to the University of Paris, where he received his doctorate in law in 1936, when he was twenty-five years old. He attended the Academy of International Law at The Hague and then joined the staff of the Mexican embassy in Sweden, finally returning in 1941 to Mexico to take a post in the Foreign Ministry.

In 1945 García Robles was a member of the Mexican delegation at the San Francisco conference that founded the United Nations. He then joined the UN Secretariat as it was being formed and remained there for eleven years, serving in the important position of director of the Division of Political Affairs. It was while leading a UN mission to the Middle East in 1949 that he met Juanita Sislo of Peru, who became his wife. They were to have two sons.

In 1957 García Robles returned to the Mexican Foreign Ministry to become director general for Europe. In the following years he was also concerned with shaping his country's policy at the Law of the Sea conferences. In 1962 he became ambassador to Brazil, serving until 1964, when he was appointed under secretary for foreign affairs in the Ministry.

disarmament: to give up or reduce armed forces and weapons supplies.

"Unfortunately the actions and more frequently the words of the chiefs of states of the nuclear powers do not seem to reflect a full awareness of what is at stake in this question of the nuclear arms race."

Alfonso García Robles, 1982

1911 García is born in Porbandar, Gujarat.

1944 García Robles is a member of the Mexican delegation at the San Francisco conference that founds the United Nations and joins the UN Secretariat.

1966 García Robles is instrumental in the signing of the Treaty of Tlatelolco, declaring Latin America "forever free of nuclear weapons."

1978 García Robles plays a leading role in the first UN Special Session on disarmament.

1981 García Robles receives the Nobel Peace Prize.

1991 García Robles dies.

The Treaty of Tlatelolco declared Latin America "forever free of nuclear weapons."

In October 1962 the conflict between the United States and the Soviet Union over Soviet missiles in Cuba alarmed Latin Americans about the danger that nuclear arms might be used in their hemisphere. It was the presidents of Brazil, Ecuador, and Bolivia who first proposed making Latin America a nuclear-free zone, but the idea made no headway until García Robles took it up. He first persuaded the president of Mexico and then other Latin American governments to join in an agreement concerning such a zone. By 1963 he had succeeded in generating widespread support for the idea among these governments and secured approval of the concept from the UN General Assembly.

In 1964, on the initiative of García Robles, a conference was held in Mexico City, which set up the Preparatory Commission for the Denuclearization of Latin America with instructions to prepare a preliminary draft of a multilateral treaty. García Robles chaired this commission with considerable skill and was chiefly responsible for the text of the draft that was ready to be signed in 1967. This was the Treaty of Tlatelolco, taking the Aztec name for the site of the Mexican Foreign Ministry, where it was signed. The treaty was the first of its kind in the world. It declared Latin America "forever free of nuclear weapons" and provided for regular reports by the signatory states and for special inspections to ensure observance of their obligations.

García Robles continued to work for disarmament as Mexico's permanent representative to the United Nations from 1971 to 1975. He was foreign minister in 1975–76, and when he left office because of a change in government, he was asked what position he would like to have. His friends, who have regarded him as "obsessed" with disarmament, anticipated his choice, which was to become Mexico's representative to the UN Disarmament Commission in Geneva, which position he still held at the time of his Nobel prize.

In this post he helped prepare for the first UN Special Session on disarmament in 1978, at which meeting he played a leading role. He coordinated the various proposals that were advanced, and he was mainly responsible for the drafting and adoption of the final document. Several of its clauses were strikingly similar to the preamble of the Treaty of Tlatelolco.

At the second Special Session in 1982, García Robles again made an important contribution. Although the results of the session were generally disappointing, García Robles did find much agreement with his proposal for a world disarmament campaign. In the following years at the UN Disarmament Commission in Geneva, where in 1987 he was the respected doyen, García Robles worked hard to promote a comprehensive test ban of nuclear weapons.

Alfonso García Robles died in 1991. ◆

Garrison, William Lloyd

DECEMBER 10, 1805–MAY 24, 1879 ● ABOLITIONIST

William Lloyd Garrison was the most outstanding and influential abolitionist writer and publisher in the United States. His weekly newspaper, *The Liberator,* which appeared for thirty-five years from 1830 to 1865, built up and encouraged antislavery feeling among abolitionists, and aroused reaction among slaveholders and their sympathizers.

Garrison began life in hardship. He was born on December 10, 1805, in Newburyport, Massachusetts. His father had been an alcoholic, and as a very young boy he was left fatherless. After brief formal schooling, he was apprenticed to a newspaper editor in Newburyport. His apprenticeship taught him printing and editing, and gave him a chance to develop skill in writing. He ran a small Newburyport newspaper, the *Free Press,* in 1828. This was not a success, but he did become friendly with a struggling young poet, John Greenleaf Whittier. The two became lifelong friends. Garrison moved to Boston where he worked for a time on a newspaper devoted to the cause of temperance. He wrote articles on many kinds of reform—antidrinking, antigambling, antiwar. While in Boston, he met Benjamin Lundy, a Quaker who was already committed to the cause of abolition.

Garrison took up the abolitionist idea rapidly. He recognized this as his life work, and plunged into an absolute, "no-holds-barred" attack on the very idea of slavery. He spent part of 1829 and 1830 in Baltimore, writing strong, even violent, attacks on slavery and slave owners. One man brought suit against him for libel and he went to jail when he couldn't pay his fine. This jail term lasted only briefly, for a New Yorker came to his help with money to pay the fine.

Garrison and a partner, Isaac Knapp, began to publish *The Liberator* on January 1, 1831. They had borrowed equipment, and they operated "on a shoestring" with very small subscription lists to support the publication. Garrison, however, set the tone for the drive on slavery in his opening issue. It included an editorial denouncing the evil of slavery and ending with his famous statement: "I am in earnest—I will not equivocate—I will not excuse—I will not retreat a single inch—and I will be heard." He lived on that principle for the next thirty-five years.

Garrison suffered personal injury and was in danger of death from mobs who opposed his uncompromising ideas. Accepting the southern argument that slavery was protected by the U.S. Constitution, he denounced the Constitution as a "covenant with death and an agreement with hell!" He argued that the free (and therefore good) northern states should secede from the Union and he went on a lecture tour through the midwestern states to argue this point. He publicly burned a copy of the Constitution and demanded the prompt and complete conversion of Americans to the doctrine of abolition. He acted more like a reforming clergyman than a political leader. He voted only once in his life, and he would have nothing to do with those who organized political parties to oppose slavery, or who supported efforts to abolish slavery gradually. He wanted immediate emancipation, with no reservations and no payments to slave owners.

Given these positions, his approach to the Republican party in 1860 was cool and detached. He did not fully support the Civil War effort until after Lincoln had published the Emancipation Proclamation. Then he did support Lincoln. Garrison's main objective was accomplished with the Thirteenth Amendment. He suggested that the antislavery societies that he had organized and helped should be dissolved, and he discontinued *The Liberator* on December 29, 1865. Garrison was not especially active in the drive for civil rights for Negroes after the Civil War; his major interest was in emancipation and the end of formal slavery. He did take up a num-

"And now let me give the sentiment which has been, and ever will be, the governing passion of my soul: 'Liberty for each, for all, and forever!' "

William Lloyd
Garrison, 1865

1805 Garrison is born in Newburyport, Massachusetts.

1828 Garrison begins running the newspaper *The Free Press*.

1831 Garrison begins publishing *The Liberator* with Isaac Knapp.

1879 Garrison dies.

ber of other reform movements after the war, and was especially active in the drives to curb alcoholic beverages, and to arrange for women's right to vote. Garrison was internationally famous. He had many friends and supporters among the English abolitionists (who had succeeded in ending slavery in the British Empire long before 1865), and with Irish and Canadian reformers as well. His single-minded drive on slavery was an extremely important and significant element in developing the antislavery movement in the United States. ◆

Garrison's single-minded drive on slavery was an important element in developing the antislavery movement in the United States.

Garvey, Marcus Mosiah

AUGUST 17, 1887–JUNE 10, 1940 ● CHAMPION OF THE BACK-TO-AFRICA MOVEMENT

Hailed in his own time as a redeemer, a "black Moses," Marcus Garvey is now best remembered as champion of the Back-to-Africa movement that swept the United States in the aftermath of World War I.

Garvey was born on August 17, 1887, in the town of St. Ann's Bay on the north coast of the island of Jamaica. He left school at fourteen, worked as a printer's apprentice, and subsequently joined the protonationalist National Club, which advocated Jamaican self-rule. He participated in the printers' union strike of 1912, and following its collapse, he went to Central America, working in various capacities in Costa Rica, Honduras, and Panama. He spent over a year in England during 1913–14, where he teamed up for a time with the pan-Negro journalist and businessman Duse Mohamed Ali, publisher of the influential *African Times and Orient Review*. After a short tour of the European continent, he returned to England and lobbied the Colonial Office for assistance to return to Jamaica.

Garvey arrived back in Jamaica on the eve of the outbreak of World War I. He lost little time in organizing the UNIA, which he launched at a public meeting in Kingston on July 20, 1914. Content at first to offer a program of racial accommodation while professing strong patriotic support for British war aims, Garvey was a model **colonial**. He soon aspired to establish a Tuskegee-type industrial training school in Jamaica. In spring

"A race without authority and power is a race without respect."
Marcus Garvey, 1923

colonial: living in a new territory with strong allegiance to the parent state.

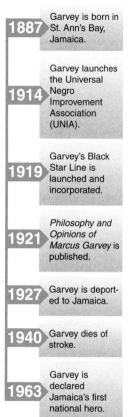

1887 Garvey is born in St. Ann's Bay, Jamaica.

1914 Garvey launches the Universal Negro Improvement Association (UNIA).

1919 Garvey's Black Star Line is launched and incorporated.

1921 *Philosophy and Opinions of Marcus Garvey* is published.

1927 Garvey is deported to Jamaica.

1940 Garvey dies of stroke.

1963 Garvey is declared Jamaica's first national hero.

Garvey envisioned a black-owned and -run shipping line to foster economic independence and serve as a symbol of black grandeur and enterprise.

1916, however, after meeting with little success and feeling shut out from political influence, he came to America—ostensibly at Booker T. Washington's invitation, though Garvey arrived after Washington died.

Garvey's arrival in America was propitious. It coincided with the dawn of the militant New Negro era, the ideological precursor of the Harlem Renaissance of the 1920s. Propelled by America's entry into World War I in April 1917, the New Negro movement quickly gathered momentum from the outrage that African Americans felt in the aftermath of the infamous East St. Louis race riot of July 2, 1917. African-American disillusionment with the country's failure to make good on the professed democratic character of American war aims became widespread.

Shortly after his arrival in America, Garvey embarked upon a period of extensive travel and lecturing that provided him with a firsthand sense of conditions in African-American communities. After traveling for a year, he settled in Harlem, where he organized the first American branch of the UNIA in May 1917.

With the end of the war, Garvey's politics underwent a radical change. His principal political goal now became the redemption of Africa and its unification into a United States of Africa. To enrich and strengthen his movement, Garvey envisioned a black-owned and -run shipping line to foster economic independence, transport passengers between America, the Caribbean, and Africa, and serve as a symbol of black grandeur and enterprise.

Accordingly, the Black Star Line was launched and incorporated in 1919. The line's flagship, the SS *Yarmouth*, rechristened the SS *Frederick Douglass*, made its maiden voyage to the West Indies in November 1919; two other ships were acquired in 1920. The Black Star Line would prove to be the UNIA's most powerful recruiting and propaganda tool, but it ultimately sank under the accumulated weight of financial inexperience, mismanagement, expensive repairs, Garvey's own ill-advised business decisions, and ultimately, insufficient capital.

Meanwhile, by 1920 the UNIA had hundreds of divisions and chapters operating worldwide. It hosted elaborate annual conventions at its Liberty Hall headquarters in Harlem and published the *Negro World*, its internationally disseminated weekly organ that was soon banned in many parts of Africa and the Caribbean.

At the first UNIA convention in August 1920, Garvey was elected to the position of provisional president of Africa. In order to prepare the groundwork for launching his program of African redemption, Garvey sought to establish links with Liberia. In 1920 he sent a UNIA official to scout out prospects for a colony in that country. Following the official's report, in the winter of 1921 a group of UNIA technicians was sent to Liberia.

Starting in 1921, however, the movement began to unravel under the economic strain of the collapse of the Black Star Line, the failure of Garvey's Liberian program, opposition from black critics, defections caused by internal dissension, and official harassment. The most visible expression of the latter was the federal government's indictment of Garvey, in early 1922, on charges of mail fraud stemming from Garvey's stock promotion of the Black Star Line, though by the time the indictment was presented, the Black Star Line had already suspended all operations.

The pressure of his legal difficulties soon forced Garvey into an ill-advised effort to neutralize white opposition. In June 1922 he met secretly with the acting imperial wizard of the Ku Klux Klan in Atlanta, Georgia, Edward Young Clarke. The revelation of Garvey's meeting with the KKK produced a major split within the UNIA, resulting in the ouster of the "American leader," Rev. J. W. H. Eason, at the August 1922 convention. In January 1923 Eason was assassinated in New Orleans, Louisiana, but his accused assailants, who were members of the local UNIA African Legion, were subsequently acquitted. Following this event and as part of the defense campaign in preparation for the mail fraud trial, Garvey's second wife, Amy Jacques Garvey (1896–1973), edited and published a small volume of Garvey's sayings and speeches under the title *Philosophy and Opinions of Marcus Garvey* (1923).

Shortly after his trial commenced, Garvey unwisely assumed his own legal defense. He was found guilty on a single count of fraud and sentenced to a five-year prison term, though his three Black Star Line codefendants were acquitted. (The year following his conviction, Garvey launched a second shipping line, the Black Cross Navigation and Trading Co., but it, too, failed.)

Thanks to an extensive petition campaign, Garvey's sentence was commuted after he had served thirty-three months in the Atlanta federal **penitentiary**. He was immediately deported to Jamaica upon release in November 1927 and never allowed

> *"The dawn of a new day is upon us and we see things differently. We see not now as individuals, but as a collective whole, having one common interest."*
> Marcus Garvey, 1923

penitentiary: a jail or prison.

Garvey's ideology inspired millions of blacks worldwide with the vision of a redeemed and emancipated Africa.

"Lose not courage, lose not faith, go forward."

Marcus Garvey

to return to America. A second and expanded volume of *Philosophy and Opinions of Marcus Garvey* was edited and published by Amy Jacques Garvey in 1925 as part of Garvey's attempt to obtain a pardon.

Back in Jamaica, Garvey soon moved to reconstitute the UNIA under his direct control. This move precipitated a major split between the official New York parent body and the newly created Jamaican body. Although two conventions of the UNIA were held in Jamaica, Garvey was never able to reassert control over the various segments of his movement from his base in Jamaica.

Although he had high hopes of reforming Jamaican politics, Garvey went down to defeat in the general election of 1930 in his bid to win a seat on the colonial legislative council. He had to content himself with a seat on the municipal council of Kingston. Disheartened and bankrupt, Garvey abandoned Jamaica and relocated to London in 1935. A short time after arriving in England, however, fascist Italy invaded Ethiopia, producing a crisis that occasioned a massive upsurge of pro-Ethiopian solidarity throughout the black world, in which movement UNIA divisions and members were at the forefront. Garvey's loud defense of the Ethiopian emperor Haile Selassie soon changed to scathing public criticism, thus alienating many of Garvey's followers.

Throughout the thirties Garvey tried to rally his greatly diminished band of supporters with his monthly magazine, *Black Man*. Between 1936 and 1938 he convened a succession of annual meetings and conventions in Toronto, Canada, where he also launched a school of African philosophy as a UNIA training school. He undertook annual speaking tours of the Canadian maritime provinces and the eastern Caribbean.

In 1939 Garvey suffered a stroke that left him partly paralyzed. The indignity of reading his own obituary notice precipitated a further stroke that led to his death on June 10, 1940. Although his last years were spent in obscurity, in the decades between the two world wars, Garvey's ideology inspired millions of blacks worldwide with the vision of a redeemed and emancipated Africa. The importance of Garvey's political legacy was acknowledged by such African nationalists as Nnamdi Azikiwe of Nigeria and Kwame Nkrumah of Ghana. In 1964 Garvey was declared Jamaica's first national hero.

While he failed to realize his immediate objectives, Garvey's message represented a call for liberation from the psychological bondage of racial subordination. Drawing on a gift for spellbinding oratory and spectacle, Garvey melded black aspirations for economic and cultural independence with the traditional American creed of success to create a new and distinctive black gospel of racial pride. ◆

Gorbachev, Mikhail Sergeyevich

MARCH 2, 1931– ● POLITICAL REFORMER

Mikhail Gorbachev, leader of the Soviet Union from 1985 to 1991, gained recognition as a force for political and social reform through his efforts to radically reconstruct the Soviet Union's economic and political system. Gorbachev's attempt to democratize his country contributed to the downfall of communism and radically changed the global political and economic climate. In 1990 he won the Nobel Peace Prize for his world peace efforts.

Gorbachev was born the son of Russian peasants in Stavropol in 1931. When he was ten years old , during World War II, the armies of Nazi Germany invaded the Soviet Union. Gorbachev's father, a farmer on a state farm in Stavropol, was forced to fight in the war and young Gorbachev took over many of his father's duties while continuing to work hard at school. Even after the war, while still a student, Mikhail Gorbachev continued to drive a combine harvester in the fields.

When Gorbachev was eighteen, he received the Order of the Red Banner of Labor award from the Communist Party for his achievements during the harvest. His experience working the land (his native region of Stavropol was one of the most agriculturally rich areas of the Soviet Union) would serve him later in life, and his ability to be both an exemplary worker

Gorbachev's attempt to democratize his country contributed to the downfall of communism and radically changed the global political and economic climate.

1931 — Gorbachev is born in Stavropol.

1955 — Gorbachev graduates with a degree in law from Moscow University.

1967 — Gorbachev receives a degree in agriculture from Stavropol Agricultural Institute.

1980 — Gorbachev becomes a full member of the Politburo.

1985 — Gorbachev is chosen to lead the Soviet Union.

1991 — Gorbachev resigns as president and the USSR dissolves.

and a successful student earned him admission to the Law School of Moscow University in 1950. He continued part-time studies at Stavropol Agricultural Institute and in 1967 he obtained a degree in agriculture to add to his first degree in law. In 1952 he became a member of the Communist Party and upon his graduation with a law degree in 1955, he began his career in the Communist Party organization in Stavropol.

Gorbachev had always been recognized for his formidable intelligence and quickly rose through the ranks to become head of the regional Communist Party in 1970. There he attracted the attention of top Soviet leaders in Moscow, most notably Yuri Andropov, at the time head of the country's secret police. When Gorbachev went to Moscow in 1978, Andropov supported his appointment as party secretary in charge of agriculture. Reform minded, Gorbachev received rapid promotion but he was far from free to implement his ideas. In 1980, when he became a full member of the politburo, the chief policy-making body of the Communist Party, he found most of the members of the party, and the ailing Soviet leader Leonid Brezhnev, opposed to his reforms.

Andropov became general secretary of the Communist Party when Brezhnev died in 1982 and again showed his support for Gorbachev's strength and intelligence by giving him greater responsibility and putting him in charge of economic policy. Andropov died in office in 1984 and his successor, Konstantin Chernenko, lasted only thirteen months before dying. Gorbachev, who had become one of the politburo's most highly active and visible members, was chosen to lead the Soviet Union in 1985. Gorbachev's reform plans met with great resistance from old-line party members.

In his first years as leader, Gorbachev's youth, as well as his open and vigorous style, raised hopes among the Soviet people that living standards would improve. He made strides in diplomacy, greatly improving Soviet-American relations, meeting often with President Ronald Reagan (his partner at five summit meetings from 1985 to 1988) and subsequently with President George Bush in 1989.

From 1918 until the mid 1980s the Union of Soviet Socialist Republics (USSR or Soviet Union) was ruled with an iron hand by the Communist Party. The centralized government controlled the economy, all social policies, and freedom of expression and information. In 1987 and 1988 Gorbachev set out to initiate deep reforms of the Soviet economic and political system. *Perestroika*, Gorbachev's program for economic and political reform, called for a reduction in the power of the Communist Party and increased power for elected bodies. Some limited free-market mechanisms were also introduced. Gorbachev's policy promoting openness in the social system, *glasnost*, changed the face of Russian culture: books that had been long suppressed were allowed to be published, and open debate began to appear in the media. Yet, despite his popularity many Communist Party members and other Soviet officials criticized him for his radical ideas. He set social, political, and economic considerations above the military, and his grand plan for the economy proved difficult to implement.

Gorbachev also supported reforms in the Soviet-bloc countries of Eastern Europe and communism began to lose power in Poland, Hungary, East Germany, and Czechoslovakia. The liberalization of these countries led to the decline of communism in Romania and Bulgaria as well. The Soviet Union allowed these communist regimes to collapse without interference.

In 1990 the Congress of People's Deputies elected Gorbachev to the newly created post of president of the USSR. In his new role, Gorbachev continued to support reform throughout the country and in the main governing body. The Soviet Union experienced more political freedom than it had ever known. The world at large benefited from Gorbachev's actions to reduce the risk of superpower conflict.

In spite of Gorbachev's reforms, the Soviet Union encountered severe economic problems and Gorbachev's authority and effectiveness declined. In 1991, after a failed coup by several Soviet communist officials, Gorbachev resigned from the Communist Party. At the same time, most of the fifteen republics that made up the Soviet Union declared independence and agreed to become part of a loose confederation of former Soviet republics. The Russian government of Boris Yeltsin assumed the functions of the collapsing Soviet government. On December 25, 1991, Gorbachev resigned as president and the Soviet Union ceased to exist.

In recent years, Gorbachev has remained active, lecturing all over the world on peace and on the environment. In 1993 he founded the Green Cross, an organization focusing on global environmental concerns. He lives in Moscow with his wife, Raisa, and they have a daughter and two granddaughters.

> *"Man has no right to seek well-being at the expense of another human being. Prosperous nations must not seek well-being at the expense of poor, developing nations, or big nations at the expense of small ones."*
>
> Mikhail Gorbachev, 1993

In recent years, Gorbachev has remained active, lecturing all over the world on peace and on the environment.

Hamer, Fannie Lou (Townsend)

Fannie Lou Townsend was born to Ella Bramlett and James Lee Townsend in Montgomery County, Mississippi, in 1917. Her parents were sharecroppers, and the family moved to Sunflower County, Mississippi, when she was two. Forced to spend most of her childhood and teenage years toiling in cotton fields for white landowners, Townsend was able to complete only six years of schooling. Despite wrenching rural poverty and the harsh economic conditions of the Mississippi Delta, she maintained an enduring optimism. She learned the value of self-respect and outspokenness through her close relationship with her mother. In 1944 she married Perry Hamer, moved with him to Ruleville, and worked as a **sharecropper** on a plantation owned by W. D. Marlowe.

During her years on the Marlowe plantation, Hamer rose to the position of time- and recordkeeper. In this position she acquired a reputation for a sense of fairness and a willingness to speak to the landowner on behalf of aggrieved sharecroppers. She began to take steps directly to challenge the racial and economic inequality that had so circumscribed her life after meeting civil rights workers from the Student Nonviolent Coordinating Committee (SNCC) in 1962. In Mississippi, SNCC was mounting a massive voter registration and desegregation campaign aimed at empowering African Americans to change their own lives.

"When I liberate others, I liberate myself."

Fannie Lou
Hamer, 1969

sharecropper: a tenant farmer who works the land in return for a share of the crop, supplies, living quarters, and food.

Inspired by the organization's commitment to challenging the racial status quo, Hamer and seventeen other black volunteers attempted to register to vote in Indianola, Mississippi, on August 31, 1962, but were unable to pass the necessary literacy test, which was designed to prevent blacks from voting. As a result of this action, she and her family were dismissed from the plantation, she was threatened with physical harm by Ruleville whites, and she was constantly harassed by local police. Eventually, she was forced to flee Ruleville and spent three months in Tallahatchie County, Mississippi, before returning in December.

In January 1963 Hamer passed the literacy test and became a registered voter. Despite the persistent hostility of local whites, she continued her commitment to civil rights activities and became a SNCC field secretary. By 1964 Hamer had fully **immersed** herself in a wide range of local civil rights activities, including SNCC-sponsored voter registration campaigns and clothing- and food-distribution drives. At that time she was a central organizer and vice chairperson of the Mississippi Freedom Democratic Party (MFDP), a parallel political party formed under the auspices of SNCC in response to black exclusion from the state Democratic party. Hamer was one of the sixty-eight MFDP delegates elected at a state convention of the party to attend the Democratic National Convention in Atlantic City in the summer of 1964. At the convention the MFDP delegates demanded to be seated and argued that they were the only legitimate political representatives of the Mississippi Democratic party because unlike the regular party that formed and operated at the exclusion of blacks, their party was open to all Mississippians of voting age.

Hamer's televised testimony to the convention on behalf of the MFDP propelled her into the national spotlight. A national audience watched as she described the economic reprisals that faced African Americans who attempted to register to vote and recounted the beating that she and five other activists had received in June 1963 in a Winona County, Mississippi, jail. Hamer's proud and unwavering commitment to American democracy and equality inspired hundreds of Americans to send telegrams supporting the MFDP's challenge to the southern political status quo. Although the MFDP delegates were not seated by the convention, Hamer and the party succeeded in mobilizing a massive black voter turnout and publicizing the racist exclusionary tactics of the state Democratic party.

immersed: having plunged into something.

1917 Hamer is born in Montgomery County, Mississippi.

1962 Hamer attempts without success to vote.

1963 Hamer becomes a registered voter.

1968 Hamer founds the Freedom Farm Corporation.

1977 Hamer dies of cancer and heart disease.

By the mid-sixties SNCC had become ideologically divided and Hamer's ties to the organization became more tenuous. However, she continued to focus her political work on black political **empowerment** and community development. Under her leadership, the MFDP continued to challenge the all-white state Democratic party. In 1964 Hamer unsuccessfully ran for Congress on the MFDP ticket, and one year later spearheaded an intense lobbying effort to challenge the seating of Mississippi's five congressmen in the House of Representatives. She played an integral role in bringing the Head Start program for children to Ruleville, and organized the Freedom Farm Cooperative for displaced agricultural workers. In 1969 she founded the Freedom Farm Corporation in Sunflower, a cooperative farming and landowning venture to help poor blacks become more self-sufficient. It fed well over 5,000 families before collapsing in 1974. Three years later, after over a decade of activism, she died from breast cancer and heart disease.

Fannie Lou Hamer was a symbol of defiance and indomitable black womanhood that inspired many in the civil rights movement. Morehouse College and Howard University, among others, have honored her devotion to African-American civil rights with honorary doctoral degrees. Her words "I'm sick and tired of being sick and tired" bear testament to her lifelong struggle to challenge racial injustice and economic exploitation. ◆

> **empowerment:** to give official power or authority.

> Hamer's words "I'm sick and tired of being sick and tired" bear testament to her lifelong struggle to challenge racial injustice and economic exploitation.

Hernández, Antonia

MAY 30, 1948– ● HISPANIC RIGHTS ACTIVIST

As president and general council for the Mexican American Legal Defense Fund (MALDEF), Antonia Hernández works to ensure equal treatment for Hispanics in education and employment, and to protect the rights of immigrants.

Hernández is herself an immigrant. She was born on May 30, 1948, in the Mexican state of Coahuila in the town of Torreón. When she was eight years old, her family moved to the United States and settled in East Los Angeles. Manuel, her father, was employed as a gardener; her mother, Nicolasa, was a homemaker who devoted herself to raising Antonia and her five younger brothers and sisters. Because Hernández did not

> *"Without affirmative action I would not have had an opportunity to go to UCLA and explore horizons that were never opened to my parents."*
>
> Antonia Hernández

Ruben Blades

Popular singer/songwriter Ruben Blades is also a Hispanic-American activist. *Siembra,* Blades's 1978 album with Willie Colon, featuring rebellious poetry about life in El Barrio, came like a cry for recognition to the Latin American community both in the United States and in Central America. Its songs went to the top of the charts in Latin America, the United States, and many parts of Europe.

Born in Panama City, Panama, Blades is well known for his albums in his native Spanish language, especially for the songs that directly highlight the political conflicts that have at times been prevalent in Panama. After he moved to New York in the mid-1970s, Blades created a new sound called "Nueva Cancion" (new song), with trombonist Willie Colon. Colon was seeking a collaborator with whom he could write songs about El Barrio, the area of Harlem in New York City that is home to most inhabitants of Puerto Rican descent.

At the height of his musical career, Blades took the time to pursue a master's degree in international law at Harvard University. After earning his law degree, Blades began appearing in films and onstage. He became widely known as an actor in such films as *The Milagro Beanfield War* and *Crossover Dreams* (both films with a social conscience), and more recently for his stage work in Paul Simon's Broadway musical, *The Capeman*, in which he portrayed the title role, a man from El Barrio who becomes involved in race riots in New York. Blades ran for president of Panama in 1994, in the first free elections in 26 years. During his campaign he performed songs that told of the future of Panama. Though he received just 20 percent of the vote, the leading parties came to realize that he and his followers are a force to be reckoned with. Blades continues to write and play music with his band, Son del Solar, and to speak out on humanitarian issues such as workers' rights, rights for the poor, care of the environment, and the life of the common people in both his native Panama and the United States.

> *"As we grow, what is the greatest challenge facing our community? Education. The issue of educating our children has to consume us night and day."*
>
> Antonia Hernández, 1998.

speak English when she came to the United States, she was forced to learn the new language by the "sink-or-swim" method. She was sent to a regular fourth-grade class and left to learn almost entirely on her own. As she told Diane Dismuke of *NEA Today,* "I remember sitting in class like a vegetable, a nonentity. I never want another kid to go through what I did." She recalls the mixed blessing of a teacher who stayed after school to help her because she was different from *"them,"* meaning the other Hispanic students in the school. Grateful for the help, Hernández also resented the implied slur.

Despite poverty, the Hernández family managed to send all six children to college. Several of Hernández's bothers and sisters became teachers, which is what Hernández intended to become when she started college. She realized her dream when she received her bachelor's degree from UCLA in 1970 and a teaching certificate in 1971. She was teaching in an Upward Bound program in February 1971 when Hispanic students in East L.A. walked out of their classrooms to protest unfair conditions. When some of the students were arrested, Hernández decided that she could do more to help Hispanics as an attorney than as a teacher. Although several of her teachers advised her to apply to Stanford or Harvard law school, Hernández chose to study at UCLA in order to stay near her family.

When she graduated from law school in 1974, Hernández took a position with the East Los Angeles Center for Law and Justice. In 1978, a year after her marriage to fellow lawyer Michael Stern, she was offered a job as staff counsel to the United States Senate Judiciary Committee, which was chaired by Senator Ted Kennedy. Though reluctant to leave her family, Hernández was finally persuaded by her husband that this was an opportunity she could not afford to miss. She would be, Stern reminded his wife, the first Hispanic woman to hold the position—and he was sure he would be able to find a job in Washington. So the couple moved to Washington, D.C., where Stern did find a job working for the Department of Justice and Hernández advised the committee about human rights and immigration and in the process gained valuable experience in drafting legislation. Hernández also spent some time as the southwest coordinator for Ted Kennedy's 1980 presidential campaign.

When Republicans won a Senate majority in 1980, Hernández lost her job. Soon after, she accepted a position as a staff attorney in MALDEF's Washington office. In 1983 she returned to Los Angeles as MALDEF's specialist on employment issues. She and her husband had two children by that time and were delighted to return to Los Angeles, where they bought a home across the street from Hernández's mother. The closeness of the Hernández family is highlighted by the fact that at the time all six of Nicolasa Hernández's children lived within a half a mile of one another. In 1985 Antonia Hernández was named president of MALDEF, succeeding Joaquin Alvila.

As president, Hernández continues to work on a variety of legal issues that affect the Hispanic population. She delivers many speeches every year on issues central to Latinos, including civil rights, **bilingual** education, and immigration. She spent a great deal of time speaking out against California's

1948 Hernández is born in Coahuila, Mexico.

1970 Hernández receives a bachelor's degree from UCLA.

1974 Hernández graduates from law school at UCLA.

1978 Hernández is offered a job as staff counsel to the U.S. Senate Judiciary Committee.

1985 Hernández becomes president of the Mexican Legal Defense Fund (MALDEF).

bilingual: able to use two languages.

controversial Proposition 187, which was intended to keep illegal immigrants from receiving educational and welfare benefits. Although the Proposition passed in November of 1994, Federal Judge Mariana Pfaelzer declared it unconstitutional in November of 1997. Before leaving office, California governor Pete Wilson vowed to overturn the judge's decision but the ruling still stood when the newly elected governor, Gray Davis, took office in 1998. As of mid-1999, Davis, an opponent of the initiative, had still not decided whether to appeal Judge Pfaelzer's decision. In the late 1990s, in the wake of attempts to end affirmative action in California, Hernández has delivered many speeches defending the practice as necessary to ensure equal education for minority students. As she said at a PBS "Fred Friendly Seminar" in March 1999, "Great good has been achieved by affirmative action in education, and there remains a great need of these programs to ensure that all talented and promising students are fairly evaluated when applying for college." ◆

Huerta, Delores

APRIL 10, 1930– ● LABOR ACTIVIST

> "I would like to be remembered as a woman who cares for her fellow humans. We must use our lives to make the world a better place, not just to acquire things. That is what we are put on the earth for."
>
> Delores Huerta

Delores Huerta, one of the most prominent Hispanic labor leaders in the United States, cofounded the United Farm Workers Union (UFW) with César Chávez. Because of her work to help the poor and disadvantaged, she has become a folk hero in many Mexican-American communities and has been depicted in murals and celebrated in *corridos* (ballads).

Huerta was born in Dawson, New Mexico, on April 10, 1930. She was the second child and only daughter of Juan and Alicia Huerta, who divorced when Huerta was five. After the divorce, Huerta's mother moved to Stockton, California, where she raised the children.

Eventually, after struggling to make ends meet as a cannery worker and waitress, Alicia Huerta bought a small hotel and restaurant and managed to earn enough to ensure a comfortable life for her family. Huerta admired her mother's ability to run her own business and credits her mother's example for her own independence of spirit. Huerta also learned compassion from her mother, who used to allow poor migrant workers to stay at the hotel for free.

Unlike many Hispanic women of her generation, Huerta was able to pursue a college education. She received an A.A. degree from Stockton College and later went on to obtain a teaching certificate. Huerta began work as a teacher but quickly became frustrated because she felt she could do little to help the barefoot and hungry children who entered her classroom.

In 1955 Huerta met Fred Ross, an organizer with the Community Service Organization (CSO), a Mexican-American self-help group. Huerta went to work for the CSO registering voters and conducting civic and educational programs; eventually she went to the state capital in Sacramento as a lobbyist.

During the late 1950s Huerta became increasingly interested in the plight of farmworkers, many of whom were poorly educated immigrants or illegal aliens who did not speak English. Owners regularly exploited workers, paying low wages, and even charging workers for drinking water as they labored under the hot sun. Fields were sprayed with pesticides so dangerous that workers died and children were born with serious birth defects. Housing was woefully inadequate and children often worked long hours in the field alongside their parents. It was during this period that Huerta met César Chávez, who was also deeply concerned about the exploitation he had seen on California's farms. Together they tried unsuccessfully to interest the CSO in issues related to farmworkers. By 1962 it was clear that the CSO was not going to respond to the need, so Huerta and Chávez founded the National Farm Workers Association, which later became the United Farm Workers (UFW).

Although Chávez has always been the better known of the pair, Huerta was an extremely valuable partner in the growth of the union. In 1965, when the union went on strike against California's grape growers, Huerta negotiated the union's first contract, despite the fact that she herself had never even seen a union contract before. During the union's boycott of table grapes in the late 1960s, Huerta was sent to New York City as the East Coast boycott coordinator. During the 1970s Huerta directed the Citizenship Participation Day Department, the political arm of the UFW. In the 1980s she helped found the union's radio station, Radio Campesina. In the late 1990s Huerta continued to work on behalf of the UFW.

Over the years, Huerta has been arrested more than twenty times and was nearly beaten to death by police in a demonstration

1930 Huerta is born in Dawson, New Mexico.

1955 Huerta goes to work for the Community Service Organization (CSO).

1962 Huerta joins with César Chávez to form the United Farm Workers (UFW).

1964 Huerta negotiates the UFW's first union contract.

1988 Huerta is injured by police in a demonstration; she wins a settlement of $825,000 from the city of San Francisco.

Although Chávez has always been the better known of the pair, Huerta was an extremely valuable partner in the growth of the United Farm Workers.

in San Francisco in 1988. That incident resulted in a record financial settlement for Huerta, who suffered a damaged spleen and six broken ribs. Police also revised their rules of crowd control as a result of what happened to Huerta.

Huerta has been married twice and now lives with Chávez's older brother Richard. She has eleven children, two by her first husband, five by her second, and four by her current partner. Huerta admits that she has had little time to spend with her children, and her second marriage was clearly a casualty of her work. But her children have all been involved with the union in some way and include an attorney, a doctor, a paralegal, a therapist, and a chef. At last count, Huerta had fourteen grandchildren and two great-grandchildren.

In her eulogy to Chávez at his funeral in April 1993, Huerta said, "Society has lost a very great man. César proved to the world that poor people can solve their problems if they stick together, and he showed the rest of society how they can participate and help the downtrodden." These words apply equally well to Huerta herself. ◆

Hume, John

JANUARY 18, 1937– ● NORTHERN IRELAND POLITICAL LEADER

Trimble, David

OCTOBER 15, 1944– ● NORTHERN IRELAND POLITICAL LEADER

Over the past thirty years, more than 3,500 people have died in Northern Ireland because of the violence resulting from the conflict between Roman Catholic groups who favor unification with the Irish Republic in the south and Protestant loyalists who prefer to remain a British province. John Hume and David Trimble are the leaders of Northern Ireland's largest Catholic and Protestant political parties: Hume is the head of the Roman Catholic nationalist Social Democratic and Labor Party, which he helped found in 1970, and Trimble heads the Protestant Ulster Unionist Party.

Good Friday Accords

In April 1998 marathon talks between the Protestant majority and Roman Catholic minority produced a landmark settlement that represents the most significant step ever taken toward peace in Northern Ireland. Called the Good Friday Accords, the agreement included a commitment to use peaceful means to resolve political differences. It called for the establishment of a Northern Ireland legislative assembly that would have control over many local matters. It also called for the establishment of a North-South Ministerial Council, which would include government representatives from Northern Ireland and Ireland, as well as a Council of the Isles, to include representatives from the Irish parliament and the various legislative assemblies of the United Kingdom. Voters in both the Irish Republic and in Northern Ireland backed the peace plan by a large majority in a May 1998 referendum.

The Good Friday agreement was the culmination of peace talks that had begun in the summer of 1996 mediated by former U.S. senator from Maine George Mitchell. "We have to start spilling our sweat, not our blood," commented John Hume, the prominent Catholic leader who is widely known as a a supporter of nonviolent civil protest. Among the other leaders in Northern Ireland expressing approval of the accord were Gerry Adams, the leader of Sinn Fein, the political wing of the paramilitary Provisional Irish Republican Army (IRA).

But these longtime political opponents became conciliators who negotiated a historic peace accord for their region, signed in April 1998, known as the Good Friday Accords. For their work to bring an end to decades, even centuries of sectarian violence in Northern Ireland, John Hume and David Trimble were jointly awarded the 1998 Nobel Peace Prize.

John Hume, born in Londonderry in Northern Ireland, was educated at St. Colomb's College, Londonderry, and at the National University of Ireland. He began his political career in 1969 as a representative in the Northern Ireland Parliament (dissolved in 1972). Since the 1970s he has traveled frequently to America to lobby American politicians to support a policy of moderation in Northern Ireland's troubles and to avoid aiding the IRA. Yet Hume was one of the few Social Democratic and Labor Party leaders Gerry Adams of Sinn Fein trusted; in 1996 Hume was instrumental in getting the IRA to agree to a ceasefire and Sinn Fein to join the peace talks. Hume is also a member of the British Parliament in London and of the European Parliament in Strasbourg, France, to which he was elected in 1979. He is married with five children and is the recipient of several honorary doctorates.

1937 Hume is born in Londonderry, Northern Ireland.

1969 Hume begins his political career as a representative in the Northern Ireland Parliament.

1996 Hume is instrumental in getting the IRA to agree to a cease-fire.

1998 Hume receives the Noble Peace Prize.

1944 — Trimble is born in Bangor, County Down.

1977 — Trimble joins the Ulster Unionists.

1990 — Trimble is elected to the British Parliament.

1995 — Trimble is made leader of the Ulster Unionist Party.

1998 — Trimble receives the Noble Peace Prize.

David Trimble was born in Bangor, a seaside resort in County Down, and educated at Bangor Grammar School and Queens University, Belfast. He is married and has four children. Like John Hume, he originally pursued an academic career. An uncompromising conservative prior to the Good Friday Accords, Trimble used to be a hardline opponent of the party he now heads, and sometimes advocated acts of violent civil disobedience. He joined the Ulster Unionists in 1977, was elected to the British Parliament in 1990, and in 1995 was made the Leader of the Ulster Unionist Party.

The Norwegian Nobel Committee said of Hume and Trimble: "The Northern Irish Nobel Laureate in Literature, Seamus Heaney, used the fable of the hedgehog and the fox to describe our two Laureates and the difference between them. 'John Hume is the hedgehog, who knew the big truth that justice had to prevail,' he wrote. David Trimble, on the other hand, 'is the fox, who has known many things, but who had the intellectual clarity and political courage to know that 1998 was the time to move unionism towards an accommodation with reasonable and honourable nationalist aspirations. In so doing, he opened the possibility of a desirable and credible future for all the citizens of Northern Ireland.'" ◆

J

Jackson, Helen Hunt

OCTOBER 15, 1830–AUGUST 12, 1885 ● NATIVE AMERICAN
RIGHTS ACTIVIST

Helen Maria Fiske Hunt Jackson was an author and noted advocate of Indian reform. Born in Amherst, Massachusetts, she was the daughter of an Amherst College language professor. She married Edward Bissell Hunt, an army lieutenant, in 1852; the couple had two sons. In 1863 her husband died while experimenting on a prototype submarine. After the subsequent death of both sons, Jackson began a professional writing career that continued for the rest of her life.

Using such pseudonyms as "No Name," "Rip Van Winkel," "Marah," and "Sax Holm" she wrote hundreds of poems, numerous travel articles, magazine and newspaper pieces, and books. Her letters and articles appeared in major New York and Boston newspapers, as well as the *Atlantic Monthly, Hearth and Home, Woman's Journal,* and *Scribner's Monthly Magazine*. Ralph Waldo Emerson once described her as the "greatest American woman poet," but she was convinced that

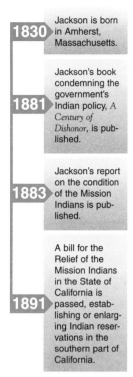

1830 Jackson is born in Amherst, Massachusetts.

1881 Jackson's book condemning the government's Indian policy, *A Century of Dishonor*, is published.

1883 Jackson's report on the condition of the Mission Indians is published.

1891 A bill for the Relief of the Mission Indians in the State of California is passed, establishing or enlarging Indian reservations in the southern part of California.

Moved by the tragic removal of the Ponca Indians, Jackson used her considerable literary and research skills to awaken the public to the mistreatment of all Native Americans.

her most important literary contributions were *A Century of Dishonor* and *Ramona,* both published under her own name. These books have been continually in print since originally published.

In the 1870s several events—a trip to Colorado Springs for health reasons; her marriage to local banker and railroad promoter, William Sharpless Jackson; her visit to Boston for the seventieth birthday of Oliver Wendell Holmes; and her chance attendance at a lecture by Ponca chief Standing Bear—changed the direction of her life. Jackson began writing articles and books on Indian-related issues, and these publications thrust her into the public eye as one of the foremost Native American policy reformers of the nineteenth century.

Moved by the tragic removal of the Ponca Indians, Jackson used her considerable literary and research skills to awaken the public to the mistreatment of all Native Americans. She criticized government policy in letters to the editors of major Boston and New York newspapers and was soon engaged in a controversial exchange of letters with Carl Schurz, secretary of the Department of the Interior.

A Century of Dishonor, published by Harper and Brothers in 1881, was a scathing indictment of the government's Indian policy. Displeased by the public's and Congress's response to the work, she wrote a protest novel, *Ramona,* hoping to "move people's heart" with the tragic story of the dispossession of California's Mission Indians. She gathered historical data while on assignment for *Century* magazine and while working as a special Interior Department agent authorized to write a comprehensive report on the condition of the Mission Indians. That report, which included eleven specific recommendations, was published in 1883.

By that time, Jackson's Indian-related articles and books had helped shape the work of several reform organizations, including the Women's National Indian Association (WNIA), the Indian Rights Association (IRA), and the Lake Mohonk Conference of the Friends of the Indians. After her death, members of both the WNIA and the IRA carried on her work, and many of her recommendations were incorporated into a January 1891 bill for the Relief of the Mission Indians in the State of California. The resulting California Mission Indian Commission established or enlarged existing Native American reservations in the southern part of the state, reservations that continue to exist. ◆

Jackson, Jesse Louis

OCTOBER 8, 1941 – ● MINISTER, POLITICIAN AND CIVIL RIGHTS ACTIVIST

J esse Jackson was born Jesse Burns in Greenville, South Carolina, to Helen Burns and Noah Robinson, a married man who lived next door. In 1943, his mother married Charles Henry Jackson, who adopted Jesse in 1957. Jesse Jackson has recognized both men as his fathers. In 1959 Jackson graduated from Greenville's Sterling High School. A gifted athlete, Jackson was offered a professional baseball contract; instead, he accepted a scholarship to play football at the University of Illinois, at Champaign-Urbana. When he discovered, however, that African Americans were not allowed to play quarterback, he enrolled at North Carolina Agricultural and Technical College in Greensboro. There, besides being a star athlete, Jackson began his activist career as a participant in the student sit-in movement to integrate Greensboro's public facilities.

> *"Where there is hope, there is life, where there is life there is possibility, and where there is possibility change can occur."*
> Jesse Jackson, 1988

Jackson's leadership abilities and charisma earned him a considerable reputation by the time he graduated with a B.S. in sociology in 1964. After graduation he married Jacqueline Brown, whom he had met at the sit-in protests. During his senior year, he worked briefly with the Congress of Racial Equality (CORE), quickly being elevated to the position of director of southeastern operations. Jackson then moved north, **eschewing** law school at Duke University in order to attend the Chicago Theological Seminary in 1964. He was later ordained to the ministry by two renowned figures: gospel music star and pastor, Clay Evans, and legendary revivalist and pulpit orator, C. L. Franklin. Jackson left the seminary in 1965 and returned to the South to become a member of the Rev. Dr. Martin Luther King Jr.'s staff of the Southern Christian Leadership Conference (SCLC).

eschewing: avoiding.

Jackson initially became acquainted with SCLC during the famous march on Selma, Alabama in 1965. In 1966 King appointed him to head the Chicago branch of SCLC's Operation Breadbasket, which was formed in 1962 to force various businesses to employ more African Americans. In 1967, only a year after his first appointment, King made Jackson the national director of Operation Breadbasket. Jackson concentrated on businesses heavily patronized by blacks, including bakeries, milk companies, soft-drink bottlers, and soup companies. He arranged a number of boycotts of businesses refusing to comply with SCLC demands of fair employment practices, and successfully negotiated compromises that soon gained national attention.

Jackson was in King's entourage when King was assassinated in Memphis in 1968. After King's death, however, Jackson's relationship with SCLC became increasingly strained over disagreements about his independence and his penchant for taking what was considered to be **undue** initiative in both public relations and organizational planning. He was also criticized for the direction in which he was leading Operation Breadbasket. Finally, in 1971, Jackson left SCLC and founded Operation PUSH, which he would lead for thirteen years. As head of PUSH, he continued an aggressive program of negotiating black employment agreements with white businesses, as well as promoting black educational excellence and self-esteem.

In 1980, Jackson had demanded that an African American step forward as a presidential candidate in the 1984 election. On October 30, 1983, after carefully weighing the chances and need for a candidate, he dramatically announced, on the television program *60 Minutes* his own candidacy to capture the White House. Many African-American politicians and community leaders, such as Andrew Young, felt that Jackson's candidacy would only divide the Democrats and chose instead to support Walter Mondale, the favorite for the nomination. Jackson, waging a campaign stressing voter registration, carried a hopeful message of empowerment to African Americans, poor people, and other minorities. This constituency of the "voiceless and downtrodden" became the foundation for what Jackson termed a "Rainbow Coalition" of Americans—the poor, struggling farmers, feminists, gays, lesbians, and others who historically, according to Jackson, had lacked representation. Jackson, offering himself as an alternative to the mainstream Democratic party, called for, among other things, a defense budget freeze, programs to stimulate full employment, **self-determination** for the Palestinians, and political empowerment of African Americans through voter registration.

Jackson's campaign in 1984 was characterized by dramatic successes and equally serious political gaffes. In late 1983 U.S. military flyer Robert Goodman was shot down over Syrian-held territory in Lebanon, while conducting an assault. In a daring political gamble, Jackson made Goodman's release a personal

---

undue: improper.

1941 Jackson is born in Greenville, South Carolina.

1966 Dr. Martin Luther King Jr. appoints Jackson to head the Chicago branch of SCLC's Operation Bread Basket.

1971 Jackson founds Operation PUSH (People United to Save Humanity).

1984 Jackson campaigns for the U.S. presidency.

1988 Jackson runs for president for the second time; he becomes president of the National Rainbow Coalition, Inc.

self-determination: determination by citizens of their own political status.

mission, arguing that if the flyer had been white, the U.S. government would have worked more diligently toward his release. Traveling to Syria, Jackson managed to meet with President Hafez al-Assad and Goodman was released shortly afterwards; Jackson gained great political capital by appearing at the flyer's side as he made his way back to the United States.

The 1984 campaign, however, was plagued by political missteps. Jackson's offhand dubbing of New York as "Hymietown" while eating lunch with two reporters cost him much of his potential Jewish support and raised serious questions about his commitment to justice for all Americans. Though Jackson eventually apologized, the **characterization** continued to haunt him, and remains a symbol of strained relations between African Americans and Jews. Another issue **galling** to many Jews and others was Jackson's relationship with Louis Farrakhan, head of the Nation of Islam. Farrakhan had appeared with Jackson and stumped for him early in the campaign. Jackson, despite advice to the contrary, refused to repudiate Farrakhan; it was only after one speech, in which Farrakhan labeled Judaism a "dirty" religion, that the Jackson campaign issued a statement condemning both the speech and the minister. Another controversy, and a source of special concern to Jews, was Jackson's previous meetings with Yasir Arafat, head of the Palestine Liberation Organization (PLO), and his advocacy of self-determination for the Palestinians.

Jackson ended his historic first run with an eloquent speech before the Democratic National Convention in San Francisco, reminding black America that "our time has come." In a strong showing in a relatively weak primary field, Jackson garnered almost 3.3 million votes out of the approximately 18 million cast.

Even more impressive than Jackson's first bid for the presidency was his second run in 1988. Jackson espoused a political vision built upon the themes he first advocated in 1984. His campaign once again touted voter registration drives and the Rainbow Coalition, which by this time had become a structured organization closely overseen by Jackson. His new platform, which included many of the planks from 1984, included the validity of "comparable worth" as a **viable** means of eradicating pay inequities based on gender, the restoration of a higher maximum tax rate, and the implementation of national health care. Jackson also urged policies to combat "factory flight" in the Sun Belt and to provide aid to farmworkers in

characterization: description.

galling: irritating.

"Our flag is red, white, and blue, but our nation is a rainbow—red, yellow, brown, black, and white—and we're all precious in God's sight."
Jesse Jackson, 1984

viable: capable of functioning.

their fight to erode the negative effect of corporate agribusiness on family farms. Further, he railed against the exploitative practices of U.S. and transnational corporations, urging the redirection of their profits from various foreign ventures to the development of local economies.

While he failed to secure the Democratic nomination, Jackson finished with a surprisingly large number of convention delegates and a strong finish in the primaries. In thirty-one of thirty-six primaries, Jackson won either first or second place, earning almost seven million votes out of the approximately twenty-three million cast. In 1988 Jackson won over many of the black leaders who had refused to support him during his first campaign. His performance also indicated a growing national respect for his oratorical skills and his willingness to remain faithful to politically progressive ideals.

Jackson's power-
ful oratorical
style impresses
and challenges
audiences
regardless of
their political
beliefs.

In the 1992 presidential campaign, Jackson, who was not a candidate, was critical of Democratic front-runners Bill Clinton and Al Gore, and did not endorse them until the final weeks of the campaign. Since his last full-time political campaign in 1988, Jackson has remained highly visible in American public life. He has crusaded for various causes, including the institution of a democratic polity in South Africa, statehood for the District of Columbia, and the banishment of illegal drugs from American society.

Jackson has also been an outspoken critic of professional athletics, arguing that more African Americans need to be involved in the management and ownership of professional sports teams and that discrimination remains a large problem for many black athletes. Further, on the college level, the institution of the NCAA's Proposition 42 and Proposition 48 has earned criticism from Jackson as being discriminatory against young black athletes. Through the medium of a short-lived 1991 television talk show, Jackson sought to widen his audience, addressing pressing concerns faced by African Americans.

oratorical: the ability to
speak eloquently in public.

Jackson's various crusades against illegal drugs and racism, while often specifically targeted toward black teenagers, have exposed millions of Americans to his message. His powerful **oratorical** style—pulpit oratory that emphasizes repetition of key phrases like "I am somebody"—often impresses and challenges audiences regardless of their political beliefs. In late 1988 Jackson became president of the National Rainbow Coalition, Inc.; he remains involved in the activities of numerous other organizations.

During the early 1990s Jackson remained largely outside the national spotlight. He was disappointed by the failure of his bid to assume leadership of the National Association for the Advancement of Colored People following the resignation of Rev. Benjamin Chavis. Jackson returned to widespread public prominence in the mid-1990s. In 1996 he was a supporter of the successful congressional campaign of his son Jesse Jackson Jr. In May 1999 Jackson helped win the release of three U. S. soldiers held captive by the Serbian government during the Kosovo hostilities.

Jackson has been the most prominent civil rights leader and African-American national figure since the death of Martin Luther King, Jr. The history of national black politics in the 1970s and 1980s was largely his story. He has shown a great ability for making alliances, as well as a talent for defining issues and generating controversy. The essential dilemma of Jackson's career, as with many of his peers, has been the search for a way to advance and further the agenda of the civil rights movement as a national movement at a time when the political temper of the country has been increasingly conservative. ◆

> Jackson has been the most prominent civil fights leader and African-American national figure since the death of Martin Luther King Jr.

Jingsheng, Wei

MAY 20, 1950– ● CHINESE HUMAN RIGHTS ACTIVIST

Many people regard Wei Jingsheng as the father of Chinese democracy. Others call him the "Nelson Mandela of China" because, like Mandela, Wei has spent a good portion of his adult life in prison for holding political opinions considered subversive by the government under which he lives.

Wei did not start out to be a counterrevolutionary. In fact, for many years he was an enthusiastic supporter of Chinese communism. Born in Beijing on May 20, 1950, Wei and his three younger brothers and sisters grew up in a staunchly communist home. As a boy, Wei was required to memorize a page of Mao's writings every day; in school he studied Mao, Marx, Engels, Stalin, and Lenin.

In 1966 Wei joined the Red Guard and participated in the Great Proletarian Cultural Revolution in which supporters of

> *"In a world filled with ignorance, thinking becomes a crime."*
>
> Wei Jingshen

Mao and his wife, Jiang Qing, closed schools, slowed production, and cut off Chinese relations with the outside world. The idea of the cultural revolution was to encourage the growth of the "new China" by eliminating all vestiges of the old. During his travels around China on behalf as a member of the Red Guard, however, Wei noticed that China was rife with the kinds of social inequalities he thought communism was supposed to eliminate. In 1968, to signal an end to the Cultural Revolution that they themselves had begun, Mao and Jiang arrested many of the leaders of the Red Guard who had carried out their program. Wei, narrowly escaping imprisonment, spent the next year in Anhui Province in central China. Here he witnessed horrors greater than any he had seen before, including starving peasants exchanging babies with other families as food. Eventually Wei concluded that Mao was to blame for China's social problems.

Wei served in the Chinese army from 1969 through 1974; he then took a job as an electrician at the Beijing zoo. Mao died in 1976 and Jiang Qing and three other leaders of the Cultural Revolution known as the Gang of Four were arrested. By 1978 a new moderate faction headed by Deng Xiaoping had come into power in China, and posters critical of the government began to be posted on a brick wall west of Tiananmen Square. On December 5, 1978, there appeared on this "Democracy Wall" an essay by Wei entitled "The Fifth Modernization: Democracy." Wei's essay was in response to Deng's proposed "Four Modernizations"—in agriculture, industry, defense, and technology. Wei asserted that none of these modernizations was possible without democracy.

Soon afterward, Wei started a **dissident** journal called *Exploration.* Six days after Deng outlawed publications critical of the government, the March 25, 1979, issue of *Exploration* published a blunt indictment of Deng. Wei declared in "Do We Want Democracy or New **Autocracy**?" that Deng would become a dictator like Mao if the Chinese people were not vigilant. On March 29 Wei was arrested and charged with passing military secrets to a foreign journalist. On October 16, 1979, he was sentenced to fifteen years in prison.

While in prison, Wei was kept from contact with other prisoners for fear he would influence them and was held in solitary confinement for at least five years, during which time he lost twelve teeth, contracted hepatitis, and developed a heart condition. In 1984 Wei was assigned to a labor camp in the moun-

> Wei noticed that China was rife with the kinds of social inequalities he thought communism was supposed to eliminate.

dissident: someone who disagrees with the establishment.

autocracy: rule by someone who has undisputed authority.

tains, because, he believes, the government hoped that the thin air would cause his heart problems to worsen. Five years later Wei was moved to the Nanpu Salt Works where he was confined to a tiny cell and prevented from bathing for months at a time.

In September 1993 Wei was released six months before the end of his term. Since China had applied to host the 2000 Summer Olympics, it appeared the early release was an attempt to curry favor with the Olympic Committee. Before he left prison Wei demanded that officials give him the letters he had written while in jail, most of which, he knew, had never been delivered. These were smuggled out of China and published in 1997 as *The Courage to Stand Alone*. Some of Wei's letters are to family and friends, some to government officials. In one, written to Deng Xiaoping after the Tiananmen Square massacre, Wei wrote with characteristic bluntness, "So, now that you've successfully carried out a military coup to deal with a group of unarmed and politically inexperienced students and citizens, how do you feel? . . . I've long known that you are precisely the kind of idiot to do something foolish like this."

A stubborn man, Wei resumed his pro-democracy activities as soon as he was released. Not surprisingly, he was rearrested on April 1, 1994, and held incommunicado for more than a year and a half before being tried and convicted of trying to overthrow the government. On December 13, 1995, he was sentenced to another fourteen years in prison. Wei's fame outside of China grew, and in the same year he was sent back to prison, he was nominated for the Nobel Peace Prize and awarded the Olof Palme Award and the European Parliament's Sakharov Prize for Freedom of Thought. Altogether, Wei has been nominated four times but has not received the Nobel Peace Prize.

In November 1997, after years of effort on the part of various human rights organizations, Wei Jingsheng was released from prison on the condition that he accept exile in the United States. Although Wei had refused earlier offers of exile, he accepted this time because he was denied medical treatment in China. He spent just six hours with his family before leaving Beijing on a Northwest Airlines flight bound for Detroit.

Wei was treated at Henry Ford Hospital in Detroit before leaving to stay with supporters in New York. He hopes to return to his homeland one day, and continues to speak out in favor of the 3,000 political prisoners still languishing in the Chinese "gulag," or system of forced labor camps. Still, life in China has changed substantially since Wei first posted his essay on the

> *"I think there are few opportunities for one person to really influence history. The opportunity is very rare. But if you give people a new, important way of thinking, this thought itself can change the world."*
> Wei Jingsheng, 1998

Wei hopes to return to his homeland one day, and continues to speak out in favor of the 3,000 political prisoners still languishing in the Chinese "gulag."

Democracy Wall. The laws Wei was accused of violating have been repealed, and pro-democracy advocates now post their criticisms of the government on the Internet. ◆

Johnson, James Weldon

JULY 17, 1871–JUNE 17, 1938 ● POET AND POLITICAL LEADER

James William Johnson, who changed his middle name to Weldon in 1913, was born in Jacksonville, Florida. James, Sr., his father, the headwaiter at a local hotel, accumulated substantial real estate holdings and maintained a private library. Helen Dillet Johnson, his mother, a native of Nassau in the Bahamas, was the only African-American woman teaching in Jacksonville's public schools. Through his parents' example, the opportunity to travel, and his reading, Johnson developed the urbanity and the personal magnetism that characterized his later political and literary career.

Johnson graduated in 1894 from Atlanta University, an all-black institution that he credited with instilling in him the importance of striving to better the lives of his people. Returning to Jacksonville, he traveled many different roads to fulfill that sense of racial responsibility. Appointed principal of the largest school for African Americans in Florida, he developed a high school curriculum. At the same time, he founded a short-lived newspaper, the *Daily American* (1895–96); studied law; passed the bar examination; and wrote lyrics for the music of his brother, J. Rosamond Johnson. In 1900 the brothers collaborated on "Lift Ev'ry Voice and Sing," a song that is regarded as the Negro national anthem.

Johnson moved to New York in 1902 to work with his brother and his brother's partner on the **vaudeville** circuit, Robert Cole. Called by one critic the "ebony Offenbachs," the songwriting team of Cole, Johnson, and Johnson was one of the most successful in the country. (The 1902 song "Under the Bamboo Tree" was their greatest success.) The team tried to avoid **stereotypical** representations of blacks and tried to invest their songs with some dignity and humanity, as well as humor.

While his brother toured with Cole, James Weldon Johnson studied literature at Columbia University and became

> In 1900 Johnson and his brother J. Rosamond Johnson collaborated on "Lift Ev'ry Voice and Sing," a song that is regarded as the Negro national anthem.

vaudeville: stage entertainment consisting of various musical, comedy, and physical acts.

stereotypical: oversimplified opinion; prejudiced attitude.

active in New York City politics. In 1904, in a political association dominated by Booker T. Washington, Johnson became the treasurer of the city's Colored Republican Club. The Republican party rewarded his service with an appointment to the United States Consular Service in 1906, and Johnson served first as United States **consul** at Porto Cabello, Venezuela, and then, from 1908 to 1913, in Corinto, Nicaragua.

In Venezuela he completed his first and only novel, *The Autobiography of an Ex-Colored Man* (1912). Published

consul: an official appointed by a government to live in a foreign country and represent commercial interests.

1871 Johnson is born in Jacksonville, Florida.

1894 Johnson graduates from Atlanta University.

1895 Johnson studies law and passes the bar exam.

1900 Johnson collaborates with his brother on "Lift Ev'ry Voice and Sing."

1916 Johnson becomes field secretary of the NAACP.

1933 Johnson publishes his autobiography, *Along This Way.*

1938 Johnson is killed in an automobile accident.

gravitated: moved toward.

dialect: a regional variety of a spoken language.

anonymously, it was taken by many readers for a true autobiography. That realism marks an important transition from the nineteenth- to the twentieth-century African-American novel. Johnson brought modern literary techniques to his retelling of the popular nineteenth-century "tragic mulatto" theme.

The election of Woodrow Wilson, a Democrat, to the presidency blocked Johnson's advancement in the consular service. He returned to New York, where, in 1914, he joined the *New York Age* as an editorial writer. While he was associated with the politics of Booker T. Washington, Johnson's instincts were more radical and he **gravitated** toward the NAACP. In 1916 the NAACP hired him as a field secretary, charged with organizing or reviving local branches. In that post, he greatly expanded and solidified the still-fledgling organization's branch operations and helped to increase its membership, influence, and revenue. He also took an active role organizing protests against racial discrimination, including the racial violence of the "Red Summer" of 1919, a phrase he coined.

Shortly after he joined the staff of the NAACP, Johnson published his first collection of poetry, *Fifty Years and Other Poems* (1917). Like the work of Paul Laurence Dunbar, Johnson's poetry falls into two broad categories: poems in standard English and poems in a conventionalized African-American dialect. While he used **dialect**, he also argued that dialect verse possessed a limited range for racial expression. His poems in standard English include some of his most important early contributions to African-American letters. Poems like "Brothers" and "White Witch" are bitter protests against lynching that anticipate the poetry of Claude McKay in the 1920s and the fiction of Richard Wright in the 1930s and 1940s.

During the 1920s Johnson's political and artistic activities came together. He was appointed secretary of the NAACP's national office in 1920. His tenure brought coherence and consistency to the day-to-day operations of the association and to his general political philosophy. He led the organization in its lobbying for the passage of the Dyer Anti-Lynching Bill and in its role in several legal cases; his report on the conditions of the American occupation of Haiti prompted a Senate investigation. Johnson's leadership helped to establish the association as a major national civil rights organization committed to accomplishing its goals through lobbying for legislation and seeking legal remedies through the courts. In 1927–28 and again in 1929, he took a leave of absence from the NAACP. During the latter period he helped organize the consortium of Atlanta University and Spelman and Morehouse colleges.

Also in the 1920s, Johnson, with such colleagues at the NAACP as W. E. B. Du Bois, Walter White, and Jessie Fauset, maintained that the promotion of the artistic and literary creativity of African Americans went hand in hand with political activism, that the recognition of blacks in the arts broke down racial barriers. Their advocacy of black artists in the pages of *Crisis,* and with white writers, publishers, and critics, established an audience for the flourishing of African-American literature during the Harlem Renaissance. Johnson himself published an anthology of African-American poetry, *The Book of Negro Poetry* (1922, rev. 1931), and he and his brother edited two volumes of *The Book of American Negro Spirituals* (1925 and 1926). In his introductions to these anthologies and in critical essays, he argued for a distinct African-American creative voice that was expressed by both professional artists and the anonymous composers of the spirituals. *Black Manhattan* (1930) was a pioneering "cultural history" that promoted Harlem as the cultural capital of black America.

Johnson was not in the conventional sense either a **pious** or a religious man, but he consistently drew on African-American religious expressions for poetic inspiration. In early poems like "Lift Ev'ry Voice and Sing," "O Black and Unknown Bards," and "100 Years," he formulated a secular version of the vision of hope embodied in spirituals and gospel songs. His second volume of poetry, *God's Trombones* (1927), drew on the African-American **vernacular** sermon. Using the rhythms, syntax, and figurative language of the African-American preacher, Johnson devised a poetic expression that reproduced the richness of African-American language without succumbing to the stereotypes that limited his dialect verse.

In 1930 Johnson resigned as secretary of the NAACP to take up a teaching post at Fisk University and pursue his literary career. His autobiography, *Along This Way,* was published in 1933; his vision of racial politics, *Negro Americans, What Now?,* was published in 1934; and his third major collection of poetry, *Saint Peter Relates an Incident,* was published in 1935. He was killed in an automobile accident on June 26, 1938. ◆

"The final measure of the greatness of all people is the amount and standard of the literature and art they have produced. The world does not know that a people is great until that people produces great literature and art."
James Weldon Johnson, 1931

pious: showing reverence for a religion or God.

vernacular: a language native to the region.

Jordan, Barbara Charline

FEBRUARY 21, 1936–JANUARY 17, 1996 ● CONGRESSWOMAN AND PROFESSOR

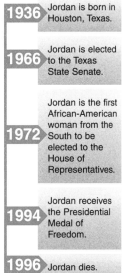

1936 Jordan is born in Houston, Texas.

1966 Jordan is elected to the Texas State Senate.

1972 Jordan is the first African-American woman from the South to be elected to the House of Representatives.

1994 Jordan receives the Presidential Medal of Freedom.

1996 Jordan dies.

impeachment: bringing accusations against or removal from office.

grassroots: the basic, local roots of society.

B arbara Jordan was born in Houston, Texas, the daughter of Arlyne Jordan and Benjamin M. Jordan, a Baptist minister. She spent her childhood in Houston, and graduated from Texas Southern University in Houston in 1956. Jordan received a law degree from Boston University in 1959. She was engaged briefly in private practice in Houston before becoming the administrative assistant for the county judge of Harris County, Texas, a post she held until 1966.

In 1962, and again in 1964, Jordan ran unsuccessfully for the Texas State Senate. In 1966, helped by the marked increase in registered African-American voters, she became the first black since 1883 elected to the Texas State Senate. The following year she became the first woman president of the Texas Senate. That year, redistricting opened a new district in Houston with a black majority. Jordan ran a strong campaign, and in 1972 she was elected to the House of Representatives from the district, becoming the first African-American woman elected to Congress from the South.

Jordan's short career as a high-profile congresswoman took her to a leadership role on the national level. In her first term, she received an appointment to the House Judiciary Committee, where she achieved national recognition during the Watergate scandal, when in 1974 she voted for articles of **impeachment** against President Richard M. Nixon. A powerful public speaker, Jordan eloquently conveyed to the country the serious constitutional nature of the charges and the gravity with which the Judiciary Committee was duty-bound to address the issues. "My faith in the Constitution is whole, it is complete, it is total," she declared. "I am not going to sit here and be an idle spectator to the diminution, the subversion, the destruction of the Constitution."

Jordan spent six years in Congress, where she spoke out against the Vietnam War and high military expenditures, particularly those earmarked for support of the war. She supported environmental reform as well as measures to aid blacks, the poor, the elderly, and other groups on the margins of society. Jordan was a passionate campaigner for the Equal Rights Amendment, and for **grassroots** citizen political action. Central to all of her concerns was a commitment to realizing the ideals of the Constitution.

Public recognition of her integrity, her legislative ability, and her oratorical excellence came from several quarters. Beginning in 1974, and for ten consecutive years, the *World Almanac* named her one of the twenty-five most influential women in America. *Time* magazine named Jordan one of the Women of the Year in 1976. Her electrifying keynote address at the Democratic National Convention that year helped to solidify her stature as a national figure.

In 1978, feeling she needed a wider forum for her views than her congressional district, Jordan chose not to seek reelection. Returning to her native Texas, Jordan accepted a professorship in the School of Public Affairs at the University of Texas at Austin in 1979, and from 1982 to 1993 she held the Lyndon B. Johnson Centennial Chair in Public Policy. Reflecting her interest in minority rights, in 1985 Jordan was appointed by the secretary-general of the United Nations to serve on an eleven-member commission charged with investigating the role of **transnational** corporations in South Africa and Namibia. In 1991 Texas governor Ann Richards appointed her "ethics guru," charged with monitoring ethics in the state's government. In 1992, although confined to a wheelchair by a **degenerative** disease, Jordan gave a keynote speech at the Democratic National Convention, again displaying the passion, eloquence, and integrity that had first brought her to public attention nearly two decades earlier.

In 1993 President Bill Clinton appointed Jordan to chair the U.S. Commission on Immigration Reform. She received the Presidential Medal of Freedom in 1994. Jordan died in 1996 from pneumonia and complications related to leukemia. ◆

"Do not call for Black power or green power. Call for brain power."
Barbara Jordan, 1977

transnational: going beyond national boundaries.

degenerative: involving deterioration of a tissue or organ.

King, Martin Luther, Jr.

JANUARY 15, 1929–APRIL 4, 1968 ● BAPTIST MINISTER AND LEADER OF THE NONVIOLENT MOVEMENT FOR CIVIL RIGHTS

Martin Luther King Jr. was the second black American to win the Nobel Peace Prize. He was, said Chairman Jahn of the Nobel committee, "the first person in the Western world to have shown us that a struggle can be waged without violence. He is the first to make the message of brotherly love a reality in the course of his struggle, and he has brought this message to all men, to all nations and races."

King was born Michael King Jr., the second child and first son of a Baptist minister in Atlanta, Georgia. When the boy was six years old, two white playmates were told not to play with him, and his mother had to explain about segregation: it was a social condition, and he was as good as anyone else. The father lifted the boy's vision higher; he told him about Martin Luther, the great leader of the Reformation, and said that from now on they would both be named after him.

Martin Luther King Jr., a very bright student, began to show his oratorical ability as early as his high school years. At fifteen he entered Morehouse College in Atlanta, the distinguished black institution, and decided to become a minister. As he said later, "I'm the son of a preacher . . . my grandfather was a

Morehouse College

Morehouse College, founded in 1867, is a small, private liberal arts college in Augusta, Georgia. It is the nation's only historically black, four-year liberal arts college for men. The Augusta Institute, as Morehouse was called in its very early days, had the primary purpose of preparing black men to serve as ministers and teachers in the nation's African-American communities following the Civil War. Today, Morehouse College has an international reputation for producing leaders who have influenced national and world history. The college is recognized for many of its alumni, including Nobel Peace Prize laureate Martin Luther King Jr., former secretary of health and human services Louis Sullivan, Olympian Edwin Moses, filmmaker Spike Lee, and others, among them several congressmen, federal judges, and college presidents. Julian Bond, noted civil rights leader and politician, was a student at Morehouse College in the early 1960s. The institution maintains a commitment to excellence in leadership and service as well as scholarship, and these men and many other Morehouse graduates have made great contributions to their professions and to the world. In recognition of its origins as a black institution, Morehouse takes a responsibility for instructing students about the history and culture of African Americans. The college emphasizes the continuing search for truth as a liberating force. In keeping with the actions and ideals of its illustrious alumni, the college supports and encourages programs that benefit all people and that seek to abolish discrimination and injustice.

preacher, my great-grandfather was a preacher, my only brother is a preacher, my daddy's brother is a preacher, so I didn't have much choice." During his senior year, when he was eighteen, King was ordained and elected assistant pastor of the Ebenezer Baptist Church, which had been established by his grandfather and where his father was then the minister.

He graduated at nineteen in sociology and went on to Crozier Theological Seminary in Chester, Pennsylvania, where he was one of only six black students in a student body of about one hundred. In three years he received the degree of bachelor of divinity, having been president of the senior class and valedictorian. With a Crozier fellowship, he entered Boston University in 1951 to study for a doctorate.

"We must pursue peaceful ends through peaceful means."
Martin Luther King Jr.

While at Crozier he first heard of Gandhi's nonviolent movement that had won independence for India, and he began to think of how such methods might be used by the black people in America. It appeared to him that Gandhi "was probably the first person to lift the love ethic of Jesus above mere interaction between individuals to a powerful effective social force on a large scale."

In his studies at Boston University, King was introduced to the leading theological ideas of the day, and he also had the opportunity to follow philosophy courses at Harvard. In Boston he met the beautiful and talented Coretta Scott, who was studying to be a concert singer at the New England Conservatory of Music, but who gave up her career to become his wife. They were married in 1953 and were to have four children. Coretta was always a great support for him, and after his death she carried on his work, becoming a national leader in her own right.

In 1954, after King had completed the course work for his Ph.D., he had job offers from colleges and churches in the North, but he felt that his place was in the South, where he could do more for his people. When he decided to answer the call from Dexter Avenue Baptist Church in Montgomery, Alabama, however, Coretta had reservations. She had grown up in Alabama only eighty miles from there, and she knew that Montgomery was still living in **hallowed** memories of its past as the first capital of the Confederacy and that they would encounter deep racial prejudices. Later she came to feel that the choice of Montgomery "was an inevitable part of a greater plan for our lives."

King officially entered upon his pastor's duties in Montgomery in September 1954. The next year he received his Ph.D. from Boston University, in November their first child was born, and a few weeks later the series of events began in Montgomery that propelled him into a greater role than he could ever have foreseen.

On December 1, 1955, Rosa Parks, a forty-year-old seamstress, refused to give up her seat in a bus to a white man as she was ordered to do by the driver. "I was just plain tired, and my feet hurt," she explained later. For this she was arrested and charged with disobeying the city's segregation ordinance.

The black community was outraged, and their pastors quickly organized a one-day boycott of the buses in protest. This was so successful that it was decided to continue the boycott until demands to desegregate the buses were met. For leadership the pastors turned to their young colleague of the Dexter Avenue Church, who had already won a reputation among them for his powerful preaching. They felt that he had not been in town long enough to make enemies and could easily relocate to another city if things went wrong. Consequently, Martin Luther King Jr. became president of the committee to conduct the boycott,

1929 — King is born in Atlanta, Georgia.

1957 — King becomes founding president of the Southern Christian Leadership Conference.

1963 — King delivers "I Have a Dream" speech at the March on Washington.

1964 — King receives the Nobel Peace Prize.

1968 — King is assassinated in Memphis, Tennessee.

1969 — King's widow establishes the Martin Luther King Jr. Center for Nonviolent Social Change in Atlanta.

1986 — A national holiday is established to honor King's birth.

hallowed: cherished.

"Life's most urgent question is: What are you doing for others ?"
Martin Luther King Jr.

Throughout the South blacks rallied at King's call, fighting segregation through marches, demonstrations, sit-ins, and other nonviolent methods.

which was hopefully called the Montgomery Improvement Association. He was then not quite twenty-seven.

In his first speech, to a mass meeting on December 5, King announced the nonviolent principles that were to guide the civil rights movement from then on. In the struggle for freedom and justice to which they were called, he said, "Our actions must be guided by the deepest principles of the Christian faith." He concluded: "If you will protest courageously, and yet with dignity and Christian love, future historians will say, 'There lived a great people—a black people—who injected new meaning and dignity into the veins of civilization.' This is our challenge and our overwhelming responsibility."

In this spirit the boycott effort persisted, despite bitter efforts to break it through all kinds of harassment, abuse, and persecution. For over a year the black community of Montgomery stayed out of the public buses—walking, car-pooling, and using all possible means of transit—until finally the United States Supreme Court ruled that segregation on the buses was unconstitutional. King was the target for arrests, constant anonymous death threats, and a night bombing of his home.

The Montgomery bus boycott drew worldwide attention to the racial struggle in the South and to King. The movement for racial justice spread beyond Montgomery, and King became the leader of the Southern Christian Leadership Conference, which coordinated the major civil rights activities. Throughout the South blacks rallied at King's call, fighting segregation through marches, demonstrations, sit-ins, and other nonviolent methods. King was always at the forefront, and he was beaten, arrested, and jailed. In one prison cell he wrote his moving "Letter from Birmingham Jail," explaining to some white ministers who counseled patience "why we can't wait."

He traveled thousands of miles, in the North as well as in the South, making speeches, raising money, appealing for support from political, labor, and business leaders. In 1963, when 250,000 persons, 75,000 of them white, took part in a march in Washington to urge Congress to pass civil rights legislation, King addressed them from the Lincoln Memorial in his most famous speech, "I Have a Dream," presenting his vision of an America living out the true meaning of its egalitarian creed. Great steps forward were taken when Congress passed the Civil Rights Act of 1964 and the Voting Rights Act of 1965, but realization of the dream was still far off.

King had not sought the leadership in Montgomery, but felt that God had directed him to take it on, and in the following years he continued to feel that he had no choice, despite the pain and suffering he endured. He sometimes thought **wistfully** of a peaceful life in a teaching post somewhere, but he put such thoughts aside. The public commendation that he received only drove him to devote more of his energies to the cause he served. He lived with danger and had premonitions of an early death, but he carried on, firm in the faith that he was meant to.

wistfully: full of yearning.

Early in 1964 King learned that he had been nominated for the Nobel Peace Prize by Swedish parliamentary deputies, and in the summer a request came from Oslo for documentation, indicating that his candidacy was being seriously considered. Possibly with an eye on the prize, arrangements were made for King to have an audience with Pope Paul VI and to visit West Berlin in September. But King expected that the award would be given to someone who was involved with international peace activities.

He returned from Berlin exhausted and checked into a hospital for a physical examination, mainly for a few days' rest. The next morning Coretta telephoned to wake him up with the news that he had won the prize. Sleepily, he thought he was still dreaming. Once awake, he called a press conference at the hospital, but first met with his wife and closest associates, explaining to them that the prize represented the international moral recognition of their whole movement, not his personal part in it. He asked them to join him in prayer for strength to work harder for their goal. At the press conference he announced that he would give the prize money of approximately fifty-four thousand dollars to the movement, which he arranged to do on his return from Oslo.

"We have written a Declaration of Independence, itself an accomplishment, but the effort to transform the words into a life experience still lies ahead."
Martin Luther King Jr., 1968

After receiving the Nobel prize King took a public stand against the American war in Vietnam, **antagonizing** political leaders who had helped with civil rights legislation and alienating former associates who thought he should keep to the one issue. He lobbied for federal assistance to the poor, insisting that the misery of poverty knows no racial distinctions, and he planned a "Poor People's March" on Washington for April 20, 1968. He was not to live to see it. On April 4 while in Memphis, Tennessee, helping striking garbage workers, Martin Luther King Jr. was assassinated.

antagonizing: provoking hostility.

Only a few months before, in a sermon at Ebenezer Baptist Church, he had spoken of his own death and funeral. He wanted no long **eulogy**:

> Say that I was a drum major for justice. Say that I was a drum major for peace. That I was a drum major for righteousness. And all of the other shallow things will not matter. I won't have any money to leave behind. I won't have the fine and luxurious things of life to leave behind. But I just want to leave a committed life behind.

In 1986, by act of Congress, the United States began the annual celebration of the birthday of Martin Luther King Jr. in January as a national holiday. ◆

Lewis, John

FEBRUARY 21, 1940– ● POLITICIAN AND CIVIL RIGHTS LEADER

John Lewis was born near the town of Troy, in Pike County, Alabama. Growing up on a small farm, Lewis was one of ten children in a poor sharecropping family. Lewis had been drawn to the ministry since he was a child, and in fulfillment of his lifelong dream, he entered the American Baptist Theological Seminary in Nashville, Tennessee, in 1957. He received his B.A. four years later. As a seminary student Lewis participated in nonviolence workshops and programs taught by James Lawson—a member of the Fellowship of Reconciliation (FOR), a pacifist civil rights organization. Lewis became a field secretary for FOR and attended Highlander Folk School, an interracial adult education center in Tennessee committed to social change, where he was deeply influenced by Septima Clark, the director of education at Highlander.

Lewis became an active participant in the growing Civil Rights Movement. He became a member of the Nashville Student Movement, and along with Diane Nash Bevel, James Bevel, and other African-American students he participated in the Nashville desegregation campaigns of 1960. Lewis was one of the founding members of the Student Nonviolent Coordinating Committee (SNCC) in 1960 and played a leading role in organizing SNCC participation in the Congress of Racial Equality's (CORE) freedom rides. He led freedom rides

"We were out to build a community, not a separate place for blacks by creating conflict and destruction. We wanted to win people over and that cannot be done with the use of violence. Nonviolence was a much better way."
Congressman John Lewis, 1998

1940 Lewis is born in Pike County, Alabama.

1960 Lewis helps found the Student Nonviolent Coordinating Committee.

1963 Lewis delivers a controversial speech at the March on Washington.

1965 Lewis marches with Dr. Martin Luther King Jr. in Selma, Alabama.

1986 Lewis defeats Julian Bond in a race for a seat in Congress from an Atlanta district.

In Congress Lewis was an advocate of civil rights and drew much praise from political observers for his political acumen.

acumen: shrewdness.

in South Carolina and Alabama, where he and the other protesters were violently attacked by southern whites.

Lewis rose to a leadership position within SNCC, serving as national chairman from 1963 to 1966. During the 1963 March on Washington, Lewis—representing SNCC—delivered a highly controversial speech that criticized the federal government's consistent failure to protect civil rights workers, condemned the civil rights bill as "too little, too late," and called on African Americans to participate actively in civil rights protests until "the unfinished revolution of 1776 is complete." Despite the fact that he had acceded to the march organizers and other participants and allowed his speech to be severely edited to tone down its militant rhetoric, it was still considered by most in attendance to be the most radical speech of the day.

In March 1965 Lewis marched with Rev. Dr. Martin Luther King Jr. in Selma, Alabama, to agitate for a voting rights act that would safeguard African Americans' access to the franchise. He was one of the many participants severely beaten by state troopers on what became known as Bloody Sunday. By 1966 Lewis's continued advocacy of nonviolence had made him an anachronism in the increasingly militant SNCC. He resigned from the organization in June of that year, to be succeeded by Stokely Carmichael as SNCC's chairperson. Lewis continued his civil rights activities as part of the Field Foundation from 1966 to 1967 and worked as director of community organization projects for the Southern Regional Council. In 1970 he was appointed director of the Voter Education Project, which promoted black empowerment through greater participation in electoral politics.

Lewis became more directly involved in the political arena six years later when he was appointed by President Carter to serve on the staff of ACTION—a government agency that coordinated volunteer activities. From 1981 to 1986, he served on the Atlanta City Council. In 1986, in a bitter race, he challenged and defeated Julian Bond—another civil rights veteran—for the seat in Congress from an Atlanta district. In Congress Lewis became an influential member of the House Ways and Means Committee. He was an advocate of civil rights and drew much praise from political observers for his political **acumen**. In 1998, he was reelected from Georgia's Fifth Congressional District for a seventh term. ◆

Lowell, James Russell

FEBRUARY 22, 1819–AUGUST 12, 1891 ● ABOLITIONIST AND AUTHOR

James Russell Lowell was an American author, teacher, and diplomat who also played a critical role in the nineteenth-century antislavery movement.

Lowell's career as a student was marked by difficulties with the authorities at Harvard: he preferred to read things of his own choice rather than the assigned books and he had a tendency to play practical jokes. Although he was officially "class poet" in 1838, he spent most of his senior year away from the college under private instruction as a disciplinary measure. Lowell then studied law and graduated from the Harvard Law School in 1840. He never enjoyed legal practice and did not follow that profession.

Lowell's early writings were books of poetry, including several antislavery poems. He met and married Maria White in December 1844. She was not only interested in poetry but was a dedicated abolitionist. Lowell's poetry became deeper and better and his interests began to focus on the evils of slavery. The newly married couple socialized with a group of young people devoted to the reforms of the day, which included abolitionism. Lowell contributed to several antislavery newspapers during the 1840s, serving as editorial writer for *The Pennsylvania Freeman* and contributing to *The National Anti-Slavery Standard*, for which he became "corresponding editor" in 1848.

James Russell Lowell also became an important literary critic and was named professor of modern languages and literature at Harvard in 1855. While holding this post, he edited the *Atlantic Monthly* and the *North American Review*, contributing many articles and reviews to both periodicals. Slavery occupied a great deal of his attention and when the Republican party was organized, Lowell was one of its first supporters. The Civil War brought forth one of his finest literary works, the *Commemoration Ode*. This was a deeply felt poem in honor of the Harvard men who had died during the war and of President Abraham Lincoln.

Following the Civil War, Lowell was designated U.S. minister to Spain; he served in that post from 1877 to 1880, when he was transferred to Great Britain. He remained as U.S. minister to Great Britain from 1880 to 1885. During these years he won praise for his work in improving diplomatic relations with Britain. ◆

> *"New occasions teach new duties; Time makes ancient good uncouth; They must upward still, and onward, who would keep abreast of Truth;"*
> James Russell Lowell, 1844

1819 Lowell is born.

1848 Lowell becomes corresponding editor of *The National Anti-Slavery Standard.*

1855 Lowell is named professor of modern languages and literature at Harvard.

1891 Lowell dies.

Lutuli, Albert John

1898–JULY 21, 1967 ● LEADER OF THE AFRICAN NATIONAL CONGRESS IN
SOUTH AFRICA

> "I have joined my people in the new spirit that moves them today, the spirit that revolts openly and boldly against injustice and expresses itself in a determined and nonviolent manner."
>
> Albert John
> Lutuli, 1952

Albert John Lutuli (this is the spelling he preferred; the name is frequently spelled "Luthuli") was descended from a line of Zulu leaders. His grandfather and his uncle had both been tribal chiefs in Natal, a province of the Republic of South Africa. His grandparents were the first Christian converts in the community, and their younger son, Lutuli's father, became a missionary in what was then Rhodesia, where Lutuli was born. After his father's death, his mother returned with her eight-year-old son to Groutville, a small town near Durban on the east coast of South Africa, where she sent him to a Congregationalist mission school and took in washing to pay for his schoolbooks.

Lutuli continued his education in missionary schools with the help of scholarships, graduating at twenty-three from Adams College in Natal, trained as a teacher. He was offered another scholarship to do graduate work, but he chose to accept a teaching position at Adams College in order to support his mother. He was one of the first two black teachers hired at Adams, and he remained there for fifteen years, teaching Zulu history and literature. In 1927 he married a fellow teacher, and in 1929 the first of their seven children was born. During this period Lutuli rose to positions of leadership among African teachers, becoming president of the African Association of Teachers in 1933. He was also active in church organizations, which led to a trip to India to attend a Christian conference and a lecture tour in the United States, sponsored by missionary societies.

In 1935 the elders of his tribe asked him to become the chief, which was an elective position subject to approval by the South African government, which paid the salary. Lutuli, who was committed to his teaching, hesitated, but finally in 1936 he accepted, and his life took a new turn. Lutuli was then thirty-eight, and he had never occupied himself with political issues. Nor did these concern him in his early years as chief of the community of five thousand Zulus in the Groutville area, where he was kept busy by his duties as civil administrator, judge, and presiding figure at tribal ceremonies. His policy was to preserve the best of the tribal culture, while fostering Christian values and giving his people the benefits of modern civilization. He also tried to improve the conditions of laborers on the sugar-cane plantations.

Meanwhile, the government of the ruling white minority had begun imposing restrictions on nonwhites. In 1936 the government disenfranchised the only Africans who had the vote, in Cape Province. In 1948 the Nationalist government adopted the policy of apartheid to keep the races apart. The Pass Laws limited where nonwhites could live and work, and their educational opportunities were reduced.

These measures brought Lutuli into active opposition. In 1944 he joined the African National Congress (ANC), which had been founded in South Africa in 1912 to secure civil rights for Africans in that country, including the vote. Members of other racial groups were invited to join the struggle. In 1945 Lutuli was elected to a position in the Natal division of the ANC, and in 1951 he became its president and helped organize nonviolent measures of resistance, such as boycotts, strikes, and noncompliance, to discriminatory policies.

The government demanded that he withdraw either from the ANC or from his office as tribal chief. Lutuli refused to do either, and in 1952 the government deposed him. He issued a declaration, "The Chief Speaks," asking, "What have been the fruits of my many years of moderation?" Only more laws limiting rights, he said, "an intensification of our subjection to ensure and protect white supremacy." Lutuli defended the ANC, whose nonviolent passive resistance campaign was not subversive and did not seek to overthrow the state. Any chief worthy of his position, he said, had no choice but to fight fearlessly against laws and conditions that tend to **debase** human personality, a God-given force. He concluded, "It is inevitable that in working for Freedom some individuals and some families must take the lead and suffer: the Road to Freedom Is via the Cross."

One month after the government dismissed him as chief, Lutuli was elected to the presidency of the ANC and became the national leader of the struggle for racial equality in South Africa. Determined to fight only with nonviolent means, he opposed extremists on the left who wanted to use violence and establish an all-black state, as well as those who wanted to compromise with the government.

The government now began a succession of bans against Lutuli to limit his freedom of expression and his movements

1898 Lutuli is born in Rhodesia.

1936 Lutuli becomes chief of the Zulu tribe.

1952 The South African government deposes Lutuli as chief; he is elected president of the African National Congress (ANC).

1960 Lutuli receives the Nobel Peace Prize.

1967 Lutuli dies.

debase: reduce status or esteem.

"We believe in the brotherhood of peoples and in respect for the value of the individual. My congress has never given expression to hatred for any race in South Africa."

Albert John Lutuli, 1958

inexplicable: not explainable.

pathological: relating to something abnormal.

beyond the limits of his home district. In 1956 when he attended an ANC congress, he was arrested, along with 155 others, and charged with treason. After spending a year in jail, he was released and the charges dropped. He testified at the trials of the remaining defendants, who were all acquitted in 1961 with a verdict acknowledging that the ANC was neither plotting violent revolution nor dominated by communists.

In 1960 a mass demonstration at Sharpeville against the pass regulations was fired on by the police, and sixty-nine people were killed and 180 wounded. Lutuli publicly burned his pass in solidarity with the victims, for which he was given a jail sentence that was suspended because of his health, and he was returned to Groutville. The ANC was then outlawed by Parliament.

Lutuli was living in Groutville under restrictions when word came that he was to receive the 1960 Nobel Peace Prize. The government newspaper condemned the award as "an **inexplicable pathological** phenomenon," but Lutuli said later that he never knew he had so many friends in South Africa, as congratulations came pouring in from people of all racial groups. Yielding to pressure, the government finally agreed to grant Lutuli a passport to go to Oslo for the ceremony, but it was good only for ten days, and he could not go anywhere else, not even to Stockholm to meet the other prize winners. Wherever his plane landed, however, Lutuli was met by enthusiastic ovations.

In presenting him with the prize, Chairman Jahn quoted Lutuli's letter to the prime minister of South Africa: "We believe in a community where the white and the non-white in South Africa can live in harmony and work for our common fatherland. . . . We believe in the brotherhood of peoples and in respect for the value of the individual. My congress has never given expression to hatred for any race in South Africa." Lutuli, said Jahn, "brings a message to all who work and strive to establish respect for human rights both within nations and between nations. Well might we ask: Will the non-whites of South Africa, by their suffering, their humiliation, and their patience, show the other nations of the world that human rights can be won without violence?"

He returned to the isolation to which his government had condemned him, but he was not forgotten. The South African Colored People's Congress nominated him for president, the National Union of South African Students elected him honorary president, and the students of Glasgow University voted to name him rector, although he declined.

Lutuli's autobiography, *Let My People Go,* appeared in 1962. Its concluding words reaffirmed his hope for Africa: "Somewhere ahead there beckons a civilization, a culture, which will take its place in the parade of God's history beside other great syntheses, Chinese, Egyptian, Jewish, European. It will not necessarily be all black; but it will be African."

He remained restricted to his home during his last years, his powers declining, no doubt saddened by the continued **intransigence** of the government and the turn away from nonviolence among many of his former followers. In 1967, while walking on a trestle near his home, he was struck by a train and killed. ◆

intransigence: refusal to compromise.

M

MacBride, Seán

JANUARY 26, 1904–JANUARY 15, 1988 ● CHAMPION OF HUMAN RIGHTS

In 1974 Seán MacBride was recognized with the Nobel Peace Prize for his great contribution to the cause of human rights. He was a fervent Irish nationalist who, after fighting for Ireland's independence in his youth, became one of the leading internationalists of his time.

MacBride was born in Paris, the son of Major John MacBride, who had led the Irish Brigade against the British in the Boer War, and the beautiful Maude Gonne MacBride, who was active both in the movement for Irish independence and the struggle for women's rights. The parents became separated shortly after their son's birth, Major MacBride returning to Dublin to join the revolutionary forces and his wife and son remaining in Paris, where the boy attended a Jesuit school until he was twelve.

In that year, 1916, Major MacBride was executed by the British after taking part in the abortive Easter Rebellion, and Seán and his mother secretly returned to Ireland. The next year the thirteen-year-old joined the Irish Republican Army (IRA) as a junior volunteer, and for the next twenty years he worked in the underground against British rule. Three times jailed, the first time when he was only fourteen, MacBride rose in the

1904 MacBride is born in Paris.

1936 MacBride becomes commander-in-chief of the Irish Republican Army.

1963 MacBride helps found and becomes chairman of Amnesty International.

1974 MacBride receives the Nobel Peace Prize.

1988 Macbride dies at the age of eighty-three.

MacBride helped found and became president of Amnesty International, the organization that defends prisoners of conscience.

ranks, receiving the Military Service Medal for Irish Independence in 1935 and becoming commander in chief of the IRA in 1936. In 1937 he withdrew from the IRA shortly before its leaders declared their intention of aiding Adolf Hitler.

During these years he had worked as a journalist, married Catalina Bulford, an Irish woman from Argentina, and visited the United States to secure support for the IRA. He had enrolled at Dublin University, but was arrested on the second day of classes. Through intermittent study over a period of seven years, however, he managed to complete the three-year lecture course for his law degree, and in 1937 he was admitted to the Irish bar. He soon became the most successful trial lawyer in Dublin, effectively defending, among others, former IRA comrades with whose policies he had disagreed.

After the Second World War, MacBride entered politics, founding the Republican party, which stood for the establishment of the Irish Republic, the end of the partition of Ireland between North and South, and a program of social welfare. In 1947 he was elected to the Irish parliament and continued to hold his seat until 1958.

From 1948 until 1951 he was foreign minister. During his tenure MacBride helped negotiate the Republic of Ireland Act, which finally established Ireland's complete independence of Britain, and he made his first appearance on the international stage, taking a leading role in the Council of Europe. He was mainly responsible for the European Convention for the Protection of Human Rights and Fundamental Freedoms, which he signed in 1950 along with the other foreign ministers of the member states. This represented the most important implementation of the UN Universal Declaration of Human Rights, with binding provisions for the signatories and setting up the European Court of Human Rights. MacBride always regarded this as his most satisfying accomplishment in law. From this moment on he was to devote his major energies to the protection of human rights, not only in Western Europe, but throughout the world.

He helped found and became president of Amnesty International, the organization that defends prisoners of conscience, and after this was well established, he served as secretary-general of the International Commission of Jurists from 1963 to 1970. This association had been founded in West Berlin to publicize acts of governmental injustice in Eastern Europe, but it expanded its work to take up violations of human rights all over the world, with jurists from over fifty countries participating.

In 1968 during the UN Human Rights Year, MacBride led a coalition of nongovernmental organizations concerned about these matters. He was also a central figure in various international peace organizations, such as the World Federation of UN Associations and the International Peace Bureau.

MacBride's practical work with these organizations was accompanied by a profusion of speeches and articles, in which he developed legal and theoretical foundations for the protection of the individual. He took the position that no state could maintain that how it treated its citizens was a matter of concern to itself alone, since human rights are the common property of all mankind and cannot be violated.

MacBride was already in his sixties when he entered a new area of activity. He became the legal adviser to Kwame Nkrumah in newly independent Ghana and helped him establish the Organization of African States. Then, with strong support from the African countries, the UN General Assembly unanimously elected him as high commissioner for Namibia, a difficult assignment, since South Africa insisted on retaining its control. He was also assistant secretary-general of the United Nations.

"Amnesty was one of my children."
Seán MacBride,
Paris, 1988

MacBride emphasized the fundamental relationship between peace and human rights and called the Universal Declaration of Human Rights "the most important declaration ever adopted by mankind." Only he would add one more right, one that had been urged by religious leaders: "the right of an individual to refuse to kill, to torture or to participate in the preparation for the nuclear destruction of humanity." He concluded, "The signpost just ahead of us is '**Oblivion.**' Can the march on this road be stopped? Yes, if public opinion uses the power it now has."

oblivion: lack of active knowledge or awareness.

In the ensuing years MacBride continued his efforts for peace and human rights and was also active in the ecumenical movement and the search for new sources of energy to replace nuclear energy. His talents as an international diplomat and mediator were drawn upon as chairman of the controversial UNESCO committee for the study of international communications and as a respected intermediary in the early days of the American hostage crisis in Iran, when he tried to get the matter moved from the political arena to the realm of international law.

In 1984, at the age of eighty, he was in the news for his MacBride principles, an antidiscrimination code aimed at requiring American companies in Northern Ireland to employ Roman Catholics on an equal basis with Protestants. In 1987 he was still active with the International Peace Bureau as president **emeritus**.

emeritus: retired from professional life.

The diversity of
MacBride's
awards testifies
to his remark-
able ability to
gain the trust
and respect of
representatives
of very different
positions.

He probably received as many honors as any individual in
our time; after the Nobel Peace Prize came the Lenin Peace
Prize, recognition by the American legal profession with the
American Medal of Justice, and the Silver Medal of UNESCO.

The diversity of his awards testifies to his remarkable ability to gain the trust and respect of representatives of very different positions. He even quietly served as an intermediary
between Irish extremists and the British government in the
troubled question of Northern Ireland. Much as MacBride traveled the world in the service of humanity, he never lost his
deep-felt love for his homeland. He died in Dublin in January
1988, at the age of eighty-three. ◆

Malcolm X

MAY 19, 1925–FEBRUARY 21, 1965 ● BLACK NATIONALIST AND LEADER

Malcolm X, born Malcolm Little and also known by his
religious name, El-Hajj Malik El-Shabbazz, was the
national representative of Elijah Muhammad's
Nation of Islam, a prominent black nationalist, and the founder of the Organization of
Afro-American Unity. He was born in
Omaha, Nebraska. His father, J. Early Little,
was a Georgia-born Baptist preacher and an
organizer for Marcus Garvey's Universal
Negro Improvement Association. His mother, M. Louise Norton, also a Garveyite, was
from Grenada. At J. Early Little's murder,
Malcolm's mother broke under the emotional and economic strain, and the children became wards of the state. Malcolm's
delinquent behavior landed him in a detention home in Mason, Michigan.

Malcolm journeyed to Boston and then
to New York, where, as "Detroit Red," he
became involved in a life of crime—numbers, peddling dope, con games of many
kinds, and thievery of all sorts, including
armed robbery. A few months before his
twenty-first birthday, Malcolm was sen-

Martin Luther King Jr. and Malcolm X.

tenced to a Massachusetts prison for burglary. While in prison, his life was transformed when he discovered through the influence of an inmate the liberating value of education, and through his family the empowering religious/cultural message of Elijah Muhammad's nation of Islam. Both gave him what he did not have: self-respect as a black person.

After honing his reading and debating skills, Malcolm was released from prison in 1952. He soon became a minister in the Nation of Islam and its most effective recruiter and apologist, speaking against black self-hate and on behalf of black self-esteem. In June 1954, Elijah Muhammad appointed him minister of Temple Number 7 in Harlem. In the temple and from the platform on street corner rallies, Malcolm told Harlemites, "We are black first and everything else second." Initially his black nationalist message was unpopular in the African-American community. The media, both white and black, portrayed him as a teacher of hate and a promoter of violence. It was an age of integration, and love and nonviolence were advocated as the only way to achieve it.

Malcolm did not share the optimism of the civil rights movement and found himself speaking to unsympathetic audiences. "If you are afraid to tell truth," he told his audience, "why, you don't deserve freedom." Malcolm relished the odds against him; he saw his task as waking up "dead Negroes" by revealing the truth about America and about themselves.

The enormity of this challenge motivated Malcolm to attack the philosophy of the Rev. Dr. Martin Luther King, Jr. and the civil rights movement head-on. He rejected integration: "An integrated cup of coffee is insufficient pay for 400 years of slave labor." He denounced nonviolence as "the philosophy of a fool": "There is no philosophy more **befitting** to the white man's tactics for keeping his foot on the black man's neck." He ridiculed King's 1963 "I Have a Dream" speech: "While King was having a dream, the rest of us Negroes are having a nightmare." He also rejected King's command to love the enemy: "It is not possible to love a man whose chief purpose in life is to humiliate you and still be considered a normal human being." To blacks who accused Malcolm of teaching hate, he retorted: "It is the man who has made a slave out of you who is teaching hate."

As long as Malcolm stayed in the Black Muslim movement, he was not free to speak his own mind. He had to represent the "Messenger," Elijah Muhammad, who was the sole and absolute authority in the Nation of Islam. When Malcolm disobeyed

befitting: appropriate for.

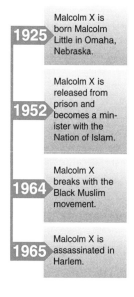

1925 Malcolm X is born Malcolm Little in Omaha, Nebraska.

1952 Malcolm X is released from prison and becomes a minister with the Nation of Islam.

1964 Malcolm X breaks with the Black Muslim movement.

1965 Malcolm X is assassinated in Harlem.

> *"I for one believe that if you give people a thorough understanding of what confronts them and the basic causes that produce it, they'll create their own program, and when the people create a program, you get action."*
>
> Malcolm X

Malcolm went to Selma, Alabama, while Martin Luther King Jr. was in jail, in support of King's efforts to secure voting rights.

Muhammad in December 1963 and described President John F. Kennedy's assassination as an instance of "chickens coming home to roost," Muhammad rebuked him and used the incident as an opportunity to silence his star pupil. Malcolm realized that more was involved in his silence than what he had said about the assassination. Jealousy and envy in Muhammad's family circle were the primary reasons for his silence and why it would never be lifted.

Malcolm reluctantly declared his independence in March 1964. His break with the Black Muslim movement represented another important turning point in his life. No longer bound by Muhammad's religious structures, he was free to develop his own philosophy of the black freedom struggle.

Malcolm had already begun to show independent thinking in his "Message to the Grass Roots" speech, given in Detroit three weeks before his silence. In that speech he endorsed black nationalism as his political philosophy, thereby separating himself not only from the civil rights movement, but more important, from Muhammad, who had defined the Nation as strictly religious and apolitical. Malcolm contrasted "the black revolution" with "the Negro revolution." The black revolution, he said, is international in scope, and it is "bloody" and "hostile" and "knows no compromise." But the so-called "Negro revolution," the civil rights movement, is not even a revolution. Malcolm mocked it: "The only revolution in which the goal is loving your enemy is the Negro revolution. It's the only revolution in which the goal is a desegregated lunch counter, a desegregated theater, a desegregated public park, a desegregated public toilet; you can sit down next to white folks on the toilet."

After his break, Malcolm developed his cultural and political philosophy of black nationalism in "The Ballot or the Bullet." Before audiences in New York, Cleveland, and Detroit, he urged blacks to acquire their constitutional right to vote, and move toward King and the civil rights movement. Later he became more explicit: "Dr. King wants the same thing I want—freedom." Malcolm went to Selma, Alabama, while King was in jail in support of King's efforts to secure voting rights. Malcolm wanted to join the civil rights movement in order to expand it into a human rights movement, thereby internationalizing the black freedom struggle, making it more radical and more militant.

During his independence, which lasted for approximately one year before he was assassinated, nothing influenced

Malcolm more than his travel abroad. His pilgrimage to Mecca transformed his theology. Malcolm became a Sunni Muslim, acquired the religious name El-Hajj Malik El-Shabbazz, and concluded that "Orthodox Islam" was incompatible with the racist teachings of Elijah Muhammad. The sight of "people of all races, colors, from all over the world coming together as one" had a profound effect upon him. "Brotherhood," and not racism, was seen as the essence of Islam.

Malcolm's experiences in Africa also transformed his political philosophy. He discovered the limitations of skin-nationalism, since he met whites who were creative participants in liberation struggles in African countries. In his travels abroad, Malcolm focused on explaining the black struggle for justice in the United States and linking it with other liberation struggles throughout the world. "Our problem is your problem," he told African heads of state: "It is not a Negro problem, nor an American problem. This is a world problem; a problem of humanity. It is not a problem of civil rights but a problem of human rights."

> *"A man has to act like a brother before you can call him a brother."*
> Malcolm X, 1964

When Malcolm returned to the United States, he told blacks: "You can't understand what is going on in Mississippi, if you don't know what is going on in the Congo. They are both the same. The same interests are at stake." He founded the Organization of Afro-American Unity, patterned after the Organization of African Unity, in order to implement his ideas. He was hopeful of influencing African leaders "to recommend an immediate investigation into our problem by the United Nations Commission on Human Rights."

Malcolm X was not successful. On February 21, 1965, he was shot down by assassins as he spoke at the Audubon Ballroom in Harlem. He was thirty-nine years old.

No one made a greater impact upon the cultural consciousness of the African-American community during the second half of the twentieth century than Malcolm X. More than anyone else, he revolutionized the black mind, transforming docile Negroes and self-effacing colored people into proud blacks and self-confident African Americans. Preachers and religious scholars created a black theology and proclaimed God as liberator and Jesus Christ as black. College students demanded and got Black Studies. Artists created a new black esthetic and proclaimed, "Black is beautiful."

No area of the African-American community escaped Malcolm's influence. Even mainstream black leaders who first dismissed him as a rabble-rouser, embraced his cultural philosophy following his death. Malcolm's most far-reaching influence, however, was among the masses of African Americans in the ghettos of American cities. Malcolm loved black people deeply and taught them much about themselves. Before Malcolm, most blacks did not want to have anything to do with Africa. But he reminded them that "you can't hate the roots of the tree and not hate the tree; you can't hate your origin and not end up hating yourself; you can't hate Africa and not hate yourself."

Malcolm X was a cultural revolutionary. Poet Maya Angelou called him a "charismatic speaker who could play an audience as great musicians play instruments." Disciple Peter Bailey said he was a "master teacher." Writer Alfred Duckett called him "our sage and our saint." In his eulogy, actor Ossie Davis bestowed upon Malcolm the title "our shining black prince." Malcolm can be best understood as a cultural prophet of blackness. African Americans who are proud to be black should thank Malcolm X. Few have played as central a role as he in making it possible for African Americans to claim their African heritage. ◆

> Few have played as central a role as Malcolm X in making it possible for African Americans to claim their African heritage.

Mandela, Nelson

JULY 18, 1918– ● SOUTH AFRICAN PRESIDENT AND CIVIL RIGHTS ACTIVIST

Nelson Mandela was born to Henry Gadla Mphakanyiswa and Nosekeni Fanny Mandela at Mbhashe in the Umtata district of the Transkei. Though a scion of the Thembu royal house, Henry Gadla was not in line for the succession. Nonetheless, he was a chief, albeit later deposed for insubordination. Fanny Mandela, a devout Methodist, was his third wife, which meant that her son, Nelson, could not inherit the chieftainship. This set the young Mandela on the course of education and urban politics and paved the way for his presidency of South Africa.

After his father's death, the nine-year-old Nelson Mandela, as arranged by his father, traveled to Mqekezweni, where the acting chief of the Ama-Thembu, Jongintaba David Dalindyebo, took charge of his education. He enrolled at the local school and eventually gained admission to Fort Hare College in 1938 but was expelled in 1940 for engaging in a strike action. In 1941 he traveled to Johannesburg, where he

> *"We must not allow fear to stand in our way. Our march to freedom is irreversible."*
>
> Nelson Mandela, upon his release from prison, 1990

African National Congress

The African National Congress (ANC) is the majority political party in South Africa. It came to power in April 1994 after the first national elections in which blacks were allowed to vote. The African National Congress was founded in 1912 in order to maintain voting rights for Coloreds (as persons of mixed race were called at the time) and Blacks in South Africa. In 1948 the majority Afrikaner National Party instituted a policy of rigid racial segregation called apartheid. The ANC Youth League, headed by Nelson Mandela, Walter Sisulu, and Oliver Tambo, initiated the Defiance Campaign, a program of nonviolent protests, strikes, boycotts, and marches. In the process, leaders of the movement became targets of police harassment and arrest.

In March of 1960, the Sharpville massacre became a turning point in the Defiance Campaign. The South African government declared the ANC illegal and it went underground and continued to organize its campaign against apartheid. The ANC announced the formation of an armed force called Umkhonto we Sizwe, with Mandela as its chief, to carry out acts of sabotage and guerrilla warfare. Mandela and other Umkhoto leaders were arrested in 1963 and were sentenced to life in prison and the liberation movement was banned. The Soweto uprising in 1976 inspired thousands of youths to join Umkhonto we Sizwe. As resistance mounted, the South African regime become more vicious. A national state of emergency was declared in 1986, under which hundreds of thousands of South Africans were detained and held.

In 1990, after years of international isolation, the government repealed the last of the laws upholding apartheid. South Africa legalized the ANC and released Mandela and other ANC leaders from prison. In 1993 the country extended voting rights to all races, and democratic elections were held the following year. Nelson Mandela, then head of the ANC, was elected president of South Africa, the first black ever to hold the office. Mandela ceded his position as head of the ANC to Thabo Mbeki in 1997.

took up temporary employment as a policeman at the mines and met Walter Sisulu, who encouraged him to study law. Mandela simultaneously enrolled for a B.A. degree by correspondence, which he obtained in 1942, and went on to study law at Witwatersrand University. Here he was exposed to Indian and white students and to radical, liberal, and **Africanist** thought. He joined the African National Congress (ANC) and in 1944 founded the ANC Youth League with Walter Sisulu and Oliver Tambo.

Africanist: allegiance to ideals, interests, and traditions of Africa.

In 1948 the Afrikaner National Party came into power and began institutionalizing racism as apartheid. A spate of racist laws were passed in quick succession, among them the Group Areas Act of 1950, which ultimately resulted in the uprooting of millions of Black, Colored, and Indian people, and the

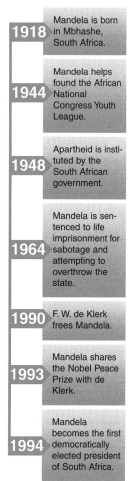

In the campaign that followed the national conference of antiapartheid groups in the early 1960s, Mandela went underground to facilitate his work and avoid arrest.

Bantu Education Act of 1953, designed to make sure that Africans remained menial laborers.

The ANC responded by adopting a program of militant action against the Nationalists. With Mandela on its executive committee, the ANC in 1951 organized a national work stoppage in cooperation with the Indian Congress. This was followed in 1952 with the Defiance of Unjust Laws Campaign, in which 8,577 volunteers defied racist laws and were imprisoned. The outbreak of violence and the six-month banning of fifty-two leaders, among them Mandela and the newly elected president-general of the ANC, Albert Lutuli, ended that campaign. Banning orders restricted the rights of movement and association. In 1953 Mandela was served with his second such order, this one for two years. A third, five-year, banning order came in 1956.

On June 25–26, 1955, the ANC and other antiapartheid organizations convened the Congress of the People in Kliptown, just outside Johannesburg, at which some 3,000 delegates adopted the Freedom Charter as a blueprint for a nonracial, democratic South Africa. Discontent within the ANC over the charter and alleged white and communist influence resulted in a split in 1958 and led to the formation of the Pan-African Congress (PAC) under the leadership of Robert Sobukwe. Meanwhile, the government declared the Freedom Charter a treasonable document and in 1956 brought to trial 156 key figures, among them Mandela and Lutuli. The trial continued until March 1961, when all of the accused against whom charges had not already been dropped were acquitted.

In 1960 a peaceful anti-pass demonstration organized by the PAC resulted in the massacre at Sharpeville, in which police killed sixty-nine protestors and injured 180. Blacks responded with a massive work stoppage; the government retaliated by declaring a state of emergency, banning the ANC and PAC and detaining thousands throughout the country, among them Mandela. After his release, he participated in the organization of a national conference of antiapartheid groupings against the government's intention to leave the British Commonwealth and establish a racist republic. In the campaign that followed the conference, he went underground to facilitate his work and avoid arrest and came to be known as the Black Pimpernel.

In 1961 Mandela, having reached the conclusion that the power of the Nationalists would never be broken through mass civil action alone, initiated Umkhonto we Sizwe (the Spear of the Nation) to organize sabotage against key state installations. December 1961 saw the first bomb blasts in South Africa against apartheid. Mandela left the country secretly and traveled to African nations incognito to raise funds and set up training bases for Umkhonto cadres. He himself underwent military training in Algeria and Tunisia.

Mandela returned to South Africa in July 1962, was arrested in August, and was sentenced in November to five years imprisonment, three for incitement to strike and two for leaving the country without a passport. In June 1964 he was sentenced to life imprisonment for sabotage and attempting to overthrow the state through violent revolution.

Mandela's personal life had seen drastic changes from 1957 to 1960. He and his first wife, Eveline, divorced in 1957. He married Winnie Madikizela in 1958, and by early 1960 they had two daughters. Imprisoned numerous times beginning in the late 1950s and subjected to a long series of bans, Winnie nonetheless persisted in her antiapartheid activities and contributed significantly in keeping her husband in the public eye. (The Mandelas were divorced in 1995. That year, Winnie Mandela was dismissed from her government position amid controversial charges of abuse of power.)

The antiapartheid struggle escalated in 1976 when African youth in the township of Soweto revolted against the enforcement of Afrikaans as a **medium** of instruction. The revolt spread to other parts of the country and brought out the workers. By 1985 the government was in crisis. In 1988 Mandela's condition of imprisonment improved significantly, and the government began negotiating with him. The last Afrikaner president, F. W. de Klerk, unbanned the ANC, PAC, and the South African Communist Party and released Mandela in 1990. (The two men shared the Nobel Prize for peace in 1993.) The first nonracial democratic elections followed in 1994, and Mandela was inaugurated as the first democratically elected president of the country. ◆

"I have cherished the ideal of a democratic and free society in which all persons live together in harmony and with equal opportunities. It is an ideal which I hope to live for and to achieve. But if needs be, it is an ideal for which I am prepared to die."
Nelson Mandela, 1964

medium: a method of conveying something.

Mann, Horace

MAY 4, 1796–AUGUST 2, 1859 ● EDUCATOR AND ADVOCATE FOR PUBLIC EDUCATION

Horace Mann, a pioneer in the development of free public schools, believed that education should be free and universal, nonsectarian, and democratic and that such education should be provided by well-trained professional teachers.

Mann grew up in an environment dominated by poverty and hardship. He was poorly schooled himself, but overcame a poor start to enter and graduate from Brown University with high honors in 1819. He graduated from a famous law school in Litchfield, Connecticut, and in 1823 he was admitted to the bar in Massachusetts. He served in the Massachusetts state legislature, first in the House and then in the Senate, from 1827 to 1837.

As president of the Senate, Mann supported and signed a new education law. The law created a new state board of education and authorized the board to have a full-time, paid secretary as its executive officer. Mann himself was named secretary in 1837 and undertook the job of remaking the state's public schools. Mann brought to his new duties such courage, vision, and wisdom that during the brief period of twelve years in which he held office, the Massachusetts school system was almost completely transformed. Massachusetts had been a pioneer in public schooling during the colonial period, but its schools were maintained by local towns and very few of them had professional teachers or good equipment. Mann's first task as secretary of the board was to increase public awareness of the purpose, value, and necessity of public education. With this end in view, he organized annual educational conventions in every county for the benefit of teachers, school officials, and the public. Realizing that there was little hope of any improvement in the schools apart from the improvement of the teaching profession, he rapidly implemented plans that led to the establishment of teachers' institutes and normal schools.

Mann led a reorganization of the public schools, with emphasis on the relation between local school boards and the state school board. As board secretary, he was able to promote adoption of new courses of study, new methods of teaching, and new systems of financing public schools. He pressed through a regulation that schools must be open at least six months a year. He was responsible for the first full-scale teacher training college in the United States, established at Lexington, Massachusetts, in 1839.

Horace Mann reentered politics in 1848 as a member of Congress from Massachusetts. After being defeated for reelection, he became president of Antioch College in Yellow Springs, Ohio. He served there from 1853 until his death.

Mann's lasting place in American history rests, however, on his services to public education. His influence in this field

1796 Mann is born.

1827 Mann serves in the Massachusetts state legislature.

1837 Mann is named secretary of the new state board of education.

1839 Mann founds the first full-scale teacher-training college in the United States.

1848 Mann becomes president of Antioch College in Ohio.

extended far beyond the boundaries of Massachusetts. Copies of his annual reports and other educational writings were widely disseminated throughout the United States with the result that one state after another sought and followed his advice. He also published a widely read magazine, *The Common School Journal*. Because of his efforts, public education began to flourish in the United States and has become a basic **tenet** of American democracy. ◆

tenet: principle.

Marshall, Thurgood

JULY 2, 1908–JANUARY 24, 1993 ● CIVIL RIGHTS LAWYER AND ASSOCIATE JUSTICE OF THE U.S. SUPREME COURT

Thurgood Marshall distinguished himself as a jurist in a wide array of settings. As the leading attorney for the National Association for the Advancement of Colored People (NAACP) between 1938 and 1961, he pioneered the role of professional civil rights advocate. As the principal architect of the legal attack against *de jure* racial segregation, Marshall oversaw the most successful campaign of social reform litigation in American history. As a judge on the United States Court of Appeals, solicitor general of the United States, and associate justice of the Supreme Court, he amassed a remarkable record as a public servant. Given the influence of his achievements over a long span of time, one can reasonably argue that Thurgood Marshall may have been the outstanding attorney of twentieth-century America.

Marshall was born in Baltimore, Maryland, where his father was a steward at an exclusive, all-white boat club, and his mother was an elementary school teacher. He attended public schools in Baltimore before proceeding to Lincoln University in Pennsylvania where he shared classes with, among others, Cabell "Cab" Calloway, the entertainer, Kwame Nkrumah, who became president of Ghana, and Nnamdi Azikiwe, who became president of Nigeria. After

1908 Marshall is born in Baltimore, Maryland.

1933 Marshall graduates first in his class from Howard University School of Law.

1939 Marshall becomes special counsel to the NAACP.

1954 In *Brown* v. *Board of Education* Marshall persuades the U.S. Supreme Court to rule that racial segregation is illegal.

1961 President John F. Kennedy nominates Marshall to a seat on the U.S. Court of Appeals for the Second Circuit in New York.

1967 President Lyndon B. Johnson nominates Marshall for a seat on the U.S. Supreme Court.

1993 Marshall dies.

"We may be losing the battle for equality because racism is broader and stronger than ever before."

Thurgood
Marshall, 1989

graduating, he was excluded from the University of Maryland School of Law because of racial segregation. Marshall attended the Howard University School of Law, where he fell under the tutelage of Charles Hamilton Houston. Houston elevated academic standards at Howard, turning it into a veritable hothouse of legal education, where he trained many of those who would later play important roles in the campaign against racial discrimination. Marshall graduated in 1933, first in his class.

After engaging in a general law practice for a brief period, Marshall was persuaded by Houston to pursue a career working as an attorney on behalf of the NAACP. Initially he worked as Houston's deputy and then, in 1939, he took over from his mentor as the NAACP's special counsel. In that position, Marshall confronted an extraordinary array of legal problems that took him from local courthouses, where he served as a trial attorney, to the Supreme Court of the United States, where he developed his skills as an appellate advocate. Over a span of two decades, he argued thirty-two cases before the Supreme Court, winning twenty-nine of them. He convinced the Court to invalidate practices that excluded blacks from primary elections (*Smith* v. *Allwright*, 1944), to prohibit segregation in interstate transportation (*Morgan* v. *Virginia*, 1946), to nullify convictions obtained from juries from which African Americans had been barred on the basis of their race (*Patton* v. *Mississippi*, 1947), and to prohibit state courts from enforcing racially restrictive real estate covenants (*Shelley* v. *Kraemer*, 1948).

Marshall's greatest triumphs arose, however, in the context of struggles against racial discrimination in public education. In 1950, in *Sweatt* v. *Painter*, he successfully argued that a state could not fulfill its federal constitutional obligation by hurriedly constructing a "Negro" law school that was inferior in tangible and intangible ways to the state's "white" law school. That same year he successfully argued in *McLaurin* v. *Oklahoma State Regents* that a state university violated the federal constitution by admitting an African-American student and then confining that student, on the basis of his race, to a specified seat in classrooms and a specified table in the school cafeteria. In 1954, in *Brown* v. *Board of Education*, Marshall culminated his campaign by convincing the Court to rule that racial segregation is invidious racial discrimination and thus invalid under the Fourteenth Amendment to the federal constitution.

In 1961, over the objections of white supremacist southern politicians, President John F. Kennedy nominated Marshall to a seat on the United States Court of Appeals for the Second Circuit in New York. Later, President Lyndon B. Johnson appointed Marshall to two positions that had never previously been occupied by an African American. In 1965 President Johnson appointed Marshall as Solicitor General, and in 1967 he nominated him to a seat on the Supreme Court.

Throughout his twenty-four years on the Court, Marshall was the most insistently liberal of the Justices, a stance that often drove him into dissent. His judgments gave broad scope to individual liberties (except in cases involving asserted claims to rights of property). Typically he supported claims of freedom of expression over competing concerns and scrutinized skeptically the claims of law enforcement officers in cases implicating federal constitutional provisions that limit the police powers of government. In the context of civil liberties, the most controversial positions that Marshall took involved rights over reproductive capacities and the death penalty. He viewed as unconstitutional laws that prohibit women from exercising considerable discretion over the choice to continue a pregnancy or to terminate it through abortion. Marshall also viewed as unconstitutional all laws permitting the imposition of capital punishment.

"Racism separates but it never liberates. Hatred generates fear, and fear, once given a foothold, binds, consumes and imprisons."
Thurgood Marshall, 1992

The other side of Marshall's **jurisprudential** liberalism was manifested by an approach to statutory and constitutional interpretation that generally advanced egalitarian policies. His judgments displayed an unstinting solicitude for the rights of labor, the interests of women, the struggles of oppressed minorities, and the condition of the poor. One particularly memorable expression of Marshall's empathy for the indigent is his dissent in *United States v. Kras* (1973), a case in which the Court held that a federal statute did not violate the Constitution by requiring a $50 fee of persons seeking the protection of bankruptcy. Objecting to the Court's assumption that, with a little self-discipline, the petitioner could readily accumulate the required fee, Marshall wrote that

jurisprudential: system of law.

In *Brown* v. *Board of Education* Marshall convinced the U.S. Supreme Court to rule that racial segregation is invalid under the Fourteenth Amendment of the federal Constitution.

> It may be easy for some people to think that weekly savings of less than $2 are no burden. But no one who has had close contact with poor people can fail to understand how close to the margin of survival many of them are . . . It is perfectly proper for judges to disagree about what the Constitution requires. But it is disgraceful for an interpretation of the Constitution to be premised upon unfounded assumptions about how people live.

Marshall retired from the Court in 1991, precipitating a contentious confirmation battle when President George Bush nominated as Marshall's successor Clarence Thomas, a conservative African-American jurist.

Marshall died on January 24, 1993. His extraordinary contributions to American life were memorialized in an outpouring of popular grief and adulation greater than that expressed for any previous justice. Marshall has been the object of some controversy since his death. Immediately after Marshall's death, a public debate opened over Marshall's instructions regarding his confidential Supreme Court papers. Ultimately, the Library of Congress opened them to public access without restriction. In 1996 newly uncovered documents demonstrated that Marshall had passed secret information to FBI Director J. Edgar Hoover during his years at the National Association for the Advancement of Colored People. These developments have not detracted from Marshall's heroic position in American history, in tribute to which he was honored by the erection of a statue in his native Baltimore in 1995. ◆

Menchú-Tum, Rigoberta

JANUARY 1959– ● GUATEMALAN CIVIL RIGHTS ACTIVIST

> *"It is said that our indigenous ancestors, Mayas and Aztecs, made human sacrifices to their gods. It occurs to me to ask: How many humans have been sacrificed to the gods of Capital in the last five hundred years?"*
>
> Rigoberta Menchú Tum, 1995

Rigoberta Menchú is a Maya-Quiché Indian woman from Guatemala and the first indigenous Latin American woman to win the Nobel Peace Prize. She is a member of the Coordinating Commission of the Committee of Peasant Unity (CUC) and a founding member of the United Representation of the Guatemalan Opposition (RUOG).

Menchú was born in Chimel, near San Miguel de Uspantán, to Vicente Menchú and Juana Tum, Maya peasants and Catholic lay leaders. Self-educated, from the age of eight she accompanied her parents to harvest export crops on south coast plantations, and later worked for two years as a domestic in Guatemala City. She participated with her parents in local pastoral activities.

In the 1970s expropriation of Indian land in El Quiché threatened Maya subsistence and prompted her family's political activism and involvement with the CUC. In the late 1970s

Menchú organized local self-defense groups, armed with rocks and machetes, in response to the government's escalated counter-insurgency war in the highlands. In January 1980 her father was burned to death in the occupation of the Spanish embassy in Guatemala City by campesinos with the support of trade unionists and students. Menchú continued organizing efforts in local Maya communities until forced to flee in 1981; since then she has lived in Mexico City.

A powerful speaker, Menchú has continued to work for peace and the rights of indigenous people in Guatemala in international forums. She has participated in the UN Working Group on Indigenous Populations, the UN Subcommission on Prevention of Discrimination and Protection for Minorities, and the UN Conference on the Decade of Women. She is a credentialed observer of the UN Human Rights Commission and the General Assembly. She serves on the board of the International Indian Treaty Council and was a member of honor at the Second Continental Gathering of the "500 Years of Resistance" Conference. Among other awards, she has received the 1988 Nonino Prize special award, the 1990 Monseñor Proaño Human Rights Prize, the 1990 UNESCO Education for Peace Prize, and the 1991 French Committee for the Defense of Freedoms and Human Rights prize. In 1992 she was awarded the Nobel Peace Prize. ◆

1959 Menchú is born in Chimel, Guatemala.

1979 Menchú organizes local self-defense groups against the government.

1980 Menchú's father is killed in Guatemala City.

1981 Menchú flees to Mexico.

1992 Menchú receives the Nobel Peace Prize.

Mfume, Kweisi

OCTOBER 24, 1948– ● POLITICIAN AND NAACP PRESIDENT

Before being appointed as president of the National Association for the Advancement of Colored People (NAACP), Kweisi Mfume was a disc jockey, a Baltimore City councilman, a United States representative, and the chair of the Congressional Black Caucus. He was also, by his own admission, a high-school dropout, an unmarried teenaged father of five, a gambler, and a small-time criminal. The story of how the boy from the mean streets of Baltimore became one of the most prominent African-American leaders of his day reads like a movie script.

Kweisi Mfume was born Frizzell Gray on October 24, 1948, in Turners Station, Maryland, an all-black enclave on the

"My decision to run for public office grew out of a simple desire to fight a system that most of the time exploited its weakest citizens."
Kweisi Mfume

The story of how the boy from the mean streets of Baltimore became one of the most prominent African American leaders of his day reads like a movie script.

1948 Mfume (Frizzell Gray) is born in Turners Station, Maryland.

1976 Mfume graduates magna cum laude from Morgan State.

1979 Mfume is elected to the Baltimore City Council.

1986 Mfume is elected to the U.S. Congress.

1992 Mfume is elected chair of the largest-ever Congressional Black Caucus.

1996 Mfume resigns from his congressional seat and becomes president of the NAACP.

shores of Chesapeake Bay, not far from Baltimore. Pee-Wee, as he was called by family and friends, was the oldest of four children born to Mary Elizabeth Willis. At the time of Mfume's birth, his mother was married to Clifton Gray, and until his mother's death sixteen years later Mfume believed Gray to be his biological father. Only after Mary Willis died did Mfume discover that his mother's friend, the kind man he knew as "Mr. Charlie" was his natural father.

When Mfume was eleven, Gray left the family and Mary Willis decided to move closer to her own family on the East Side of Baltimore. While the move made economic sense, it was hard on Mfume, who was suddenly uprooted from a friendly rural environment and transplanted to a tough urban world where he was daily forced to prove himself as a man.

Mfume was close to his mother, whom he credits for raising him with a strict moral and behavioral code. Thus, when Willis died of cancer in 1965, Mfume was cut adrift in more ways than one. He dropped out of school, worked three jobs, and in his spare time shot dice and worked as a courier in the numbers racket, an illegal gambling scheme popular among the urban poor. It was during this period that Mfume fathered five boys out of wedlock, by three different mothers.

In his autobiography, *No Free Ride*, Mfume says that he was saved from a life on the streets by an event that was nothing short of miraculous. One evening while shooting dice, he saw his mother in a vision that persuaded him to change his life and become the son she had wanted.

Mfume got his general education diploma (GED) and enrolled at Community College of Baltimore, where he was editor of the college newspaper and vice president of the Black Student Union. As he had changed his life, he decided to change his name as well. He became Kweisi Mfume, which is "conquering son of kings" in the Ibo language.

In 1972 the newly christened Mfume married Linda Shields. While going to school, he also worked as a disc jockey at WEBB, a radio station owned by singer James Brown. Mfume, who was supposed to be playing popular music, dubbed his program *Ebony Reflections* and often played music with a social message and read speeches by Malcom X and poems by Nikki Giovanni. Brown repeatedly tried to fire Mfume, who was saved from this fate by the station manager, who would literally hide Mfume whenever Brown came to town.

After completing two years at Baltimore Community College, Mfume transferred to Morgan State University to complete his bachelor's degree. He became involved in student government and helped launch the college's new radio station, WEAA. During this period Mfume and his wife drifted apart, and the marriage ended in divorce.

After graduating magna cum laude from Morgan State in 1976, he became program director for WEAA and hosted his own talk show. His criticism of Baltimore mayor William Donald Schaefer led listeners to encourage Mfume to run for city council against **incumbent** Emerson Julian. Mfume began his campaign by occupying Julian's chair at a council meeting and declaring to watching reporters and television cameras that he claimed the seat "for the people." In an unfortunate turn of events Julian died two months after the beginning of the campaign, and others entered the race. Nevertheless, on September 11, 1979, Kweisi Mfume was elected to the Baltimore city council by a three-vote margin. He served for seven years, during which time he continued to host his talk show and managed to complete a master's degree at Johns Hopkins University.

incumbent: existing officeholder.

In 1986 Mfume made a successful run for Maryland's 7th District congressional seat. His Republican opponent, the Reverend Saint George Crosse, tried to discredit Mfume by revealing that he had fathered five boys out of wedlock. Mfume, though he had not married the boys' mothers, had been an active, involved father, and his children were quick to rally to his defense, which caused Crosse's strategy to backfire.

Mfume quickly made a name for himself in Congress and in 1992 he was elected chair of the largest-ever Congressional Black Caucus. The Maryland congressman used his power to gain tax credits for the working poor and to persuade President Clinton to restore exiled Haitian president Jean-Bertrand Aristide to power.

Mfume used his power to gain tax credits for the working poor and to persuade President Clinton to restore exiled Haitian president Jean-Bertrand Aristide to power.

In a move that surprised many, Mfume resigned his congressional seat on February 18, 1996, and on February 20 took over as president of the NAACP, a post that had been vacant since 1994. Some thought Mfume unwise to give up a position of steadily increasing political power to head an organization that had suffered a loss of prestige over the years and that was heavily in debt. But Mfume took the challenge and began quickly to make many important changes. He erased the $3.5-million **deficit**, consolidated regional offices, computerized the

deficit: when spending exceeds revenue.

membership list, revived *The Crisis*, a publication begun by W. E. B. Du Bois, and established a new web page.

Mfume, never one to pass up a fight, relishes the challenges posed by his job. "I'm absolutely convinced," he says, "that there is a very special future ahead for us." ◆

Mitchell, Clarence Maurice, Jr.

MARCH 8, 1911–MARCH 18, 1984 ● LAWYER AND CIVIL RIGHTS LEADER

> *"In those days, Clarence Mitchell was called the 101st senator, but those of us who served here then knew full well that this magnificent lion in the lobby was a great deal more influential than most of us with seats in the chamber."*
>
> Senator Howard Baker, upon the death of Clarence Mitchell, 1984

Born in Baltimore, Maryland, Clarence Mitchell was the son of Clarence Maurice Mitchell, Sr., a chef in a fancy Annapolis restaurant, and Elsie Davis Mitchell. He attended Lincoln University in Pennsylvania, where he received an A.B. degree in 1932. The following year, he joined the *Baltimore Afro-American* as a reporter/columnist, covered the trials of the Scottsboro Boys, and reported on racial violence in Princess Anne County, Maryland. In 1934 he ran unsuccessfully for the Maryland House of Delegates on the socialist party ticket. In 1937 Mitchell spent a year doing graduate work at the Atlanta School of Social Work. That year, he briefly became Maryland State Director of the Negro National Youth Administration, during which time he married activist Juanita Jackson. The couple had four children, two of whom were later elected to local office in Baltimore.

In 1938 Mitchell was named executive secretary of the National Urban League branch in St. Paul, Minnesota, where he established his expertise in labor questions. In 1942 Mitchell became assistant director of Negro Manpower Service in the War Manpower Commission, and at the same time served on the Fair Employment Practices Committee (FEPC). The next year, he joined the FEPC full time, and became associate director of its Division of Field Operation. He supervised antidiscrimination efforts until it was disbanded in 1946.

In 1946 Mitchell joined the NAACP as labor secretary in the organization's Washington bureau, where he cemented ties with organized labor and lobbied for civil rights legislation. Mitchell organized the National Council for a Permanent FEPC, and pushed for enforcement of executive orders banning discrimination. In 1949 he blocked the United Nations Food and Agricultural Organization from locating at the University of Maryland because of discriminatory University practices. The following year, Mitchell became head of the bureau.

In November 1949 Mitchell called a National Emergency Civil Rights Mobilization conference, in order to form a broad-based, interracial pressure group for equality which would be built on the nucleus of the National Council for a permanent FEPC. In January 1950 delegates from sixty organizations met and formed a steering committee, the Leadership Conference on Civil Rights. Mitchell was appointed legislative chairman, and served in that role for the next twenty-eight years. As the chief civil rights lobbyist on Capitol Hill, Mitchell was such a ubiquitous figure in Congress that he was often known as "the 101st senator." A courteous, gentle man, Mitchell formed alliances with both Democrats (notably senator and later president Lyndon B. Johnson) and Republicans (such as Senator Everett Dirksen). In 1957 Mitchell marshaled support for a Civil Rights Bill, the first since Reconstruction. He aided the passage of the Civil Rights Acts in 1960, 1964, and 1968, as well as the 1965 Voting Rights Act and its extension in 1975.

Mitchell was known for his devotion to legal processes. He once explained that "when you have a law, you have an instrument that will work for you permanently," whereas private agreements were more **ephemeral**. He was also willing to protest personally against discrimination. In 1956, he became nationally known when he was arrested in Florence, Alabama, for using a whites-only door to the railroad station, an incident that became a cause célèbre. In 1958, he entered the University of Maryland's evening law school, where he obtained his law degree in 1962. In 1968 Mitchell opposed the efforts of civil rights supporters to procure an executive order banning housing discrimination, and pushed President Lyndon Johnson to recommend congressional legislation. For his success in bringing about the Civil Rights Act of 1968, which provided legal protection against discrimination in rental housing, the NAACP awarded him the Spingarn Medal in 1969.

In 1975 Mitchell was named a member of the United States delegation at the United Nations by President Gerald Ford. After his retirement in 1978 Mitchell served as a consultant and operated a law practice. In 1980 President Jimmy Carter awarded him the Presidential Medal of Freedom. He died in Washington, D.C., in 1984. The following year, the Baltimore city courthouse was named in his honor. ◆

1911 Mitchell is born in Baltimore, Maryland.

1945 Mitchell joins the NAACP as labor secretary in Washington.

1950 The Leadership Conference on Civil Rights is formed and Mitchell is appointed legislative chairman.

1969 Mitchell receives the NAACP's Spingarn Medal.

1980 Mitchell receives the Presidential Medal of Freedom.

1984 Mitchell dies in Baltimore.

ephemeral: lasting a short time.

Montezuma, Carlos

1865?–1923 ● NATIVE AMERICAN PHYSICIAN, EDITOR,
AND POLITICAL REFORMER

> "American Indians are not free. We are not free! We are hoodwinked, duped more and more every year; we are made to feel that we are free when we are not. We are chained hand and foot; we stand helpless, innocently waiting for the fulfillment of promises that will NEVER be fulfilled in the overwhelming great ocean of civilization."
>
> Carlos Montezuma, 1915

assimilate: to blend into a culture or society.

Carlos Montezuma, a Yavapai Indian, was born in Arizona. In 1871 he was captured by the Pima Indians who sold him to Carlos Gentile, a photographer. After traveling to New York with Gentile, Montezuma was raised by a series of white foster parents and eventually enrolled in the medical school at the University of Illinois. Following his graduation in 1889, he engaged in private practice and then joined the Indian Health Service. He worked in North Dakota, at the Western Shoshone Agency in Nevada, and finally at the Colville Agency in Washington. From 1894 to 1896 he served as the physician at Carlisle Indian School in Pennsylvania.

Montezuma resigned from the Indian Health Service to return to private practice in Chicago. He devoted much of the remainder of his career to social and political reform. Considerably influenced by the Progressive movement, he believed that the reservation system prevented Native Americans from acculturating and that residency on reservations isolated Indian people from the mainstream of American life. Along with other Native American Progressives, he blamed United States Indian policy and the Bureau of Indian Affairs for the Indians' failure to **assimilate** and charged that the BIA was staffed by "generally incompetent and broken-down white derelicts" who "squeezed the life-blood out of the Indians." He further asserted that only the abolition of the bureau and the reservation system would guarantee that Native American people would achieve an equitable position in American society.

Gertrude Simmons Bonnin, Charles Daganett, and other Indian Progressives formed the Society of American Indians in 1911; Montezuma waited two years before joining the group because of his fears that the Bureau of Indian Affairs had too much influence on the organization. In 1916 he began the publication of *Wassaja*, a journal advocating the abolition of the BIA and the integration of Indian people into the mainstream of American life. He continued to edit and publish *Wassaja* until 1922, when he became disenchanted with the society and charged that its leadership had lost its militancy and had acquiesced to the BIA.

Disillusioned by political fragmentation among the ranks of Indian Progressives and suffering from tuberculosis, Montezuma moved from Chicago to the Yavapais' Fort McDowell reservation in central Arizona in 1922. Although he previously had condemned the reservation system, he spent the final months of his life defending the Yavapais' residency at Fort McDowell. When the Bureau of Indian Affairs urged the Yavapais to join the Pimas on the Salt River reservation, Montezuma opposed the move and championed the Yavapais' claims to water from the Verde River. He died of tuberculosis at Fort McDowell.

Montezuma's life mirrored the hopes and frustrations of acculturated, educated Native Americans during the first quarter of the twentieth century. Influenced by the Progressive movement, they hoped to implement reform through the federal government but were thwarted by a federal bureaucracy reluctant to make any meaningful changes. Although the Society of American Indians proved ineffective at promoting reform, it did provide the foundation for other pan-Indian political movements that developed later in the century. ◆

1865 Montezuma is born in Arizona.

1889 Montezuma graduates from the University of Illinois medical school.

1894 Montezuma begins serving as physician at Carlisle Indian School in Pennsylvania.

1913 Montezuma joins the Society of American Indians.

1916 Montezuma begins publishing the journal *Wassaja*.

1923 Montezuma dies of tuberculosis at Fort McDowell.

Moreno, Luisa

1906–1992 ● POET AND TRADE UNION AND CIVIL RIGHTS ACTIVIST

Luisa Moreno was born in Guatemala. Her elite parents christened her Blanca Rosa Rodríguez López. (When she began organizing in the United States, she took the name Luisa Moreno.) As a teenager, Moreno moved to Mexico where she worked as a journalist and pursued her talents as a poet. At the age of twenty-one, she published her critically acclaimed collection of poems, *El Venedor de Cocuyos (Seller of Fire-flies)*, in Mexico City. That year, she married artist Angel De León, and the couple moved to New York City. In 1928 Moreno gave birth to her only child, a daughter, Mytyl.

During the Great Depression, Moreno struggled to support her infant daughter and unemployed husband by bending over a sewing machine in Spanish Harlem. She organized

Moreno became the first Latina vice president of a major U.S. labor union.

her *compañeras* into La Liga de Costureras, a Latina garment workers' union. In 1935 the American Federation of Labor hired her as a professional organizer. Leaving her abusive husband behind, Moreno, with Mytyl in tow, boarded a bus for Florida where she unionized African American and Latina cigar rollers. Within two years, she joined the Congress of Industrial Organizations (CIO), and in 1938 she became affiliated with the United Cannery, Agricultural, Packing, and Allied Workers of America (UCAPAWA-CIO).

From 1938 to 1947 Moreno organized Mexican farm and food-processing workers throughout the southwest. Her most notable success was among southern California cannery workers, 75 percent of whom were women. Under UCAPAWA, Mexican, Jewish, and Anglo women secured higher wages and innovative benefits including equal pay for equal work. During the 1940s Moreno became the first Latina vice president of a major U.S. labor union and the first Latina member of the California CIO Council.

Moreno also served as the principal organizer for the first national civil rights assembly among Latinos, El Congreso de Pueblos de Habla Española (Spanish-speaking Peoples' Congress). Meeting in Los Angeles in April 1939, Congreso delegates drafted a comprehensive platform. Many of its planks (for example, political representation, immigrants rights, and bilingual education) resonate with as much force today as they did more than a half century ago. El Congreso also called for an end to segregation in public facilities, housing, education, and employment. The projected national network of local chapters never developed, however, and the organization was further weakened by red-baiting.

From 1945 to 1950 UCAPAWA, which had become a target of conservative politicians and trade unionists, slowly disintegrated. Marrying former labor organizer Gray Bemis, Moreno retired from public life in 1947. A year later she faced deportation proceedings. Journalist Cary McWilliams and newspaper editor Ignacio López headed her defense committee. She was offered citizenship in exchange for testifying at the deportation hearing of labor leader Harry Bridges, but she refused to be "a free woman with a **mortgaged** soul." She left the United States in 1950 under terms listed as "voluntary departure under warrant of deportation" on the grounds that she had once been a member of the Communist party. After four decades of political

1906 Moreno is born in Guatemala.

1935 The American Federation of Labor hires Moreno as a professional organizer.

1939 El Congreso de Pueblos de Habla Espanola drafts a comprehensive platform; Moreno is a principal organizer.

1950 Moreno leaves the United States under warrant of deportation.

1992 Moreno dies in her native Guatemala.

mortgaged: subject to claim or obligation.

activism in Guatemala, Cuba, and Mexico, she died in her native Guatemala on November 4, 1992. ◆

Moses, Robert Parris

JANUARY 23, 1935– ● CIVIL RIGHTS ACTIVIST AND EDUCATOR

Bob Moses was born in New York City and raised in Harlem. He graduated from Hamilton College in 1956 and began graduate work in philosophy at Harvard University, receiving his M.A. one year later. Forced to leave school due to his mother's death, Moses taught mathematics at a private school in New York City. He first became active in the Civil Rights Movement in 1959, when he worked with Bayard Rustin, a prominent Southern Christian Leadership Conference (SCLC) activist, on organizing a youth march for integrated schools. A meeting with civil rights activist Ella Baker inspired Moses to immerse himself in the civil rights movement that was sweeping the South. In 1960 Moses joined the Student Nonviolent Coordinating Committee (SNCC) and became the fledgling organization's first full-time voter registration worker in the deep south.

Moses, who often worked alone facing many dangerous situations, was arrested and jailed numerous times. In McComb, Mississippi, he spearheaded black voter registration drives and organized Freedom Schools. He grew to play a more central role in SNCC, and in 1962 he became the strategical coordinator and project director of the Congress of Federated Organizations (COFO)—a statewide coalition of the Congress of Racial Equality (CORE), SNCC, and the National Association for the Advancement of Colored People (NAACP). In 1963, COFO, with Moses as the guiding force, launched a successful **mock** gubernatorial election campaign—"the Freedom Ballot"—in which black voters were allowed to vote for candidates of their choosing for the first time. Its success led Moses to champion an entire summer of voter registration and educational activities to challenge racism and segregation in 1964, the Freedom Summer, with the purpose of capturing national attention forcing federal intervention in Mississippi.

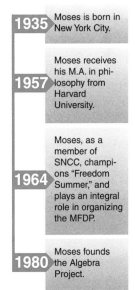

1935 Moses is born in New York City.

1957 Moses receives his M.A. in philosophy from Harvard University.

1964 Moses, as a member of SNCC, champions "Freedom Summer," and plays an integral role in organizing the MFDP.

1980 Moses founds the Algebra Project.

mock: imitation.

During the Freedom Summer, Moses played an integral role in organizing and advising the Mississippi Freedom Democratic Party.

During the Freedom Summer, Moses played an integral role in organizing and advising the Mississippi Freedom Democratic Party (MFDP)—an alternative third party that challenged the legitimacy of the all-white Democratic party delegation at the Democratic National Convention in Atlantic City. After the 1964 summer project came to an end, SNCC erupted in factionalism. Moses's staunch belief in the Christian idea of a beloved community, nonhierarchical leadership, grassroots struggle, local initiative, and pacifism made him the leading ideologue in the early years of SNCC. Finding himself unwillingly drawn into the factional struggle, Moses left the organization and ended all involvement in civil rights activities. Later that year, he adopted Parris—his middle name—as his new last name, to elude his growing celebrity.

A conscientious objector to the Vietnam War, Moses fled to Canada to avoid the draft in 1966. Two years later he traveled with his family to Tanzania, where he taught mathematics. In 1976 Moses returned to the United States and resumed his graduate studies at Harvard University. Supplementing his children's math education at home, however, led him away from the pursuit of his doctorate and back into the classroom. In 1980 he founded the Algebra Project, with grants received from a MacArthur Fellowship, to help underprivileged children get an early grounding in mathematics to better their job opportunities in the future.

Moses viewed the Algebra Project—whose classes were directly modeled on Freedom Schools and Citizenship Schools from the early 1960s—as an integral continuation of his civil rights work. He personally oversaw all teacher training to insure that the emphasis was placed on student empowerment, rather than dependence on the teachers. Creating a five-step learning method to help children translate their concrete experiences into complex mathematical concepts, Moses pioneered innovative methods designed to help children become independent thinkers. After proven success in raising students' standardized test scores in Massachusetts public schools, the project branched out to schools in Chicago, Milwaukee, Oakland, and Los Angeles, and Moses was once again propelled into the public eye. In 1992, in what he saw as a spiritual homecoming, Moses returned to the same areas of Mississippi where he had registered African-American voters three decades earlier, and launched the Delta Algebra project to help ensure a brighter future for children of that impoverished region. ◆

"One of the central things we're saying is that the ongoing struggle for citizenship and equality for minority people is now linked to an issue of math and science literacy."
Robert P. Moses, 1994

Mother Teresa

AUGUST 27, 1910–SEPTEMBER 5, 1997 ● NOBEL PRIZE WINNER AND MISSIONARY

Mother Teresa was a Roman Catholic nun who received the 1979 Nobel Peace Prize for her work with the poor. She was admired around the world for her compassion and for her commitment to providing care and comfort to the poor, the sick, the destitute, and the dying.

Mother Teresa was born Agnes Gonxha Bojaxhiu on August 26, 1910, to Nikola and Dranafile (Bernai) Bojaxhiu in Skopje, in what is now Macedonia. Her father was a building contractor and merchant, and her family was among the small minority of Roman Catholics in a predominantly Muslim region. Dranafile was deeply religious and she took her three children to church daily. She was known for her hospitality to the poor, who would frequently join the Bojaxhiu family for meals. In 1917 Agnes's father died, and her mother, left to support three children, set up a business selling embroidered red cloth.

As a child, Agnes was tidy, obedient, and thoughtful. She enjoyed praying and liked to be in church. After school hours she was engaged in church activities. She joined a Christian society for girls, and at meetings she learned about the lives of saints, and sometimes heard inspiring letters from missionaries who worked among the poor and sick in India.

Agnes first felt her life's calling as a nun at the age of twelve. She decided to become a missionary nun in India, and at eighteen, she left home to join the Sisters of Loreto, an Irish Catholic order with a mission in Calcutta, India. After a few months of training and learning English in Dublin she was sent to Darjeeling at the foot of the Himalayas in India, where she took her initial vows as a nun in 1929 and took the name Teresa. In 1937 she committed herself to her vows of poverty, chastity, and obedience, and became Sister Teresa.

After taking her vows Sister Teresa taught at St. Mary's High School outside Calcutta. The suffering and poverty she

> *"I must be willing to give whatever it takes not to harm other people and, in fact, to do good to them. This requires that I be willing to give until it hurts. Otherwise, there is not true love in me and I bring injustice, not peace, to those around me."*
>
> Mother Teresa, 1994

witnessed on the streets of Calcutta deeply impressed her, and she felt inspired to work among the poor in the slums of Calcutta. In 1948 she left the Loreto community, exchanged her convent habit for a simple white sari with a blue border, and began her life's work among the poor. She became an Indian citizen that year at the age of thirty-eight.

Mother Teresa began her work by first learning nursing, feeling that medical training was indispensable to her task of caring for people. Her first facility for the poor was an open-air school for homeless children. She gradually expanded her work, joined by volunteers and supported by donations from various religious organizations, individuals, and the government.

In 1950 Mother Teresa received permission from the church to start her own order, "The Missionaries of Charity," whose main task was to love and care for people in need. Over the years she set up orphanages, schools in slums, and homes for sick and dying homeless people. In all her endeavors Mother Teresa emphasized the importance of giving the deprived and the sick a feeling of dignity through personal contact. The order grew tremendously and by the early 1990s it comprised about 4,000 nuns and novices, 400 priests and brothers, and hundreds of thousands of lay workers. It worked at 450 sites throughout the world, including shelters for the homeless, centers for the malnourished, hospices for lepers, mobile health clinics, homes for drug addicts and alcoholics, and relief centers for people hit by natural catastrophe.

One of her best known missions abroad occurred in 1982 when Mother Teresa traveled to war-torn Beirut to assist the war victims there. At that time the city was crippled by fighting between the Muslims and the Christians. Crossing the line that separated Christian East Beirut from Muslim West Beirut, she rescued dozens of mentally ill Muslim children who were trapped in a hospital without food or water.

Mother Teresa's work drew considerable attention throughout the world, and she received a number of awards, including the Pope John XXIII Peace Prize in 1971 and India's Jawaharlal Nehru Award for International Understanding in 1972 for her promotion of international peace and understanding. She also received the 1979 Nobel Peace Prize for her work to overcome poverty and distress in the world, which the Nobel Committee recognized as a constant threat to peace. Mother Teresa used the prize money that accompanied the award—the equivalent of $190,000—for building homes for the **destitute**.

1910 Mother Teresa is born Agnes Gonxa Bojaxhiu in Uskup in present-day Macedonia.

1928 Agnes joins the Sisters of Loretto.

1937 Agnes takes her final vows and chooses the name Teresa.

1948 Teresa leaves the convent to work with the poor.

1950 Teresa and her helpers form the Missionaries of Charity.

1966 Mother Teresa's work becomes widely noticed when she is interviewed on the BBC.

1997 Mother Teresa dies in Calcutta.

destitute: lacking possessions and resources.

Mother Teresa was not without critics. Some were concerned that she was trying to idealize poverty. Others were dismayed by her strong opposition to abortion, divorce, and the use of contraceptives. She was also criticized for her view that women belonged in the home.

Most people, however, knew Mother Teresa for her piety, humility, organizational talents, energy, and practicality. Throughout the years she declined offers of regular income, because she did not want her work to become a business. She also forbade fund-raising at her order, partly because such an activity would require accounting and would take away from time spent with the needy. She and her order lived a life of poverty, eating the same food as the poor and typically rising at 4:40 A.M. and working until 9 P.M. with only thirty minutes rest. The women who joined her order were expected to sever family ties and only return home on a rare occasion to attend an important family event. A cheerful disposition was required of all who worked with her, as was a show of respect for the worth and dignity of the individual human being.

In 1990 Mother Teresa experienced heart problems that caused her to resign as head of her order. But the order could not agree on a successor and reelected her to her post. In March 1997 her failing health caused her to step down from her post. She died in Calcutta on September 5, 1997, after suffering cardiac arrest. ◆

> Most people know Mother Teresa for her piety, humility, organizational talents, energy, and practicality.

Mott, Lucretia Coffin

JANUARY 3, 1793–NOVEMBER 11, 1880 ● ABOLITIONIST AND WOMEN'S
RIGHTS REFORMER

L ucretia Mott was a leader of the American abolitionist movement as well as instrumental in pioneering women's rights. Mott's parents were Quakers, as were most of her forebears. She was a student and then a teacher at the Friends' boarding school in Poughkeepsie, New York. In 1811 she returned home to Philadelphia where she married James Mott, a fellow teacher at Nine Points and her father's business partner. She became a minister of the Society of Friends and was known as an eloquent speaker. Many of her sermons and speeches concerned social reform, especially temperance, peace, women's rights, and antislavery.

> *"There is nothing of greater importance to the well-being of society at large—of man as well as woman—than the true and proper position of woman."*
>
> Lucretia Mott, 1849

Mott became quite active in the abolitionist movement. In 1833 she helped found the American Anti-Slavery Society and the Philadelphia Female Anti-Slavery Society. She took a public stand against slavery at a time when some Quaker leaders did not oppose slavery, so she was at the center of a controversy among her own religious colleagues. In 1840 Mott went to London as a delegate to the World Anti-Slavery Convention. The men who controlled the meeting refused to seat her and the other women delegates. Mott met Elizabeth Cady Stanton at the convention and the two women were furious about the rebuff, vowing to take action about the unjust treatment of women.

Mott helped Stanton organize the first women's rights convention, held on July 19 and 20, 1848, in Seneca Falls, New York.

Quakers

Throughout its history, the Society of Friends (commonly known as Quakers) has called for peace, nonviolence, and social equality. The early Quakers were distinguished by a belief in the "inner light," or indwelling of God, in every individual; pacifism; simplicity of dress; the use of "yes" or "no" instead of taking a legally required oath; and a refusal to tip their hats to social superiors.

William Penn, a wealthy Quaker who was disturbed by the persecution of the Friends in England, resolved to establish a refuge for his fellow believers in the New World. After receiving the colony of Pennsylvania from Charles II in 1681 in payment of a debt of £16,000 owed to his father by the crown, he began his "holy experiment," a colony devoted to full religious toleration. Under his protection the Quaker community in Pennsylvania moved from intense mysticism to practical, ethical religion and middle-class respectability. During the 18th century the Quakers became progressively more concerned with the issue of slavery and under the leadership of such "traveling friends" as John Woolman managed to end the evil among their own membership by about 1785. Pennsylvania Quakers established the first antislavery society in 1775.

Famous Quakers include Lucretia Mott, a leader of the abolitionist and women's rights movements in the United States; Susan B. Anthony, a reformer and one of the first leaders in the women's suffrage movement; and John Greenleaf Whittier, often referred to as the "Quaker poet," because his poems show the influence of his Quaker upbringing.

The convention launched the women's rights movement in the United States. Mott and Stanton remained an influence in that movement for many years.

Mott continued to speak out for abolition and women's rights for the rest of her life. She lectured widely and served as president of the Philadelphia Anti-Slavery Society. After the passage of the Fugitive Slave Law of 1850, the Motts' home became a sanctuary for runaway slaves. ◆

Muhammad, Elijah

OCTOBER 10, 1897–FEBRUARY 25, 1975   ● RELIGIOUS LEADER

Born Robert Poole in Sandersville, Georgia, Muhammad was one of thirteen children of an itinerant Baptist preacher and sharecropper. In 1919 he married Clara Evans and they joined the black migration to Detroit, where he worked in the auto plants. In 1931 he met Master Wallace Fard (or Wali Farad), founder of the Nation of Islam, who eventually chose this devoted disciple as his chief aide. Fard named him "Minister of Islam," dropped his slave name, Poole, and restored his true Muslim name, Muhammad. As the movement grew, a Temple of Islam was established in a Detroit storefront. It is estimated that Fard had close to 8,000 members in the Nation of Islam, consisting of poor black migrants and some former members from Marcus Garvey's Universal Negro Improvement Association and Noble Drew Ali's Moorish Science Temple.

After Fard mysteriously disappeared in 1934, the Nation of Islam was divided by internal schisms and Elijah Muhammad led a major faction to Chicago, where he established Temple of Islam No. 2 as the main headquarters for the Nation. He also instituted the worship of Master Fard as Allah and himself as the Messenger of Allah and head of the Nation of Islam, always addressed with the title "the Honourable." Muhammad built on the teachings of Fard and combined aspects of Islam and Christianity with the black nationalism of Marcus Garvey into a "proto-Islam," an unorthodox Islam with a strong racial slant. The Honorable Elijah Muhammad's message of racial separation focused on the recognition of true black identity and stressed economic independence. "Knowledge of self" and "do

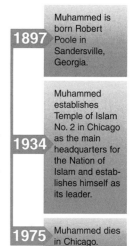

1897 Muhammed is born Robert Poole in Sandersville, Georgia.

1934 Muhammed establishes Temple of Islam No. 2 in Chicago as the main headquarters for the Nation of Islam and establishes himself as its leader.

1975 Muhammed dies in Chicago.

"The education and training of our children must not be limited to the 'Three R's' only. It should instead include the history of the black nation, the knowledge of civilizations of man and the Universe, and all sciences."

Elijah Muhammed, 1962

for self" were the rallying cries. The economic ethic of the Black Muslims has been described as a kind of black puritanism—hard work, frugality, the avoidance of debt, self-improvement, and a conservative lifestyle. Muhammad's followers sold the Nation's newspaper, *Muhammad Speaks,* and established their own educational system of Clara Muhammad schools and small businesses such as bakeries, grocery stores, and outlets selling fish and bean pies. More than 100 temples were founded. The disciples also followed strict dietary rules outlined in Muhammad's book *How to Eat to Live,* which enjoined one meal per day and complete abstention from pork, drugs, tobacco, and alcohol. The Nation itself owned farms in several states, a bank, trailer trucks for its fish and grocery businesses, an ultramodern printing press, and other assets.

Muhammad's ministers of Islam found the prisons and streets of the ghetto a fertile recruiting ground. His message of self-reclamation and black manifest destiny struck a responsive chord in the thousands of black men and women whose hope and self-respect had been all but defeated by racial abuse and denigration. As a consequence of where they recruited and the militancy of their beliefs, the Black Muslims have attracted many more young black males than any other black movement.

Muhammad had an uncanny sense of the vulnerabilities of the black psyche during the social transitions brought on by two world wars; his *Message to the Black Man in America* diagnosed the problem as a confusion of identity and self-hatred caused by white racism. The cure he prescribed was radical surgery through the formation of a separate black nation. Muhammad's 120 "degrees," or lessons, and the major doctrines and beliefs of the Nation of Islam all elaborated on aspects of this central message. The white man is a "devil by nature," absolutely unredeemable and incapable of caring about or respecting anyone who is not white. He is the historic, persistent source of harm and injury to black people. The Nation of Islam's central theological myth tells of Yakub, a black mad scientist who rebelled against Allah by creating the white race, a weak, hybrid people who were permitted temporary dominance of the world. Whites achieved their power and position through devious means and "tricknology." But, according to the Black Muslim apocalyptic view, there will come a time in the not-too-distant future when the forces of good and the forces of evil—that is to say, blacks versus whites—will clash in a "Battle of Armageddon," and the blacks will emerge victorious to

The Black Muslims have attracted many more young black males than any other black movement.

recreate their original hegemony under Allah throughout the world.

After spending four years in a federal prison for encouraging draft refusal during World War II, Elijah Muhammad was assisted by his chief protégé, Minister Malcolm X, in building the movement and encouraging its rapid spread in the 1950s and 1960s. During its peak years, the Nation of Islam had more than half a million devoted followers, influencing millions more, and accumulated an economic empire worth an estimated $80 million. Besides his residence in Chicago, Muhammad also lived in a mansion outside of Phoenix, Arizona, since the climate helped to reduce his respiratory problems. He had eight children with his wife, Sister Clara Muhammad, but also fathered a number of illegitimate children with his secretaries, a circumstance that was one of the reasons for Malcolm X's final break with the Nation of Islam in 1964.

With only a third-grade education, Elijah Muhammad was the leader of the most enduring black **militant** movement in the United States. He died in Chicago and was succeeded by one of his six sons, Wallace Deen Muhammad. After his death, Muhammad's estate and the property of the Nation were involved in several lawsuits over the question of support for his illegitimate children. ◆

With only a third grade education, Elijah Muhammed was the leader of the most enduring black militant movement in the United States.

militant: aggressive.

Muir, John

APRIL 21, 1838–DECEMBER 24, 1914 ● CONSERVATIONIST

The most influential **conservationist** in America, John Muir first explored the wilderness as an escape from the grim and austere home of his fanatically Calvinist father. His experiences in the schools of his native Scotland were no better, although his teachers recognized him as exceptionally bright. The educational system, he later wrote, was "founded on leather." Muir's escapes into the out-of-doors germinated lifelong habits. "When I was a boy in Scotland," his autobiography revealed, "I was fond of everything that was wild, and all my life I've been growing fonder and fonder of wild places and wild creatures."

His family's move to Wisconsin in 1849 placed Muir beyond the reaches of public schools, but he taught himself

conservationist: a person who advocates preservation of natural resources.

John Muir

1838 John Muir is born in Scotland.

1890 Yosemite National Park is created.

1892 Muir and friends found the Sierra Club, dedicated to the preservation of the Yosemite and Sierra wilderness areas.

1914 Muir dies.

1916 The National Park Service is created.

advanced mathematics and developed a passion for reading, especially the travels of western explorer Alexander von Humboldt. A tinkerer and an inventor, Muir won first place in a science competition in Madison, Wisconsin, in 1860. He caught the attention of a University of Wisconsin professor, who invited Muir to take classes. At the university, he discovered the Transcendentalist writings of Ralph Waldo Emerson and Henry David Thoreau and the scientific writings of Louis Agassiz and Asa Gray, all of which had a profound impact on his thinking. Muir left school in his junior year to begin a series of "wanderings"; the first trek took him through southeastern Canada and the north-central United States. Supporting himself with odd jobs that allowed time for his wilderness studies, Muir next traveled, in 1867, from Indiana to Cedar Key, Florida, a journey he recorded along with his environmental observations as "A Thousand-Mile Walk to the Gulf."

Muir moved to California and its Yosemite Valley in 1868, where he lived intermittently for several years, traipsing the mountains and recording his observations of their geology and botany. Recalling the glaciology lessons of his college days, Muir concluded that the Yosemite Valley was a product of glacial actions, not the result of cataclysmic convulsions as many believed. The articles he published on his theories earned him the scorn of some (he was labeled an "ignoramus" by leading geologists), but twentieth-century science explorations of the valley proved him correct.

In the mid-1870s Muir began studies of the great sequoias. He concluded that rather than seeking out wet areas, the giant trees actually created such areas by capturing water that would otherwise roar on to lower regions in destructive floods. In practical terms, Muir saw the destruction of the Sierra forests by lumber companies as a threat not only to the region's beauty but also to the maintenance of the region's watershed. His long campaign for a federal forest-conservation policy resulted from his studies.

Throughout the late 1870s Muir explored Washington, Oregon, and Utah. The lure of unknown Alaska, purchased by the United States in 1865, was so great that Muir postponed his engagement to his future wife, Louis Wanda. He headed off for his first of five trips to Alaska in May 1879.

Muir became a successful farmer in the 1880s, but in his prosperity, he continued his writing on and advocacy of environmental causes. He fought for the establishment of Yosemite National Park, created in 1890. Two years later Muir and friends founded the Sierra Club. Originally an alpine club encouraging camping and climbing, the new organization was dedicated to the preservation of the Yosemite and Sierra wilderness areas. Muir served as its first president and led the fight against big business's designs on Yosemite's lumber, mining, and grazing resources.

The Sierra Club's success, however, was short-lived. By 1900 San Francisco began casting about for more water for its growing population. The city settled on the Hetch Hetchy Valley, northeast of Yosemite Valley. The dam the city proposed would create a reservoir that fluctuated 240 feet for each season, turning the beautiful valley into a monstrous eyesore. Preservationists initially blocked court applications for the use of the valley, but by 1905 Gifford Pinchot announced that President Theodore Roosevelt's administration would support the dam's construction. The Sierra Club continued the battle against the "Hetch Hetchy Steal," as it was called, but the dam was built in 1913.

Muir, however, had other successes. President Grover Cleveland established thirteen forest reserves in 1897 to protect the lands from commercial exploitation. After President Roosevelt joined Muir in a camping trip through Yosemite in 1903, the president began his conservation programs in earnest. Muir's work and his Sierra Club influenced the creation of the National Park Service in 1916, but Muir himself had died two years before.

> *"Thousands of tired, nerve-shaken, over-civilized people are beginning to find out that going to the mountains is going home; that wildness is a necessity; and that mountain parks and reservations are useful not only as fountains of timber and irrigating rivers, but as fountains of life."*
> John Muir, 1875

Muir fought for the establishment of Yosemite National Park, created in 1890.

"Who publishes the sheet-music of the winds or the music of water written in river-lines?"

John Muir, 1875

John Muir ardently believed that a nation of increasingly urbanized people—"tired, nerve-shaken, over-civilized"—required wilderness areas as a respite from their city lives. His writings, more than sixty-five magazine articles and four books, as well as his advocacy sparked tremendous growth in the environmental field in the late 1800s and early 1900s. His leadership of the Sierra Club helped turn the organization into a powerful lobby for the protection of the environment and wilderness lands. His influence was hardly diminished a century later. ◆

Myrdal, Alva

JANUARY 31, 1902–FEBRUARY 1, 1986 ● NOBEL PEACE PRIZE WINNER, AUTHOR, AND DIPLOMAT

Alva Myrdal received the 1982 Nobel Peace Prize, along with Alfonso García Robles of Mexico, for her work in the international movement toward disarmament. Myrdal headed the Swedish delegation to the United Nations Disarmament Committee from 1962 and had written one of the best books on the disarmament race, *The Game of Disarmament.*

The list of Alva Myrdal's accomplishments over her long life is all the more remarkable because her record of achievement was made in a man's world. She pointed out: "I had not held my first important position until I was almost forty years old." Thereafter she had carried on two careers of distinction, one in her own country and one abroad, before she took up the cause of disarmament at the age of fifty-nine.

She and her husband first won acclaim as scholars and social reformers. She was a sociologist and educator, and Gunnar Myrdal was an economist who later won the Nobel Memorial Prize in Economics (they are the only married couple who won Nobel prizes in different fields). Together the Myrdals played an important role in the shaping of the Swedish welfare state. Later their individual work made it necessary for them to live apart for some periods, but they tried to make these as short as possible.

Alva Reimer was born in Uppsala in 1902, the daughter of a self-taught building contractor who was a Social Democrat and active in social welfare matters and the cooperative movement. She grew up in the little town of Eskilstuna, where very

"I have, despite all disillusionment, never, never allowed myself to feel like giving up. This is my message today; it is not worthy of a human being to give up."

Alva Myrdal, 1980

Alva Myrdal in 1982, after winning the Nobel Peace Prize.

early her qualities of mind and spirit became apparent. She developed a passion for reading, and a friendly secondhand book dealer let her read anything she chose. Girls in Eskilstuna were supposed to finish the seventh grade at age fourteen and then prepare themselves to be farmers' wives. The high school was only for boys. But Alva was determined to continue her education. She learned office skills in a commercial school and when she was fifteen, she took a job in the local tax office, operating an adding machine. For two years she saved her earnings, spending money only for books and to contribute to the family income. Then she persuaded her father to talk the local school board into setting up classes for a group of girls, the same courses that the boys were taking, but for a tuition fee, and the girls were not allowed in the school buildings.

On one summer day three university students on a bicycling trip stopped at the Reimer farm and asked to sleep in the hayloft. One was a law student named Gunnar Myrdal, who was much taken with this highly intelligent and beautiful young woman, as was she with him, so much so that she did something unheard of. Not telling her parents, she accepted his invitation to join the bicycle tour.

The Myrdals played an important role in the shaping of the Swedish welfare state.

With Gunnar's encouragement, Alva made her way to Stockholm University. She received her degree in 1924, when she was twenty-two, and in the same year she and Gunnar were married. They were to be parents of a son and two daughters.

In the following years they pursued advanced studies in Stockholm, London, Leipzig, Geneva, and the United States, before settling down in Sweden in 1932. In 1934 they published *The Crisis of the Population Question,* which had an important influence on social policies throughout Scandinavia and led to Alva Myrdal's participation in government commissions on population and housing.

In 1936 Alva Myrdal founded the Training College for Nursery and Kindergarten Teachers and directed its work until 1948, gaining a reputation as an expert in early childhood education. A member of the Social Democratic party, she served on its program planning committee and also on a number of government commissions. At the same time, she was prominent in the struggle for equal rights for women.

From 1938 to 1940 she accompanied her husband to the United States, where Gunnar Myrdal was engaged in research for his classic study of American race relations, *An American Dilemma.* She was busy with her own projects, lecturing, writing and investigating American education and social problems. In 1939 the Swedish government appointed her to the board responsible for Swedish participation in the New York World's Fair.

During the Second World War, in which Sweden remained **neutral**, Alva Myrdal became concerned with the plight of refugees both in her own country and elsewhere in Europe. For her war work she was later decorated by both Finland and Norway.

After the war Alva Myrdal entered upon a second career, in international relations. She was an early supporter of the United Nations Organization and served on the board of the World Federation of United Nations Associations. In 1949 she was appointed director of the UN Department of Social Affairs and was the highest ranking woman in the UN Secretariat. In 1951 she moved to UNESCO as the director of the Department of Social Services.

In the councils of these world bodies Alva Myrdal showed such unusual skill in dealing with people in international relationships that in 1955 the Swedish government appointed her as ambassador to India, with responsibilities for the neighboring countries as well. Swedish businessmen were at first apprehen-

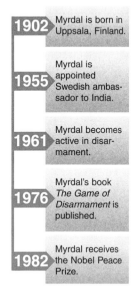

1902 Myrdal is born in Uppsala, Finland.

1955 Myrdal is appointed Swedish ambassador to India.

1961 Myrdal becomes active in disarmament.

1976 Myrdal's book *The Game of Disarmament* is published.

1982 Myrdal receives the Nobel Peace Prize.

neutral: not engaged on either side.

sive because of her socialist background, but they were soon applauding her expertise in trade matters. She achieved a special relationship with Prime Minster Jawaharlal Nehru and cultivated wide acquaintanceships throughout Indian society. Her diplomatic reports on India were considered models.

It was in March 1961, after her service in India had ended, that Alva Myrdal was "drafted" into disarmament, as she put it. She was then at the disposal of the Foreign Office, with the title of ambassador-at-large, and the foreign minster, who was looking toward his final appearance at the UN General Assembly, asked her to serve as his special assistant on disarmament and to draft a speech on that subject for him. She replied that she had no detailed knowledge of disarmament and asked for two weeks to study the subject before the appointment became public. Her inventive mind came up with four proposals, of which he selected one on nuclear-free zones. She emerged from the exercise so engaged with the problem that she declared, "Disarmament is my main preoccupation for the foreseeable future."

In 1962 she became a member of the upper chamber of the Swedish parliament and was invited to join the cabinet, first without portfolio and then as minister both for disarmament and for church affairs. She was a member of the cabinet for twelve years in all and was fondly called the "Grand Old Lady of Swedish Politics." In the cabinet and in the parliament she had an important influence on Sweden's **unilateral** renunciation in 1968 of nuclear weapons and shortly thereafter all chemical and biological means of warfare. In 1973, at the age of seventy-one, she resigned from all her government positions.

From 1962 to 1973 she was a member of the Swedish delegation to the UN General Assembly, serving on the Political Committee, where disarmament matters were dealt with. Also during these years she headed the Swedish delegation to the UN Disarmament Committee in Geneva, where she became the leader of the representatives from **nonaligned** nations. Now in her sixties, she cut a striking figure in these UN meetings in New York and Geneva. Small and vivacious, her fair hair now gray, her blue eyes alight and her bright laughter always at the ready, she combined charm with determination, and, with an impressive mastery of scientific and technical detail, she used her powers of analysis and explication with convincing effect. They called her "the conscience of the disarmament movement," and the U.S. representative to the Political Committee

Myrdal's colleagues in the UN called her "the conscience of the disarmament movement."

unilateral: done by one side or one person.

nonaligned: not allied with any nation.

later remarked, "I bear many scars testifying to her effectiveness."

On the basis of this experience she produced one of the best studies of the nuclear arms race ever written, *The Game of Disarmament*, published in 1976. Her sharp critique of the superpowers as chiefly responsible for the failure of disarmament efforts was underlined in the subtitle, *How the United States and Russia Run the Arms Race*. While her many articles and books brought home the nuclear danger and made carefully considered recommendations for reasonable policies, she was at the same time particularly proud of some "concrete" achievements. She had successfully prevailed upon her government to appropriate funds both for seismological research to improve verification techniques for observing test ban treaties and for the establishment of the Swedish International Peace Research Institute, aimed at **buttressing** peace and disarmament efforts with scholarly data and documentation.

buttressing: strengthening a cause.

Alva Myrdal used her half of the Nobel prize, the equivalent of $78,500, for peace causes and to provide herself with a secretary. She continued to work for peace as long as she was able, writing, sending out copies of the 1982 edition of *The Game of Disarmament*, even making appearances at peace demonstrations in Stockholm. During the last two years of her life she was hospitalized, and she died in February 1986, the day after her eighty-fourth birthday. ◆

Nader, Ralph

Consumer activist Ralph Nader has worked to make cars, toys, and airlines safer. He has lobbied for stricter regulation of meat processing, nuclear energy, and television advertising. He was instrumental in the formation of the Occupational Safety and Health Administration, the Environmental Protection Agency, the Consumer Product Safety Commission, and he helped to pass at least eight major consumer protection laws. Today, Ralph Nader's name is synonymous with consumer activism.

Nader was born in Winsted, Connecticut, on February 27, 1934, to Lebanese immigrant parents. His father, Nadra, came to the United States in 1912 to escape the oppressive rule of the Ottoman Turks; his mother, Rose, came five years later. The Naders settled in Winsted, where they owned and operated the Highland Arms Restaurant, which was always as much a source of conversation as it was of food. "You pay ten cents for a cup of coffee," boasts Nadra Nader, "and you also get a dollar's worth of conversation." The Nader family was widely known for its community activism as well as for its lively dinner-table debates, both at home and in the restaurant.

Nader once shamefacedly confessed to his father that he had failed to stand up for his beliefs when a teacher expressed a contrary opinion. Nadra lectured the boy on the importance of using his precious right as an American to freedom of speech. What good is freedom, his father demanded, if people fail to take advantage of it? By the time he was a freshman at Princeton in 1951, however, Nader had learned his lesson well. When he found dead birds surrounding campus trees that had been

"The most important office in America for anyone to achieve is fulltime citizen."
Ralph Nader

1934 Nader is born in Winsted, Connecticut.

1965 Nader publishes *Unsafe at Any Speed.*

1969 Staff nicknamed "Nader's Raiders."

1992 Nader runs for the presidency as an independent.

1996 Nader runs for president as the Green Party's candidate.

1998 Nader founds "Commercial Alert."

Nader's investigations led to reforms in everything from meatpacking to coal mining.

sprayed with pesticides, Nader tried to ban the use of such chemicals on campus. He also tried to organize a protest to help a hot-dog vendor whose license was challenged by local restaurateurs.

Upon graduation from Princeton, Nader enrolled in Harvard Law School, where he became interested in the lack of safety standards in the automobile industry. In 1959 he published an article entitled "The Safe Car You Can't Buy," in which he noted that "Detroit today is designing automobiles for style . . . but not—despite the 5,000,000 reported accidents, nearly 40,000 fatalities, 1,100,000 permanent disabilities and 15,000,000 injuries yearly—for safety."

Nader briefly practiced law in Hartford, Connecticut, but in 1963 he hitchhiked to Washington, D.C., where he worked at a variety of jobs, including one as an advisor to a Senate subcommittee on automobile safety. From this experience and his law school research came what is probably still Nader's most significant accomplishment, his 1965 book *Unsafe at Any Speed: The Designed-in Dangers of the American Automobile*. The book lambasted the entire automobile industry for its safety record but it focused particular attention on the faulty suspension system of General Motors' Corvair. Nader's book had only modest sales until it was revealed that GM had hired private detectives to investigate and attempt to discredit him. GM's president, John Roche, was called before a congressional subcommittee to apologize to Nader, who afterward successfully sued GM for invasion of privacy. Sales of Nader's book skyrocketed, and Nader himself was seen across America as a David to GM's Goliath—a lone individual heroically battling big business.

Nader continued his crusade for protection of individual Americans against abuse and neglect by corporations and governmental agencies. His investigations led to reforms in everything from meatpacking to coal mining. As his fame grew, idealistic law school graduates began to arrive in Washington anxious to work with and learn from Nader. In 1969 William Greider of the *Washington Post* coined the nickname "Nader's Raiders" to describe these young people, and by 1970 Nader had 30,000 applicants for 200 open positions among his dedicated young staffers, who worked long hours for low pay on various task forces Nader established to investigate consumer issues. By 1972 Nader's task forces had written seventeen books exposing problems across the nation.

Nader continued to found new organizations such as the Center for Auto Safety and the Public Interest Research Group. Nader does not head these organizations himself; in fact, he has developed many of this generation's leading activists by creating new organizations for young staffers to lead. Over the years, he and the organizations he has founded have supported and encouraged ordinary citizens at the grassroots level to recognize and use the power they have as American citizens.

Nader's personal life has contributed to the legend of "Saint Ralph." It is said that Nader does not own a car or a television set, does not use credit cards, lives in a sparsely furnished apartment, never breaks traffic laws, and donates most of what he earns to the various organizations he has founded. He has never married because he feels that his work would interfere with family life.

Nader's reputation for frugality and integrity encouraged some to consider him the ideal candidate for the presidency. In 1992 Nader ran as an independent and again in 1996 as the Green Party's candidate. While he did not expect to win in either election, Nader wanted to draw attention to what he calls America's political "duopoly"—the two party-system that excludes other viewpoints and discourages grassroots campaigns. He refused campaign contributions and advocated campaign finance reform.

In 1998 Nader founded a new organization called Commercial Alert, designed to help citizens do battle with corporations that advertise and market harmful products. In a press release, Nader indicted companies who "transmit tawdry commercial values into homes and schools, undermining home values, pitting children against their own parents and pulling families apart." Nader has also announced plans to build a museum of tort law in his home state of Connecticut that will feature products that Nader helped to remove from the market—including silicone breast implants, flammable pajamas, and the infamous Ford Pinto, whose gas tank exploded in rear-end collisions. ◆

> *"The concept of an individual with a conscience is one whose highest allegiance is to his fellow men."*
> Ralph Nader

Nation, Carry Amelia Moore

NOVEMBER 25, 1846–JUNE 9, 1911 ● TEMPERANCE REFORMER AND
CHAMPION OF WOMEN'S RIGHTS

Carry Nation, temperance and women's rights champion, was born in Garrard County, Kentucky. Her family moved to Missouri in 1856 and Texas in 1867. There she married Charles Gloyd, a young physician and an alcoholic. After their marriage failed, she returned to Missouri and became a schoolteacher. In 1877 she married David A. Nation, preacher, editor, lawyer, and Civil War veteran. The couple

moved to Texas, and after her husband failed at farming, the family moved to Medicine Lodge, Kansas, in 1889, where she and other members of the Woman's Christian Temperance Union rallied anti-alcohol residents to close Medicine Lodge's illegal saloons in 1899. Nation blamed alcohol for destroying marriages and family life and believed that she was divinely ordained to wipe out strong drink.

After passive methods of preaching and confronting saloon customers failed, she used a hatchet for the first time to smash saloons in Kiowa, Kansas, in 1900. Later that year she wrecked the bar at the Carey Hotel in Wichita, Kansas. She described her actions as "hatchetations," but police called them "disturbing the peace." Late in 1901 her husband, David Nation, was granted a divorce.

Between 1901 and 1908 Carry Nation took her crusade across Kansas and into Missouri, Texas, Michigan, Montana, and Washington, D.C. She appeared at Chautauqua gatherings, county fairs, and even burlesque shows. During this period she wrote her autobiography and started several publications, including the *Hatchet, Smasher's Mail,* and *Home Defender.* By 1909 these publications had failed, and her own health was declining. She moved from Washington, D.C., to Arkansas. In 1911, after suffering a stroke, she was admitted to a sanitarium in Leavenworth, Kansas, where she died. She was buried in the family plot at Belton, Missouri, not far from the town of Peculiar. Nearly forgotten when national prohibition became law in 1920, she is today remembered as a larger-than-life figure who promoted temperance and prohibition and the rights of women. ◆

> *"Smash, ladies, smash!"*
> Carry Nation, her battle cry, 1900–1910

Newman, Paul

JANUARY 26, 1925– ● ACTOR AND PHILANTHROPIST

A merican actor Paul Newman rose to fame as one of the most respected and popular performers of his generation. He starred in such films as *Cat on a Hot Tin Roof*

(1958), *The Long Hot Summer* (1958), *The Hustler* (1961), *Hud* (1963), *Cool Hand Luke* (1967) *Butch Cassidy and the Sundance Kid* (1969), *The Sting* (1973), *The Verdict* (1982), and *The Color of Money* (1986), for which he won an Academy Award as Best Actor. In 1982 Newman founded Newman's Own, a successful line of food products that has earned over $150 million for charity.

Paul Newman was born and raised in Cleveland Ohio, the son of a successful sporting goods store owner. After serving in the Navy Air Corps during the last year of World War II, Newman graduated from Kenyon College in Ohio. He spent a year in the Yale Drama School graduate program from 1951–52 and attended the famous New York Actors Studio. He often played a rebel in his early screen work, which led to a career playing the fascinating outsider on film. His intense good looks, sexual charisma, and charm appeal to moviegoers the world over.

In 1958, after his first failed marriage, Newman married his costar in *The Long Hot Summer*, Joanne Woodward. Newman has starred in sixty-five movies throughout his five-decade Hollywood career including his most recent, *Message in a Bottle* (1999). He has also directed six others including *Rachel, Rachel* (1968) and *The Effect of Gamma Rays on Man-in-the-Moon Marigolds* (1972).

Paul Newman's homemade salad dressing was always popular among friends and acquaintances. In 1982 Newman and long-time friend A. E. Hotchner decided to bottle and sell the salad dressing for charity under the brand name Newman's Own. The company was an immediate success. Over the years, Newman's Own has expanded from salad dressing to pasta sauces, salsas, popcorn, lemonade, ice cream and steak sauces, and cookies.

Newman has always insisted on top quality products without artificial ingredients or preservatives. His goal is to create nutritious, all-natural versions of his favorite foods. He attributes the success of Newman's Own to this commitment to quality and to his promise to give all profits to educational and charitable organizations. Over 1,000 charities have received donations from Paul Newman as a result of the sale of Newman's Own products worldwide.

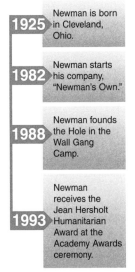

1925 Newman is born in Cleveland, Ohio.

1982 Newman starts his company, "Newman's Own."

1988 Newman founds the Hole in the Wall Gang Camp.

1993 Newman receives the Jean Hersholt Humanitarian Award at the Academy Awards ceremony.

Hollywood and Social Change

Throughout history humanitarians have become famous for their good works. With the dawning of the entertainment age and the growth of Hollywood as a cultural influence, many who have achieved fame in motion pictures have gone the opposite route, using their "star power" to make changes in the world.

Hollywood has a long list of socially and politically active celebrities who over the years have been able both to use film itself as a tool for change and also to capitalize on their power to bring attention to issues of national and global concern.

Paul Newman, for example, began his product line, Newman's Own, in 1982. One hundred percent of the after-tax profits from the sale of Newman's Own products goes to charitable and educational organizations. Stanley Kubrick, the noted film director, contributed to public awareness of nuclear war with *Dr. Strangelove*, a film that was controversial in its depiction of Soviet-American relations and brought to light, through highly sophisticated satire, the potential for global nuclear disaster.

Other notable liberal activists in Hollywood include directors Sidney Lumet (*12 Angry Men, Serpico, Dog Day Afternoon, Network*) and Mike Nichols (*Silkwood*), director of photography Haskell Wexler (notably, the antiwar film *Coming Home*), and the film actors Tim Robbins, Warren Beatty, and Susan Sarandon.

"Spaghetti sauce and salad dressing are useful sometimes."

Paul Newman, 1998

A project close to Newman's heart is the Hole in the Wall Gang Camp, which he founded in 1988 with Ursula and A. E. Hotchner. It is a sleep-away camp for seriously ill children, providing year-round activities for kids with cancer and other serious blood diseases. The camp is subsidized by profits from Newman's Own but Newman solicits private donations for the majority of the operating costs. The Hole in the Wall Discovery Center, created in 1992, brings inner-city and suburban fifth graders together in a camp setting to have fun while developing an appreciation of cultural and personal diversity.

As a tribute to his charitable work, Paul Newman received the Jean Hersholt Humanitarian Award at the 1993 Academy Awards ceremony.

The intensely private Newman consistently deflects attention and praise for his humanitarian work as well as for his film work. "Once you allow your face to adorn a bottle of salad dressing, there's no way you can take yourself seriously," Newman jokes with characteristic modesty. "It's been wonderfully humbling." ◆

Newton, Huey P.

FEBRUARY 17, 1942 – AUGUST 22, 1989 ● RADICAL POLITICAL ACTIVIST

Huey Newton was born in Monroe, Louisiana. His family moved to Oakland, California, when he was young. Newton was the youngest of seven siblings. He attended Merritt College in Oakland and participated in the groundswell of political activities that were erupting on college campuses nationwide. He joined the increasing number of blacks who questioned the ability of the civil rights movement to deal with the problems of housing, unemployment, poverty, and police brutality that plagued urban African Americans.

In college, Newton and his friend Bobby Seale were active in the effort to diversify the curriculum at Merritt, as well as lobbying for more black instructors. Newton joined the Afro-American Association but soon became a vocal critic of the organization's advocacy of capitalism. Instead, he sought inspiration from Robert Williams, a former head of the Monroe, North Carolina, NAACP, who advocated guerrilla warfare, and from Third World revolutionaries such as Cuba's Fidel Castro, China's Mao Ze Dong, and Algeria's Franz Fanon. Newton believed that blacks were an oppressed colony being exploited economically and disfranchised politically within U.S. borders and argued that blacks should launch a liberation movement for self-empowerment.

In 1966 Newton and Seale founded the Black Panther Party for Self-Defense. Newton took on the title of minister of defense and acted as leader of the organization. Among the points raised in their initial program was the right to bear arms to defend their community from police repression.

In November Newton and Seale, armed with shotguns—which were legal at the time as long as they were not concealed—instituted "justice patrols" to monitor the actions of the police and inform blacks of their rights when stopped by the police. The police responded with resentment and harassment. On October 28, 1967, in culmination of a year of hostile and antagonistic relations between the Panthers and the police, Newton was arrested and charged in the shooting of one police officer and the murder of another. Events of this incident are unclear and conflicting. Newton claimed to be unconscious after being shot by one of the policemen.

> *"We stand for the transformation of the decadent, reactionary, racist system, that exists at these times."*
>
> Huey Newton

> In 1966 Newton and Seale founded the Black Panther Party for Self-Defense.

cause célèbre: famous cause.

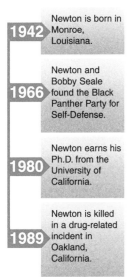

1942 ▸ Newton is born in Monroe, Louisiana.

1966 ▸ Newton and Bobby Seale found the Black Panther Party for Self-Defense.

1980 ▸ Newton earns his Ph.D. from the University of California.

1989 ▸ Newton is killed in a drug-related incident in Oakland, California.

Newton's trial became a cause célèbre, and "Free Huey" became a slogan that galvanized thousands of people on the New Left.

Newton's arrest heightened the awareness of police brutality in the black community. While in prison Newton was considered a political prisoner; rallies and speeches focused attention on his plight. His trial became a **cause célèbre**, and "Free Huey" became a slogan that galvanized thousands of people on the New Left. Massive rallies and demonstrations at the courthouse demanding his release were organized by BPP members.

Newton remained active in prison, issuing speeches and directives. He was convicted in September 1968 of voluntary manslaughter, and was sentenced to two to fifteen years in prison. His conviction was overturned by the Court of Appeals, because of procedural errors during his first trial. Newton, after being released from prison, tried to revive the organization. However, during the early 1970s, the BPP had declined due to legal problems, internal tensions, and a factional split among BPP members on the East and West Coasts. This division was fostered by the disinformation campaign launched by the FBI, which created a climate of distrust and suspicion within the BPP. Many on the East Coast believed the ideology of Eldridge Cleaver—who had become the public spokesperson for the BPP during Newton's incarceration and who advocated politically motivated armed actions. Newton articulated the feelings of many on the West Coast by arguing that the BPP, by becoming too militant, had moved onto a plane with which average blacks could no longer identify. He wanted to focus more on community programs and political education. Newton ordered a series of purges, which debilitated the party further.

Although Newton remained publicly identified with the party, many people no longer looked to him as leader. Increasingly isolated, Newton cultivated a small band of supporters. In 1974 Newton was accused of murder in the killing of a woman. Newton fled to Cuba, feeling that he would not get a fair trial here. In 1977 he returned to the United States to resume leadership of the weakened and splintering party. In his absence, Elaine Brown had assumed leadership of the organization and taken it in new directions. Newton's role in the organization continued to diminish. He was retried in the 1967 killing of the policeman and convicted, but that conviction was later overturned. He also faced trial for the murder of the woman, but the charge was dropped after two hung juries.

In 1980 Newton received a Ph.D. from the University of California. His thesis was "War Against the Panthers—A Study of Repression in America." While Newton remained politically active, his visibility as a public figure was waning. He was arrested in 1985 for embezzling funds from a nutritional program he headed. Three years later, he was convicted of possessing firearms. Increasingly addicted to drugs and involved in the drug trade, he was killed in a drug-related incident on the streets of Oakland in 1989. ◆

Noel-Baker, Philip

NOVEMBER 1, 1889–OCTOBER 8, 1982 ● FOUNDER OF THE LEAGUE OF NATIONS AND UNITED NATIONS

Philip Noel-Baker won the Nobel Peace Prize in 1959 for a lifetime of work for peace and disarmament. He was present at the creation of the League of Nations and the United Nations and also participated in the Disarmament Conference in 1932, playing an important role on each occasion. Moreover, Noel-Baker was one of the world's leading authorities on disarmament, the major cause with which he was associated during his life.

The source of the drive that carried him through almost seven decades of peacemaking lay in his Quaker background. His family had been Quakers almost since the beginning of the Society of Friends in the seventeenth century. His father, Joseph Baker, was a well-to-do businessman, whose social concern took him into politics. In Parliament Joseph Baker was a staunch advocate of peace, and the outbreak of the war in 1914 found him in Germany at an international peace congress he had helped organize through the churches.

Philip Alan Baker grew up in an atmosphere of Quakerism, Liberal politics, and peacemaking. So many foreign guests were entertained at his home that it was called the "International Hotel." He went to Quaker schools and spent a year at the Quaker college of Haverford near Philadelphia. He returned to take his degree at Cambridge University, where he excelled in history and economics, as well as in debating and athletics. He captained the Cambridge track team and in 1912 ran in the Olympics, despite a taped, dislocated foot.

After Cambridge he was appointed vice principal at Ruskin College, Oxford, but after a few months the war began. With

> The source of the drive that carried Noel-Baker through almost seven decades of peacemaking lay in his Quaker background.

his Quaker convictions he could not join the army, so with the support of his father and other Friends, he helped organize the Friends Ambulance Unit and became its first commandant in France, where the unit was loosely attached to the Red Cross and provided medical services at the front. One of the ambulance drivers was a pretty English girl named Irene Noel whom Baker married in 1915, later adding her name to his to become Noel-Baker. In 1916 the army decided to tighten its control over the Friends Ambulance Unit and requested that its leader be commissioned as an officer. This Noel-Baker could not conscientiously do, so he left to organize the British Ambulance Unit to work on the Italian front, where he spent the remainder of the war.

At war's end Noel-Baker had a collection of medals for valor from both France and Italy and a burning desire to do something to prevent war from happening again. At Cambridge he had twice been named Whewell Scholar in international law and had also briefly studied in both Paris and Munich. Thus he was qualified for an appointment with Lord Robert Cecil, who was looking for a bright young man to help him draw up plans for postwar peace machinery. Noel-Baker went with Cecil to Paris to work on the Covenant of the League of Nations and the charter of the International Labor Organization and was then appointed to the secretariat of the League. He was thirty-one.

repatriating: to return to the country of origin.

There is a story that Lloyd George got the idea that the new League should take on the job of **repatriating** prisoners of war and asked the young man in the secretariat who could do it. Noel-Baker replied, "Fridtjof Nansen," and Lloyd George said, "Get him." However it all began, Noel-Baker was indeed the messenger sent to Norway to persuade the famous explorer to take the job, and Nansen accepted. In the following years Noel-Baker continued to assist and advise Nansen in his work for refugees and as Norway's delegate in the Assembly. Noel-Baker himself was principal adviser to Sir Eric Drummond, the first secretary-general of the League, from 1920 to 1922, and then secretary to the British delegation. In 1927 Nansen wrote to Noel-Baker, "All I have done in the League has been done with you, and could not have been done without you. . . . Oh, dear friend, how much you have done for me and for the League during many years."

Noel-Baker kept up his League connections even after leaving Geneva in 1924 for a major academic appointment as the first Sir Edward Cassell Professor of International Relations at the University of London, only the second such chair in the British Isles. In his five years in that position Noel-Baker firmly established the department of international relations and published his first scholarly works, including *Disarmament*, in 1926, which became a peace classic.

The preparatory work was under way for the League's Disarmament Conference, and the book was written "to show the complexity of the problems to those who think them simple; and to suggest solutions to those who think them insoluble." He based his account on his "personal experience of debates among soldiers, sailors and other experts who have had to consider at Paris, Geneva, and elsewhere the practical realization of disarmament policy." As in all his books, he devoted much space to the arguments against disarmament, which he sought to answer with ample documentation and careful reasoning. He did not claim that disarmament would be a **panacea** in itself, but regarded it as a vital component in the development of intergovernmental cooperation: "When a general treaty of disarmament is signed, the central bastion of the enemy defences will be captured." He foresaw a slow, painful "struggle against the age-long misery of war," and he felt victory had to be won first "in the minds and hearts of men." Of this he remained hopeful, and for the rest of his life he remained a major force in the movement for disarmament, never abandoning this hope until perhaps at the very end of his life.

It was a great setback to his hopes when the League Disarmament Conference, which was finally convened in 1932, was a failure almost from the start. Noel-Baker always blamed this on the Conservatives, who had replaced the more pro-League Labour government just before the conference began. Noel-Baker was now a Labour politician himself, having left the university in 1929 to win a seat in the House of Commons and to become parliamentary secretary to the foreign secretary, Arthur Henderson. At the Disarmament Conference he was principal assistant to Henderson, who was chairman, and he worked hard to support him in what was a losing cause.

In 1933 he came to America again to lecture at Yale and to receive the Howland Prize for "distinguished work in the sphere of government." In 1936 Noel-Baker helped his old friend Cecil organize the Peace Ballot of the League of Nations Union, which showed strong backing for the League. In the same year Noel-Baker was elected to Parliament from Derby, which he continued to represent until he retired in 1970, after almost

panacea: a remedy for all ills.

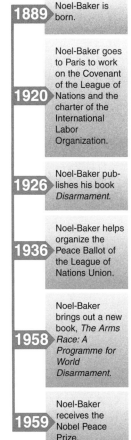

1889 Noel-Baker is born.

1920 Noel-Baker goes to Paris to work on the Covenant of the League of Nations and the charter of the International Labor Organization.

1926 Noel-Baker publishes his book *Disarmament*.

1936 Noel-Baker helps organize the Peace Ballot of the League of Nations Union.

1958 Noel-Baker brings out a new book, *The Arms Race: A Programme for World Disarmament.*

1959 Noel-Baker receives the Nobel Peace Prize.

"Defeatism about the feasibility of plans for disarmament and ordered peace has been the most calamitous of all the errors made by democratic governments in modern times."

Noel-Baker, *The Arms Race*, 1958

imperative: extremely important.

forty years in the House of Commons and having become a leader of his party.

During World War II Noel-Baker served as a top government official in the Ministry of Transport. When Labour returned to power, he held a number of posts, including cabinet rank, but the position of foreign secretary always eluded him. Perhaps his unyielding peace position disturbed some of his Labour colleagues. On the other hand, his fellow Quakers were very uncomfortable when he was appointed secretary of state for air, but pleased when he moved to the Commonwealth Relations Office, where he served for three years and made a significant contribution in the transition from empire to commonwealth.

At the formal closing session of the League of Nations, Noel-Baker had declared, "Geneva has been the first Parliament of the World. Our work has not ended; it has only begun." When the UN Preparatory Commission was formed in 1944, he was sent as the British delegate, for he was singularly fitted to share his unparalleled experience with the League. He was at San Francisco in 1945 to help draft the charter of the United Nations and then became a member of the British delegation to the General Assembly. He helped develop policies for the UN Secretariat and also lent a hand at meetings of the Food and Agricultural Organization and the Economic and Social Council.

With the introduction of nuclear weapons, disarmament became more **imperative** than ever. In 1958 Noel-Baker brought out a new book, *The Arms Race: A Programme for World Disarmament*, updating his *Disarmament* of 1926 for the nuclear age, although with a preface that was very much the same. Once again, Noel-Baker's book became something of a basic primer on the subject, and it won the Albert Schweitzer Book Award. It certainly strengthened his candidacy for the Nobel Peace Prize, which was awarded to him in the year following its publication.

Another honor came to Noel-Baker in 1960, when he was made president of UNESCO's International Council of Sport and Physical Recreation. He was the only winner of a Nobel medal who had also won a medal in that other international competition, the Olympic Games, having won the silver in the 1500-meter event at Antwerp in 1920. He had captained the British team again at the 1924 Olympics, and he always kept up with athletics. He played tennis most of his life and took long walks until arthritis stiffened his legs and he had to use a cane.

In his old age many honors came: in 1976 the French awarded him the Legion of Honor; in 1977 he was made a life peer, Baron Noel-Baker of Derby, his longtime constituency; and in the same year he became a Papal Knight of Sylvester, an unusual honor for a Quaker. When he retired from the House of Commons in 1970 at the age of eighty-one, he declared, "While I have the health and strength, I shall give all my time to the work of breaking the **dogmatic** sleep of those who allow the nuclear, chemical, biological, and conventional arms race to go on."

dogmatic: strong opinion.

In October 1982 Noel-Baker died at his home in London, shortly before his ninety-third birthday. ◆

Pankhurst, Emmeline

JULY 14, 1858–JUNE 14, 1928 ● BRITISH SUFFRAGIST

English suffragist Emeline Pankhurst's father, Robert Goulden, was a Manchester textile manufacturer and a friend of the political radical Dr. Richard Pankhurst, who had drafted the first women's suffrage bill in the late 1860s. Goulden and Dr. Pankhurst were campaigning together in 1875, when the doctor met Emmeline, recently returned from college in Paris. They were married the following year.

During her early married life, Pankhurst was occupied with bringing up their four children. When she returned to public activities, she became increasingly involved with her husband's parliamentary work, and in 1889 they established the Women's Franchise League.

Beginning in 1895, Emmeline Pankhurst held several municipal posts in Manchester, but when Dr. Pankhurst died suddenly in 1898, she retreated from active politics. It was her eldest daughter, Christabel, who led her back into the suffrage campaign, and in 1903 she founded the Women's Social and Political Union. The WSPU gained widespread recognition in 1905 when two of its members were thrown out of a hall where the prime minister and several cabinet ministers were holding a meeting. These two demonstrators were arrested in the street for technical assault on the police, and after having refused to pay a fine, the suffragettes—a name coined by the press—were imprisoned.

A year later, when Pankhurst moved to London, the campaign intensified. Neither the Liberal government nor the Labour opposition was taking the suffragettes' cause seriously. "Votes for women would do more harm than good," said Prime Minister Herbert Asquith. "Parliament is not elected on the basis of universal **suffrage**—children are not represented there." Reluctantly, the WSPU resorted to militant tactics. At first they were not violent, merely vociferous and obstructive. Nevertheless, in the year 1908–09, Pankhurst was imprisoned three times.

In 1909 the WSPU began using hunger strikes as a political weapon. A truce was called a year later, but when the government blocked a franchise bill, the suffragettes launched a period of violent militancy. Arson attacks, directed from Paris by Christabel Pankhurst, were making the headlines. Under the notorious Cat and Mouse Act of 1913, Emmeline was arrested, released, and rearrested twelve times in one year.

It was a surprise to her colleagues when, at the outbreak of World War I, Emmeline Pankhurst immediately called off the campaign and urged the suffragettes to stand loyally with the government and England. She traveled around the country advocating national service for women, and wrote her autobiography, *My Own Story*, in 1914.

By 1915 there were severe problems keeping the factories open and producing and David Lloyd George, the minister of munitions, asked Mrs. Pankhurst to organize a march that would demonstrate women's readiness to fill men's places at work. Thousands marched under the slogan "We Demand the Right to Serve," and consequently a national register of women was compiled.

The war years gave women the chance to exercise their vital social power; finally, after the war, they were afforded the political power they had demanded for over five decades. An act in 1918, allowing women over thirty to vote, gave the franchise to women for the first time.

During the postwar years, Mrs. Pankhurst lived in the United States, Canada, and Bermuda. She returned to England in 1926 and was immediately chosen as a Conservative candi-

suffrage: the right to vote.

1858 Pankhurst is born in Manchester, England.

1876 Emmeline marries Richard Pankhurst, who drafted the first women's suffrage bill.

1889 Pankhurst and her husband establish the Women's Franchise League.

1903 Pankhurst founds the Women's Social and Political Union.

1918 Women over thirty years of age are granted the right to vote in England.

1928 Pankhurst dies just before the Representation of the People Act extends the vote to women on terms equal to male suffrage.

date for a London constituency. Her declining health prevented her from being elected. She died in 1928, only a few weeks after the Representation of the People Act extended the vote to women on terms equal to male suffrage.

Her two daughters were also leaders of the women's suffrage movement. The fiery Christabel Pankhurst (1880–1958) was a militant suffragette who won an adoring following. Thrown out of the House of Commons, she screamed at a policeman, "I shall assault you, I shall spit at you!" For a time beginning in 1912, she was responsible for an arson campaign for which she was imprisoned. She became an evangelist and eventually was recognized by the establishment when created a dame of the British Empire in 1936.

Sylvia Pankhurst (1882–1960) opposed the institution of marriage and defended the right to be an unmarried mother (she was one herself). In the 1930s she was active in behalf of Ethiopian independence. ◆

Her two daughters, Christabel and Sylvia Pankhurst, were also leaders of the women's suffrage movement.

Parks, Rosa

FEBRUARY 4, 1913– ● CIVIL RIGHTS ACTIVIST

Rosa Parks's refusal to give up her seat to a white man on a segregated bus in Montgomery, Alabama, on December 1, 1955, ignited the chain of events that led to the nationwide civil rights movement. Parks was not simply a woman who was too tired to stand up after a long day at work. She had spent years as an active volunteer for the local National Association for the Advancement of Colored People (NAACP) out of a deep conviction that the laws that segregated African Americans in the South must be changed.

Rosa Parks was born Rosa McCauley in Tuskegee, Alabama. Her father was a carpenter and builder, her mother a schoolteacher. Parks grew up in her mother's parents' home in Pine Level, Alabama, near Montgomery. Her grandfather, Sylvester Edwards, was one of the few African Americans who owned a small farm in the rural community, and he was determined that his children receive an education so they would not have to go into domestic service. "My grandfather was the one who instilled in my mother and her sisters that you don't put up with

"To Rosa Parks, whose creative witness was the great force that led to the modern stride toward freedom."

Martin Luther King Jr.

Congressional Gold Medal

The Congressional Gold Medal is Congress's highest honor. On May 4, 1999, President Clinton signed a bill awarding the Congressional Gold Medal to Rosa Parks, whose refusal in 1955 to give up her seat on a bus to a white man sparked the civil rights movement in the United States. Parks, 86, received the medal on June 15, 1999.

Each medal, three inches in diameter and minted in gold, bears the image of the recipient. Others who have been awarded a Congressional Gold Medal include Mother Teresa, Nelson Mandela, the Reverend Billy Graham and his wife, Ruth Graham, and a group of nine black students in Little Rock, Arkansas, who were instrumental in integrating Central High School in 1957.

"The only tired I was, was tired of giving in."

Rosa Parks

bad treatment from anybody," she wrote in *Rosa Parks: My Story.* "It was passed down almost in our genes."

Parks started school in a one-room schoolhouse in Pine Level. Schools for African-American children were in session for only five months a year, since many children had to help their parents plow and plant in spring and harvest in fall. Parks herself worked as a field hand on a neighboring plantation, picking and chopping cotton. When she was eleven she lived with relatives and went to junior high school in Montgomery, where she encountered for the first time the full impact of the segregation laws in the South. Very few African Americans obtained a high school education, since there was no public high school for African Americans in Montgomery. Parks attended the laboratory high school at Alabama State Teacher's College for Negroes, graduating in 1933. She had earned her diploma, but there were no jobs for African-American women that required a diploma. She took in sewing and worked as a tailor's assistant at a department store.

Parks first became active in civil-rights work after her marriage to Raymond Parks, a barber, in 1932. She and her husband supported the Scottsboro defendants, a notorious case in which nine African-American youths were convicted in 1931 on questionable evidence for raping two white women. In 1943 Parks became one of the first women to join the Montgomery NAACP. As an adviser to the NAACP Youth Council, one of her projects was an attempt to persuade the main Montgomery library to allow African-American students to take out books. This attempt failed. She also worked as secretary of the Montgomery NAACP from 1943 to 1956. Among her duties was keeping a record of cases of discrimination or acts of violence against African Americans.

Often called the mother of the civil rights movement, Parks is best known for her refusal to give up her bus seat to a white man in early December 1955. Her arrest for violating the segregated seating laws was the incident that sparked the Montgomery bus boycott, an organized boycott of city buses by African Americans, who made up over 70 percent of the ridership. Lasting for over a year, this first massive nonviolent protest brought the struggle for African-American equality to national attention.

"I had felt for a long time, that if I was ever told to get up so a white person could sit, that I would refuse to do so," Parks said in 1955. She was asked to be on the executive committee of the Montgomery Improvement Association (MIA), which was created to direct the boycott and was led by the young minister Martin Luther King Jr. Parks gave out clothing and shoes to people who walked to and from work, served as a dispatcher for the MIA transportation committee, and gave speeches around the country to raise money. The boycott continued for 381 days, until December 21, 1956, the day after written notice was received from the U.S. Supreme Court that Montgomery's segregated bus seating was unconstitutional.

Both Parks and her husband lost their jobs as a result of the boycott. In 1957 they moved to Detroit, where she worked for several years at a small clothing factory. From 1965 to 1988 she was an administrative assistant in the Detroit office of African-American congressman John Conyers.

Parks has never stopped working for equal rights for African Americans. She travels frequently to speak about the bus boycott and tell the story of the civil rights movement. She was an active member of the Southern Christian Leadership Conference (SCLC), which Dr. King and others formed to fight segregation. In 1987, ten years after her husband's death, Parks founded the Rosa and Raymond Parks Institute for Self-Development in Detroit. The organization is dedicated to helping young African Americans continue their education and pursue careers.

In 1999 Parks was awarded the Congressional Gold Medal of Honor. She is also the recipient of ten honorary degrees and numerous other honors and awards, including the NAACP's prestigious Spingarn Medal (1979). In her autobiography, *Rosa Parks: My Story*, she singled out a tribute she received in Montgomery, where it all started:

> The bus on which I was arrested back on December 1955 was part of the Cleveland Avenue line. Today, Cleveland Avenue is named Rosa Parks Boulevard. ◆

Often called the mother of the civil rights movement, Parks is best known for her refusal to give up her bus seat to a white man in early December 1955.

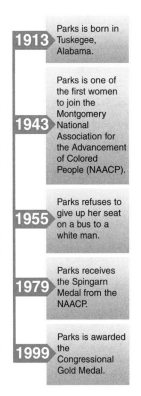

1913 Parks is born in Tuskegee, Alabama.

1943 Parks is one of the first women to join the Montgomery National Association for the Advancement of Colored People (NAACP).

1955 Parks refuses to give up her seat on a bus to a white man.

1979 Parks receives the Spingarn Medal from the NAACP.

1999 Parks is awarded the Congressional Gold Medal.

Paul, Alice

JANUARY 11, 1885–JULY 9, 1974 ● SUFFRAGIST AND WOMEN'S RIGHTS ACTIVIST

A lice Paul was a leader of the American women's suffrage movement and a lifelong activist for women's rights. She composed and introduced the first equal rights amendment to the American Constitution. A believer in nonviolent social protest, Paul remained active until a stroke disabled her in 1974.

> *"I always feel the movement is a sort of mosaic. Each of us puts in one little stone, and then you get a great mosaic at the end."*
>
> Alice Paul

Alice Paul was born in Moorestown, New Jersey, the eldest of four children of William Mickle Paul, a banker and real estate investor, and Tacy Parry. Paul's earliest memory is accompanying her mother to a women's suffrage meeting.

Paul attended Quaker schools in Moorestown and attended Swarthmore College where she earned a B.S. in biology in 1905. She was elected to Phi Beta Kappa and Pi Gamma Mu in recognition of academic excellence. In 1907 Paul earned an M.A. degree in sociology from the University of Pennsylvania and began research on the legal status of women. In the fall of 1907 she continued her studies in social work on a Quaker Fellowship in Woodbridge, England.

While working as a London caseworker, Paul became involved in the British suffrage movement as a protégée of Christabel, Emmeline, and Sylvia Pankhurst. With American suffragist Lucy Burns, Paul learned the more defiant tactics of the Women's Social and Political Union that the two later employed to secure passage of the Nineteenth Amendment to the American Constitution (women's right to vote).

Paul returned to the United States in 1910 and resumed her graduate studies at the University of Pennsylvania. In 1912 she completed a Ph.D. in sociology. Paul continued suffrage work within the ranks of the National American Woman Suffrage Association (NAWSA). After a disagreement on strategy with Carrie Chapman Catt and other NAWSA leaders, Paul and Burns founded the Congressional Union of

The Equal Rights Amendment

First proposed as an addition to the U.S. Constitution by Alice Paul in 1923, the Equal Rights Amendment (ERA) stated that "equality of rights under the law shall not be denied or abridged by the United States or by any state on account of sex." Supporters argued that the Constitution must include the principle of equality of rights for women and that such an amendment would remove sex-based discrimination. Opponents to the amendment objected, as did some women's rights advocates who feared it would jeopardize recent legislation providing female industrial workers minimum protection against exploitative working conditions. The Supreme Court had upheld protective legislation for women in *Muller* v. *Oregon* (1908) but not for men, claiming the need to protect citizens able to bear children. Convinced that Congress would not extend protection to men and that the Court would therefore deny it to women if the amendment passed, organized labor opposed the ERA. It remained in the House Judiciary Committee for forty-seven years despite efforts to secure passage.

The 1960s brought renewed attention to the amendment. Hopes had faded that the Supreme Court would use the equal protection clause of the Fourteenth Amendment to subject laws that discriminated on the basis of sex to the same strict scrutiny applied to laws discriminating on the basis of race. When protective legislation was revealed to have harmed the very group it was intended to protect, liberal feminists had an additional reason for urging passage of the ERA. After massive lobbying, Congress in March 1972 voted overwhelmingly to submit the ERA as the Twenty-seventh Amendment to the states. Twenty-two states rushed to ratify; by 1975, however, momentum had slowed. Even after the original period for ratification was extended to 1982 supporters could secure favorable votes from only thirty-five of the thirty-eight states needed for passage. Five states meanwhile rescinded their endorsements. In December 1981 a federal judge ruled that those rescissions were legal and that Congress had acted illegally in extending the ratification deadline. Before ERA supporters could appeal the ruling to the Supreme Court, the deadline for ratification, July 30, 1982, expired, leaving opponents of the amendment victorious.

the NAWSA in 1913, which became an independent organization the following year.

The "New Suffragists" decided to employ the more **strident** tactics of the British feminists, but because of Paul's Quaker beliefs, without the violence. Paul founded the National Woman's Party (NWP) in 1916, serving as chairperson until 1921, and was instrumental in gaining women's voting rights in 1920. Actively involved in protests, Paul served time in jail for her participation in demonstrations. Like many suffragists, Paul was charged with disturbing the peace and unlawful assembly.

After the Nineteenth Amendment was ratified in 1920, Paul, with characteristic single-mindedness, decided to press

strident: harsh and insistent.

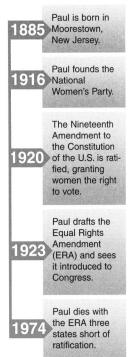

1885 Paul is born in Moorestown, New Jersey.

1916 Paul founds the National Women's Party.

1920 The Nineteenth Amendment to the Constitution of the U.S. is ratified, granting women the right to vote.

1923 Paul drafts the Equal Rights Amendment (ERA) and sees it introduced to Congress.

1974 Paul dies with the ERA three states short of ratification.

on for equal rights for women in all areas of life. In the midst of harsh criticism from those who favored protective legislation for women, Paul wrote the Equal Rights Amendment (ERA) in 1923 and saw it introduced in Congress for the first time that December. Meanwhile, Paul continued her education. She earned three law degrees: an LL.B. from Washington College of Law (1922) and an LL.M. (1927) and D.C.L. (1928) from American University. A small income from her father's estate allowed Paul to devote all of her time and legal expertise to women's rights.

In the 1930s she served on the executive committee of Equal Rights International. Her goal was to obtain an international equal rights treaty. By the late 1930s Paul had garnered enough support to found the World Party for Equal Rights for Women, or the World Women's Party. After serving for two years as chair of the WWP in Geneva, Paul returned to the United States in 1941.

There is no evidence that Paul ever considered marriage. Paul's work for equality allowed little time for long-term relationships. After returning to the United States in 1941, she resided with her sister Helen. When Helen passed away, Paul and her closest friend, feminist Elsie Hill, shared a home until Elsie's death in the late 1960s.

Paul's intensity and the ranks of the NWP would not allow the ERA to die; it was repeatedly introduced in Congress until it passed in 1972 and was sent to the states for ratification. As late as 1969 Paul still protested on the front lines, both for women's equality and against the Vietnam War. She remained committed to nonviolent civil protest. Paul continued to lobby for the ERA until a stroke disabled her in 1974. She died in Moorestown, erroneously believing that, with only three additional states needed for ratification, the Equal Rights Amendment would soon become a reality. ◆

Pauling, Linus

FEBRUARY 28, 1901–AUGUST 19, 1994 ● SCIENTIST AND PEACE ACTIVIST

It was the dropping of the atomic bombs on Japan in 1945 that first awakened in Linus Pauling what became a compelling sense of social concern. Up to that time Pauling had been a distinguished scientist, enjoying a happy family life, whose driving force was his insatiable curiosity about the world of nature.

He remembers a critical incident when he was a high school freshman in Portland, Oregon. One afternoon a school-mate took him home to show off a brand new chemistry set. Pauling watched in amazement as his friend mixed colored powders in solutions that fizzed and smelled and then combined something with some table sugar, added a drop of acid, and the sugar burst into flame. It was not long before Pauling was put-ting together his own chemistry set to try experiments himself. This was the beginning of a long road he was to travel. As he wrote years later, "I was simply entranced by chemical **phe-nomena,** by the reactions in which substances, often with strik-ingly different properties, appear; and I hoped to learn more and more about this aspect of the world."

phenomena: observable facts or events.

At high school he took all available science and mathe-matics courses. When he was refused permission to finish his requirements quickly so that he could enter college early, he dropped out before the last term and went off to college anyway. Many years later the high school was proud to award its most famous alumnus his missing diploma.

Pauling entered Oregon Agricultural College (now Oregon State University) when he was sixteen and worked his way through. His last and best summer job was as state inspector of paved roads. While still an undergraduate he was made an instructor of quantitative chemistry, and it was in his classroom that he encountered an intelligent and attractive student named Ava Helen Miller. A romance quickly developed that soon led to an engagement and a wedding the following year, when Pauling was twenty-two. It was a happy marriage that was to produce four children and to last for fifty-eight years until Ava Helen died in 1981.

"I feel sure that we are going to win out in the fight against nuclear war, and against the reliance on force for the solution of world problems."
Linus Pauling, 1961

By 1923 Pauling had finished his first year of graduate work at the California Institute of Technology and had published his first scientific paper on molecular structure of crystals. He pub-lished four more in his second year and was awarded his Ph.D. in 1925. This was followed by a Guggenheim grant to study in Europe, and when he returned in 1927, Caltech made him assistant professor, at twenty-six the youngest member of the faculty.

When he was thirty, Pauling published a paper, "The Nature of the Chemical Bond," that became a classic. In this and sub-sequent papers he explained for the first time the structure of

1901 > Pauling is born in Oregon.

1927 > Pauling becomes, at 26, the youngest member of the faculty at California Institute of Technology.

1945 > The atomic bombings of Hiroshima and Nagasaki awaken Pauling's sense of social concern.

1954 > Pauling is awarded the Nobel Prize for chemistry.

1958 > Pauling publishes his book *No More War!*

1963 > Pauling receives the Nobel Peace Prize; the limited Test Ban Treaty goes into effect.

1994 > Pauling dies at the age of 93.

vilification: slandering or abusing in public

Pauling was appalled by the atomic bomb's destructive potential.

molecules in terms of quantum mechanics. For this he was given the Nobel Prize for chemistry in 1954. Meanwhile he had gone on to a succession of important discoveries, making connections among physical sciences, biology, and medicine.

After the bombing of Hiroshima, Pauling began to speak out against the atomic bomb. He was appalled by the bomb's destructive potential. He joined Albert Einstein's Emergency Committee of Atomic Scientists and began to speak out against war and nuclear testing. In the cold war mood of the time, a supporter of a policy of peace was all too readily suspected of being pro-communist, and Pauling suffered such indignities as having the State Department refuse him a passport and having to face congressional committees and declare that he was not a communist. On one such occasion he tried to explain why he was independent of any political line: "Nobody tells me what to think—except Mrs. Pauling." Despite such harassment and **vilification** by the press, Pauling refused to be silent. "I kept on going to keep the respect of my wife," he says today.

In April 1957 Albert Schweitzer issued his Declaration of Conscience from Oslo, describing the human damage done by radioactive fallout and asking for the cessation of nuclear tests. On May 15 Pauling echoed this appeal in a speech at Washington University in Saint Louis, and the response was so enthusiastic that that very evening Pauling, encouraged by several colleagues, wrote the Scientists' Bomb-Test Appeal, calling for a test-ban treaty, and sent it out to the scientific community. Within two weeks two thousand American scientists had signed the appeal, and Pauling began to solicit signatures from other countries. Eventually over eleven thousand scientists from forty-nine countries signed the document, and Pauling and his wife were able to present the petition to the United Nations in January 1958 as the opinion of the great majority of the world's scientists.

In 1958 Pauling published *No More War!*, an exposition of the scientific facts of nuclear weapons in clear and simple language and an appeal to prevent their use in war. (It was reprinted twenty-five years later, with little need to revise its basic explanation and message.) In 1959 at a conference on nuclear weapons in Hiroshima, Pauling wrote the resolution calling for a ban on their testing and development.

The Paulings then circulated an appeal against the proliferation of nuclear weapons and convened an international conference on the subject in Oslo in May 1961. Among the sponsors were Albert Schweitzer, Philip Noel-Baker, Lord Bertrand Russell, and other notables. Sixty distinguished scientists from fifteen countries attended the conference, which was financed by funds from Pauling's Nobel Prize in chemistry and private contributions.

In September 1961 Pauling sent telegrams to both President Kennedy and Premier Khrushchev, urging them to sign a ban on testing. In November he was invited to Moscow to attend the second centenary celebration of the Soviet Academy of Science, and he used the occasion to speak against new nuclear tests by the Soviet Union. He sent Khrushchev two letters and the draft of a test-ban treaty, which was strikingly similar to the form of the treaty that was finally signed in 1963. The treaty went into effect on October 10, 1963, the day Pauling was notified that he was to receive the Nobel Peace Prize. ◆

> *"You can contribute, and you can't be sure how great your contribution is, but you can contribute, so do it."*
> Linus Pauling, 1990

Pérez Esquivel, Adolfo

NOVEMBER 26, 1931– ● ARGENTINE SCULPTOR AND PEACE ACTIVIST

A dolfo Pérez Esquivel is the coordinator of the Service for Peace and Justice (SERPAJ), Latin America's principal organization promoting societal change through nonviolence. In 1980 he received the Nobel Peace Prize for his work with SERPAJ.

Born in Buenos Aires, Pérez Esquivel was educated in Catholic schools and was deeply influenced by the writings of Saint Augustine and Thomas Merton, was well as by the pacifist example of Mohandas Gandhi. Trained in sculpture at the National School of Fine Arts, he later taught there for fifteen years. He abandoned his successful career as a sculptor in the early 1970s to promote nonviolence as the most appropriate response to the violence that was afflicting Latin America as a result of increasing pressures for change.

In 1974 Pérez Esquivel joined with other Catholic activists to form SERPAJ, an agency for the dissemination of knowledge of nonviolent strategies and for the promotion of greater observance of human rights, participatory models of economic development, greater political participation especially among the poor, disarmament, and demilitarization. That year Pérez Esquivel became the general coordinator of SERPAJ, traveling

> *"Our first step is always to make people aware that they are human beings and deserving of dignity."*
> Adolfo Pérez Esquivel, 1981

The Disappeared

In 1976 the military in Argentina seized control of the government, sharply curtailed political activity, and launched a campaign that eventually crushed the leftist opposition. Human rights groups estimate that between 5,000 and 15,000 Argentines vanished during the 1970s. The missing are called Los Desaparecidos (the Disappeared). Many humanitarians, including Nobel Peace Prize winner Adolfo Pérez Esquivel, took up the cause of the disappeared and their families.

The Mothers of the Plaza de Mayo began demonstrating in the Buenos Aires Plaza de Mayo in 1977. Dressed in black, they demanded to know the fate of their loved ones. Marching around the statue of liberty, in front of the presidential palace, they tied white handkerchiefs around their heads with names of disappeared sons and daughters and carried signs emblazoned with photographs. Even though the military regime responsible for the atrocities fell in 1983, the Mothers of the Plaza de Mayo still continue to demonstrate every Thursday at 3:30 in the afternoon. They vow to continue until all of the missing are identified.

throughout Latin America and elsewhere to promote nonviolence. As a result of his work he was jailed for fourteen months in 1977–78 by the Argentine military government. Upon his release he resumed his work promoting nonviolence as the most effective way of creating a democratic and liberating social order. ◆

Phillips, Wendell

November 29, 1811–February 2, 1884 ● Abolitionist

Wendell Phillips was one of the most powerful and individual orators of his time. An inspiring speaker, he stirred the hearts of many nineteenth-century audiences, inspiring them to join the antislavery movement.

Phillips was born into a wealthy and important family in Salem, Massachusetts. He attended Boston Latin School where he was honored for his speaking ability. He graduated from Harvard College in 1831 and attended Harvard Law School. In 1837 he married Ann Greene.

Wendell Phillips became very skillful as a platform speaker, working before audiences with great physical charm and excellent voice. In the nineteenth century, orators depended very

Wendell Phllips was one of the most powerful and individual orators of his time.

ANTI-SLAVERY MEETING ON THE COMMON.

much on the personal impact of their speeches for effect, and Phillips was an effective speaker. After graduation from Harvard and early success as a lawyer, Wendell Phillips became interested in the abolition of slavery. In December 1837 Phillips's spontaneous address condemning the murder of Elijah P. Lovejoy at a public meeting in Boston's Faneuil Hall caught the imagination and stirred the hearts of the audience. His reputation as an eloquent speaker was established and he became a leader of the antislavery protest.

Phillips worked with William Lloyd Garrison and denounced slavery as a complete evil. In fact, Phillips went to the extent of charging that the U.S. Constitution was evil for protecting slavery, and he suggested that the free states of the North ought to secede from the Union. During the Civil War he was impatient with the Lincoln policy that looked for a reunion of the states and that delayed acting to abolish slavery.

Lecturing on lyceum platforms, Phillips traveled from place to place denouncing slavery. He also wrote pamphlets and editorials from Garrison's *Liberator* but his primary contribution to the movement was as an orator.

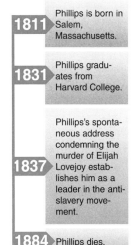

1811 Phillips is born in Salem, Massachusetts.

1831 Phillips graduates from Harvard College.

1837 Phillips's spontaneous address condemning the murder of Elijah Lovejoy establishes him as a leader in the anti-slavery movement.

1884 Phillips dies.

The Abolition Movement

The movement to end slavery, which began in the United States as early as the 1600s and grew with the efforts of Patrick Henry and others during the American Revolution, is known as the abolition movement. Though most abolition activity took place in the United States and Britain, there have been antislavery operations in many other parts of the world as well. Some of the most famous abolitionists came from New England, which was an area of much antislavery activity. William Lloyd Garrison published an antislavery newspaper called *The Liberator* in 1831 and the poets James Russell Lowell and John Greenleaf Whittier were active abolitionists. Lucretia Mott, Wendell Phillips, and Sarah and Angelina Grimke were among the many who were great influences in the abolition movement.

Phillips's zeal as a reformer and skill as a speaker continued after the Civil War for causes that he adopted. He was a strong advocate of Prohibition and he felt that the American Indians had not been fairly treated. Phillips was also impressed by the mistreatment of many laboring people. He argued against the profit motive in organizing and conducting business, because he linked profits with unfair treatment of workers. He was nominated by the Labor Reform and the Prohibition parties for the governorship of Massachusetts in 1870 but his candidacy was unsuccessful. He continued to lecture throughout his life until his death in 1884. ◆

Picotte, Susan LaFlesche

1866–1915 ● NATIVE AMERICAN PHYSICIAN, REFORMER, AND CIVIC LEADER

Picotte created for herself a unique role as a civic leader, doctor, missionary, and spokesperson for the Omaha Indians.

Susan LaFlesche Picotte was born on the Omaha reservation in Nebraska. The daughter of Joseph LaFlesche, "progressive" chief of the Omaha Indians, and his wife, Mary Gale, Susan LaFlesche was educated at the reservation mission school, a young ladies' academy in New Jersey, and Hampton Institute in Virginia. With the help of the Connecticut branch of the Women's National Indian Association, a philanthropic reform group, she then attended the Woman's Medical College in Philadelphia, from which she graduated in March 1889 as the first Native American woman physician in the United States.

After her graduation she returned to the Omaha reservation where she planned to open a hospital. In 1894 she married

Henry Picotte, a French Sioux, with whom she had two sons; after her husband died in 1905, she moved to the newly incorporated town of Walthill, Nebraska.

Picotte created for herself a unique role as civic leader, doctor, missionary, and spokesperson for the Omaha Indians. She was an avid supporter of prohibition, a founder of Walthill's Presbyterian church, president of the local board of health, and a member of the local women's club, the Thurston County Medical Association, the State Medical Society, and the Nebraska Federation of Women's Clubs. Her major satisfaction, however, always came from her work for the Omahas. In addition to treating as many as one hundred patients a month, she assisted countless people with financial or personal problems. She made maximum use of her contacts to cut through government red tape and always blended her concrete assistance with advice firmly rooted in Protestant Christianity and Victorian morality.

In 1913 Picotte saw her dream realized when the Presbyterian Board of Home Missions established a hospital in Walthill. When she died two years later at the age of forty-nine, the hospital was renamed in her honor. ◆

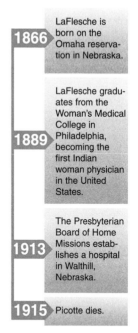

1866 LaFlesche is born on the Omaha reservation in Nebraska.

1889 LaFlesche graduates from the Woman's Medical College in Philadelphia, becoming the first Indian woman physician in the United States.

1913 The Presbyterian Board of Home Missions establishes a hospital in Walthill, Nebraska.

1915 Picotte dies.

Purvis, Robert

AUGUST 4, 1810–APRIL 19, 1898 ● ABOLITIONIST AND POLITICAL LEADER

Robert Purvis was born in Charleston, South Carolina, the second of three sons of William Purvis, a British cotton merchant, and Harriet Judah, a free woman of color. A staunch opponent of slavery, William Purvis instilled his hatred of the "peculiar institution" in his sons. Robert Purvis gave his first antislavery speech when he was seventeen.

In 1819 William Purvis sent his family to Philadelphia, intending eventually to settle with them in England. The children were enrolled in the Pennsylvania Abolition Society's Clarkson School, and Robert later attended Amherst College in Massachusetts. In 1826 William Purvis died, leaving the bulk of his fortune—some $200,000—to his sons. When the eldest son died without issue, his brothers received his share. A shrewd businessman, Robert Purvis put his legacy to good use, investing in bank stock and real estate.

Robert Purvis gave his first antislavery speech when he was seventeen.

Purvis sheltered runaway slaves and conveyed them to the next "safe house" in his carriage.

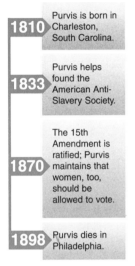

1810 ▶ Purvis is born in Charleston, South Carolina.

1833 ▶ Purvis helps found the American Anti-Slavery Society.

1870 ▶ The 15th Amendment is ratified; Purvis maintains that women, too, should be allowed to vote.

1898 ▶ Purvis dies in Philadelphia.

disheartened: dispirited.

Light-skinned and wealthy, Purvis rejected suggestions that he relocate and "pass." In 1831 he married Harriet Forten, the daughter of African-American businessman and abolitionist James Forten. With his Forten in-laws he threw himself into the antislavery struggle. A tireless member of the Philadelphia Vigilance Committee, he sheltered runaways and conveyed them to the next "safe house" in his carriage. With William Lloyd Garrison, he was a founding member of the American Anti-Slavery Society in 1833, and in 1834 he crossed the Atlantic to meet leaders of the British antislavery movement. With his father-in-law, he helped steer white abolitionists, among them Garrison and Arthur Tappan, away from African colonization and toward a sweeping program designed to achieve racial equality. Purvis also had a profound influence on his young niece, educator and social reformer Charlotte Forten, who spent much of her early life in the Purvis household.

For two decades the Purvises lived in an elegant home in Philadelphia, where they entertained abolitionists from the United States and Europe. In 1842, with racial violence escalating, they moved to an estate in Byberry, some twelve miles outside Philadelphia.

Purvis welcomed the outbreak of the Civil War, demanding that President Abraham Lincoln make emancipation his goal. With the end of the war came an invitation to head the Freedmen's Bureau. However, Purvis declined the offer, fearing that this was a ploy by President Andrew Johnson to keep the support of African-American voters even as he set about destroying the bureau.

Initially a staunch Republican, Purvis became **disheartened** as the party retreated from the principles it espoused during Reconstruction. In the Philadelphia mayoral race of 1874, his endorsement of the Democratic candidate was denounced by other African-American leaders. He was also criticized for his stance on the Fifteenth Amendment, which was ratified in 1870. A lifelong champion of women's rights, Purvis contended that African-American men should not be enfranchised unless women received the vote.

In the last two decades of his life Purvis assumed the role of an elder statesman, tending his garden, orchard, and livestock. He died in Philadelphia at the age of eighty-seven, survived by his second wife and four of his eight children. ◆

Randolph, Asa Philip

APRIL 15, 1889–MAY 16, 1979 ● LABOR AND CIVIL RIGHTS LEADER

The younger son of James William Randolph (a minister in the African Methodist Episcopal Church), A. Philip Randolph was born in Crescent City, Florida, and raised in Jacksonville. In 1911, after graduating from the Cookman Institute in Jacksonville, the twenty-two-year-old Randolph migrated to New York City and settled in Harlem, then in an early stage of its development as the "Negro capital of the world." While working at odd jobs to support himself, he attended the City College of New York (adjoining Harlem), where he took courses in history, philosophy, economics, and political science. During his enrollment at CCNY, he also became active in the Socialist party, whose leader, Eugene Debs, was one of his political heroes.

Between 1914 and the early 1920s Randolph belonged to a group of young African-American **militants** in New York, the "Harlem radicals," who regarded themselves as the New Negro political avant-garde in American life. Some of them, including Randolph, combined race radicalism with socialism. Others, such as Marcus Garvey, who arrived in Harlem in 1916, emphasized an Africa-oriented black nationalism—they were **averse** to movements that advocated social reform or racial integration within the mainstream of American society. But all Harlem radicals defied the old establishment of African-American leadership, though it included so distinguished a member as W. E. B. Du Bois.

To race radicalism and socialism Randolph soon added an interest in trade unionism, which was to form a basic part of his

> *"Nothing counts but pressure, pressure, more pressure, and still more pressure through broad organized aggressive mass action."*
> A. Philip
> Randolph, 1942

militants: group acting aggressively for a cause.

averse: having an active feeling of distaste.

245

approach to the struggle for black progress. In 1917 he and his closest socialist comrade in Harlem, Chandler Owen, founded and began coediting *The Messenger*, a monthly journal that subtitled itself "The Only Radical Magazine Published by Negroes." The *Messenger* campaigned against lynchings in the South; opposed America's participation in World War I; counseled African Americans to resist the military draft; proposed an economic solution to the "Negro problem"; and urged blacks to ally themselves with the socialist and trade-union movements. For its **irreverent** editorial stands, the *Messenger* came under the close surveillance of the federal government. In 1918 Postmaster General Albert Burleson revoked the magazine's second-class mailing privileges, and in 1919 a Justice Department report ordered by Attorney General A. Mitchell Palmer described the *Messenger* as being "by long odds the most able and most dangerous of the Negro publications."

irreverent: lacking proper respect.

In 1917 Randolph also helped to organize the Socialist party's first black political club in New York, located in Harlem's Twenty-first Assembly District. And in 1920, the party recognized his growing importance as a spokesman by naming him its candidate for New York State **comptroller**, one of the highest positions to which a black socialist had been named. He lost in the November elections but polled an impressive 202,361 votes, about a thousand fewer than Eugene Debs polled in New York that year as the Socialist party's candidate for president.

comptroller: an official who audits public accounts.

In the early 1920s Randolph began dissolving his formal ties to the party when it became clear to him that the black masses were not as responsive to the socialist message as he had hoped. This was partly because of their traditional distrust for ideologies they deemed to be un-American; partly because black nationalism was, emotionally and psychologically, more appealing to them; and partly because the Socialist party failed to address the special problems of black exclusion from the trade-union movement. But despite his retirement from formal party activities, Randolph was always to consider himself a democratic socialist.

In 1925 a delegation of Pullman porters approached Randolph with a request that he organize their workforce into a legitimate labor union.

In 1925 a delegation of Pullman porters approached him with a request that he organize their workforce into a legitimate labor union, independent of employer participation and influence. Randolph undertook the task—a decision that launched his career as a national leader in the fields of labor and civil rights. But establishing the Brotherhood of Sleeping Car Porters was a far more difficult task than he had anticipated. The Pullman Company had crushed a number of earlier efforts at organizing its porters, and for the next twelve years it remained contemptuous of Randolph's. Not until 1937, after Congress had passed enabling labor legislation, did the Pullman executives recognize the Brotherhood of Sleeping Car Porters as a certified bargaining agent.

This victory gained the brotherhood full membership in the American Federation of Labor (AFL). It also gave Randolph— as the brotherhood's chief delegate to annual AFL conventions—an opportunity to answer intellectuals in Harlem who had criticized him for urging blacks to ally themselves with the trade-union movement. The black **intelligentsia** then regarded the AFL as a racist institution, most of whose craft unions barred nonwhite membership. How then (his critics argued) could Randolph call on blacks to invest their economic aspirations in organized labor? Randolph maintained, however, that trade unionism was the main engine of economic advancement for the working class, the class to which a majority of the black population belonged. He believed, moreover, that the achievement of political rights, for which all blacks were struggling, would be meaningless without comparable economic gains.

Throughout his tenure as a delegate to the annual conventions of organized labor (in 1955 he became a vice president of the merged AFL-CIO), Randolph campaigned relentlessly against unions that excluded black workers. When he retired as a vice president in 1968, the AFL-CIO had become the most integrated public institution in American life, though pockets of resistance remained. Randolph was not the sole instrument of that revolution, but he was its opening wedge, and much of it was owed to his unyielding agitation.

The brotherhood's victory in 1937 also **inaugurated** Randolph's career as a national civil rights leader; he emerged from the struggle with Pullman as one of the more respected figures in black America. In 1937 the recently formed National Negro Congress (NNC), recognizing Randolph's potential as a mass leader, invited him to be its president. In accepting, he himself saw the NNC as a potential mass movement. But he was obliged to resign the NNC's presidency in 1940, when he discovered that much of the organization had fallen under communist control. He was to be a resolute anticommunist for the rest of his life. He wrote to a colleague in 1959:

1889 Randolph is born in Crescent City, Florida.

1911 Randolph graduates from Cookman Institute in Jacksonville and moves to Harlem.

1917 Randolph and Chandler Owen found and begin coediting the *Messenger – The Only Radical Magazine Published by Negroes.*

1925 Randolph begins organizing the Brotherhood of Sleeping Car Porters.

1937 Randolph becomes president of the NNC.

1955 Randolph becomes vice president of the AFL.

1964 Randolph receives the Presidential Medal of Freedom.

1979 Randolph dies.

intelligentsia: political elite.

inaugurate: to bring about the beginning.

They [communists] are not only undemocratic but anti-democratic. They are opposed to our concept of the dignity of the human personality, the heritage of the Judeo-Christian philosophy, and hence they represent a totalitarian system in which civil liberties cannot live.

"Freedom is never given; it is won."
A. Philip Randolph, 1937

Randolph's withdrawal from the NNC freed him to organize, early in 1941, the March on Washington Movement based on the Gandhian method of nonviolent direct action. It achieved its first major victory in June of that year. Faced with Randolph's threat to lead a massive invasion of the nation's capital, President Franklin D. Roosevelt issued an executive order banning the exclusion of blacks from employment in defense plants—the federal government's earliest commitment to the policy of fair employment. That breakthrough brought Randolph to the forefront of black mass leadership, making him "the towering civil rights figure of the period," according to James Farmer, one of his younger admirers. The March on Washington Movement disintegrated by the end of the 1940s. But by then Randolph had secured another historic executive order—this one from President Harry S Truman, in 1948, outlawing segregation in the armed services. Scholars were to see his movement as one of the most remarkable in American history. Aspects of its influence went into the formation of Farmer's Congress of Racial Equality (1942) and Rev. Dr. Martin Luther King's Southern Christian Leadership Conference (1957), both of which helped to lead the great nonviolent protest movement of the 1960s.

Randolph was the elder statesman of the nonviolent protest movement of the 1960s, a unifying center of the civil rights coalition.

Randolph was the elder statesman of that movement, a unifying center of the civil rights coalition that composed it. His collaboration with its various leaders culminated in the 1963 March on Washington, the largest demonstration for racial redress in the nation's history. Randolph had conceived that event. And it is appropriate that he should have called it a March for Jobs and Freedom; it represented his two-pronged approach, political and economic, to the black struggle.

After 1963 Randolph the architect of black mass pressure on the federal government faded gradually from the scene. In 1964 President Lyndon B. Johnson awarded him the Presidential Medal of Freedom, the nation's highest civilian honor. He spent the remaining years of his active life chiefly as a vice president of the AFL-CIO. He died in 1979, at the age of ninety. ◆

Rankin, Jeannette

JUNE 11, 1880–MAY 18, 1973 ● WOMAN SUFFRAGIST, PACIFIST, AND THE FIRST WOMAN ELECTED TO THE U.S. CONGRESS

Jeannette Rankin was born on a ranch near Missoula, Montana. The eldest of seven children, she graduated from the University of Montana in 1902, worked in a settlement house in San Francisco, and studied at the New York School of Philanthropy. After gaining political skills during her work for the National American Woman Suffrage Association in Washington, New York, California, and several other states, she returned to Montana to spearhead its successful women's suffrage campaign in 1914. In 1916, using the political base she had created in the suffrage fight, Rankin ran for the U.S. House of Representatives on the Republican ticket. Her promising political career was arrested by her first vote in the House of Representatives, in which she joined fifty-five other members of Congress who voted against the United States' entry into World War I. Although her position was supported by many Montanans, it ultimately led to her defeat in a 1918 bid for the U.S. Senate.

In 1924 Rankin moved to Georgia and began working as a grassroots peace activist. In 1940, with war again looming on the American horizon, she returned to Montana, where she had continued to own property. Once again Montanans elected her to the House of Representatives. In 1941 she cast the sole vote against the U.S. declaration of war against Japan, thus becoming the only person in the history of Congress to vote against U.S. entry into both world wars. This vote, which was widely unpopular, put an end to her political career.

Between 1942 and the late 1960s Rankin led a life of semi-retirement. She traveled extensively and studied the philosophy and techniques of pacifism; she was especially influenced by Gandhi. In 1968 she led the Jeannette Rankin Brigade, a phalanx of women protesters, in a march against the Vietnam War. In 1972 the National Organization of Women chose her as the first inductee into the Susan B. Anthony Hall of Fame. Rankin died a year later, having lived a life remarkable for its adherence to principle over political gain. ◆

1880 Rankin is born near Missoula, Montana.

1924 Rankin moves to Georgia and begins working as a peace activist.

1941 Rankin becomes the only person in the history of Congress to vote against U.S. entry into both world wars.

1968 Rankin leads the Jeannette Rankin Brigade in protest of the Vietnam War.

1972 Rankin is chosen by NOW as the first inductee to the Susan B. Anthony Hall of Fame.

1973 Rankin dies.

Rankin was the only person in the history of the Congress to vote against U.S. entry into both world wars.

Reeve, Christopher

SEPTEMBER 25, 1952– ● ACTIVIST FOR PEOPLE WITH DISABILITIES

> *"The time has come when you don't have to despair anymore. Help is on the way. I think what we all want most in the world is for what we do to be useful, you know, to be recognized, or to be able to make some kind of difference."*
>
> Christopher Reeve, 1999

The actor Christopher Reeve rose to fame as the star of the *Superman* movies, four films about the cartoon superhero. With Susan Sarandon, Ron Silver, and other activists from the entertainment industry, Reeve founded and served as copresident of the Creative Coalition, a pro-arts and environmentalist lobbying force. The organization supported the National Endowment for the Arts and campaigned for safe water and recycling in New York City. Reeve escorted political leaders on flights, piloting his own plane, over timberlands in Maine to give them a firsthand look at clear-cut forests. He traveled to Santiago to stand with actors threatened with execution by the Pinochet government in Chile.

When he was thrown from a horse while competing in a combined training equestrian event on Memorial Day 1995, he landed on his head, shattering his top cervical vertebra, breaking the second, and severing and wounding nerves in his spinal cord. The accident meant weeks in intensive care, high-risk surgery, months in rehabilitative therapy, and years, perhaps a lifetime, as a quadriplegic on a respirator. Like others who have suffered similar accidents is Reeve's determination and the grace with which he has learned to live his new life. He now lends his celebrity to the cause of disabled people everywhere and to those suffering from spinal cord injuries in particular.

Born in New York City on September 25, 1952, Reeve is the son of Franklin d'Olier Reeve, a professor at Wesleyan University in Middletown, Connecticut, and Barbara Pitney Lamb, a debutante. The marriage ended in divorce and Christopher and his brother, Ben, both preschoolers, moved to Princeton, New Jersey, with their mother.

Growing up, Reeve threw himself into backstage crew work at Princeton's McCarter Theatre. He took every opportunity to perform in plays at school and was

The Asian and Pacific Decade of Disabled Persons

The governments of the Asian and Pacific region made a collective commitment to improving the lives of citizens with disabilities by declaring the period 1993-2002 as the Asian and Pacific Decade of Disabled Persons. This unique regional initiative supports the inclusion of people with disabilities in society to reach the decade goal of full participation and equality of people with disabilities. Hong Kong issued a statement at a regional conference on the issue supporting further progress in the areas of legislation, public awareness, disability prevention, human resource development, rehabilitation services, equalization of opportunities, accessibility, social integration, and community-based initiatives. The statement also advocated increased awareness of disability issues. Rehabilitation International and Inclusion International, two international organizations for the disabled, released a joint statement in June 1998 supporting affirmative action for people with disabilities. It urged national level organizations and government ministries join together to promote and implement activities that minimize the negative effects of disabilities through rehabilitation and equalization of opportunities.

eventually given roles in McCarter's repertory company. He apprenticed at the Williamstown Theatre Festival, and was hired by the Harvard Summer School Repertory Theatre. He attended Cornell University, where he majored in drama, and persuaded the theater department to allow him to finish his degree work at the Juilliard School at New York's Lincoln Center. At Juilliard he studied with Michael Kahn and Marian Seldes and made a friend for life of the actor Robin Williams.

Reeve was performing on the New York stage when he auditioned for *Superman,* an action adventure film based on the classic comic strip character. The film and its three sequels made Reeve an international star. He went on to perform in a dozen other films and in fourteen made-for-television movies and small-screen productions, but none captured the public imagination in quite the same way as the *Superman* series. He continued to work on Broadway and in regional theatre and pursued his love of horses and competitive equestrian events.

Reeve credits his wife, singer Dana Morosini, with giving him the will to live immediately following his accident. Morosini reminded Reeve that he was still himself despite his multiple disabilities. His family and friends inspired him to build and continue a daily regimen of exercise so that his body will be prepared for the cure for his condition that he has come to expect.

Reeve began to find a way to begin a new professional life when he journeyed from the rehabilitation center to the stage

1952 Reeve is born in New York City.

1989 Reeve and others found The Creative Coalition.

1995 Reeve suffers a horseback riding accident that leaves him a quadriplegic.

1996 Reeve founds the Christopher Reeve Foundation.

at the Pierre Hotel to present an award to his friend Robin Williams at the Creative Coalition's annual banquet. Sharing the stage and wisecracking along with Williams's comic antics, Reeve found himself basking in the love and admiration of colleagues. He began his new life of service when he spoke at the 1996 Academy Awards, inspiring millions with his lighthearted remarks in the face of his devastating accident.

After a speech to the American Paralysis Association, in which he set a personal goal to begin walking by his fiftieth birthday, Reeve was chosen as APA's board chairman. As a spokesperson for the disabled, he lobbies Congress for increased funding to the National Institutes of Health, speaks out against unfair practices by insurance companies, and supports worldwide symposia and research on finding a cure for those with spinal cord injuries. In 1996 he founded the Christopher Reeve Foundation, whose mission is to raise funds for medical research and to support quality-of-life programs for people with disabilities. The foundation helps people get better wheelchairs and works to make sure that restaurants, businesses, and shops comply with the American Disabilities Act. Reeve's work is making a difference. *The Wall Street Journal* called the dramatic increase in funding for spinal cord research between 1995 and 1999 "the Reeve effect."

Reeve does daily battle against depression as he endures hours of conditioning and care from the professionals who must dress him, bathe him, and move him from bed to chair in the morning and back again at night. He says often, "I'm the president of a club I wouldn't want to join, but that's the way it goes." His determination, optimism, and focus inspire awe as he maintains a rigorous schedule of machine-aided exercise, travel, and public appearances. By personal example, as much as by his activism, Christopher Reeve redefines heroism. ◆

> By personal example, as much as by his activism, Christopher Reeve redefines heroism.

Rockefeller, John Davison

July 8, 1839–May 23, 1937 ● Industrialist

John Davison Rockefeller was born in Richford, Tioga County, New York, where his father traded in lumber and salt. At a very early age, Rockefeller showed an aptitude for numbers, displaying an attention to detail, especially where money was concerned. At the age of seven, he had his first successful business venture—selling turkeys. The family then moved to Ohio, and at age sixteen, Rockefeller went to work in Cleveland for a produce firm. In 1859 he formed a partnership with Colonel Maurice Clark to trade produce. When Clark discovered oil, they began trading Pennsylvania oil. The idea of accruing instant wealth from oil caught their fancy. In 1863, when a new railroad line put Cleveland in a position to compete, refineries sprang into existence. At first, Rockefeller thought refining would be merely a sideline. In 1865, after repeated arguments about expansion, he bought out his partner, Clark, for $12,500. With the purchase of the refinery, Rockefeller began to expand the business and poured his profits, plus borrowed money, into building a second refinery. He decided to open additional markets, and in 1866 put his brother William in charge of another firm in New York as the manager of the Atlantic coast trade and the export of kerosene. The growing popularity of the refining business led Rockefeller to comment: "All sorts of people went into it; the butcher, the baker, and the candlestick maker began to refine oil." His success was a result of his ability to cut costs as well as a ruthlessness in stifling competition.

In 1867 Rockefeller and his new partner, Andre, brought Henry Flagler into the business as a third partner. Flagler became a valued colleague and a close friend. In 1870 Rockefeller and a few of his people incorporated the Standard Oil Company (Ohio) and the company prospered. Rockefeller bought out his competitors by using a new method of purchase—he gave stock in his company to acquire other companies. He never owned more than 27 percent of Standard Oil stock, but even so, he became the wealthiest man in the United States with a personal fortune exceeding one billion dollars.

By the early 1880s Standard Oil had bought out or driven out of business most of its competition in Ohio. The company used its leverage to obtain reduced freight rates. It then bought pipelines and terminals, and began to buy competing refineries in other cities until Standard Oil almost had a **monopoly**. The company exploited every avenue to increase income and lower expenses. It not only received reduced freight rates but was also getting "drawbacks," collecting a percentage of the freight costs paid by the competition. This practice led to the enactment of antimonopoly laws, first by the states and then by Congress. The Sherman Antitrust Act was passed by Congress in 1890, and the law was upheld in the Ohio Supreme Court in 1892.

Rockefeller was able to work around the law for a while by eliminating the Standard Oil "Trust" and renaming the com-

"The most important thing for a young man is to establish credit— a reputation, character."

John D. Rockefeller

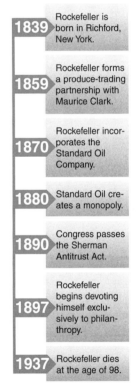

1839 Rockefeller is born in Richford, New York.

1859 Rockefeller forms a produce-trading partnership with Maurice Clark.

1870 Rockefeller incorporates the Standard Oil Company.

1880 Standard Oil creates a monopoly.

1890 Congress passes the Sherman Antitrust Act.

1897 Rockefeller begins devoting himself exclusively to philanthropy.

1937 Rockefeller dies at the age of 98.

monopoly: commodity controlled by one company.

pany Standard Oil Company of New Jersey. The new company was the largest and most efficient producer of petroleum products. Standard Oil of New Jersey operated throughout the world, until 1911, when the Supreme Court ruled that the company was in violation of the Sherman Antitrust Act.

"I believe it is every man's religious duty to get all he can honestly and to give all he can."

John D. Rockefeller, 1850

Rockefeller was a generous philanthropist. As a pious Baptist he began by making relatively small contributions to the Baptist church. In 1892 he was instrumental in founding the University of Chicago. It was suggested that Rockefeller gave his spare change to the university—amounting to thirty-five million dollars. From 1897 he devoted himself exclusively to philanthropy, joined by his son John (1894–1960). They created the Rockefeller Institute for Medical Research, later renamed Rockefeller University. In his lifetime, John D. Rockefeller contributed over half a billion dollars to charity.

In his later years, Rockefeller was well known for his habit of carrying a pocketful of shiny new dimes that he would give to the small children he met in his travels. Despite his great wealth, he was frugal with regard to personal expenses. He would wear suits until they became shiny. When he died at the age of ninety-eight, he was worth twenty-six million dollars, including a single share in Standard Oil worth $43.94. ◆

Roosevelt, Eleanor

OCTOBER 11, 1884–NOVEMBER 7, 1962 ● FIRST LADY, POLITICAL ACTIVIST, AND HUMANITARIAN

Born into a branch of the prominent Roosevelt family (she was Theodore Roosevelt's niece), Anna Eleanor Roosevelt experienced an unhappy childhood, a formative education abroad, and a brief stint teaching in a social settlement in New York City before marrying her third cousin Franklin D. Roosevelt in 1905. She devoted the following years to domesticity, bearing six children (five of whom lived), and supporting her husband's career. Her discovery in 1918 of his affair with her social secretary, Lucy Mercer, altered her domestic priorities. Thereafter, her marriage became a "business partnership," and she sought emotional sustenance primarily among a circle of women political friends.

In 1921 Franklin Roosevelt became paralyzed from poliomyelitis. At the urging of Louis Howe, Roosevelt's mentor and campaign manager, Eleanor Roosevelt joined New York women's political and advocacy groups, ostensibly to keep Roosevelt's name before the public. The leadership positions she attained in these groups not only brought her new friends but enabled her to pursue important reform issues such as unionization and protective legislation for women. In 1928, during Alfred E. Smith's presidential campaign, she headed the women's division of the national Democratic committee. These experiences influenced the evolution of her political views and honed her speaking, writing, and organizational skills.

As the president's wife, Eleanor Roosevelt represented the views of reformers to White House administrators, influenced federal appointments of women, and made certain that New Deal programs included women. In 1936 she began a syndicated newspaper column, "My Day," that reported on her travels to gather support for New Deal programs and collect information for the president. She also went on paid lecture tours.

Some of her activities drew criticism. Called a "busybody," she was told that a proper First Lady should confine herself to White House ceremonial functions. Criticism mounted when she invested her earnings in "Arthurdale," a subsistence homestead scheme for West Virginia miners, and when she took unpopular stands for free speech or against racial discrimination. During World War II, she served as codirector of the Office of Civilian Defense but resigned when the social-service programs she devised were ridiculed. Her travels on the president's behalf to bring comfort to troops were more appreciated although still censured for being costly. Criticism upset her, but it did not deter her public activities. Within the limits imposed by her marital status, she was the most independent, activist of all First Ladies.

After Franklin Roosevelt's death, President Harry S Truman appointed her a delegate to the United Nations. She helped defeat Soviet delegate Andrei Vishinsky's position on refugee repatriation and later led the struggle to hammer out the Universal Declaration of Human Rights. When Dwight D. Eisenhower became president, she resigned but remained politically active; she helped form Americans for Democratic

"No one can make you feel inferior without your consent."
Eleanor Roosevelt

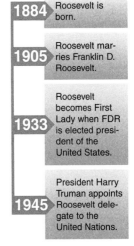

1884 Roosevelt is born.

1905 Roosevelt marries Franklin D. Roosevelt.

1933 Roosevelt becomes First Lady when FDR is elected president of the United States.

1945 President Harry Truman appoints Roosevelt delegate to the United Nations.

Action, opposed Senator Joseph McCarthy's anticommunist witch-hunts, supported presidential candidate Adlai E. Stevenson, and represented the American Association for the United Nations. President John F. Kennedy appointed her chair of his Commission on the Status of Women. Although she died before it completed its work, her role as chair provided fitting closure to a life that had been committed so fully to women's and other social concerns. ◆

Roosevelt, Theodore

OCTOBER 27, 1858–JANUARY 6, 1919 ● PRESIDENT OF THE UNITED STATES, CONSERVATIONIST, AND REFORMER

"Get action. Seize the moment. Man was never intended to become an oyster."

Theodore Roosevelt

"Teddy" Roosevelt, as he was nicknamed, was the son of a New York merchant. He suffered from asthma attacks and was a frail boy. His family gave him good training and care, and he was himself determined to be strong and healthy. By sheer will power and constant exercise, he did what he had set out to do. By the time he reached college age, he was in excellent condition. His favorite sport was boxing.

Roosevelt was a good student. He won election to Phi Beta Kappa, the national honor fraternity for college students, before he graduated from Harvard in 1880. Roosevelt tried law study for awhile after graduation, but gave it up to become a writer. His first book, *The Naval War of 1812*, a history, appeared in 1882 and was well received.

In that same year, Theodore Roosevelt entered politics in New York City. He was the Republican candidate for the State Assembly and he won. He had a flair for publicity, and also for independence. He would not take orders from his political party leaders, and he saw to it that whatever he did was promptly reported to the newspapers. In the State legislature, he supported reform legislation that the Democratic governor, Grover Cleveland, recommended. Roosevelt himself showed a great deal of interest in civil service reform, and in laws concerning labor and business.

Roosevelt suffered a terrible personal blow in 1884. On Valentine's Day, February 14, both his young wife (whom he had married in 1880) and his mother died within a few hours of each other. He had already lost his father. He decided to leave New York (at least for a time) and he invested some money in ranchland far out west, in the badlands area of the Dakota territory. There he spent nearly two years, running a ranch, living with cowboys, and loving every minute of the strenuous work, the outdoor life, and his beautiful surroundings. He lost most of the money he had invested, for his cattle died during a very severe winter, but he returned east in 1887 refreshed and ready to tackle any problem. He set to work writing and turned out six books, including the first volumes of *The Winning of the West*, books about the early pioneers who faced dangers in the west and turned them into opportunities for themselves and for the United States. He remarried in 1886 and returned to politics, working for Benjamin Harrison's election in 1888.

Roosevelt's reward for helping the Harrison campaign was an appointment to the U.S. Civil Service Commission. He worked in this office from 1889 to 1895, as his appointment was renewed by the Democrat, Grover Cleveland, reelected president in 1894. Roosevelt won a reputation for fairness and for quick action. Meanwhile, he was friendly with important Washington figures, including such leaders as John Hay and Henry Adams. He returned to New York in 1895 to head the New York City Police Commission. Again, he publicized his work. He tried earnestly to reward and advance honest policemen and to punish those who were dishonest or lazy. To some, he was a snooping nuisance. They made fun of his eyeglasses and called him "four eyes." Most people who knew him considered him a man they could trust.

He returned to Washington in 1897 when William McKinley was sworn in as president. Roosevelt had helped in the 1896 campaign, but the top leaders in the Republican party did not especially approve of independence and frankness. He was given the post of **undersecretary** of the navy, where he might be conveniently forgotten, but since the secretary did not manage things very closely, Roosevelt became a very prominent figure. He was caught up in the movement to intervene in the Cuban revolution to force Spain out of Cuba. He argued strongly

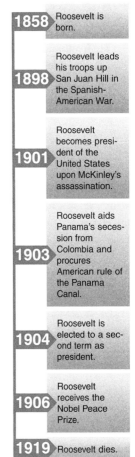

1858 Roosevelt is born.

1898 Roosevelt leads his troops up San Juan Hill in the Spanish-American War.

1901 Roosevelt becomes president of the United States upon McKinley's assassination.

1903 Roosevelt aids Panama's secession from Colombia and procures American rule of the Panama Canal.

1904 Roosevelt is elected to a second term as president.

1906 Roosevelt receives the Nobel Peace Prize.

1919 Roosevelt dies.

undersecretary: official directly underneath the secretary.

"[W]e cannot afford to take part in or be indifferent to oppression or maltreatment of any man who . . . has by his own industry, energy, self-respect, and perseverance struggled upward to a position which would entitle him to the respect of his fellows, if only his skin were of a different hue."

Theodore Roosevelt, 1905

franchise: a special privilege granted to a group.

for intervention and denounced President McKinley's cautious and peaceful approach as unmanly. Eventually, McKinley, a four-year veteran of fighting in the Civil War, was backed into a declaration of war on Spain. Roosevelt promptly resigned from his desk job in Washington and looked for active duty.

With Leonard Wood as colonel, Roosevelt helped recruit a regiment of volunteer cavalry for the U.S. Army. He became its lieutenant-colonel, but in the eyes of the public, he was the leader of the outfit, which was made up of cowhands, college boys, and friends of T. R. The Rough Riders, as they were called, went to Cuba and were part of the campaign against Santiago. They charged up one side of San Juan Hill on July 1, 1898 (they charged on foot, for a number of reasons), with Roosevelt personally in charge. Although the Rough Riders were only part of the division that captured San Juan Hill, the American public regarded the battle as Teddy Roosevelt's own victory.

After the fighting ended, Roosevelt became a special nuisance to his army superiors. He saw to it that the public learned of the terrible sanitary conditions in the camps in Cuba, which were causing the sickness and death of many soldiers. Roosevelt was soon back in his home state. The New York State Republicans now found themselves with a genuine war hero, as well as an independent, reform-minded politician. Without much enthusiasm, the party nominated him for governor of New York.

The 1899 campaign for governor turned into a Teddy Roosevelt show. He campaigned all over the state with an escort of his wartime buddies, the Rough Riders. He swept the election and became governor. In office, he used his personal influence and his political power to further civil service reform. He backed a program to tax some of the large companies in the state that used public property in their business (**franchises** for the use of streets by street railways, for instance.). The Progressive Era was under way, and Theodore Roosevelt was soon recognized as a very progressive governor.

The New York party was furious with him by 1900. They were looking for ways to get him out of the state. Vice President Garret Hobart had died in office, but President McKinley was to run again in 1900. The New York party leaders managed to have Roosevelt named for the vice president's position, hoping to get him out of New York and into a position of no power for the next four years. Roosevelt accepted the nomination, and he carried the chief burden of the 1900 campaign for the

Republicans. He was sworn in as vice president in March 1901. He was worried whether he might be permanently "on the shelf" in that position.

In September 1901, while Roosevelt was on a hunting trip in the Adirondack Mountains wilderness, President William McKinley was shot. The vice president hurried back to make contact with the rest of the government, just in time to learn that McKinley had died. On September 14, 1901, Theodore Roosevelt was sworn in as president of the United States. He was not quite forty-three years old, the youngest man ever to take office as president. His political foes in New York were devastated. The "cowboy" they had tried to get rid of was now in the White House.

When Theodore Roosevelt became president, there was a great deal of discontent among Americans. The Populists had fought against some abuses suffered by American farmers and debtors, and their party had disappeared into the Democratic party. Many of the abuses they had fought against continued. Civil service was a problem that was beginning to yield to the work of successive presidents. Trusts, which were combinations of the wealthiest and most powerful businessmen, seemed to control many of the industries in the country. The little businessman, the laborer, and the farmer often felt that they were at the mercy of the big businessman, especially if he controlled a major railroad or a large bank.

Roosevelt announced that he intended to see that every American, rich or poor, had a "square deal." The term comes from card games, where cards can be dealt unfairly or honestly. Americans in 1901 used the word "square" for "honest," and T. R. threatened to use the power of the president to make sure that people got exactly a square deal.

He led Congress to pass important laws to regulate business. The Elkins Act (1903), for example, required railroads to charge the same rates to all customers, and not to favor anyone by "rebates"—that is, paying back parts of freight rates to big customers. A few years later, Roosevelt's Justice Department lawyers sued the Standard Oil Company of Indiana under the Elkins Act for having received rebates. Roosevelt was not satisfied just to have a law passed; he tried to use the law to prevent companies from taking unfair advantage.

Labor problems attracted a great deal of attention. There were many questions over whether unions should be helped, permitted to exist, or stopped by government action. The most

> Roosevelt announced that he intended to see that every American, rich or poor, had a "square deal."

"There is a homely adage which runs: 'Speak softly and carry a big stick; you will go far.'"
Theodore
Roosevelt, 1901

important labor problem that Theodore Roosevelt had to solve came in 1902. The United Mine Workers called a great strike against the hard-coal (anthracite) mines in Pennsylvania. The mine owners refused to deal with the union for many months. Finally, President Roosevelt decided that the public interest required the mines to open. He called on both sides to permit a government arbitrator to decide the dispute. The union agreed to this, but the mine owners refused. Roosevelt then threatened to have the army take over and operate the mines, and he called on important bankers to persuade the mine owners to agree. The pressure worked, and the mine strike was settled. The most important conclusion to be drawn from this event was that the federal government would henceforth represent the interest of the public in the case of a major strike.

Progressives were especially worried bout the concentration of money, or power over money, in a few hands. One outstanding example of this was the Northern Securities Company, an organization that controlled most of the railroads north and west of Chicago. Roosevelt ordered his attorney general to charge Northern Securities with violating the antitrust laws, and in 1904 the U.S. Supreme Court agreed that the Northern Securities Company had to be broken up. In this and similar cases, Roosevelt was supported by a large majority of Americans who praised him as a "Trustbuster." He himself thought that a trust that operated fairly was perfectly all right, but he was determined to destroy unfair trusts.

Roosevelt, the outdoors enthusiast, was interested in the conservation of American natural resources. He pushed this program the entire time he was president. In 1902 he helped put through the Newlands Act. This provided for the start of federally sponsored **irrigation** projects in the arid parts of the country. He was responsible for withdrawing about a quarter of a billion acres of forest and mineral lands from misuse, and he required a full appraisal of the value of public lands before permitting them to be sold off. He was interested in extending national parks and forests, and probably had more influence on American history because of his conservation interests than for anything else. Gifford Pinchot was Roosevelt's chief aide in conservation matters.

Roosevelt's policies were very popular with American voters, who returned him to the White House in the 1904 election by a wide margin. He continued his attention to progressive reforms during his second term. During that term, he was

irrigation: supplying with water.

annoyed by the "muckrakers" (he gave them that name himself) who could only write about the bad side of American life, and not of the healthy and good side. However, he acted on some of the muckrakers' complaints. For example, during his second term the Pure Food and Drug Act was passed (June 30, 1906). This law established minimum standards for healthy foods and for the purity of drugs to treat the ill. It was another effort to protect the public and make sure that Americans got a "square deal" when they bought meat or medicine. At the very end of his term as president, Roosevelt signed the first law in the United States to prohibit the free sale of opium and other narcotics.

One other aspect of American life attracted Roosevelt's attention. His experience in the Spanish-American War convinced him that the U.S. Army needed a thorough overhauling. A general staff was provided for the army, beginning in 1903. Roosevelt hoped that it would make for a more efficient army in case of future wars. He was also interested in pushing the U.S. Navy to a peak of efficiency. He sponsored the building of additional modern battleships for the fleet and made the navy one of the important naval forces of the world.

Theodore Roosevelt was interested in every form of innovation and invention. While he was president, the army was permitted to purchase and operate the first dirigible balloons (balloons with engines that could drive them through the air). He was the first American president to ride in an automobile during a parade. After he left the White House, he was the first to fly in an airplane—at a time when airplanes were little more than powered kites. The first wireless messages were flashed across the Atlantic while Roosevelt was president, and he encouraged his naval and military officers to investigate the uses of radio for military purposes.

Strictly speaking, Theodore Roosevelt never retired. After his personally selected Republican successor, William Howard Taft, was elected in 1908, Roosevelt went off on hunting trips and lectured and wrote extensively. But by 1912 he had completely soured on his old friend Taft. He believed that Taft had not continued the Roosevelt policies, especially in conservation and trust matters. So after an attempt to win the Republican nomination himself, T. R. set up his own personal party and ran for president in 1912.

In that election, the Roosevelt party was known as the Progressive or "Bull Moose" party. (Roosevelt had said that he

His experience in the Spanish-American War convinced him that the U.S. Army needed a thorough overhauling.

"The nation behaves well if it treats its natural resources as assets which it must turn over to the next generation increased, and not impaired, in value."

Theodore Roosevelt, 1910

felt strong as a "bull moose" in returning to the political wars.) His campaign was marked by an attempted assassination; a man later judged to be insane shot a bullet into Roosevelt's chest in Milwaukee. The bullet was slowed down by a heavy eyeglass case, and he was only lightly wounded. When the votes were counted, Roosevelt had not won the presidency. He had diverted enough Republican votes, however, for Woodrow Wilson to win—the second Democrat since the Civil War to become president.

Roosevelt turned again to exploring, nature study, and writing. He headed an **expedition** into the Brazilian jungles in 1914, an expedition in which he contracted fevers that left him permanently weakened. The trip is commemorated on the map by the Rio Teodoro, named in his honor. When World War I broke out, Roosevelt originally was a neutral, friendly to both English and German leaders. However, he quickly decided that the Germans were wrong, and he began to insist that the United States should help the Allies. When Wilson maintained neutrality, Roosevelt denounced him and the Congress for following him. After the United States actually entered the war, Roosevelt approached Wilson in the hope of being named to a high command of American forces in Europe. Wilson turned him down, and the ex-president had to sit out the war.

expedition: journey.

Theodore Roosevelt's philosophy of facing danger and conquering it inspired his own sons, as it did many others. During World War I, his son Quentin was one of America's earliest fighter pilots, and was killed in action. Long after the president's death, his son and namesake, General Theodore Roosevelt, was the first general officer ashore in the American invasion of Normandy in World War II, where he died of a heart attack. A third son, Kermit Roosevelt, died in service in Alaska during World War II.

Above all,
Roosevelt left
the nation the
idea of a square
deal—of every
man's right to
start off fairly
with others, and
of the government's duty to
see to it that its
citizens were
started off fairly.

Teddy Roosevelt made a tremendous impression on American history. He believed in developing the powers of a man, or a nation, and using those powers for what he thought was right. He was firmly convinced that his country should extend its influence around the world in the interests of what seemed right. He built his own strength from a puny boyhood to a point at which he outrode cavalry officers, and suffered severe eye injury at his favorite sport of boxing. Above all, Roosevelt left the nation the idea of the square deal—of every man's right to start off fairly with others, and of the government's duty to see to it that its citizens were started off fairly. His contribution to the American conservation movement is enormous. Rough-speaking leader of men though he was, he delighted in his own children and in having other children visit him. He was entertained and pleased to hear that the "teddy bear" had been named after him. ◆

Rustin, Bayard

MARCH 17, 1910–AUGUST 24, 1987 ● CIVIL RIGHTS LEADER AND PACIFIST

B ayard Rustin was a civil rights leader, pacifist, political organizer, and controversial public figure. He was born in West Chester, Pennsylvania, in 1910, the last of nine children. He accumulated a colorful personal history, beginning with his youthful discovery that the woman he had assumed was his older sister was actually his mother. Reared by his mother and grandparents, local caterers, he grew up in the relatively privileged setting of a large mansion in town. Like the rest of his family, Rustin became a Quaker, maintaining an enduring commitment to personal pacifism as a way of life. Tall, thin, usually bushy-haired, and with an acquired West Indian accent, Rustin was noticed wherever he appeared.

He attended college at West Chester State, then moved to Harlem during the 1930s, where he cultivated a **bohemian** lifestyle, attending classes at City College, singing with jazz groups and at night clubs, and gaining a reputation as a chef. His most notable activity, however, was aligning with the Communist party through the Young Communist League, a decision based on the party's position on race issues. In 1941 when asked by the party to abandon his program to gain young black recruits in favor of a singular emphasis on the European war effort, Rustin quit the party.

His public personality and organizing skills subsequently brought him to the attention of A. Philip Randolph, who recruited him to help develop his plans for a massive March on Washington to secure equal access to defense jobs. The two men, despite brief skirmishes, remained lifelong friends. When President Franklin D. Roosevelt capitulated to Randolph's threat

"To be afraid is to behave as if the truth were not true."
Bayard Rustin, 1973

bohemian: a person living an unconventional lifestyle.

pacifist: actively opposed to conflict and war.

to hold the march—though Rustin believed that Randolph should not have canceled the march—Randolph arranged for Rustin to meet with A. J. Muste, the head of the radical **pacifist** Fellowship of Reconciliation (FOR). Muste came to regard the younger man almost as a son, naming him in 1941 as a field staff member for FOR while Rustin also continued as a youth organizer for the March on Washington Movement.

Now possessed of a reputation as an activist in the politics of race, Rustin was able to offer advice to the members of the FOR cell who became the nucleus for a new nonviolent action organization, the Congress of Racial Equality (CORE). Until 1955 Rustin remained a vital figure in the FOR/CORE alliance, holding a variety of offices within both groups, conducting weekend and summer institutes on nonviolent direct action in race relations, and serving as a conduit to the March on Washington Movement for ideas and techniques on nonviolence. In 1947 he worked closely with Randolph again in a movement opposing universal military training and a segregated military, and once again believed Randolph wrong in abandoning his strategies when met with a presidential executive order intended to correct the injustice. They argued briefly and publicly, then reconciled. Rustin is sometimes credited with persuading Randolph to accept nonviolence as a strategy.

Rustin's dual commitment to nonviolence and racial equality cost him dearly. In the summer of 1942, refusing to sit in the Jim Crow section of a bus going from Louisville, Kentucky, to Nashville, Tennessee, he was beaten and arrested. The following year, unwilling to accept either the validity of the draft or conscientious objector status—though his Quaker affiliation made that option possible—he was jailed as a draft resister and spent twenty-eight months in prison. Following his release, in 1947 he proposed that a racially integrated group of sixteen CORE/FOR activists undertake a bus trip through the Upper South to test a recent Supreme Court decision on interstate travel.

Termed the Journey of Reconciliation, the trip was essentially peaceful, although participants encountered violence outside Chapel Hill, North Carolina, where Rustin and three others were charged with violating the segregation laws. In a **sham** trial, Rustin and the others were convicted and sentenced to thirty days hard labor on a chain gang. His continuing visible role in racial policies brought him additional arrests and beatings.

1910 Rustin is born in West Chester, Pennsylvania.

1941 Rustin becomes field staff member for Fellowship of Reconciliation (FOR).

1942 Rustin is beaten and arrested for refusing to sit in the back of a bus.

1947 Rustin organizes the racially integrated Journey of Reconciliation.

1963 Rustin successfully organizes the March on Washington.

1964 Rustin is named executive director of the A. Philip Randolph Institute.

sham: not genuine.

After his release from the chain gang, Rustin traveled to India, where he was received by Mohandas K. Gandhi's sons. He had earlier blended strands of Gandhian nonviolence into his conception of pacifism. When the bus boycott developed in Montgomery, Alabama, Rustin appeared on the scene to offer support, advice, and information on nonviolence. Martin Luther King Jr. accepted his help. But when word leaked of Rustin's former ties to the Communist party and his 1953 conviction on a morals charge—allegedly for homosexual activity—he was rushed out of town. The gossip led to Rustin's resignation from both CORE and FOR in 1955, although he continued the pacifist struggle in the War Resisters League.

A 1952 visit to countries in north and west Africa convinced him of the need to assist Africans in their independence struggle. And he continued to be an active though less visible force in the effort to achieve racial justice, invited by King to assist in the creation of the Southern Christian Leadership Conference and to serve as a publicist for the group. Conservative members, however, eventually sought his ouster, and from 1960 until 1963 Rustin had little contact with King.

In 1963, as Randolph renewed his plans for a massive March on Washington, he proposed Rustin as the coordinator for the national event. Though initially opposed by some major civil rights leaders and under surveillance by the FBI, Rustin successfully managed the complex planning for the event and avoided violence. He was named executive director of the A. Philip Randolph Institute in 1964, while continuing to lead protests against militarism and segregation.

After the mid-1960s, Rustin's calls for blacks to work within the political system and his close ties with Jewish groups and labor unions made him the target of attacks by younger radicals, while his support for American investment and educational efforts in South Africa during the 1970s and 1980s outraged opponents of the apartheid regime. Following his death, the Bayard Rustin High School for the Humanities in New York City was named in his honor. ◆

Rustin was named executive director of the A. Philip Randolph Institute in 1964, while continuing to lead protests against militarism and segregation.

Sakharov, Andrei

MAY 21, 1921–DECEMBER 14, 1989 ● NOBEL PEACE PRIZE WINNER,
PHYSICIST, AND HUMAN RIGHTS ACTIVIST

The Nobel Committee gave the 1975 peace prize to Andrei Sakharov, the first Soviet citizen so honored, calling him "one of the great champions of human rights in our age." Once again the committee recognized that peace must be based upon the respect for human rights, as it had done in such prizes as those for Albert Lutuli, René Cassin, and Martin Luther King Jr. The October announcement declared, "Sakharov's fearless personal commitment in upholding the fundamental principles for peace between men is a powerful inspiration for all true work for peace. Uncompromisingly and with unflagging strength Sakharov has fought against the abuse of power and all forms of violation of human dignity."

Andrei Dimitriyevich Sakharov was born in Moscow a few years after the **Bolshevik** Revolution to a family of the Russian intelligentsia. His father was a physicist who taught and wrote textbooks and popular books on science. The family lived in a large communal apartment building, where most of the other tenants were relatives who shared a love for science, literature, and music. Sakharov's father was an excellent pianist and had once supported himself by playing the piano accompaniment to silent films. His grandmother, who had taught herself English when she was fifty, used to read aloud English novels and plays in the original to her little grandchildren. In this setting Sakharov had his first lessons at home, and when he went to school, he found some difficulty in adjusting to the other children.

In his studies Sakharov always performed brilliantly. In 1938, when he was seventeen, he graduated with distinction

> *"All of this triggers an irrational yet very strong emotional impact. How not to start thinking of one's responsibility at this point?"*
>
> Andrei Sakharov, following the test of the first Soviet superbomb in 1955

Bolshevik: member of the extremist wing of the Russian Socialist Democratic party after the Russian Revolution in 1917.

Nuclear Weapons

On August 6, 1945, during World War II, the United States military dropped the first of two atomic bombs on Japan. The city of Hiroshima was the first target, where a bomb was dropped in the center of the city, instantly killing 70,000 to 80,000 people and injuring an estimated 70,000 more, while destroying half of the city's buildings. Three days later, on August 9, 1945, another bomb was dropped on Nagasaki, killing between 40,000 and 70,000 people, injuring just as many, and destroying half of the city's buildings. Within another five years, 75,000 to 125,000 more had died from the aftereffects of the bomb (cancer, radiation illness, and related causes). People in Hiroshima and Nagasaki to this day experience the devastating effects, many dying of cancer and others of genetic problems caused by the radiation.

In the years after the war, many scientists, including Linus Pauling and Andrei Sakharov, spoke out against the use of nuclear weapons. Scientists began urging a test ban shortly after the first atomic test in 1945. In 1963 the three nuclear powers (the Soviet Union, the United States, and the United Kingdom) signed and ratified the Partial Test Ban Treaty, which disallowed nuclear tests in the atmosphere, under water, and in outer space. In 1996 a Comprehensive Test Ban Treaty (CTBT) was endorsed at the United Nations in New York City. The treaty bans all explosive tests, including underground tests. Over 150 nations have signed the treaty including the United States, Russia, and China. As of May 1999 the United States had not ratified the treaty. Without U.S. ratification, the treaty cannot be enforced.

from secondary school and entered the Faculty of Physics in Moscow University.

In 1945 Sakharov, now twenty-four, entered the Physics Institute of the Academy of Sciences, where he studied under the great theoretical physicist Igor Tamm, who was later to win the Nobel Prize for physics. In two years Sakharov was ready to defend his thesis, attaining the equivalent of an American Ph.D.

In 1948 Sakharov joined Tamm's team of nuclear scientists, working first in Moscow and later at a secret research center, and for the next twenty years he was occupied with the development of nuclear weapons. He worked under conditions of highest security, and he enjoyed all the special privileges the Soviet Union accords its top scientists.

Another group of scientists developed the Soviet atomic bomb by 1949, four years after the completion of the American bomb. Tamm, Sakharov, and their colleagues had the task of inventing the hydrogen bomb before American scientists did, which they accomplished in 1953. Sakharov has been called

> Sakharov worked under conditions of highest security, and he enjoyed all the special privileges the Soviet Union accords its top scientists.

the "father" of the Soviet hydrogen bomb, but he has always protested that this was a collaborative effort. He was, however, awarded the coveted Stalin Prize, after having been decorated several times with the Order of Socialist Labor; in that same year of 1953 he was made a full member of the Soviet Academy of Sciences at the unprecedented early age of thirty-two. His mentor Tamm was granted full membership at the same time after twenty years of association with the academy in an associate capacity, which was the normal procedure.

In 1957 Sakharov was influenced by the public statements of Albert Schweitzer and Linus Pauling about the dangers of radioactive fallout from nuclear bomb testing, for which he came to feel that he bore some responsibility. In 1958 he tried in vain to persuade the Soviet government to call off a series of tests, and in 1961 he tried again, approaching the Soviet leader, Nikita Khrushchev, personally. Sakharov was again rebuffed, Khrushchev declaring: "Sakharov is a good scientist. But leave it to us, who are specialists in this tricky business, to make foreign policy." Sakharov, however, did not give up, and he feels that he may have had some influence on the conclusion of the Partial Test Ban Treaty of 1963.

Sakharov continued to develop his ideas, and early in 1968 he wrote a tract entitled *Thoughts on Progress, Coexistence, and Intellectual Freedom*. Here he formulated the thesis that the only alternative to general nuclear destruction was the cooperation of the socialist and capitalist systems, which he saw as converging, in the control of nuclear arms, technological and scientific development, and assistance to the third world. Along with this international program, he called for a liberalization of Soviet society.

This manifesto was circulated in the Soviet Union through copies passed from hand to hand; it was then published in translation abroad and widely commented upon. As a result, Sakharov was barred from secret research in 1968, and the following year he was sent back to the Physics Institute, with reduced salary and privileges. Not long afterward he suffered a personal loss when his wife died.

From 1970 on Sakharov directed more and more of his attention to the defense of human rights and the support of individual dissidents who were facing political trials. He founded with two colleagues the Committee for Human Rights and began to attend the trials, standing outside in moral support when no longer permitted in the courtroom.

1921 — Sakharov is born in Moscow.

1953 — Sakharov and a group of scientists invent the hydrogen bomb.

1961 — Sakharov tries to persuade Khrushchev to ban nuclear bomb tests.

1975 — Sakharov receives the Nobel Peace Prize.

1980 — Sakharov is exiled to Gorki.

1986 — President Gorbachev releases Sakharov from exile.

1989 — Sakharov dies.

Sakharov founded the Committee for Human Rights and began to attend the trials, standing outside in moral support when no longer permitted in the courtroom.

Zionist: supporter of a Jewish state in Israel.

slander: utterance of false charges or misrepresentations.

In his association with dissident circles, Sakharov met Elena Bonner, whom he married in 1971. He was then fifty, and she was two years younger, the daughter of an Armenian Old Bolshevik who had been arrested along with his Jewish wife in Stalin's purges and who had died in prison.

Sakharov remained a member of the Academy of Sciences, even though attacked by the press and harassed by the secret police. Because of his scientific accomplishments and his reputation abroad, however, the government was reluctant to take punitive action against him. Instead, an effort was made to break him by persecuting his wife. The press denounced Bonner as a **Zionist** CIA agent who had ensnared "this spiritually unbalanced man" and was responsible for his "misguided" activities. Measures were also taken against Bonner's children, of whom Sakharov had become very fond. His own children had been encouraged to distance themselves from him.

In the summer of 1975 Bonner, after twice being refused, was finally given permission to travel to Italy for medical treatment of her eye condition. At the same time, Sakharov finished his second essay, *My Country and the World,* which was soon published abroad. He urged the Western powers to unite in their dealings with the USSR and to bring pressure on its leaders for a greater openness in Soviet society. So long as the Soviet Union was a totalitarian form of state capitalism, with a party–state monopoly of economic affairs and all other aspects of life, any détente with the West could be only a "false détente," and the Soviet leaders would exploit disarmament agreements for their own purposes.

After receiving the peace prize Sakharov continued to work for human rights in the Soviet Union, making statements to the West through Western reporters in Moscow. For the Soviet government, Sakharov's public opposition to the Soviet invasion of Afghanistan was the last straw. Early in 1980, without any charges or trial, he was sent into internal exile in Gorki, a closed city 250 miles east of Moscow, where he was isolated from all contacts. Bonner served as courier for a time, bringing his messages to Moscow, but in 1984 she was convicted of **slander** against the Soviet state and sentenced also to exile in Gorki.

In 1981 the couple went on a hunger strike for seventeen days to secure a permit for Bonner's daughter-in-law to join her husband in the United States. As Bonner's health deteriorated, Sakharov repeated such hunger strikes several times before

Bonner was given permission to leave the Soviet Union in 1985 for heart surgery in Boston, close to her family.

After Mikhail Gorbachev came to power, he announced a policy of limited liberalization. In December 1986 a hitherto forbidden telephone was suddenly installed in the Sakharov apartment in Gorki, and the next day a personal call came from Gorbachev himself. He informed Sakharov that he and Bonner could go back to Moscow and that Sakharov was to return to the Physics Institute "to work for the public good." Sakharov used the occasion to remind Gorbachev of the letter he had sent him some months before, asking **amnesty** for prisoners of conscience. He made no agreement to abandon his work for human rights when he returned to Moscow.

amnesty: pardon granted to large numbers of individuals.

Sakharov's *Memoirs* were published posthumously in 1990. ◆

Schweitzer, Albert

JANUARY 14, 1875–SEPTEMBER 4, 1965 ● ACTIVIST, PHILOSOPHER, AND MEDICAL MISSIONARY

Albert Schweitzer was the son of a Protestant pastor in the village of Günsbach in Alsace, born a few years after Alsace–Lorraine had passed from French to German rule as a consequence of the Franco-Prussian War. He grew up in a harmonious and religious home, learning to play the organ in his father's church when his feet could hardly reach the pedals. Very early in his life he began to feel uncomfortable that he was so privileged while many of his schoolmates lived in miserable peasant huts, were ill clad, and did not have enough to eat.

When he went off to the University of Strasbourg at eighteen, he rejoiced in his theological studies and his music, but he still could not help thinking of those who were less fortunate. Then, as he tells in his autobiography, one brilliant summer morning when he was twenty-one and home at Günsbach for the Whitsuntide holidays:

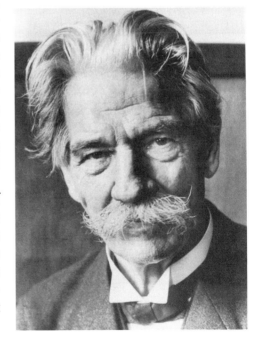

[T]here came to me, as I awoke, the thought that I must not accept this happiness as a matter of course, but must give something in return for it. Proceeding to think the matter out at once with calm deliberation, while the birds were singing outside, I settled with myself before I got up, that I would consider myself justified in living till I was thirty for science and art, in order to devote myself from that time forward to the direct service of humanity.

1875 Schweitzer is born in Alsace.

1913 Schweitzer becomes a qualified physician; he and his wife set out to be missionaries in Africa.

1952 Schweitzer receives the Nobel Peace Prize.

1957 Schweitzer's "Declaration of Conscience" is broadcast over radio in protest of nuclear testing.

1965 Schweitzer dies in Africa.

Schweitzer felt that he now understood the words of Jesus that "whoever shall lose his life for my sake shall save it": "In addition to the outward, I now found inward happiness."

Just how he would serve was not yet clear to him. He continued with his studies, earning his first doctorate, in philosophy, at the age of twenty-four with a dissertation on the religious philosophy of Immanuel Kant, and his second, in theology, with a treatise on the Synoptic Gospels. At the age of thirty he received a doctorate in music for his definitive work on J. S. Bach. Meanwhile, he had become ordained and served as professor and preacher at the theological College of St. Thomas at the University of Strasbourg and at the same time managed to commute to Paris to study organ and to become a celebrated concert organist.

In 1904, several months before his thirtieth birthday, Schweitzer happened upon an appeal of the Paris Missionary Society for missionaries to go to French Equatorial Africa. He felt immediately that this was the work for humanity he had been seeking. He decided that first he should train as a doctor so that he could serve the Africans in the capacity for which there was clearly the greatest need.

expostulated: reasoned vigorously.

His friends and relatives **expostulated** with him, arguing that he was on the verge of a brilliant career and that he would be wasting his gifts in the jungle. Could he not help the Africans more by raising money with organ concerts? Schweitzer only deplored that "people who passed for Christians" could oppose his desire to "serve the love preached by Jesus." One university student at Strasbourg agreed with his plan—Helene Bresslau, who became his wife and trained as a nurse while he was doing his medical studies.

Schweitzer was a man of inexhaustible energy. He had to give up his preaching, but during his seven years as a medical student he continued his writing and published a book on organ building and two works of biblical scholarship, including the brilliant and provocative *Quest for the Historical Jesus*. To the members of the Paris Missionary Society, his unorthodox writings raised the question whether they could accept someone who, as Schweitzer put it, "had only Christian love," but did not "hold also the correct Christian belief." Schweitzer reassured them by agreeing not to preach when he got to Africa.

After completing his medical studies, Schweitzer set out in 1913 with his wife for the missionary station of Lambaréné, on the banks of the Ogawé River in the Gabon, two days by river steamer from the coast. The site was well chosen for the tiny hospital he built, since patients could come with their canoes on hundreds of waterways that stretched into the jungle. They came with all kinds of diseases—malaria, dysentery, leprosy, elephantiasis—and with sores and ulcers and animal bites. Schweitzer had to treat them in primitive conditions after first winning their confidence. He toiled from morning to night in the torrid heat, his only relaxation the time he could find to play on the special piano-organ the Bach Society of Paris sent to him. In the late night hours he worked on a philosophy of civilization.

The First World War reached even into Schweitzer's jungle, however. He and his wife first were subjected to restrictions as German citizens in French territory; then they were taken to France in 1917 and interned as enemy aliens. Schweitzer emerged from this experience in 1918 depressed and ailing, but Archbishop Söderblom, who was to become the first religious peace laureate, arranged for him to lecture at the University of Uppsala in Sweden, where he regained his health and spirits.

Schweitzer spent the next years supporting his family and raising money for Lambaréné by presenting concerts and lectures throughout Europe and writing major autobiographical, religious, and philosophical works. When he returned to Lambaréné in 1924, after an absence of seven years, he spent the first months repairing and rebuilding the old structures. Now that he and his work were well known in Europe, however, contributions and gifts began to arrive, as well as doctors and nurses to help with the increasing numbers of patients.

After 1927 Schweitzer returned a number of times to Europe, where he could lecture, give concerts, and write at Günsbach, but his base remained the hospital at Lambaréné. On a trip to Europe in 1939, he got as far as Bordeaux, where he learned of the worsening international situation. Fearing that the coming war would prevent his return to Lambaréné, he ordered supplies for the hospital and went back immediately. During the conflict he received supplies from the United

"You ask me for a motto. Here it is: 'SERVICE.'"
Albert Schweitzer

He toiled from morning to night in the torrid heat, his only relaxation the time he could find to play the special piano-organ the Bach Society of Paris sent to him.

States, where the Albert Schweitzer Fellowship had been formed to support his work. He finally visited America in 1949 to speak at the two-hundredth anniversary celebration of the birth of Goethe, held in Aspen, Colorado.

One day late in 1953 at Lambaréné, Schweitzer's nephew, Dr. Guy Schweitzer, burst into his room to congratulate his uncle. "For what?" Albert Schweitzer asked. "Has my black cat finally had her kittens?" Dr. Guy told him that the radio station in Brazzaville had just announced that Schweitzer had been awarded the Nobel Peace Prize. Schweitzer was delighted to learn that he would receive about $33,000, enough to build and equip the hospital for lepers that he had dreamed of.

In his address accepting the Nobel Peace Prize, Schweitzer referred only very generally to the threat of nuclear war. He had been urged to use the occasion to speak out, but he had always wanted to keep **aloof** from political questions; besides, this was a subject on which he felt he had little scientific knowledge. But Schweitzer did feel that now that he had been given the Nobel Peace Prize, he "should do something to earn it." He began to consider carefully the suggestions he received from world leaders like Bertrand Russell and Pablo Casals that he take a public stand, and characteristically, he set out to acquire technical information about radiation and its effects upon health.

In was Norman Cousins, the American editor, who finally convinced Schweitzer that he had the responsibility to give a message to the world. In January 1957 Cousins traveled to Lambaréné to discuss the matter with Schweitzer, and he persuaded him to make a public statement opposing nuclear tests. Schweitzer decided that this should be read over Radio Oslo "of the city of the Nobel Peace Prize," and the Norwegian Nobel Committee agreed to sponsor the broadcast.

On April 24, 1957, Chairman Jahn read in Norwegian the text of what has become known as Schweitzer's Declaration of Conscience, and later that evening it was broadcast in the major European languages. "I raise my voice," Schweitzer had written, to warn of the catastrophe for the human race that increasing radioactive fallout represents and to appeal for an international agreement to stop atomic testing: "The end of further experiments with atom bombs would be like the sunrays of hope which suffering humanity is longing for."

Schweitzer's declaration was broadcast from 150 transmitters all over the world. It contributed to the movement among

---

aloof: removed.

"I raised my voice," Schweitzer had written, "to warn of the catastrophe for the human race which increasing radioactive fallout represents and to appeal for an international agreement to stop atomic testing."

scientists to oppose atomic testing, which Linus Pauling coordinated in 1957 and which eventually led in 1963 to the international agreement to ban atomic tests in the atmosphere. Schweitzer took an active part in this crusade and had come so far from his earlier position of avoiding political issues that in his last public statement, made shortly before his death, he supported an appeal for a cease-fire in Vietnam.

He died in Lambaréné in 1965 at the age of ninety and was buried there. He had said once that it would not matter whether his grave was in Günsbach or Lambaréné—it is "God's earth." ◆

Seale, Robert George (Bobby)

OCTOBER 22, 1936– ● ACTIVIST

B obby Seale was born to George and Thelma Seale in Dallas. Before he had reached the age of ten, his family moved to California, where his father continued in his profession as a building carpenter. At the age of eighteen, Bobby Seale was accepted into the Air Force and sent to Amarillo, Texas, for training as an aircraft sheet-metal mechanic. After training for six months, he graduated as an honor student from the Technical School Class of Air Force Training. He was then sent to Ellsworth Air Force Base in Rapid City, South Dakota, where he served for three and a half years and was discharged as a corporal. He attended Merrit College in Oakland, California, after his discharge.

When he enrolled in college in 1961, Seale intended to study engineering. He joined the Afro-American Association, an organization formed by young militant African Americans in Oakland to explore the various problems confronting the black community. Influenced by the association's regular book-discussion sessions, Seale became interested in the works of Mao Zedong and Kwame Nkrumah, and he also began to read W. E. B. Du Bois and Booker T. Washington. His awareness of and involvement in the Afro-American Association were shaped by a fellow student, Huey Newton, whose **articulation** of the social problems victimizing the black community attracted his interest.

With Newton, Seale formed the Soul Students Advisory Council, which was concerned with ending the drafting of

"You don't fight racism with racism, the best way to fight racism is with solidarity."
Bobby Seale, 1970

articulation: ability to express oneself clearly.

1936   Seale is born in Dallas, Texas.

1966   Seale and Huey Newton form the Black Panther party.

1973   Seale runs for mayor of Oakland, California.

1974   Seale resigns from the Black Panther party.

black men into the service to fight in the Vietnam War. Fired by nationalist zeal, especially after he heard Malcolm X speak, Seale invited three friends, Kenny, Isaac, and Ernie, to create the Revolutionary Action Movement to organize African Americans on the West Coast for black liberation. In October of 1966, he and Huey Newton formed the Black Panther party in Oakland. The party's objectives were reflected in its ten-point platform and program, which emphasized freedom, full employment, and equality of opportunity for African Americans. It called for an end to white racism and police brutality against black people. Although the FBI under J. Edgar Hoover's directorship declared Seale's party to be the greatest threat to the internal security of the United States, the party's programs for the poor won it broad support from the community as well as praise from civic groups. The Black Panther party also recognized the need for political participation by African Americans. To this end, it frequently organized voter-registration drives.

Three years after the formation of the party, Seale shifted his philosophical and ideological stance from race to class struggle, stressing the unity of the people and arguing that the Panthers would not "fight racism with more racism." In 1973 he ran for mayor of Oakland, forcing a runoff with John Reading, the incumbent, who defeated him. In 1974 he resigned as the chairman of the Black Panther party, perhaps in an effort to work within the mainstream political system. Since the late 1980s Seale has been involved in an organization called Youth Employment Strategies, of which he was founder, and in encouraging black youth to enroll in doctoral programs. He is based in Philadelphia. ◆

Stanton, Elizabeth Cady

NOVEMBER 12, 1815–OCTOBER 26, 1902 ● WOMEN'S RIGHTS LEADER

Elizabeth Cady Stanton was a leader in social reforms and in the drive to improve the legal status of women in the nineteenth century. She studied under Emma Willard, an earlier reformer, at Troy Female Seminary. For a time, Stanton studied law with her own father, Daniel Cady, who was one of New York State's leading authorities on property law cases. She was convinced that women were not treated properly under the existing laws of the country. When she married notable abolitionist Henry Brewster Stanton in 1840, she insisted that the ceremony must exclude "and obey" from the usual marriage vow to "love, honor, and obey" a husband.

Stanton was influenced by her husband to take up the cause of abolition. In London, she and other female abolitionists were denied seats at an abolition convention because of their sex. This led her to begin her long campaign to secure equal rights for women. Lucretia Mott, another of the Americans barred from the London convention, joined Stanton in the work. During July 19–20, 1848, the first women's rights convention in the United States was held at Seneca Falls, New York. Elizabeth Cady Stanton, who made the opening speech, read a "Declaration of Sentiments," modeled after the Declaration of Independence, setting forth the grievances of women against existing law and Custom. Due to Stanton's insistence, the document included a resolution demanding the right to vote for women.

Other conventions devoted to women's rights soon followed, and Stanton always played a leading role. She also wrote many articles, led protests, organized petitions, and lectured in public and before legislative bodies in the interest of temperance, abolition, and woman's rights. As the years passed she devoted more and more of her time to the cause of women.

From 1851, when she first met Susan B. Anthony and recruited her to enlist in the crusade for woman's rights, the two women worked together, a remarkably efficient pair whose partnership ended only with Stanton's death. Together they planned campaign programs, speeches and addresses, appearing upon public and convention platforms to plead for women's rights.

Elizabeth Cady Stanton served as president of the National Woman Suffrage Association (1869–90) and of the National American Woman Suffrage Association (1890–02).

In 1898 she published her memoirs, *Eighty Years and More*. But her monumental undertaking was the compilation, with

> *"The strongest reason why we ask for woman a voice in the government under which she lives is because of her birth-right to self-sovereignty; because, as an individual, she must rely on herself."*
>
> Elizabeth Cady Stanton, before the congressional Judiciary Committee, 1892

coeditors Susan B. Anthony and Matilda Joslyn Gage, of the first three volumes of the *History of Woman Suffrage* (1881–86). In the cause of woman's rights Stanton was undoubtedly one of the most influential leaders of her day. ◆

Steinem, Gloria

MARCH 25, 1934– ● WOMEN'S RIGHTS ACTIVIST

G loria Steinem is best known for her role as a leading spokeswoman for the "second wave" of feminism in the United States, the women's liberation movement of the late 1960s and 1970s. She founded *Ms.* magazine in 1972, which appealed to a wide audience with its articles, fiction, and poetry on women's issues.

> *"Myths of feminine inferiority have been used to suppress the talents and strengths of half the human race."*
>
> Gloria Steinem, 1971

Gloria Steinem was born to Leo and Ruth (Nuneviller) Steinem in Toledo, Ohio, on March 25, 1934, the second of two daughters. Her parents lost most of their money in the stock market crash of 1929. Her mother sold their house in Toledo to pay for Steinem's tuition at Smith College, where Steinem earned a B.A. in government in 1956.

Upon graduating from Smith, Steinem spent a year in India on a fellowship. With a group of Gandhi's followers, she walked through villages in the Ramnad region in southern India in an effort to halt **caste** riots. Her early participation in nonviolent social protest influenced Steinem's later work in the women's movement.

caste: hereditary social class in India.

In 1958 Steinem returned to the United States and embarked on a career as a freelance writer in New York City. During the 1960s she wrote for the magazines *Esquire*, *Show*, *The New York Times Magazine*, and *Vogue* as well as for the television show *That Was the Week That Was*, which presented a satirical look at the news. In 1968 she achieved her ambition to write about politics and serious social issues. She began contributing a regular column, "The City Politic," to *New York Magazine*, of which she was a founding editor.

During the 1960s Steinem was an active volunteer worker in many political causes. She organized writers to withhold a portion of their income taxes in protest of the Vietnam War and campaigned for George McGovern's presidential nomination in 1968. She also supported César Chávez and the movement on behalf of the farmworkers, organizing a benefit at Carnegie Hall and helping publicize a march in California to draw attention to the plight of the farmworkers.

By the mid sixties *Newsweek* magazine was calling Steinem "as much a celebrity as a reporter." In the following years she used her influence to draw attention to the women's movement. Her 1969 *Look* magazine article "After Black Power, Women's Liberation" won a Penney-Missouri Journalism Award. Her appearances on television and at colleges and universities in the early 1970s made her one of the most visible feminists in America.

In 1971 Steinem and other leaders of the women's movement created the National Women's Political Caucus to encourage women to run for political office. Also in that year Steinem cofounded the Women's Action Alliance, an organization to help women fight discrimination.

The following year, Gloria Steinem founded Ms., a magazine published and edited by women. The success of the magazine led to the general acceptance of "Ms." as a title that does not reveal a woman's marital status. The magazine's glossy design and wide-ranging content appeal to women of every age, class, and race, with articles covering such topics as child-rearing, welfare, women in the professions, and women in politics.

In 1972 Steinem's face was on the cover of the traditional woman's magazine *McCall's* as "Woman of the Year"—and on the cover of *New Woman* as well. In attempting to reach as many women as possible, however, Steinem and Ms. magazine were frequently the target of criticism, from radical feminists who found the magazine too middle class in its outlook and conservative feminists who disliked any departure from mainstream ideas.

In 1987 Ms. was sold to an Australian media company and Steinem accepted a post as contributing editor at Random House. She had previously published a collection of articles, *Outrageous Acts and Everyday Rebellions* (1983), and *Marilyn* (1986), a biography of the movie star Marilyn Monroe. In addition she has written a book of essays, *Moving Beyond Words* (1994), and *Revolution from Within: A Book of Self-Esteem* (1992), which reflects her conviction that "feminism is about strengthening women from the inside too." She continues to raise money for the Ms. Foundation, which she cofounded in 1972 to support programs for women. ◆

1968 Steinem begins writing a regular political column, "The City Politic," for *New York* magazine.

1971 Steinem helps create the National Women's Political Caucus and the Women's Action Alliance.

1972 Steinem helps found *Ms Magazine*.

1977 Steinem participates in the National Women's Conference in Houston, Texas.

Steinem's appearances on television and at colleges and universities in the early 1970s made her one of the most visible feminists in America.

Stone, Lucy

AUGUST 13, 1818–OCTOBER 18, 1893 ● SUFFRAGIST
AND ANTISLAVERY ACTIVIST

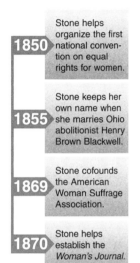

1850 — Stone helps organize the first national convention on equal rights for women.

1855 — Stone keeps her own name when she marries Ohio abolitionist Henry Brown Blackwell.

1869 — Stone cofounds the American Woman Suffrage Association.

1870 — Stone helps establish the *Woman's Journal.*

A pioneer in the women's rights movement, Lucy Stone was one of the first women in America to lecture in support of women's right to vote. A magnetic speaker who was often able to sway a hostile audience, Stone was, as Elizabeth Cady Stanton said, "the first person by whom the heart of the American public was deeply stirred on the woman question."

Stone was born near West Brookfield, Massachusetts, on August 13, 1818. Her father, Francis Stone, was a prosperous farmer who sent his sons to college but believed that girls had no need of higher education. When her father refused to aid her financially, Stone determined to put herself through college. At sixteen she began earning a dollar a week teaching children at a district school. In the following years she taught at the Wesleyan Academy in Wilbraham, Massachusetts, and at Mount Holyoke Female Seminary. By 1843, when she was twenty-five, she had saved enough money to enter Oberlin College.

Stone's commitment to equal rights for women and African Americans deepened during her years at Oberlin. Shortly after her graduation in 1847, when she became one of the first Massachusetts women to hold a degree, she gave her first public lecture on women's rights. In 1848 she became a lecturer for the Massachusetts Antislavery Society, which allowed her to devote time each week to speaking out on behalf of women. Stone often faced antagonistic crowds.

Stone helped organize one of the first national conventions on equal rights for women, held in Worchester, Massachusetts, in 1850, and remained active in organizing women's rights conventions throughout the 1850s. She continued to work for equal rights for African Americans, but she put women's rights first, saying, "I was a woman before I was an Abolitionist."

In 1855 Stone married Henry Brown Blackwell, an Ohio merchant and the brother of Elizabeth Blackwell, America's first woman physician. Blackwell had been an active member of the abolitionist movement. He promised Stone that after their marriage he would join in her efforts for women's rights. Stone protested the unequal status of married women by omitting the

Stone continued to work for equal rights for African Americans, but she put women's rights first, saying, "I was a woman before I was an Abolitionist."

word "obey" from the marriage ceremony. She was probably the first American woman to keep her own name. She refused to open mail addressed to Mrs. Henry Blackwell.

Stone and Blackwell lived in New Jersey for more than ten years and worked for women's suffrage, helping to form the New Jersey Woman Suffrage Association in 1867. In the spring of that year, the legislature of Kansas was the first state legislature to pass amendments to a state constitution granting voting rights to women and African-American men. Stone and Blackwell spent two months campaigning in Kansas and were bitterly disappointed when the voters failed to ratify the amendments.

In 1869 Stone and Blackwell moved to Boston. In November they helped found the American Woman Suffrage Association. More conservative than the National Woman Suffrage Association formed by Susan B. Anthony and Elizabeth Cady Stanton in the spring of 1869, Stone's suffrage organization centered its efforts on state legislatures. Twenty years later, Stone's daughter, Alice Stone Blackwell, was instrumental in uniting the two organizations as the National American Woman Suffrage Association. ◆

"Make the world better."
Lucy Stone's last words to her daughter, Alice Stone Blackwell

Terrell, Mary Eliza Church

SEPTEMBER 26, 1863–JULY 24, 1954 ● CIVIL RIGHTS ACTIVIST
AND WOMEN'S RIGHTS ADVOCATE

Terrell was born in Memphis, into a prosperous family of former slaves; she graduated from Oberlin College (1884) at the head of her class, then taught at Wilberforce University (1885–87) and briefly in a high school in Washington, D.C. After receiving an M.A. from Oberlin (1888), she traveled in Europe for two years, studying French, German, and Italian. In 1891 she married Robert Terrell, who was appointed judge of the District of Columbia Municipal Court in 1901.

The overlapping concerns that characterized Terrell's life—public-education reform, women's rights, and civil rights—found expression in community work and organizational activities. She served as the first woman president of Bethel Literary and Historical Association (1892–93). She was the first black woman appointed to the District of Columbia Board of Education (1895–1901, 1906–11).

In spite of elements of racism and nativism, Terrell was an active member of the National American Woman Suffrage

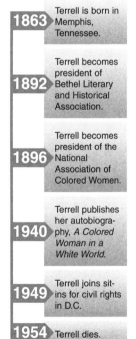

1863 ▶ Terrell is born in Memphis, Tennessee.

1892 ▶ Terrell becomes president of Bethel Literary and Historical Association.

1896 ▶ Terrell becomes president of the National Association of Colored Women.

1940 ▶ Terrell publishes her autobiography, *A Colored Woman in a White World.*

1949 ▶ Terrell joins sit-ins for civil rights in D.C.

1954 ▶ Terrell dies.

Association and addressed their convention in 1898 and 1900. She joined the Woman's Party picket line at the White House, and after the achievement of suffrage, was active in the Republican party.

Women's international affairs involved her as well. She addressed the International Council of Women (Berlin, 1904) in English, German, and French, the only American to do so; she was a delegate to the Women's International League for Peace and Freedom (Zurich, 1919) and a vice president of the International Council of Women of the Darker Races; and addressed the International Assembly of the World Fellowship of Faiths (London, 1937).

Terrell participated in the founding of the National Association for the Advancement of Colored People (NAACP) and was vice president of the Washington, D.C., branch for many years. Her various causes coalesced around her concern with the quality of black women's lives. In 1892 she helped organize and headed the National League for the Protection of Colored Women in Washington, D.C.; she was the first president of the National Association of Colored Women, serving three terms (1896–1901) before being named honorary president for life and a vice president of the National Council of Negro Women.

Terrell worked for the unionization of black women and for their inclusion in established women's affairs. In 1919 she campaigned, unsuccessfully, for a Colored Women's Division within the Women's Bureau of the Department of Labor, and to have the First International Congress of Working Women directly address the concerns of black working women.

Age did not diminish Terrell's activism. Denied admission to the Washington chapter of the American Association of University Women (AAUW) in 1946 on racial grounds, she entered a three-year legal battle that led the national group to clarify its bylaws to read that a college degree was the only requirement for membership. In 1949 Terrell joined the sit-ins that challenged segregation in public accommodations, a landmark civil rights case, as well as serving as chairwoman of the Coordinating Committee for the Enforcement of the District of Columbia Anti-Discrimination Laws.

In addition to her picketing and sit-ins, Terrell wrote many magazine articles treating disfranchisement, discrimination, and racism, as well as her autobiography, *A Colored Woman in a White World* (1940). ◆

Tibbles, Susette LaFlesche

1854–MAY 26, 1903 ● NATIVE AMERICAN RIGHTS ACTIVIST

Susette LaFlesche Tibbles was born on the Omaha reservation in Nebraska, the eldest daughter of "progressive" Omaha chief Joseph LaFlesche and his wife, Mary Gale. Educated at the Presbyterian mission school on the reservation and at the Elizabeth Institute for Young Ladies in New Jersey, she later obtained a post as an assistant teacher in the government school on the reservation.

Her claim to fame, however, resulted from her challenge to one of the saddest examples of U.S. government exploitation of Native Americans. Eager to confine all Indians to reservations, government officials had thoughtlessly transferred Ponca Indian lands to their enemies, the Sioux, and then had forcibly removed the Poncas to the unfamiliar Indian Territory (in present-day Oklahoma). After a third of the tribe died there, Ponca chief Standing Bear led a desperate group of his followers back to their homeland only to be arrested and ordered to return to the Indian Territory. In hopes of stopping removals and raising money for legal efforts to protect the Poncas, Thomas Tibbles, a journalist in Omaha, Nebraska, arranged to take Standing Bear on a speaking tour of eastern cities. LaFlesche, who accompanied them ostensibly as Standing Bear's interpreter, became a strong voice for Indian reform in her own right. LaFlesche, known to fascinated audiences as Bright Eyes, and Standing Bear fanned the flames of outrage that attracted influential easterners, including Helen Hunt Jackson and Alice Cunningham Fletcher, to the cause of Indian reform.

In 1881 LaFlesche married Tibbles, and for the next several years the two continued to bring the message of Indian reform to audiences in the northeast and in England and to U.S. congressional committees in Washington, D.C. They lent considerable support to the allotment policy proposed by Senator Henry Laurens Dawes, whose Dawes Act, a major shift in U.S. Indian policy, was enacted in 1887.

In later years, Susette LaFlesche Tibbles lived in Lincoln, Nebraska, where she wrote and illustrated children's stories and contributed editorials to her husband's populist newspaper. In 1902 she moved to her allotment near Bancroft, Nebraska, where she died in 1903, at the age of forty-nine. ◆

> LaFlesche's claim to fame resulted from her challenge to one of the saddest examples of U.S. government exploitation of Native Americans.

1854 Tibbles is born Susette LaFlesche on the Omaha reservation in Nebraska.

1881 LaFlesche marries Thomas Tibbles; they work toward Indian reform.

1887 The Dawes Act is instituted.

1903 Tibbles dies in Bancroft, Nebraska.

Truth, Sojourner

c. 1797–1883 ● ABOLITIONIST, SUFFRAGIST, AND SPIRITUALIST

*"I come from
another field—the
country of the
slave. They have
got their liberty—
so much good luck
to have slavery
partly destroyed;
not entirely. I
want it root and
branch
destroyed."*

Sojourner Truth,
1850

Sojourner Truth was born Isabella Bomefree in Ulster County, New York, the second youngest of thirteen children born in slavery to Elizabeth (usually called Mau-Mau Bett) and James Bomefree. The other siblings were either sold or given away before her birth. The family was owned by Johannes Hardenbergh, a patroon and Revolutionary War patriot, the head of one of the most prominent Dutch families in late eighteenth-century New York.

Mau-Mau Bett was mystical and unlettered but imparted to her daughter strong faith, filial devotion, and a strong sense of individual integrity. Isabella Bomefree, whose first language was Dutch, was taken from her parents in 1808 and sold to an English-speaking owner, who maltreated her because of her inability to understand English. Through her own defiance— what she later called her "talks with God"—and her father's intercession, a Dutch tavern keeper soon purchased her. Kindly treated but surrounded by the rough tavern culture and probably sexually abused, the girl prayed for a new master. In 1810 John I. Dumont of New Paltz, New York, purchased Isabella Bomefree for three hundred dollars.

Isabella remained Dumont's slave for eighteen years. Dumont boasted that Belle, as he called her, was "better to me than a man." She planted, plowed, cultivated, and harvested crops. She milked the farm animals, sewed, weaved, cooked, and cleaned house. But Mrs. Dumont despised and tormented her, possibly because Dumont fathered one of her children.

Isabella had two relationships with slave men. Bob, her first love, a man from a neighboring estate, was beaten senseless for "taking up" with her and was forced to take another woman. She later became associated with Thomas, with whom she remained until her freedom. Four of her five children survived to adulthood.

Song in the Quest for Freedom

African culture, particularly music, played a significant role in the history of slavery. As early as 1619, when the first Africans were brought as slaves to Jamestown, Virginia, the traces of a unique musical vernacular are evident. Music and songs show the displeasure that early slaves felt with this country and their plight. Slaves dreamed of freedom, and eventually their music became a kind of "double speak" or code that was undecipherable by the white slave owners. Often, slaves would sing about physical freedom in the context of religious songs. In the fields the African slave would sing about the God who would deliver him and the day he would go to heaven and be finally free. Slave owners felt no threat, believing the Africans to be singing about a better life in heaven. But these songs, which provided a safe means of expressing injustice and promoting emotional health within the slave community, also contained plans and clandestine communications that would enable the slaves to escape to freedom in the north. The Underground Railroad, the informal system that helped slaves escape to the northern states and Canada during the mid 1800s, often used a system of "call and response" songs in order to relay slaves to safety.

Although New York slavery ended for adults in 1827, Dumont promised Isabella her freedom a year earlier. When he refused to keep his promise, she fled with an infant child, guided by "the word of God" as she later related. She took refuge with Isaac Van Wagenen, who purchased her for the remainder of her time as a slave. She later adopted his family name.

Isabella Van Wagenen was profoundly shaped by a religious experience she underwent in 1827 at Pinkster time, the popular early summer African-Dutch slave holiday. As she recounted it, she forgot God's deliverance of his people from bondage and prepared to return to Dumont's farm for Pinkster: "I looked back in Egypt," she said, "and everything seemed so pleasant there." But she felt the mighty, luminous, and wrathful presence of an angry God blocking her path. Stalemated and momentarily blinded and suffocated under "God's breath," she claimed in her *Narrative*, Jesus mercifully intervened and proclaimed her salvation. This conversion enabled Isabella Van Wagenen to claim direct and special communication with Jesus and the Trinity for the remainder of her life, and she subsequently became involved with a number of highly spiritual religious groups.

A major test of faith followed Isabella Van Wagenen's conversion when she discovered that Dumont had illegally sold her son Peter. Armed with spiritual assurance and a mother's rage, she scoured the countryside, gaining moral and financial support

> Isabella Van Wagenen was profoundly shaped by a religious experience she underwent in 1827 at Pinkster time, the popular early summer African-Dutch slave holiday.

Isabella also began to attract attention for her extraordinary preaching, praying, and singing.

from prominent Dutch residents, antislavery Quakers, and local Methodists. She brought suit, and Peter was eventually returned from Alabama and freed.

In 1829 Isabella, now a Methodist, moved to New York City. She joined the African Methodist Episcopal Zion Church, where she discovered a brother and two sisters. She also began to attract attention for her extraordinary preaching, praying, and singing, though these talents were mainly employed among the Perfectionists (a sect of white radical mystics emerging from the Second Great Awakening who championed millennial doctrines and equated spiritual piety with morality and social justice with true Christianity). As housekeeper for Perfectionist Elijah Pierson, Isabella was involved in "the Kingdom," a sect organized by the spiritual zealot Robert Matthias. Among other practices he engaged in "spirit-matching," or wife swapping, with Ann Folger, wife of Pierson's business partner. Elijah Pierson's unexplained death brought public outcries of foul play. To conceal Ann Pierson's promiscuity, the Folgers suggested that there had been an erotic attachment between Matthias and Isabella Van Wagenen and that they murdered Pierson with poisoned blackberries. Challenging her accusers, Isabella Van Wagenen vowed to "crush them with the truth." Lack of evidence and prejudice about blacks testifying against whites led to dismissal of the case. Isabella Van Wagenen triumphed by successfully suing the Folgers for slander. Though chastened by this experience with religious extremism, the association with New York Perfectionists enhanced her biblical knowledge, oratorical skills, and commitment to reform.

Isabella Van Wagenen encouraged her beloved son Peter to take up seafaring to avoid the pitfalls of urban crime. In 1843 his vessel returned without him. Devastated by this loss, facing (at forty-six) a bleak future in domestic service, and influenced by the millenarian (known as the Millerite movement) ferment sweeping the northeast at the time, she decided to radically change her life. She became an itinerant preacher and adopted the name Sojourner Truth because voices directed her to sojourn the countryside and speak God's truth. In the fall of 1843 she became ill and was taken to the Northampton utopian community in Florence, Massachusetts, where black abolitionist David Ruggles nursed her at his water-cure establishment. Sojourner Truth impressed residents, who included a number of abolitionists, with her slavery accounts, scriptural interpretations, wit, and simple oral eloquence.

1797 Truth is born Isabella Bomefree, a slave, in Ulster County, New York.

1827 Truth undergoes a religious experience.

1829 Truth joins the African Methodist Episcopal Zion Church.

1846 Truth joins the abolitionist circuit.

1851 Truth delivers a speech that becomes famous as "Ain't I a Woman?"

1864 Truth meets Abraham Lincoln.

1883 Truth dies in Michigan.

By 1846 Sojourner Truth had joined the antislavery circuit, traveling with Abby Kelly Foster, Frederick Douglass, William Lloyd Garrison, and British M.P. George Thompson. An electrifying public orator, she soon became one of the most popular speakers for the abolitionist cause. Her fame was heightened by the publication of her *Narrative* in 1850, related and transcribed by Olive Gilbert. With proceeds from its sale she purchased a Northampton home. In 1851, speaking before a National Women's Convention in Akron, Ohio, Sojourner Truth defended the physical and spiritual strength of women in her famous "Ain't I a Woman?" speech. In 1853 Sojourner's antislavery, spiritualist, and temperance advocacy took her to the midwest, where she settled among spiritualists in Harmonia, Michigan.

"I cannot read a book," said Sojourner Truth, "but I can read the people." She dissected political and social issues through parables of everyday life. The Constitution, silent on black rights, had a "little **weevil** in it." She was known for her captivating one-line retorts. An Indiana audience threatened to torch the building if she spoke. Sojourner Truth replied, "Then I will speak to the ashes." In the late 1840s, grounded in faith that God and moral suasion would **eradicate** bondage, she challenged her despairing friend Douglass with "Frederick, is God dead?" In 1858, when a group of men questioned her gender, claiming she wasn't properly feminine in her demeanor, Sojourner Truth, a bold early feminist, exposed her bosom to the entire assembly, proclaiming that shame was not hers but theirs.

During the Civil War Sojourner Truth recruited and supported Michigan's black regiment, counseled freedwomen, set up employment operations for freedpeople willing to relocate, and initiated desegregation of streetcars in Washington, D.C. In 1864 she had an audience with Abraham Lincoln. Following the war, Sojourner Truth moved to Michigan, settling in Battle Creek, but remained active in numerous reform causes. She supported the Fifteenth Amendment and women's suffrage.

Disillusioned by the failure of Reconstruction, Sojourner Truth devoted her last years to the support of a black western homeland. In her later years, despite decades of interracial cooperation, she became skeptical of collaboration with whites and became an advocate of racial separation. She died in 1883 in Battle Creek, attended by the famous physician and breakfast cereal founder John Harvey Kellogg. ◆

An electrifying public orator, Truth soon became one of the most popular speakers for the abolitionist cause.

weevil: beetle.

eradicate: to do away with completely.

Tutu, Desmond Mpilo

OCTOBER 7, 1931– ● SOUTH AFRICAN RELIGIOUS LEADER AND CIVIL RIGHTS
ACTIVIST

*"You are either
for or against
apartheid, and
not by rhetoric.
You are either in
favor of evil, or
you are in favor of
good. You are
either on the side
of the oppressed
or on the side of
the oppressor. You
can't be neutral."*

Desmond Tutu,
1984

Born in Klerksdorp in the Transvaal, Desmond Mpilo Tutu became a high school teacher in 1955 after having graduated from the Pretoria Bantu College in 1953. He obtained a bachelor of arts degree from the University of South Africa in 1958. After a serious illness, and under the influence of Father Trevor Huddleston of the Community of the Resurrection, Tutu studied for the priesthood at Saint Peter's College, Johannesburg. He was ordained deacon in 1960 and priest the following year. From 1962 to 1965 he studied at King's College, University of London, obtaining a bachelor's degree in divinity and a master's degree in theology. From 1967 to 1969 he lectured at the Federal Theological Seminary in Alice, Cape, and from 1970 to 1972, at the universities of Botswana, Lesotho, and Swaziland (in Roma, Lesotho). From 1972 to 1975 he was associate director of the Theological Education Fund of the World Council of Churches, based in England.

Having been elected dean of Johannesburg in 1975, he returned to South Africa. In 1976 he was consecrated bishop of Lesotho, but two years later he accepted appointment as the general secretary of the South African Council of Churches. During his tenure in this office he became an international spokesperson in the struggle against apartheid and was awarded the Nobel Peace Prize in 1984. The same year he was elected bishop of Johannesburg, and in 1986 he became archbishop of Cape Town. He retired from this office in June 1996. In January 1996 he was appointed the chairperson of the Commission on Truth and Reconciliation by President Nelson Mandela. Recipient of many honorary doctorates and other awards, Tutu was elected president of the All Africa Conference of Churches in 1987, and reelected to that office in 1993. After the unbanning of the liberation movements in South Africa in February 1990, Tutu played a major role in facilitating peace, reconciliation, and national reconstruction in South Africa. Tutu is married to Leah Nomalizo Shenxane; the couple has four children. ◆

1931 Tutu is born in Klerksdorp, South Africa.

1961 Tutu is ordained a priest.

1976 Tutu is consecrated bishop of Lesotho.

1984 Tutu receives the Nobel Peace Prize.

1996 Nelson Mandela appoints Tutu chairperson of the Commission on Truth and Reconciliation.

Wałesa, Lech

SEPTEMBER 29, 1943– ● LEADER OF SOLIDARITY, POLISH TRADE UNION
MOVEMENT

L ech Wałesa received the Nobel Peace Prize in 1983 for
his work as a campaigner for human rights. In his case,
it was the human right, as defined by the United
Nations, of the freedom of workers to organize. Wałesa was a
leader of Solidarity, a trade union movement.

Lech Wałesa was born during the
German occupation of World War II in a
village near Lipno, close to the Vistula
River. The Wałesas had long been peasants
in the region, once with sizable land holdings, but these had been divided up generation after generation by large families, and
Bolek, Wałesa's father, was left with only a
small plot. He became a carpenter, building
barns and cowsheds, and although he was a
skilled craftsman and worked hard, life was
difficult with four children to care for.
Toward the end of the war, before Wałesa
was two years old, his father died from mistreatment in a German prison. Wałesa's
mother married Bolek's brother, and after
the war conditions improved. There were
three more children, and the family moved
from its clay cottage to a more substantial
brick house. After the children were grown,
the parents went to visit relatives in the

"We are a very special generation. We have a wonderful opportunity to establish world peace and economic prosperity. That requires us to be more active, to put more order in the world."
Lech Wałesa, 1999

comely: beautiful.

United States, where Wałesa's mother died in a traffic accident. The stepfather did not return to Poland.

Wałesa went to primary school in a neighboring town and then to the secondary trade school in Lipino. His report cards show nothing outstanding about his schoolwork. His lowest marks were in deportment, and it was recorded that he was punished three times for smoking cigarettes in the school dormitory. He was remembered, however, for being a leader among his classmates.

Wałesa finished school at the age of eighteen, worked for a time at the State Machinery Center, did his military service, and then in 1967 went to Gdansk to earn more money in the shipyards. Becoming an electrician, he learned fast and was a good worker. In 1969, now twenty-six, he married the bright and **comely** Danuta, a florist's assistant. The next year Bogdan was born, and the little family lived in a rented room, with the help of a subsidy from the shipyard.

It was in 1970 that Wałesa first emerged as an activist. In December the shipyard workers went on strike to protest the government's raising food prices. Wałesa, an outspoken member of the strike committee, was chosen as a member of the delegation to meet with the authorities in Warsaw and later was elected an officer of the union. He was leading a march of the workers when they were confronted by government forces and fifty-five of his comrades were killed. Wałesa felt responsible for their deaths, and on every anniversary, unless prevented by the government, he has returned to the scene outside the gate of the shipyard, for an act of remembrance.

A reporter who interviewed Wałesa in 1970 for the union paper wrote that this twenty-seven-year-old electrician was much talked about in the shipyard. He had been at the very center of the strike activity and was now experienced and mature for his years. He had even read books about the psychology of crowds.

allotted: assigned a portion.

In 1972 Wałesa and his family were **allotted** better living quarters in a small flat, but his union activities and his criticisms of the government brought him into difficulties with the authorities. He was dismissed from three jobs on various pretexts, and the police began to keep watch on him and often took him in for questioning.

Wałesa was unemployed in August 1980 when once again the shipyard workers started a protest against higher food prices. A crowd of workers was assembled to listen to the explanations of the director, when Wałesa climbed over the twelve-foot steel fence of the shipyard, which he was no longer permitted to enter, jumped on a piece of machinery, and asked them, "Do you recognize me? I've been working for ten years in the shipyard and feel that I am still a shipyard man. . . . We're now beginning a sit-in strike!"

Wałesa then became the leader of the workers' movement, which spread along the coast. He was head of the interfactory committee and chief negotiator with the government representative who was sent from Warsaw. In August 1980 the government accepted the workers' demands, which went beyond economic improvements to include the right to strike, the right to organize unions free of government control, and freedom of expression, liberties unprecedented in the Soviet Union and its satellites.

Over the loudspeakers at the shipyard, where Wałesa reported the progress of the negotiations, his gravelly voice was heard with respect and affection by the workers, and the short, stocky man with the reddish brown walrus mustache and twinkling eyes, always wearing on his lapel the medallion of the Black Madonna of Czestochowa, became a familiar figure in their midst, as well as on television screens and newsmagazine covers in the West. Wałesa talked the language of the workers—"We eat the same bread," he told them—and knew how to use humor and homely anecdotes in the frank and persuasive speeches he gave at meetings. His down-to-earth shrewdness endeared him to the workers and made him a formidable negotiator with the authorities. His religious devotion and his profound love of his country he shared with the great majority of his fellow citizens.

The movement spread throughout Poland to unions of workers and other associations, which were consolidated under the name of Solidarity, with Wałesa as chairman. The Catholic church gave its support to Solidarity, whose members numbered well over nine million. The government declared that the August agreement with the shipyard workers applied to the rest of the country, but it was slow to implement all the provisions, for it feared Soviet intervention if it appeared to be losing control. Consequently, strikes and protests continued, and the economy was crippled. To strengthen the government's hand, General Wojciech Jaruzelski became both prime minister and head of the Communist party. The radicals in Solidarity pressed for further political gains. Wałesa, however, was always a force for moderation, adamant that the government remain true to its pledges, but realistic about the threat from the East. He always argued for negotiation and insisted on peaceful means.

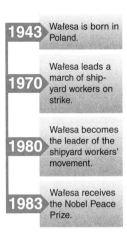

1943 Wałesa is born in Poland.

1970 Wałesa leads a march of shipyard workers on strike.

1980 Wałesa becomes the leader of the shipyard workers' movement.

1983 Wałesa receives the Nobel Peace Prize.

Wałesa talked the language of the workers—"we eat the same bread," he told them—and knew how to use humor and homely anecdotes in the frank and persuasive speeches he gave at meetings.

In December the extremists in Solidarity's leadership, to Wałesa's dismay, put through a proposal to hold a national referendum, asking whether there should be free elections and calling into question the authority of the Communist party and the military alliance with the Soviet Union. The next day General Jaruzelski proclaimed martial law, banned strikes and public gatherings, imposed a blackout on communications, and arrested Wałesa and the other Solidarity leaders. At the first sign of the government action, Wałesa had angrily rebuked the radicals, "Now you've got the confrontation you've been looking for!" In the face of effective military measures, Solidarity's call for a nationwide strike went **unheeded**.

unheeded: ignored.

After December 1981 Jaruzelski's military dictatorship, established in the name of law and order, jailed all Solidarity leaders it could lay its hands on and suppressed all dissent. There was satisfaction in the Kremlin but outrage in Western countries, and the United States applied economic sanctions. Eventually martial law was lifted, although strict controls remained, and after eleven months of detention Wałesa was released, his seventh child having been born in his absence. In view of his international reputation Wałesa was treated more leniently than the others, but he was largely cut off from the other Solidarity leaders, who were in exile, in jail, or in the underground.

In 1981 Jaruselski's military dictatorship, established in the name of law and order, jailed all Solidarity leaders it could lay its hands on and suppressed all dissent.

Wałesa himself was careful not to provoke the government. He continued to ask for dialogue with Jaruzelski and he even took a public stand against the United States' sanctions. In 1983, he decided against going to Oslo to receive the Nobel Peace Prize thinking of his comrades in jail, but fearing that he might not be allowed to return to Poland. Instead, he sent his wife and thirteen-year-old Bogdan to represent him.

Danuta Wałesa had been out of Poland only once before, when she accompanied her husband on a visit to the Pope, but from the moment she stepped off the plane at the Oslo airport and gracefully accepted Chairman Aarvik's bouquet, she impressed everyone with her poise and her intelligence. At her press conference she handled difficult questions **adroitly**, and at the ceremony she gave such an effective reading of her husband's speech that Wałesa, who heard it in Gdansk in a Radio Free Europe broadcast, told reporters afterward that he had fallen in love with her all over again. He got his champagne after all, a bottle sent from Poznan, and he drank to Solidarity

adroitly: showing skill in handling situations.

and to Danuta. That evening Walesa attended mass in Gdansk and the American chargé d'affaires came from Warsaw to convey congratulations from President Ronald Reagan. In Oslo's frigid air the former florist's assistant stood with her son on the balcony of the Grand Hotel to receive the tribute of the torchlight procession below, banner after banner of the trade unions of Norway passing by.

Danuta and Bogdan Walesa left the cheering crowds of Oslo to return to a grim reception in Warsaw, with militia standing by. Watched by the police the Walesas drove to the shrine of Our Lady of Czestochowa, where Lech deposited the Nobel medal and diploma on the altar where Polish kings had laid their crowns and generals their medals. Walesa prayed, "Everything I do, I do for you. Guide me so I can accomplish my service and multiply your glory." On the way back to Gdansk they were stopped thirteen times by the police and subjected to a body search.

Walesa had left the prize money, the equivalent of about $195,000, in Oslo intending to contribute it to a fund the Catholic church planned to establish for grants to private farmers. When the government blocked this plan, the money was used to provide much needed medical supplies to Polish hospitals.

In 1990 Walesa was elected president of Poland by a landslide. As president, Walesa helped guide Poland through its first free parliamentary elections (1991) and watched as successive ministries converted Poland's state-run economy into a free-market system. He was defeated in the 1995 presidential election. Walesa remains a symbol of hope and freedom for the Polish people. ◆

> *"In this land throughout the centuries the Polish and Jewish people lived together through good and evil. The will of the oppressor ended this. The human conscience must never forget."*
> Lech Walesa, 1988

Washington, Booker Taliaferro

C. 1856–1915 ● EDUCATOR

Founder of Tuskegee Institute in Alabama and prominent race leader of the late nineteenth and early twentieth centuries, Booker T. Washington was born a slave on the plantation of James Burroughs near Hale's Ford, Virginia. He spent

ramshackle: ready to collapse.

his childhood as a houseboy and servant. His mother was a cook on the Burroughs plantation, and he never knew his white father. With Emancipation in 1865, he moved with his family—consisting of his mother, Jane; his stepfather, Washington Ferguson; a half brother, John; and a half sister, Amanda—to West Virginia, where he worked briefly in the salt furnaces and coal mines near Malden. Quickly, however, he obtained work as a houseboy in the mansion of the wealthiest white man in Malden, General Lewis Ruffner. There, under the tutelage of the general's wife, Viola Ruffner, a former New England schoolteacher, he learned to read. He also attended a local school for African Americans in Malden.

From 1872 to 1875 Washington attended Hampton Institute, in Hampton, Virginia, where he came under the influence of the school's founder, General Samuel Chapman Armstrong, who inculcated in Washington the work ethic that would stay with him his entire life and that became a hallmark of his educational philosophy. Washington was an outstanding pupil during his tenure at Hampton and was placed in charge of the Native American students there. After graduation he returned to Malden, where he taught school for several years and became active as a public speaker on local matters, including the issue of the removal of the capital of West Virginia to Charleston.

In 1881, Washington founded a school of his own in Tuskegee, Alabama. Beginning with a few **ramshackle** buildings and a small sum from the state of Alabama, he built Tuskegee Institute into the best-known African-American school in the nation. While not neglecting academic training entirely, the school's curriculum stressed industrial education, training in specific skills and crafts that would prepare students for jobs. Washington built his school and his influence by tapping the generosity of northern philanthropists, receiving donations from wealthy New Englanders and some of the leading industrialists and businessmen of his time, such as Andrew Carnegie, William H. Baldwin Jr., Julius Rosenwald, and Robert C. Ogden.

In 1882 Washington married his childhood sweetheart from Malden, Fanny Norton Smith, a graduate of Hampton Institute, who died two years later as a result of injuries suffered in a fall from a wagon. Subsequently Washington married Olivia A. Davidson, a graduate of Hampton and the Framingham State Normal School in Massachusetts, who held the title of lady principal of Tuskegee. She was a tireless worker for the school and an effective fund-raiser in her own right. Always in rather frail health, Davidson died in 1889. Washington's third wife, Margaret James Murray, a graduate of Fisk University, also held the title of lady principal and was a leader of the National Association of Colored Women's Clubs and the Southern Federation of Colored Women's Clubs.

Washington's reputation as the principal of Tuskegee Institute grew through the late 1880s and the 1890s; his school was considered the exemplar of industrial education, viewed as the best method of training the generations of African Americans who were either born in slavery or were the sons and daughters of freed slaves. His control of the purse strings of many of the northern donors to his school increased his influence with other African-American schools in the South. His fame and recognition as a national race leader, however, resulted from the impact of a single speech he delivered before the Cotton States and International Exposition in Atlanta in 1895. This important speech, often called the Atlanta Compromise, is the best single statement of Washington's philosophy of racial advancement and his political accommodation with the predominant racial ideology of his time. For the next twenty years, until the end of his life, Washington seldom deviated publicly from the positions taken in the Atlanta address.

In his speech, Washington urged African Americans to "cast down your bucket where you are"—that is, in the South—and to accommodate to the segregation and discrimination imposed upon them by custom and by state and local laws. He said the races could exist separately from the standpoint of social relationships but should work together for mutual economic advancement. He advocated a gradualist advancement of the race, through hard work, economic improvement, and self-help. This message found instant acceptance from white Americans, north and south, and almost universal approval

1856 Washington is born a slave in Hale's Ford, Virginia.

1881 Washington founds his own school, Tuskegee Institute, in Alabama.

1895 Washington delivers a speech now known as the Atlanta Compromise.

1900 Washington founds the National Negro Business League.

1901 Washington publishes his autobiography, *Up from Slavery*.

1915 Washington dies in Tuskegee.

This speech, often called the Atlanta Compromise, is the best single statement of Washington's philosophy of racial advancement.

Washington became the most powerful African-American politician of his time as an adviser to presidents and as a dispenser of Republican party patronage.

informant: a person who gives information to an investigator.

Horatio Alger success: success achieved through self-reliance and hard work.

among African Americans. Even W. E. B. Du Bois, later one of Washington's harshest critics, wrote to him immediately after the Atlanta address that the speech was "a word fitly spoken."

While Washington's public stance on racial matters seldom varied from the Atlanta Compromise, privately he was a more complicated individual. His voluminous private papers, housed at the Library of Congress, document an elaborate secret life that contradicted many of his public utterances. He secretly financed test cases to challenge Jim Crow laws. He held great power over the African-American press, both north and south, and secretly owned stock in several newspapers. While Washington himself never held political office of any kind, he became the most powerful African-American politician of his time as an adviser to presidents Theodore Roosevelt and William Howard Taft and as a dispenser of Republican party patronage.

Washington's biographer, Louis R. Harlan, called the Tuskegean's extensive political network "the Tuskegee Machine" for its resemblance to the machines established by big-city political bosses of the era. With his network of **informants** and access to both northern philanthropy and political patronage, Washington could make or break careers, and he was the central figure in African-American public life during his heyday. Arguably no other black leader, before or since, has exerted similar dominance. He founded the National Negro Business League in 1900, to foster African-American business and create a loyal corps of supporters throughout the country. Indirectly he influenced the National Afro American Council, the leading African-American civil rights group of his day. The publication of his autobiography, *Up from Slavery*, in 1901 spread his fame even more in the United States and abroad. In this classic American tale, Washington portrayed his life in terms of a **Horatio Alger success** story. Its great popularity in the first decade of the twentieth century won many new financial supporters for Tuskegee Institute and for Washington personally.

Washington remained the dominant African-American leader in the country until the time of his death from exhaustion and overwork in 1915. But other voices rose to challenge his conservative, accommodationist leadership. William Monroe Trotter, the editor of the *Boston Guardian*, was a persistent gadfly. Beginning in 1903 with the publication of Du Bois's *The Souls of Black Folk*, and continuing for the rest of his life, Washington was criticized for his failure to be more publicly aggressive in fighting the deterioration of race relations in the United States, for his avoidance of direct public support for civil rights legislation, and for his single-minded emphasis on industrial education as opposed to academic training for a "talented tenth" of the race. Washington, however, was adept at outmaneuvering his critics, even resorting to the use of spies to infiltrate organizations critical of his leadership, such as the Niagara Movement, led by Du Bois. His intimate friends called Washington "the Wizard" for his mastery of political intrigue and his exercise of power.

Washington's leadership ultimately gave way to new forces in the twentieth century, which placed less emphasis on individual leadership and more on organizational power. The founding of the National Association for the Advancement of Colored People (NAACP) in 1909 and of the National Urban League in 1911 challenged Washington in the areas of civil rights and for his failure to address problems related to the growth of an urban black population. The defeat of the Republican party in the presidential election of 1912 also spelled the end of Washington's power as a **dispenser** of political patronage. Nevertheless, he remained active as a speaker and public figure until his death, in 1915, at Tuskegee.

dispenser: someone who distributes.

Washington's place in the pantheon of African-American leaders is unclear. He was the first African American to appear on a United States postage stamp (1940) and commemorative coin (1946). While he was eulogized by friend and foe alike at the time of his death, his **outmoded** philosophy of accommodation to segregation and racism in American society caused his historical reputation to suffer. New generations of Americans, who took their inspiration from those who were more outspoken critics of segregation and the second-class status endured by African Americans, rejected Washington's leadership role. While much recent scholarship has explored his racial philosophy and political activity in considerable depth, he remains a largely forgotten man in the consciousness of the general public, both black and white. In recent years, however, there has been some revival of interest in his economic thought by those who seek to develop African-American businesses and entrepreneurial skills. Indeed, no serious student of the African-American experience in the United States can afford to ignore the lessons that can be gleaned from Washington's life and from the manner in which he exercised power. ◆

outmoded: old fashioned; out of date.

Weld, Theodore Dwight

NOVEMBER 23, 1803–FEBRUARY 3, 1895 ● ABOLITIONIST

Theodore Weld is often considered the single most influential individual abolitionist.

Theodore Weld is often considered the single most influential individual abolitionist because he recruited so many of the eventual leaders of the antislavery movement. His converts included James G. Birney, Lyman Beecher, Harriet Beecher Stowe, Henry Ward Beecher, Angelina Grimké (his future wife), Gamaliel Bailey, Joshua Giddings, and Edwin M. Stanton and Henry B. Stanton (husband of Elizabeth Cady Stanton).

Theodore Weld, son of a Congregational minister, grew up with strong religious feelings, As a young man in Utica, New York, he became a friend and student of an English reformer, Charles Stuart. Stuart was a forceful preacher, and Weld gathered young men together to listen to Stuart's teachings. In their early years, Weld and his followers were especially interested in the question of **temperance** and the dangers of excessive drinking. By the late 1820s Weld was one of the most powerful temperance advocates in the country.

temperance: abstinence from the use of alcohol.

Weld was persuaded to fight against slavery by Stuart, who returned to England in 1829 to take part in the campaign to abolish slavery in the British Empire. As Weld studied the question, he became an ardent abolitionist and turned his whole mind and will toward converting others to abolitionism. He moved his center of activity to Lane Theological Seminary in Cincinnati, Ohio. There he met a body of students whom he converted to the cause and trained as agents of the American Anti-Slavery Society. In the process, he also converted the president of the seminary, Reverend Lyman Beecher, and his two dynamic children, Henry Ward Beecher and Harriet Beecher (who later married Calvin Ellis Stowe and who wrote *Uncle Tom's Cabin*).

After leaving Lane Seminary, Weld continued to recruit and train agents of the American Anti-Slavery Society. By 1836 seventy members of his heroic band gathered in New York for **pentecostal** training in abolitionism. One of the new agents at this conference was Angelina Grimké, Weld's future wife. They married in 1838.

Pentecostal: expressive worship and evangelism.

Weld was never a public figure during the abolition controversy. He was almost morbidly modest and worked anonymously, writing and publishing many pamphlets against slavery. Yet he had wider influence than William Lloyd Garrison, whose work was so much better known, because Weld's followers went out into the small towns and countryside of the northern states to preach abolition. As the abolitionist movement grew, Weld's disciples rose to leadership in nearly every district.

Weld went to Washington, D.C., in 1841 to head a group of antislavery insurgents in Congress who broke with the Whigs on slavery and sought to repeal the gag rule that restricted consideration of antislavery petitions in Congress. Basically, however, Weld worked behind the scenes, especially among Presbyterian and Congregationalist clergymen. ◆

Wells-Barnett, Ida Bell

JULY 6, 1862 – MARCH 25, 1931 ● JOURNALIST AND CIVIL RIGHTS ACTIVIST

Ida Bell Wells was born to Jim and Elizabeth Wells in Holly Springs, Mississippi, the first of eight children. Her father, the son of his master and a slave woman, worked on a plantation as a carpenter. There he met his future wife, who served as a cook. After Emancipation, Jim Wells was active in local Reconstruction politics.

Young Ida Wells received her early education in the grammar school of Shaw University (now Rust College) in Holly Springs, where her father served on the original board of trustees. Her schooling was halted, however, when a yellow fever epidemic claimed the lives of both her parents in 1878 and she assumed responsibility for her siblings. The next year, the family moved to Memphis, Tennessee, with an aunt. There Wells found work as a teacher. She later studied at Fisk University and Lemoyne Institute.

A turning point in Wells's life occurred on May 4, 1884. While riding a train to a teaching assignment, she was asked to leave her seat and move to a segregated car. Wells refused, and she was physically ejected from the railway car. She sued the railroad, and though she was awarded $500 by a lower court, the Tennessee Supreme Court reversed the decision in 1887. In the same year, she launched her career in journalism, writing of her experiences in an African-American weekly called *The Living Way*. In 1892 she became the co-owner of a small black newspaper in Memphis, the *Free Speech*. Her articles on the

"We must do something and we must do it now. We must educate the white people out of their two hundred and fifty years of slave history."

Ida B. Wells-Barnett, 1928

1862 ▸ Wells is born in Holly Springs, Mississippi.

1884 ▸ Wells sues over being thrown from a railway car.

1892 ▸ Wells becomes co-owner of *Memphis Free Speech* and joins antilynching crusade.

1896 ▸ Wells-Barnett helps found the National Organization of Colored Women.

1913 ▸ Wells-Barnett organizes the Alpha Suffrage Club in Chicago.

1930 ▸ Wells-Barnett runs for the Senate.

1931 ▸ Wells-Barnett dies in Chicago.

exposé: formal statement of fact.

lynching: killing by hanging, without legal sanction.

injustices faced by southern blacks, written under the pen name "Iola," were reprinted in a number of black newspapers, including the *New York Age,* the *Detroit Plain-Dealer,* and the *Indianapolis Freeman.*

In March 1892 the lynching of three young black businessmen, Thomas Moss, Calvin McDowell, and Henry Steward, in a suburb of Memphis focused Wells's attention on the pressing need to address the increasing prevalence of this terrible crime in the post–Reconstruction South. Her approach was characteristically forthright. She argued that though most lynchings were fueled by accusations of rape, they actually were prompted by economic competition between whites and blacks. Wells infuriated most whites by asserting that many sexual liaisons between black men and white women were not rape but mutually consensual.

She urged African Americans in Memphis to move to the West (where, presumably, conditions were more favorable) and to boycott segregated streetcars and discriminatory merchants. Her challenges to the prevailing racial orthodoxy of the South were met by mob violence, and in May 1892, while she was out of town, the offices of the *Free Speech* were destroyed by an angry throng of whites.

After her press was destroyed, Wells began to work for the *New York Age.* There, Wells continued to write extensively on lynching and other African-American issues. She penned **exposés** of southern injustice and decried the situation before European audiences in 1893 and 1894. During these European tours, she criticized some white American supporters of black causes for their halfhearted opposition to **lynching**. Wells's most extended treatment of the subject, *A Red Record: Tabulated Statistics and Alleged Causes of Lynchings in the United States,* appeared in 1895. This was the first serious statistical study of lynchings in the post–Emancipation South. She continued this work for the rest of her life. Some of her more widely read articles in this area include "Lynching and the Excuse for It" (1901) and "Our Country's Lynching Record" (1913). Perhaps her greatest effort in this arena was her tireless campaign for national antilynching legislation. In 1901 she met with President McKinley to convince him of the importance of such legislation. Her appeal was to no avail.

Another issue that provoked Wells's ire was the decision not to permit an African-American pavilion at the 1893 World's Fair. Wells, with the financial support of Frederick

Douglass, among others, published a widely circulated booklet entitled *The Reason Why the Colored American Is Not in the World's Exposition* (1893).

In 1895 Wells married Chicago lawyer-editor Ferdinand L. Barnett, who was appointed assistant state attorney for Cook County in 1896. The couple had four children. Chicago would remain their home for the rest of their lives, and though she was a devoted mother and homemaker, Wells-Barnett's political and reform activities were unceasing. She served as secretary of the National Afro-American Council from 1898 to 1902 and headed its Antilynching Speakers Bureau. She organized and played an important role in the founding of the National Association of Colored Women in 1896. In 1910 she founded the Negro Fellowship League in Chicago, which provided housing and employment for black male migrants. As early as 1901 the Barnetts challenged restrictive housing covenants when they moved to the all-white East Side of Chicago. Her concern for the welfare of Chicago's black community led Wells-Barnett to become, in 1913, the first black woman probation officer in the nation. She lost her appointment in 1916, when a new city administration came to power.

Wells-Barnett was also active in the fight for women's suffrage. In 1913 she organized the Alpha Suffrage Club, the first black women's suffrage club in Illinois. That year, and again in 1918, she marched with suffragists in Washington, D.C. On the former occasion she insisted on marching with the Illinois contingent, integrating it over the objection of many white women marchers.

Wells-Barnett's militant opposition to the southern status quo placed her at odds with Booker T. Washington and his strategy of accommodationism. She was much more sympathetic to the ideology of W. E. B. Du Bois and in 1906 she attended the founding meeting of the Niagara Movement. She was a member of the original Executive Committee of the National Association for the Advancement of Colored People (NAACP) in 1910. She was, however, uneasy about the integrated hierarchy at the organization and felt their public stance was too tempered, and she ceased active participation in 1912.

In 1916 Wells-Barnett began an affiliation with Marcus Garvey's Universal Negro Improvement Association (UNIA). In December 1918, at a UNIA meeting in New York, Wells-Barnett was chosen along with A. Philip Randolph to represent the organization as a delegate to the upcoming Versailles

Her concern for the welfare of Chicago's black community led Wells-Barnett to become, in 1913, the first black woman probation officer in the nation.

Conference. Both representatives were repeatedly denied U.S. State Department clearance, however, so they never attended the meeting. Wells-Barnett, however, did speak on behalf of the UNIA at Bethel AME Church in Baltimore at the end of December 1918. Her continued affiliation with the organization after this was less public.

In the last decades of her life, Wells-Barnett continued to write about racial issues and American injustice. The East St. Louis race riot of July 1917 and the Chicago riot of July and August 1919 provided the impetus for impassioned **denunciations** of the treatment of African Americans in the United States. She wrote *The Arkansas Race Riot* in 1922 in response to the accusation of murder aimed at several black farmers, an accusation that was said to have instigated the disturbance. Most of her later work targeted social and political issues in Chicago. In 1930 Wells-Barnett ran unsuccessfully as an independent candidate for the Senate from Illinois.

She died the next year, on March 25, 1931. In 1941 the Chicago Housing Authority named one of its first low-rent housing developments the Ida B. Wells Homes. In 1990 the U.S. Postal Service issued an Ida B. Wells stamp. ◆

denunciations: public condemnations.

White, Walter Francis

JULY 1, 1893–MARCH 21, 1955 ● CIVIL RIGHTS LEADER

Walter White, executive secretary of the National Association for the Advancement of Colored People (NAACP) from 1931 to 1955, was born in Atlanta, Georgia. Blond and blue-eyed, he was an African American by choice and social circumstance. In 1906, at age thirteen, he stood, rifle in hand, with his father to protect their home and faced down a mob of whites who had invaded their neighborhood in search of "nigger" blood. He later explained: "I knew then who I was. I was a Negro, a human being with an invisible pigmentation which marked me a person to be hunted, hanged, abused, discriminated against, kept in poverty and ignorance, in order that those whose skin was white would have readily at hand a proof of their superiority, a proof patent and inclusive, accessible to the moron and the idiot as well as to the wise man and the genius."

"Intolerance can grow only in the soil of ignorance: from its branches grow all manner of obstacles to human progress."
Walter White, *The Rope and the Faggot*, 1929

In 1918, when the NAACP hired him as assistant executive secretary to investigate lynchings, there were sixty-seven such crimes committed that year in sixteen states. By 1955, when he died, there were only three lynchings, all in Mississippi, and the NAACP no longer regarded the problem as its top priority. White investigated forty-two lynchings mostly in the Deep South and eight race riots in the North that developed between World War I and after World War II in such cities as Chicago, Philadelphia, Washington, D.C., Omaha, and Detroit.

In August 1946 he helped to create a National Emergency Committee Against Mob Violence. The following month, he led a delegation of labor and civil leaders in a visit with President Harry S Truman to demand federal action to end the problem. Truman responded by creating the President's Committee on Civil Rights, headed by Charles E. Wilson, chairman and president of General Electric. The committee's report, "To Secure These Rights," provided the blueprint for the NAACP legislative struggle.

The NAACP's successful struggle against segregation in the armed services was one of White's major achievements. In 1940, as a result of the NAACP's intense protests, President Franklin D. Roosevelt appointed Judge William H. Hastie as civilian aide to the secretary of war, promoted Colonel Benjamin O. Davis, the highest-ranking black officer in the army, to brigadier general, and appointed Colonel Campbell Johnson special aide to the director of Selective Service. As significant as these steps were, they did not satisfy White because they were **woefully** inadequate. So he increasingly intensified the NAACP's efforts in this area.

White then attempted to get the U.S. Senate to investigate employment discrimination and segregation in the armed services, but the effort failed. He therefore persuaded the NAACP board to express its support for the threat by A. Philip Randolph, president of the Brotherhood of Sleeping Car Porters, to lead a march on Washington in demand for jobs for blacks in the defense industries and an end to segregation in the military. To avoid the protest, President Roosevelt on June 25, 1941, issued Executive Order 8802, barring discrimination in the defense industries and creating the Fair Employment Practice Committee. That was the first time a U.S. president acted to end racial discrimination, and the date marked the launching of the modern civil rights movement. Subsequently,

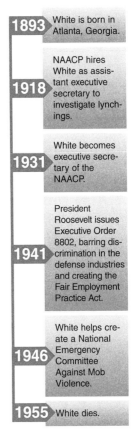

1893 — White is born in Atlanta, Georgia.

1918 — NAACP hires White as assistant executive secretary to investigate lynchings.

1931 — White becomes executive secretary of the NAACP.

1941 — President Roosevelt issues Executive Order 8802, barring discrimination in the defense industries and creating the Fair Employment Practice Act.

1946 — White helps create a National Emergency Committee Against Mob Violence.

1955 — White dies.

woefully: lamentably bad.

the NAACP made the quest for presidential leadership in protecting the rights of blacks central to its programs.

As a special war correspondent for the *New York Post* in 1943 and 1945, White visited the European, Mediterranean, Middle Eastern, and Pacific theaters of operations and provided the War Department with extensive recommendations for ending racial discrimination in the military. His book *A Rising Wind* reported on the status of black troops in the European and Mediterranean theaters.

White was as much an internationalist as a civil rights leader. In 1921 he attended the second Pan-African Congress sessions in England, Belgium, and France, which were sponsored by the NAACP and led by W. E. B. Du Bois. While on a year's leave of absence from the NAACP in 1949 and 1950, he participated in the "Round the World Town Meeting of the Air," visiting Europe, Israel, Egypt, India, and Japan.

> In 1945 White, W. E. B Du Bois, and Mary McLeod Bethune urged that the United Nations recognize equality of the races and that it adopt a bill of rights for all people.

In 1945 White, Du Bois, and Mary McLeod Bethune represented the NAACP as consultants to the American delegation at the founding of the United Nations in San Francisco. They urged that the colonial system be abolished; that the United Nations recognize equality of the races; that it adopt a bill of rights for all people; and that an international agency be established to replace the colonial system. Many of their recommendations were adopted by the United Nations.

menial: a servant.

White similarly protested the **menial** roles that blacks were forced to play in Hollywood films and sought an end to the harmful and dangerous stereotypes of the race that the industry was spreading. He enlisted the aid of Wendell Willkie, the Republican presidential candidate who was defeated in 1940 and who had become counsel to the motion picture industry, in appealing to Twentieth Century-Fox, Warner Brothers, Metro-Goldwyn-Mayer, and other major studios and producers for more representative roles for blacks in films. He then contemplated creating an NAACP bureau in Hollywood to implement the organization's programs there. Although the bureau's idea fizzled, the NAACP did create a Beverly Hills-Hollywood branch in addition to others in California.

poll tax: a tax of a fixed amount per person to vote.

During White's tenure as executive secretary, the NAACP won the right to vote for blacks in the South by getting the Supreme Court to declare the white Democratic primary unconstitutional; opposed the **poll tax** and other devices that were used to discriminate against blacks at the polls; forged an alliance between the organization and the industrial trade unions; removed constitutional roadblocks to residential integration; equalized teachers' salaries in the South; and ended segregation in higher education institutions in addition to winning the landmark *Brown* v. *Board of Education* decision in 1954, overturning the Supreme Court's "separate but equal" doctrine. Overall, White led the NAACP to become the nation's dominant force in the struggle to get the national government to uphold the Constitution and protect the rights of African Americans.

White was a gregarious, sociable man who courted on a first-name basis a vast variety of people of accomplishment and influence like Willkie, Eleanor Roosevelt, Harold Ickes, and Governor Averell Harriman of New York. In 1949 he created a furor by divorcing his first wife, Gladys, and marrying Poppy Cannon, a white woman who was a magazine food editor.

In addition to his many articles, White wrote two weekly newspaper columns. One was for the *Chicago Defender*, a respected black newspaper, and the other for white newspapers like the Sunday *Herald Tribune*. He wrote two novels, *The Fire in the Flint* (1924) and *Flight* (1926); *The Rope and the Faggot* (1929, reprint 1969), an exhaustive study of lynchings; *A Man Called White* (1948), an autobiography; and *A Rising Wind* (1945). An assessment of civil rights progress, *How Far the Promised Land?* was published shortly after White's death in 1955. ◆

> White led the NAACP to become the nation's dominant force in the struggle to get the government to uphold the Constitution and protect the rights of African Americans.

Wiesel, Elie

SEPTEMBER 30, 1928– ● SURVIVOR OF NAZI CONCENTRATION CAMPS AND LEADING INTERPRETER OF THE HOLOCAUST

E lie Wiesel, concentration camp survivor and eloquent spokesman for the suffering of the Jews during the Holocaust, was awarded the 1986 Nobel Peace Prize.

Elie(zer) Wiesel was born in Romania in the Transylvanian town of Sighet in the Carpathian Mountains near the Ukrainian border. His father, Shlomo, was a shopkeeper and a leading member of the large Jewish community in the town. Elie grew up deeply rooted in Jewish traditions. He studied the Hebrew scriptures, the Talmud, and the Hassidic teachings, and he delighted in the Hassidic tales told by his grandfather. From his father he also learned about Western rationalism and

Never Again

Remarks Made by Elie Wiesel, Chairman of the President's Commission on the Holocaust, at the National Civic Holocaust Commemoration Ceremony on April 24, 1979:

Allow me to tell you a story.

Once upon a time, far away, somewhere in the Carpathian mountains, there lived a small boy, a Jewish boy, whose dreams were filled with God, prayer, and song.

Then one day, he and his family, and all the Jews of his town, were rounded up and exiled to a dark and evil kingdom. They arrived there at midnight. Then came the first separation, the first selection.

As the boy stood with his father, wondering whether his mother and sisters would come back, an inmate came to tell them the truth; this road led to the final destination of the Jewish people; the truth was there: in the fire, the ashes, the truth was in death. And the young boy refused to believe him; it had to be a lie, a nightmare perhaps, this could not be happening, not here, not now, not in the heart of civilized Europe, not in the middle of the twentieth-century. "Father," said the boy, "if this were true, the world would not be silent. . . ." "Perhaps the world does not know," said the father. And father and son walked on, part of an eerie nocturnal procession, toward mysterious flames of darkness.

Thirty-five years later—almost to the day—the same Jewish boy stands before you with a deep sense of privilege, to remind our contemporaries that in those times of anguish and destruction, only one people—the Jewish people—were totally, inexplicably abandoned— only one people were simply, cynically handed over to their executioners.

And we, the few survivors, were left behind to bear witness and tell the tale.

humanism. He was always a bookish youth, and when he was only about twelve he wrote a set of commentaries on the Bible.

After the war began in 1939, Transylvania became part of Hungary, and in 1944, in accordance with orders from Germany, the Jews of Hungary were rounded up and sent to the death camps. Elie, then fifteen, with his parents and his three sisters was transported in a cattle car to the concentration camp of Auschwitz in Poland, where his mother and little sister were killed. He and his father managed to survive amid unspeakable conditions until the camp was evacuated in 1945 as the Soviet Army moved westward. They were taken to the concentration camp of Buchenwald in Germany, where Elie watched his father die from dysentery and starvation.

In April 1945 the survivors in the camp were liberated by American soldiers. From a photograph of the inmates lying in their rude bunks, Elie Wiesel's emaciated and worn face peers at the camera. The starving men threw themselves upon the food they were given. Three days after the liberation, Elie was in the hospital from food poisoning and almost died. He has told of looking at himself in a mirror for the first time since the deportation: "From the depths of the mirror, a corpse looked back at me. The look in his eyes, as they stared into mine, has never left me."

Alone now in the world—it was only later that he found the two sisters who survived—he was brought to Normandy in France by a relief organization, which later helped him settle in Paris to study philosophy at the Sorbonne. He lived frugally, supporting himself with jobs as choir director, camp counselor, Bible teacher, and translator. Finally he was hired by the foreign desk of a French newspaper, and he traveled to many countries, including India, where he worked on his English, and Palestine, where he reported on the establishment of the state of Israel in 1948. He then became the foreign correspondent of a Tel Aviv daily, which sent him to New York City to report on the United Nations.

In 1956 Wiesel was hit by a taxi in Times Square and seriously injured. During his long **convalescence**, he decided to apply for U.S. citizenship, which he received in 1963. In 1957 he became a feature writer for the Yiddish-language *Jewish Daily Forward* in New York, but he had already published his first book about his experiences in the camps and was to become a celebrated author. In 1969 he married Marion Erster Rose, also a concentration camp survivor, and they have one son, Shlomo Elisha.

When Wiesel left Buchenwald, he had vowed not to speak of his experiences for at least ten years: "How does one describe the indescribable? How can one be sure that the words . . . will not betray, distort the message they bear?" Then, in 1954, when Wiesel went to interview the Catholic writer François Mauriac for his Tel Aviv newspaper, he found himself interviewed instead, and after Mauriac heard Wiesel's story, he persuaded him that it was wrong not to speak out. One year later Wiesel sent Mauriac a manuscript. Published in France as *La Nuit* (*Night*) in 1958, the book has been translated into many lan-

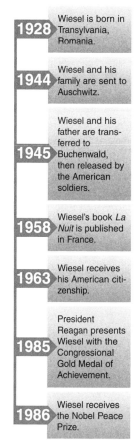

1928 ▸ Wiesel is born in Transylvania, Romania.

1944 ▸ Wiesel and his family are sent to Auschwitz.

1945 ▸ Wiesel and his father are transferred to Buchenwald, then released by the American soldiers.

1958 ▸ Wiesel's book *La Nuit* is published in France.

1963 ▸ Wiesel receives his American citizenship.

1985 ▸ President Reagan presents Wiesel with the Congressional Gold Medal of Achievement.

1986 ▸ Wiesel receives the Nobel Peace Prize.

convalescence: period in which health and strength are recovered gradually.

"Be sensitive in every way possible about everything in life. Be sensitive. Insensitivity brings indifference and nothing is worse than indifference."

Elie Wiesel, 1996

Hassidic: a Jewish sect devoted to the strict observance of ritual law.

intercede: to intervene between parties in order to reconcile differences.

guages and has become the most noted and perhaps the most influential personal account of the Holocaust ever written.

Once released from his self-imposed vow, Wiesel became a prolific writer, no longer fearing that his words might do less than justice to the victims of the Holocaust, but feeling it his duty to witness to their suffering, to keep their memory alive and try to prevent anything like it from ever happening again. A stream of some thirty books has come from his pen—novels, short stories, plays, essays. His prose is poetic and no words are wasted. His fiction has often taken the form of the **Hassidic** tales of his youth.

No one has more vividly conveyed the horrors of the Holocaust or gone more deeply into its implications. He has condemned the world's indifference—*Night* was first entitled *And the World Remained Silent*—probed the nature of God and of evil, and moved compassionately from concern with Jewish suffering to concern with all human suffering. This has taken him not only to the Soviet Union to give moral support to Soviet Jews and to work for their right of emigration but to African and Latin American countries to **intercede** for victims of injustice and brutality.

Wiesel's mother tongue was Yiddish, but he writes in French, and his French literary prizes stand at the top of the long list of awards he has received. At the same time, he has attained a mastery of English that has equipped him to become an effective teacher in American universities and a popular lecturer.

In recognition of his work for human rights, his contributions to literature, and his service as chairman of the United States Holocaust Memorial Council, President Ronald Reagan presented him in April 1985 with the Congressional Gold Medal of Achievement in a ceremony at the White House. He received the Nobel Peace Prize in 1986. ◆

Wilkins, Roy Ottoway

AUGUST 30, 1901–SEPTEMBER 8, 1981 ● CIVIL RIGHTS LEADER AND JOURNALIST

Born in a first-floor flat in a black section of St. Louis, Missouri, Roy Wilkins got his middle name from the African-American physician who delivered him, Dr. Ottoway Fields. At age four, following his mother's death,

Wilkins went to St. Paul, Minnessota to live with his aunt Elizabeth (Edmundson) and uncle Sam Williams. The Williamses wrested legal guardianship of Roy, his brother, Earl, and sister, Armeda, from their absentee, footloose father, William.

After graduating from the University of Minnesota (1923) and following a stint as night editor of the college newspaper and editor of the black weekly, the *St. Paul Appeal,* Wilkins moved to Kansas City where he was editor of the *Kansas City Call* for eight years. In 1929 in Kansas City he married Aminda Badeau. In St. Paul and Kansas City, he was active in the local National Association for the Advancement of Colored People chapters during a period when the NAACP was waging a full-scale attack against America's Jim Crow practices. Under Wilkins's stewardship the *Call* gave banner headline coverage to NAACP (Acting) Executive Secretary Walter White's 1930 campaign to defeat President Herbert Hoover's nomination of Circuit Court Judge John J. Parker to the United States Supreme Court. Parker, in a race for North Carolina governor ten years earlier, had declared his **antipathy** toward blacks. The *Call* published Parker's photo alongside his quote during the campaign: "If I should be elected Governor . . . and find that my election was due to one Negro vote, I would immediately resign my office." The *Kansas City Call* editorialized that "for a man who would be judge, prejudice is the unpardonable sin. . . ." The NAACP's success in blocking Parker's ascension to the U.S. Supreme Court gave Walter White national prominence and a friendship was forged between White, in New York, and Wilkins, in Kansas City.

antipathy: aversion or dislike.

"Slowly we have lifted ourselves by our own boot-straps. Step by halting step, we have beat our way back."

Roy Wilkins, speech given to the NAACP, New York, 1955

In 1931 White invited Wilkins to join the national staff of the NAACP in New York as assistant secretary. Wilkins accepted the post with great excitement and anticipation, regarding the NAACP at the time as "the most militant civil rights organization in the country." Wilkins, in his autobiography, recalled that the NAACP during the 1920s and '30s, had "pounded down the South's **infamous** grandfather clauses, exposed lynchings, and pushed for a federal anti-lynching law" and had "exposed the spread of peonage among black sharecroppers in the South, prodded the Supreme Court into throwing

infamous: notorious.

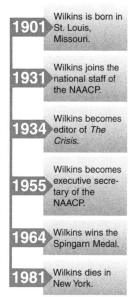

1901 Wilkins is born in St. Louis, Missouri.

1931 Wilkins joins the national staff of the NAACP.

1934 Wilkins becomes editor of *The Crisis.*

1955 Wilkins becomes executive secretary of the NAACP.

1964 Wilkins wins the Spingarn Medal.

1981 Wilkins dies in New York.

sway: persuade.

out verdicts reached by mob-dominated juries, and blotted out residential segregation by municipal ordinance." The NAACP was overturning the racial status quo and Wilkins wanted to be involved.

But there was also dissent within the NAACP. In 1934, following a blistering public attack on Walter White's leadership and on the NAACP's integrationist philosophy from NAACP cofounder W. E. B. Du Bois, who subsequently resigned as editor of the NAACP's penetrating and influential magazine, *The Crisis,* Wilkins succeeded Du Bois as editor of *The Crisis* while he continued in his post as assistant secretary. Wilkins was editor of *The Crisis* for fifteen years (1934–49).

Du Bois's open flirtation with voluntary segregation did not alter the NAACP's course; throughout the 1930s, '40s, and '50s the NAACP continued to attack Jim Crow laws and to work on behalf of blacks' full integration into American society. But by 1950 Walter White's leadership was on the wane; in that year Wilkins was designated NAACP administrator. White lost key support because of a divorce and his remarriage to a white woman; failing health made him especially vulnerable to his detractors. Upon White's death in 1955, Wilkins became executive secretary of the NAACP in the wake of its momentous victory in *Brown* v. *Board of Education of Topeka, Kansas* (1954), where NAACP lawyers had successfully argued that racially separate public schools were *inherently* unequal.

Wilkins served as the NAACP's executive secretary/director for twenty-two years, longer than any other NAACP leader. His tenure characterized him as a pragmatist and strategist who believed that reasoned arguments, both in the courtroom and in public discourse, would **sway** public opinion and public officials to purposeful actions on behalf of racial equality. During the 1960s, Wilkins was widely regarded as "Mr. Civil Rights," employing the NAACP's huge nationwide membership of 400,000 and lawyers' network to back up the direct-action campaigns of more fiery leaders like the Rev. Dr. Martin Luther King Jr. and James Farmer. The NAACP supplied money and member support to the massive March on Washington in 1963. Always moderate in language and temperament, and lacking a charismatic personal style, Wilkins was most comfortable as a strategist and adviser, had meetings with presidents from Franklin D. Roosevelt to Jimmy Carter, and was a friend of President Lyndon B. Johnson. Major civil rights legislation was signed into law in Wilkins's presence, including the Civil

Rights Act of 1964, the Voting Rights Act of 1965, and the Fair Housing Act of 1968.

As standard-bearer of integration, the NAACP during the turbulent 1960s and throughout the 1970s was pilloried with criticism from black separatists and from whites who opposed school busing and affirmative action programs. Wilkins steered a steady course, however, eschewing racial quotas but insisting on effective legal remedies to purposeful and systemic racial discrimination that included race-conscious methods of desegregating schools, colleges, and the work place. He simultaneously took to task the **exponents** of black nationalism. During the height of the Black Power movement, in 1966, Wilkins denounced calls for black separatism, saying black power "can mean in the end only black death." Although one of America's most influential and well-known leaders, Wilkins refused to arrogate to himself the plaudits due him because of his successes. He was a frugal administrator and humble individual who routinely took the subway to work and back home.

exponents: supporters.

By 1976, after forty-five years with the NAACP, Wilkins, at age seventy-five, was barely holding on to his post at the NAACP's helm. A year later, in failing health, he retired to his home in Queens, New York, where he spent his last years in the company of his wife. The winner of the NAACP's Spingarn Medal in 1964, and the recipient of many other awards, including over fifty honorary degrees, Wilkins died in September 1981. At his funeral in New York City hundreds of mourners, black and white, remembered him as a man who refused to bend to fashion. ◆

Williams, Jody

OCTOBER 9, 1950– ● ANTI–LAND MINE ACTIVIST

Jody Williams is the world's leading anti–land mine activist. She helped to found the International Campaign to Ban Landmines (ICBL) and coordinated its effort to ban the production, transfer, and deployment of antipersonnel land mines and to enforce their removal. For their efforts, Williams and ICBL were named corecipients of the 1997 Nobel Peace Prize.

"Nobody can define what makes a difference for you. You have to figure out what makes a difference for you . . . . What matters is that it gives you joy. I firmly believe that people make the most important contribution in the world that they can make if it brings them joy every day."

Jody Williams, 1998

detonator: a device used to cause bombs to explode.

antipersonnel: designed for use against military personnel.

The second of five children, Jody Williams was born and raised in Brattleboro, Vermont, a town in southeast Vermont on the Connecticut River with a tradition of social activism. Williams's brother, Stephen, was born deaf after their mother developed German measles in the first trimester of pregnancy. When other children cruelly made fun of Stephen's inability to talk as a child, Jody Williams became her brother's defender, and continued to do so when he developed schizophrenia later in adolescence. In interviews she frequently traces the origin of her compassion for the downtrodden to her childhood experiences protecting her brother.

Williams attended the University of Vermont as an undergraduate, where she majored in psychology, and spent some time after college traveling in Mexico. Later she moved to Washington, D.C., and obtained a master's degree at the Johns Hopkins School of Advanced International Studies in Baltimore, Maryland. After graduate school, Williams coordinated the Nicaragua-Honduras Education Project and she later became the associate director of Medical Aid to El Salvador, an organization based in Los Angeles.

During her many trips to Central America, Williams witnessed firsthand the devastating effects of land mines on civilians. In 1991 Vietnam Veterans of America Foundation hired Williams to coordinate a campaign against the use of land mines. A land mine is an explosive device hidden in the earth that sits indefinitely until the weight of an object or a step triggers its **detonator**. An individual land mine costs between $3 and $30 and is a far cheaper method of guarding hostile borders than having soldiers stand sentry. Some land mines are detonated by the massive weight of tanks or large trucks, but others, called **antipersonnel** land mines, are triggered by the weight of a human step. In many Third World countries antipersonnel land mines are deployed in civilian areas where ordinary people carry on the tasks of daily life — next to watering holes, along the banks of rivers, or in the crop fields. According to ICBL, there are between 80 and 110 land mines deployed worldwide, and they kill or maim 26,000 people annually, most of whom are unarmed civilians. Some of these land mines have been in place ever since World War II.

Throughout the 1990s Williams worked mostly from her home in Vermont, rising at dawn to send thousands of e-mails to government leaders, diplomats, and humanitarian groups in Europe and Asia. Williams is widely credited with doing more than any other person in the world to raise public consciousness about the dangers of antipersonnel land mines, helping to influence personalities as diverse as the late Princess Diana, Senator Patrick Leahy, and General Norman Schwarzkopf to take up the cause.

Years of public information campaigns by Jody Williams and ICBL led to talks that in December 1997 resulted in the signing of a treaty in Ottawa, Canada, by some 120 countries to stop the production, deployment, stockpiling, and sale of antipersonnel land mines. Immediately after the Williams and ISBL received the Nobel Peace Prize in October 1997, Russian president Boris Yeltsin reversed his long-held position and agreed to ban land mines. Since 1997 fifteen countries have agreed to sign the treaty bringing the total to 135. Of the world's superpowers, only China and the United States have not signed the treaty. In February 1998 Williams announced that she was leaving ICBL to write a new book about the anti–land mine campaign. ◆

1950 Williams is born in Brattleboro, Vermont.

1991 The Vietnam Veterans Association hires Williams to coordinate a campaign against the use of land mines.

1997 Williams receives the Nobel Peace Prize.

Winnemucca, Sarah

1844–1891 ● NATIVE AMERICAN RIGHTS ACTIVIST

Born in western Nevada into a band of Paiutes led by her father, Chief Winnemucca, and centered around Humboldt and Pyramid lakes, Sarah Winnemucca (Tocmetone, or Shell Flower) became a champion of Indian rights and the author of the influential *Life among the Paiutes: Their Wrongs and Claims* (1883). When her mother and sister were killed in 1865 during disturbances that followed the Paiutes' confinement to a reservation around Pyramid Lake, Winnemucca blamed Indian agents for causing the troubles. She served as an interpreter and messenger for General Oliver Otis Howard during the Paiute and Bannock hostilities of 1877 and 1878 when the general could find no man willing to negotiate with the Indians. Instrumental in persuading Chief Winnemucca to lead his band out of the war camp, she traveled with her father to Washington, D.C., in 1879 and 1880 to seek permission for the Paiutes to leave the Washington Territory and return to the Malhuer reservation in Nevada. Although the secretary of the interior granted the request, the Yakima

"Oh, my dear good Christian people, how long are you going to stand by and see us suffer at your hands?"

Sarah Winnemucca, 1872

Ableza

Ableza is a Native American arts and film institute dedicated to promoting, preserving, and protecting traditional and contemporary arts by Native American peoples. Ableza works to create a true picture of Native American people to counteract the stereotypes reinforced by Hollywood and American culture. Through education, the organization encourages self-esteem and an understanding of the Native American identity, both for the Native American communities and for non-Indians.

The institute's purpose is to use the arts in education by, about, and for the Native American community. This includes not only arts-oriented learning, but also youth programs designed to promote health, self-esteem, and a sense of cultural identity for young Native Americans. The organization calls for the development of films and dramatic works oriented toward Native Americans, and supports the development and recording of native music as well as other Native American arts, including writing and any other creative activities by and about Native Americans. Another important aspect of Ableza is its focus on youth literacy and the development of programs for that purpose. Ableza's work fosters an understanding and acceptance of all Native American cultures and their ways, their arts, and their writings. By acceptance of the diversity in the Native American community, Ableza promotes the unification of native peoples, helping to heal the sacred hoop. As young and old alike seek ties to their ethnic roots, Ableza hopes to counteract the stereotypical images suffered by Native American people over the last 500 years. Ableza provides a place for Native Americans to reclaim and tell their stories in ways that promote cultural truths and dignity through artistic excellence.

1844 Winnemucca is born in western Nevada.

1879 Winnemucca travels to Washington, D.C., to request the return of the Paiutes to the Malhuer reservation in Nevada.

1883 Winnemucca publishes *Life Among the Paiutes: Their Wrongs and Claims.*

1891 Winnemucca dies in Montana.

Indian agent thwarted the move, which only hardened Winnemucca's dislike of such men. Back East in 1881 and 1882, she lectured in Boston and other cities. Condemning the practices of Indian agents, she won sympathy for her people and the indignations visited upon them and converted many to the new Indian reform movement just then coming into full swing.

Winnemucca was married three times. The first marriage, to Lieutenant Edward Bartlett, lasted scarcely a year. When her second marriage to a Paiute also failed, she married Lieutenant Lambert H. Hopkins, probably an officer in the volunteers, who assisted her in the writing of her book. Her attacks on Indian agents led to savage countercharges that she was a liar and a "drunken prostitute," but these were refuted by General Howard and other distinguished officers, who praised her for the brave work she had done with them in the field. Money from her speaking tours allowed her to buy land in Nevada and to establish, near Lovelock, an Indian school, which she ran for three years. But in 1886 her husband died of tuberculosis, and

Winnemucca—afflicted with psychological and emotional problems, her physical health failing—retired to Monida, Montana, to live with her sister. Hailed as "the most famous Indian woman on the Pacific Coast" by the whites, called "Mother" by her Paiute tribe, Sarah Winnemucca died in Montana of tuberculosis on October 16, 1891. ◆

Woodhull, Victoria

SEPTEMBER 23, 1838–JUNE 10, 1927 ● SUFFRAGIST

One of the most flamboyant and unconventional of American reformers, Victoria Woodhull was an eloquent champion for woman's suffrage. In 1872 she was the first woman ever to run for the presidency of the United States.

"All this talk of women's rights is moonshine. Women have every right. They have only to exercise them . . . ."

Victoria Woodhull

Woodhull was born in the small town of Homer, Ohio, on September 23, 1838, one of ten children of Reuben and Roxanna (Hummel) Claflin. Her father was a poor itinerant peddler and her mother a spiritualist who believed that it was possible to communicate with the spirits of the dead. During part of her childhood Woodhull traveled through Ohio with her family in a medicine and fortune-telling show. They sold a patent medicine, Elixir of Life, with her sister Tennessee Claflin's portrait on the bottle. In 1853, just before she turned sixteen, Victoria married Dr. Canning Woodhull, but continued with her sister Tennessee to give demonstrations in clairvoyance.

In 1868, after divorcing her husband, Woodhull moved with her sister and other members of her family to New York City. A mutual interest in spiritualism brought Woodhull and Tennessee to the attention of the railroad magnate Cornelius Vanderbilt. With his advice and support, the two sisters were the first women to establish a stock brokerage firm, Woodhull, Claflin, & Co., in the financial district of

1870 Woodhull establishes first woman's brokerage firm, Woodhull, Claflin, & Co., in New York City.

1870 With her sister, Woodhull founds the radical journal *Woodhull and Claflin's Weekly.*

1871 Woodhull speaks in favor of woman's suffrage before the U.S. House Committee on the Judiciary.

1872 Woodhull is the first woman to run for president of the United States.

antagonized: provoked hostility.

compelling: demanding attention.

muckraking: searching out and publicly exposing misconduct.

New York in 1870. At this time Woodhull also became interested in a socialist group called the Pantarchy, which rejected conventional marriage and advocated free love and communal management of children and property.

In 1870 the two sisters launched *Woodhull and Claflin's Weekly*, a journal that supported among other causes equal rights for women and a single standard of morality for men and women. Woodhull's advocacy of free love **antagonized** many leaders of the women's suffrage movement, but her eloquent address in favor of women's right to vote before the U.S. House Committee of the Judiciary in January 1871 won their approval. Woodhull argued that no new amendment on women's suffrage was needed since the Fourteenth Amendment had actually enfranchised women when it asserted the rights of citizenship without making any reference to gender. She urged women to register, to vote, and, if challenged, to take their cases to court.

A **compelling** speaker on workers' rights as well as on women's rights, Woodhull ran for president of the United States on the Equal Rights party ticket in 1872 with the African-American activist Frederick Douglass as her running mate. Woodhull sympathized with the poor and with workers, and she engaged in **muckraking** attacks on American business. Her campaign had few supporters, however, and by the end of 1872 she was near financial ruin. Both Woodhull and her sister spent periods in jail but were acquitted.

Woodhull continued to write and lecture after her marriage to John Biddulph Martin. With her daughter, Zula Maud Woodhull, she published a magazine, the *Humanitarian*, from 1892 to 1910. Even in old age, she remained an advocate of innovation and change. She was an early and enthusiastic patron of aviation, offering in 1914 a prize of $5,000 for the first transatlantic flight. ◆

Wu, Harry (Wu Hongda)

1937– ● CHINESE HUMAN RIGHTS ACTIVIST

The man known in the United States as Harry Wu was born Wu Hongda in China in 1937. Imprisoned as a "counterrevolutinary rightist" when he was just twenty-one years old, Wu spent the next nineteen years in forced labor camps. Since his immigration to the United States in 1985, Wu has dedicated his life to exposing to the world the evils of the *laogai*, the Chinese system of forced labor camps.

Wu had a privileged childhood. His father was a well-to-do banker and his stepmother a kind and compassionate woman. He attended the Jesuit-run St. Francis School in Shanghai, where he was nicknamed "Harry" and baptized a Catholic. When the time came for Wu to attend college, he chose to study geology because of a report he had read in the *People's Daily* detailing the importance of geologists to China's future.

Wu applied and was accepted to the Beijing Geology Institute, where he began his studies in 1955. Although he was a good student and the founder and captain of the institute's championship baseball team, Wu's middle-class background soon caught up with him. In 1957 Communist party chairman Mao Zedong initiated a campaign called "Let a Hundred Flowers Bloom" that encouraged citizens to criticize the Communist party in order to improve it. Already suspect because of his family background, Wu **dutifully** criticized the Soviet invasion of Hungary. Despite having been ordered to make the comments, Wu later found they were held against him. Constantly **scrutinized** and criticized at mandatory political meetings, Wu finally determined that he had no option but to try to leave China if he wished to be successful in his career. Before the escape could be undertaken, however, Wu was summoned to yet another meeting at which he was forced to confess his crimes. Unsure of what he had done, Wu kept trying to find a formula that would satisfy his accusers. Finally he "confessed" to being a "counterrevolutionary rightist." That, apparently, was the right answer, and in 1960 Wu Hongda was sentenced to "**reeducation** through hard labor." Thus began nineteen years of torture, starvation, humiliation, and reeducation.

As he was hauled away to the first of many forced-labor camps, Wu wrote a note to his stepmother. He found out only when he was released from prison in 1979 that his stepmother had committed suicide when she received the letter.

While in prison Wu learned how to survive. Starving, he caught snakes and frogs, ripped their skin off with his teeth, and cooked them in makeshift pots in latrines. A wily peasant, Big-Mouth Xing, taught Wu how to find where rats hide their food; one such discovery yielded two pounds of corn, two pounds of

"I cannot turn my back on the people in the [Chinese forced labor] camps. I am free. They are not."

Harry Wu

dutifully: filled with a sense of obligation.

scrutinized: to be inspected closely.

reeducation: rehabilitation through education.

1937 Wu Hongda is born in Shanghai.

1960 Wu is sentenced to forced labor.

1979 Wu is released from camps.

1985 Wu is allowed to immigrate to the United States.

1995 Wu is arrested at the Chinese border.

Wu says that his research reveals that there are at least 1,100 prison camps in China with between six and ten million prisoners.

soybeans, and a pound of rice that the two men shared. But occasional nourishment could not alter the fact that the steamed buns, called wotou, that formed the basic diet of the prisoners were made of an indigestible mixture of flour, sorghum, chaff, and ground corncobs. By 1961 Wu was so near death that he was sent to a unit for sick prisoners. He weighed only eighty pounds, one of his lungs was filled with fluid, and he had nearly lost the will to live. When one of his friends died and Wu witnessed how the guards unceremoniously dumped his body into a hole in the ground, he decided that he had to live. As he says in his autobiography, *Bitter Winds*, "I could not simply slide into nothingness and join Chen Ming. I had to use my life purposefully and try to change the society. In that way my own existence would not be mere dust but would have some value."

Finally freed from imprisonment in 1979 Wu taught math and English at Shanxi College. In 1981 he applied for a visa to visit a sister who had immigrated to San Francisco. Four years later, in 1985, the visa was granted, and Wu sold everything he owned to pay for the plane ticket to the United States. With $40 in his pocket, Wu began life in America sleeping on park benches and working in a doughnut bakery. Eventually he accepted a position at Stanford University's Hoover Institute, where he conducted research into China's prison system. He also established the Laogai Research Foundation, whose stated mission is to compile "factual information about life within the Laogai—China's vast network of forced labor camps."

Wu says that his research reveals that there are at least 1,100 prison camps in China with between six and ten million prisoners, 10 percent of whom are political prisoners. Other researchers say that these numbers may be exaggerated but that there is no way to determine exactly how many people suffer under this system. Since he has been in the United States, Wu has traveled undercover to China four times with the purpose of documenting some of the human rights abuses there. In 1991 he and his wife, Ching-lee, risked arrest by filming an exposé for *60 Minutes* that documented the fact that China exports goods produced by forced labor. In later trips, Wu uncovered the practice of Chinese prison guards selling for transplant the organs of executed prisoners, sometimes harvesting organs before execution, sometimes delaying executions to wait for a buyer. On his fourth trip to China, on June 19, 1995, Wu was arrested as he tried to enter China at the Kazakhstan border. The Chinese

held Wu for more than two months before convicting him of
espionage. Bowing to pressure from the United States, however, the Chinese sentenced Wu to serve his term in exile—in
the United States. Since his release, Wu has continued to speak
out against human rights abuses in China. He has recently
joined with American labor unions to protest companies that
purchase Chinese goods from factories run by the military on
the assumption that the workers may be forced laborers. ◆

espionage: the practice
of spying.

Young, Andrew

OCTOBER 23, 1932– ● CIVIL RIGHTS ACTIVIST AND POLITICIAN

Andrew Young was born in New Orleans. His father was an affluent, prominent dentist, and Young was raised in a middle-class black family in a racially mixed neighborhood. He attended Howard University in Washington, D.C., and graduated in 1951. Young pursued his growing commitment to religion at Hartford Theological Seminary in Connecticut and was awarded a bachelor of divinity degree in 1955. He was ordained a Congregational minister, and from 1955 to 1959 he preached in churches in Georgia and Alabama. In the course of this work, Young experienced firsthand the wrenching poverty that shaped the lives of African Americans in the rural South. He became active in challenging racial inequality, joined the local civil rights movement and helped organize a voter-registration drive in Thomasville, Georgia, one of the first of its kind in southern Georgia.

In 1959 Young went to New York to become an assistant director of the National Council of Churches and help channel New York City philanthropic money into southern civil rights activities. Two years later, he returned to Georgia and joined the Southern Christian Leadership Conference (SCLC), a civil rights organization headed by the Rev. Dr. Martin Luther King Jr. Young became an active participant in SCLC, building a reputation for coolness and rationality and often providing a **moderating** influence within the movement. From 1961 to 1964, he served as funding coordinator and administrator of SCLC's Citizenship Education Program—a program aimed at increasing black voter registration among African Americans in the South.

"Chaos occurs when human rights are not respected."
Andrew Young,
July 1977

moderating: lessening intensity.

323

1932 Young is born in New Orleans, Louisiana.

1964 Young is named executive director of SCLC.

1972 Young is the first African American elected to the House of Representatives from Georgia since 1870.

1982 Young is elected mayor of Atlanta.

1994 Young publishes his memoir, *A Way Out of No Way.*

1996 Young serves as cochairman of the Atlanta Committee for the Olympic Games.

In 1972 Young turned his energies to the political arena and launched a successful campaign to become the first African American elected to the House of Representatives from Georgia since 1870.

Young grew to be one of King's most trusted aides. In 1964 he was named executive director of SCLC and three years later took on additional responsibility as executive vice president. During his tenure, he focused on creating social and economic programs for African Americans to broaden the scope of SCLC's activism. In 1970 Young relinquished his executive positions. However, he continued his affiliation with SCLC—serving on the board of directors—until 1972.

In 1972 Young turned his energies to the political arena and launched a successful campaign to become the first African American elected to the House of Representatives from Georgia since 1870. In Congress, he served on the House Banking Committee and became familiar with the national and international business markets. In 1976 he vigorously supported the candidacy of fellow Georgian Jimmy Carter for president and vouched for Carter's commitment to black civil rights to many who were skeptical of supporting a white Democrat from the Deep South. Upon Carter's election, Young resigned his congressional seat to accept an appointment as the United States Ambassador to the United Nations.

As ambassador, Young focused on strengthening the ties between the United States and the Third World. In 1979 he was forced to resign his position when it was revealed that he had engaged in secret negotiations with representatives of the Palestine Liberation Organization (PLO) in violation of U.S. policy. Young's supporters argued that Young was merely doing the job of a diplomat by speaking to all interested parties in sensitive negotiations. Many Jews and other supporters of Israel, however, believed that Young's actions gave the PLO unwarranted legitimacy. The furor that surrounded his actions forced him to submit his resignation.

In 1982 Young mounted a successful campaign for mayor of Atlanta. During his administration, he faced the same urban problems that plagued other big-city mayors, including a shrinking tax base, rising unemployment, and rising costs—all of which required difficult decisions in fund allocation. Despite these constraints, he was able to increase business investment in Georgia. He successfully ran for reelection in 1986, despite growing criticism from some African-American critics who argued that black Atlantans had been hurt by his economic development programs. In 1990, after he ran unsuccessfully for the Democratic gubernatorial nomination, Young reentered private life. He served as chairman of Law International, Inc., until 1993, when he was appointed vice chairman of their parent company, Law Companies Group, an internationally respected engineering and environmental consulting company based in Atlanta.

During the course of his career, Young has received many awards, including the Presidential Medal of Freedom—America's highest civilian award—and more than thirty honorary degrees from universities such as Yale, Morehouse, and Emory. In 1994 his spiritual memoir, *A Way Out of No Way*, was published. Young lobbied successfully to bring the 1996 Summer Olympics to Atlanta and served as cochairman of the Atlanta Committee for the Olympic Games. ◆

Yzaguirre, Raul

JULY 22, 1939– ● HISPANIC–AMERICAN ACTIVIST

Raul Yzaguirre is president of the National Council of La Raza, considered the largest advocacy group for Latinos in the United States. In addition to working for the civil and economic rights of Latinos, the organization conducts applied research and policy analysis in connection with Latino-related issues.

Yzaguirre was born on July 22, 1939, in San Juan, Texas, in the Rio Grande Valley. A sixth-generation American citizen, he grew up in poverty. At age fifteen he founded a youth auxiliary of a Hispanic veterans organization called the American G.I. Forum. After graduating from high school in 1958, he served for four years in the U.S. Air Force Medical Corps. Yzaguirre established the National Organization for Mexican American Services (NOMAS) in 1964. The following year he obtained a bachelor of science degree from George Washington University. Subsequently, he worked as a program analyst for the U.S. Office of Economic Opportunity,

established as part of President Lyndon B. Johnson's War on Poverty.

The National Council of La Raza was founded in 1968, based on an idea written up by Yzaguirre for NOMAS. Its goals were to reduce poverty among, and discrimination against, Latinos, and to improve their economic opportunities. At first he served La Raza as a consultant. Yzaguirre became part of the organization as its executive director in 1974, and became its president in 1978.

Under Yzaguirre's leadership, La Raza became the most influential and respected Latino organization in the country. Based in Washington, D.C., with field offices in Los Angeles, Phoenix, Chicago, and San Antonio, in the late 1990s it had over 200 formal affiliates in thirty states, Puerto Rico, and the District of Columbia. In the areas including HIV/AIDS, employment and training, health, housing, and community development, La Raza helped community-based Latino organizations to assess community needs, develop programs, raise money for them, develop and test model projects, and operate and manage programs effectively. Its Policy and Analysis Center is a Latino think tank that does applied research, policy analysis, and advocacy work.

La Raza is also a lobbying group for Latino civil rights. Yzaguirre was the first Latino to sit on the executive committee of the Leadership Conference on Civil Rights, a coalition of groups promoting equal rights for minorities and women. In a 1996 interview he stated that bigotry was the single biggest issue for Latinos. Among the consequences of that bigotry, he argued, is the fact that Latinos have the lowest per capita income and that they are the most segregated minority in the schools. He claimed that Latinos experience more employment discrimination than African Americans, and that the cost is around $12 billion a year in lost Latino wages.

For his work, Yzaguirre has received considerable recognition. In 1979 he became the first Latino to win a Rockefeller Public Service Award for Outstanding Public Service from the trustees of Princeton University. Nine years later Common Cause gave him its Public Service Award. In 1989 and 1990 Yzaguirre was one of the first Latino Fellows of the Institute of Politics at the John F. Kennedy School of Government at Harvard University. In 1993 he received the Order of the Aztec Eagle, the highest honor given to noncitizens by the government of Mexico. ◆

1939 Yzaguirre is born in San Juan, Texas.

1964 Yzaguirre establishes the National Organization for Mexican American Services.

1978 Yzaguirre becomes president of La Raza.

1979 Yzaguirre receives the Rockefeller Public Service Award for Outstanding Public Service, becoming the first Hispanic to win the prize.

1993 Yzaguirre receives the Order of the Aztec Eagle award form the government of Mexico.

Anti-Slavery Declaration (1833)

Adopted at the founding of the American Anti-Slavery Society in Philadelphia. Led by the fiery abolitionist William Lloyd Garrison, the Society pledged to end slavery in the United States.

We have met together for the achievement of an enterprise, without which that of our fathers is incomplete; and which, for its magnitude, solemnity, and probable results upon the destiny of the world, as far transcends theirs as moral truth does physical force.

In purity of motive, in earnestness of zeal, in decision of purpose, in intrepidity of action, in steadfastness of faith, in sincerity of spirit, we would not be inferior to them....

Their grievances, great as they were, were trifling in comparison with the wrongs and sufferings of those for whom we plead. Our fathers were never slaves—never bought and sold like cattle—never shut out from the light of knowledge and religion—never subjected to the lash of brutal taskmasters.

But those, for whose emancipation we are striving—constituting at the present time at least one-sixth part of our countrymen—are recognized by law, and treated by their fellow-beings, as brute beasts; are plundered daily of the fruits of their toil without redress; really enjoy no constitutional nor legal protection from licentious and murderous outrages upon their persons; and are ruthlessly torn asunder—the tender babe from the arms of its frantic mother—the heartbroken wife from her weeping husband—at the caprice or pleasure of irresponsible tyrants. For the crime of having a dark complexion, they suffer the pangs of hunger, the infliction of stripes, the ignominy of brutal servitude. They are kept in heathenish darkness by laws expressly enacted to make their instruction a criminal offence.

These are the prominent circumstances in the condition of more than two million people, the proof of which may be found in thousands of indisputable facts, and in the laws of the slave-holding States.

Hence we maintain—that, in view of the civil and religious privileges of this nation, the guilt of its oppression is unequalled by any other on the face of the earth; and, therefore, that it is bound to repent instantly, to undo the heavy burdens, and to let the oppressed go free . . .

It is piracy to buy or steal a native African, and subject him to servitude. Surely, the sin is as great to enslave an American as an African.

Therefore we believe and affirm—that there is no difference, in principle, between the African slave trade and American slavery:

That every American citizen, who detains a human being in involuntary bondage as his property, is, according to Scripture, (Ex. xxi, 16,) a manstealer.

That the slaves ought instantly to be set free, and brought under the protection of law:

That if they had lived from the time of Pharaoh down to the present period, and had been entailed through successive generations, their right to be free could never have been alienated, but their claims would have constantly risen in solemnity:

That all those laws which are now in force, admitting the right of slavery, are therefore, before God, utterly null and void; being an audacious usurpation of the Divine prerogative, a daring infringement on the law of nature, a base overthrow of the very foundations of the social compact, a complete extinction of all the relations, endearments and obligations of mankind, and a presumptuous transgression of all the holy commandments; and that therefore they ought instantly to be abrogated.

We further believe and affirm—that all persons of color, who possess the qualifications which are demanded of others, ought to be admitted forthwith to the enjoyment of the same privileges, and the exercise of the same prerogatives, as others; and that the paths of preferment, of wealth and of intelligence, should be opened as widely to them as to persons of a white complexion.

We maintain that no compensation should be given to the planters emancipating their slaves:

Because it would be a surrender of the great fundamental principle, that man cannot hold property in man:

Because slavery is a crime, and therefore is not an article to be sold:

Because the holders of slaves are not the just proprietors of what they claim; freeing the slave is not depriving them of property, but restoring it to its rightful owner; it is not wronging the master, but righting the slave—restoring him to himself:

Because immediate and general emancipation would only destroy nominal, not real property; it would not amputate a limb or break a bone of the slaves, but by infusing motives into their breasts, would make them doubly valuable to the masters as free laborers; and

Because, if compensation is to be given at all, it should be given to the outraged and guiltless slaves, and not to those who have plundered and abused them.

We regard as delusive, cruel and dangerous, any scheme of expatriation which pretends to aid, either directly or indirectly, in the emancipation of the slaves, or to be a substitute for the immediate and total abolition of slavery.

We fully and unanimously recognize the sovereignty of each State, to legislate exclusively on the subject of the slavery which is tolerated within its limits; we concede that Congress, under the present national compact, has no right to interfere with any of the slave States, in relation to this momentous subject:

But we maintain that Congress has a right, and is solemnly bound, to suppress the domestic slave trade between the several States, and to abolish slavery in those portions of our territory which the Constitution has placed under its exclusive jurisdiction.

We also maintain that there are, at the present time, the highest obligations resting upon the people of the free States to remove slavery by moral and political action, as prescribed in the Constitution of the United States. They are now living under a pledge of their tremendous physical force, to fasten the galling fetters of tyranny upon the limbs of millions in the Southern States; they are liable to be called at any moment to suppress a general insurrection of the slaves; they authorize the slave owner to vote for three-fifths of his slaves as property, and thus enable him to perpetuate his oppression; they support a standing army at the South for its protection; and they seize the slave, who has escaped into their territories, and send him back to be tortured by an enraged master or a brutal driver. This relation to slavery is criminal, and full of danger: It must be broken up.

These are our views and principles—these our designs and measures. With entire confidence in the overruling justice of God, we plant ourselves upon the Declaration of our Independence and the truths of Divine Revelation, as upon the Everlasting Rock.

Seneca Falls Declaration (1848)

The Seneca Falls Convention, the first modern woman's rights convention, called through the initiative of Lucretia Mott and Elizabeth Cady Stanton, was held in the Wesleyan Methodist Church at Seneca Falls, N.Y., July 19–20, 1848. At the gathering Stanton read a "Declaration of Sentiments," listing the many discriminations existing against women, and the convention adopted a series of eleven resolutions, one of them calling for woman suffrage. This convention launched the organized modern woman's rights movement.

When, in the course of human events, it becomes necessary for one portion of the family of man to assume among the people of the earth a position different from that which they have hitherto occupied, but one to which the laws of nature and of nature's God entitle them, a decent respect to the opinions of mankind requires that they should declare the causes that impel them to such a course.

We hold these truths to be self-evident: that all men and women are created equal; that they are endowed by their Creator with certain inalienable rights; that among these are life, liberty, and the pursuit of happiness; that to secure these rights governments are instituted, deriving their just powers from the consent of the governed. Whenever any form of government becomes destructive of these ends, it is the right of those who suffer from it to refuse allegiance to it, and to insist upon the institution of a new government, laying its foundation on such principles, and organizing its powers in such form, as to them shall seem most likely to effect their safety and happiness. Prudence, indeed, will dictate that governments long established should not be changed for light and transient causes; and accordingly all experience hath shown that mankind are more disposed to suffer, while evils are sufferable, than to right themselves by abolishing the forms to which they were accustomed. But when a long train of abuses and usurpations, pursuing invariably the same object, evinces a design to reduce them under absolute despotism, it is their duty to throw off such government, and to provide new guards for their future security. Such has been the patient sufferance of the women under this government, and such is now the necessity which constrains them to demand the equal station to which they are entitled.

The history of mankind is a history of repeated injuries and usurpations on the part of man toward woman, having in direct object the establishment of an absolute tyranny over her. To prove this, let facts be submitted to a candid world.

He has never permitted her to exercise her inalienable right to the elective franchise.

He has compelled her to submit to laws, in the formation of which she had no voice.

He has withheld from her rights which are given to the most ignorant and degraded men—both natives and foreigners.

Having deprived her of this first right of a citizen, the elective franchise, thereby leaving her without representation in the halls of legislation, he has oppressed her on all sides.

He has made her, if married, in the eye of the law, civilly dead.

He has taken from her all right in property, even to the wages she earns.

He has made her, morally, an irresponsible being, as she can commit many crimes with impunity, provided they be done in the presence of her husband. In the covenant of marriage, she is compelled to promise obedience to her husband, he becoming to all intents and purposes, her master—the law giving him power to deprive her of her liberty, and to administer chastisement.

He has so framed the laws of divorce, as to what shall be the proper causes, and in case of separation, to whom the guardianship of the children shall be given, as to be wholly regardless of the happiness of women—the law, in all cases, going upon a false supposition of the supremacy of man, and giving all power into his hands.

After depriving her of all rights as a married woman, if single, and the owner of property, he has taxed her to support a government which recognizes her only when her property can be made profitable to it.

He has monopolized nearly all the profitable employments, and from those she is permitted to follow, she receives but a scanty remuneration. He closes against her all the avenues to wealth and distinction which he considers most honorable to himself. As a teacher of theology, medicine, or law, she is not known.

He has denied her the facilities for obtaining a thorough education, all colleges being closed against her.

He allows her in Church, as well as State, but a subordinate position, claiming Apostolic authority for her exclusion from the ministry, and, with some exceptions, from any public participation in the affairs of the Church.

He has created a false public sentiment by giving to the world a different code of morals for men and women, by which moral delinquencies which exclude women from society, are not only tolerated, but deemed of little account in man.

He has usurped the prerogative of Jehovah himself, claiming it as his right to assign for her a sphere of action, when that belongs to her conscience and to her God.

He has endeavored, in every way that he could, to destroy her confidence in her own powers, to lessen her self-respect, and to make her willing to lead a dependent and abject life.

Now, in view of this entire disfranchisement of one-half the people of this country, their social and religious degradation—in view of the unjust laws above mentioned, and because women do feel themselves aggrieved, oppressed, and fraudulently deprived of their most sacred rights, we insist that they have immediate admission to all the rights and privileges which belong to them as citizens of the United States.

In entering upon the great work before us, we anticipate no small amount of misconception, misrepresentation, and ridicule; but we shall use every instrumentality within our power to effect our object. We shall employ agents, circulate tracts, petition the State and National legislatures, and endeavor to enlist the pulpit and the press in our behalf. We hope this Convention will be followed by a series of Conventions embracing every part of the country.

Dawes General Allotment Act (1887)

From the colonial period to the late 19th century the United States Government pursued an Indian Policy of containment. Allotments and small individual reservations were granted to chiefs of American Indian tribes and were increasingly used to win approval from them for the cession of parts of their tribal reserves.

Between 1850 and 1887, fifty treaties or agreements with various tribes provided for allotments of 80 to 320 acres. In the latter year a combination of greedy westerners, who were anxious to hasten the process of breaking up the remaining reservations through allotments, whether or not the Indians wished to take them (many did not), and misguided, but well-meaning humanitarians, put the Dawes General Allotment Act through Congress. With later amendments the act applied to all tribes with reservations in the public land states. It provided for the breakup of the Indian tribal relationship and the abandonment of the domestic nation theory. Reservations were to be surveyed and allotments of 40 to 160 acres assigned to heads of families, orphans, and children; the surplus lands were to be opened to white settlement. That the assignment of allotments to the Indians had wholly failed to convert them to the acquisitive society of the whites based on private ownership was well known but disregarded by Congress. Although the allotments were inalienable for twenty-five years, they quickly fell into the hands of whites, who thus acquired the best lands within the reservations, leaving in diminished reserves the least useful tracts.

Allotment proved a tragic blunder. In 1934 the allotment policy was halted by the Indian Reorganization Act, and efforts were made to restore tribal organization and to recover some of the lost land. For a time reconstitution of tribal organization progressed, but in the early 1950s another shift of policy took place. A series of termination acts was passed to break up the tribes and to effect their assimilation, despite the fact that past history had shown the futility of such a policy. Termination was as disastrous as the Dawes Act and was soon ended.

An Act To Provide For The Allotment Of Lands In Severalty
To Indians On The Various Reservations, And To Extend
The Protection Of The Laws Of The United States And The Territories Over The
Indians, And For Other Purposes (Approved, February, 8, 1887).

Be it enacted by the Senate and House of Representatives of the United States of America in Congress assembled, That in all cases where any tribe or band of Indians has been, or shall hereafter be, located upon any reservation created for their use, either by treaty stipulation or by virtue of an act of Congress or executive order setting apart the same for their use, the President of the United States be, and he hereby is, authorized, whenever in his opinion any reservation or any part thereof of such Indians is advantageous for agricultural and grazing purposes, to cause said reservation, or any part thereof, to be surveyed, or resurveyed if necessary, and to allot the lands in said reservation in severalty to any Indian located thereon in quantities as follows:

To each head of a family, one-quarter of a section;
To each single person over eighteen years of age, one-eighth of a section;
To each orphan child under eighteen years of age, one-eighth of a section; and
To each other single person under eighteen years now living, or who may be born prior to the date of the order of the President directing an allotment of the lands embraced in any reservation, one-sixteenth of a section:

Provided, That in case there is not sufficient land in any of said reservations to allot lands to each individual of the classes above named in quantities as above provided, the lands embraced in such reservation or reservations shall be allotted to each individual of each of said classes pro rata in accordance with the provisions of this act: And provided further, That where the treaty or act of Congress setting apart such reservation provides the allotment of lands in severalty in quantities in excess of those herein provided, the President, in making allotments upon such reservation, shall allot the lands to each individual Indian belonging thereon in quantity as specified in such treaty or act: And provided further, That when the lands allotted are only valuable for grazing purposes, an additional allotment of such grazing lands, in quantities as above provided, shall be made to each individual.

SEC. 2. That all allotments set apart under the provisions of this act shall be selected by the Indians, heads of families selecting for their minor children, and the agents shall select for each orphan child, and in such manner as to embrace the improvements of the Indians making the selection. Where the improvements of two or more Indians have been made on the same legal subdivision of land, unless they shall otherwise agree, a provisional line may be run dividing said lands between them, and the amount to which each is entitled shall be equalized in the assignment of the remainder of the land to which they are entitled under this act: Provided, That if any one entitled to an allotment shall fail to make a selection within four years after the President shall direct that allotments may be made on a particular reservation, the

Secretary of the Interior may direct the agent of such tribe or band, if such there be, and if there be no agent, then a special agent appointed for that purpose, to make a selection for such Indian, which selection shall be allotted as in cases where selections are made by the Indians, and patents shall issue in like manner.

SEC. 3. That the allotments provided for in this act shall be made by special agents appointed by the President for such purpose, and the agents in charge of the respective reservations on which the allotments are directed to be made, under such rules and regulations as the Secretary of the Interior may from time to time prescribe, and shall be certified by such agents to the Commissioner of Indian Affairs, in duplicate, one copy to be retained in the Indian Office and the other to be transmitted to the Secretary of the Interior for his action, and to be deposited in the General Land Office.

SEC. 4. That where any Indian not residing upon a reservation, or for whose tribe no reservation has been provided by treaty, act of Congress, or executive order, shall make settlement upon any surveyed or unsurveyed lands of the United States not otherwise appropriated, he or she shall be entitled, upon application to the local land-office for the district in which the lands are located, to have the same allotted to him or her, and to his or her children, in quantities and manner as provided in this act for Indians residing upon reservations; and when such settlement is made upon unsurveyed lands, the grant to such Indians shall be adjusted upon the survey of the lands so as to conform thereto; and patents shall be issued to them for such lands in the manner and with the restrictions as herein provided. And the fees to which the officers of such local land-office would have been entitled had such lands been entered under the general laws for the disposition of the public lands shall be paid to them, from any moneys in the Treasury of the United States not otherwise appropriated, upon a statement of an account in their behalf for such fees by the Commissioner of the General Land Office, and a certification of such account to the Secretary of the Treasury by the Secretary of the Interior.

SEC. 5. That upon the approval of the allotments provided for in this act by the Secretary of the Interior, he shall cause patents to issue therefor in the name of the allottees, which patents shall be of the legal effect, and declare that the United States does and will hold the land thus allotted, for the period of twenty-five years, in trust for the sole use and benefit of the Indian to whom such allotment shall have been made, or, in case of his decease, of his heirs according to the laws of the State or Territory where such land is located, and that at the expiration of said period the United States will convey the same by patent to said Indian, or his heirs as aforesaid, in fee, discharged of said trust and free of all charge or incumbrance whatsoever: Provided, That the President of the United States may in any case in his discretion extend the period. And if any conveyance shall be made of the lands set apart and allotted as herein provided, or any contract made touching the same, before the expiration of the time above mentioned, such conveyance or contract shall be absolutely null and void: Provided, That the law of descent and partition in force in the State or Territory where such lands are situate shall apply thereto after patents therefor have been executed and delivered, except as herein otherwise provided; and the laws of the State of Kansas regulating the descent and partition of real estate shall, so far as practicable, apply to all lands in the Indian Territory which may be allotted in severalty under the provisions of this act: And provided further, That at any time after lands have been allotted to all the Indians of any tribe as herein provided, or sooner if in the opinion of the President it shall be for the best interests of said tribe, it shall be lawful for the Secretary of the Interior to negotiate with such Indian tribe for the purchase and release by said tribe, in conformity with the treaty or statute under which such reservation is held, of such portions of its reservation not allotted as such tribe shall, from time to time, consent to sell, on such terms and conditions as shall be considered just and equitable between the United States and said tribe of Indians, which purchase shall not be complete until ratified by Congress, and the form and manner of executing such release prescribed by Congress: Provided however, That all lands adapted to agriculture, with or without irrigation so sold or released to the United States by any Indian tribe shall be held by the United States for the sole purpose of securing homes to actual settlers and shall be disposed of by the United States to actual and bona fide settlers only tracts not exceding one hundred and sixty acres to any one person, on such terms as Congress shall prescribe, subject to grants which Congress may make in aid of education: And provided further, That no patents shall issue therefor except to the person so taking the same as and homestead, or his heirs, and after the expiration of five years occupancy thereof as such homestead; and any conveyance of said lands taken as a homestead, or any contract touching the same, or lieu thereon, created prior to the date of such patent, shall be null and void. And the sums agreed to be paid by the United States as purchase money for any portion of any such reservation shall be held in the Treasury of the United States for the sole use of the tribe or tribes Indians; to whom such reservations belonged; and the same, with interest thereon at three per cent per annum, shall be at all times subject to appropriation by Congress for the education and civilization of such tribe or tribes of Indians or the members thereof. The patents aforesaid shall be recorded in the General Land Office, and afterward delivered, free of charge, to the allottee entitled thereto. And if any religious society or other organization is now occupying any of the public lands to which this act is applicable, for religious or educational work among the Indians, the Secretary of the Interior is hereby authorized to confirm such occupation to such society or organization, in quantity not exceeding one hundred and sixty acres in any one tract, so long as the same shall be so occupied, on such terms as he shall deem just; but nothing herein contained shall change or alter any claim of such society for religious or educational purposes heretofore granted by law. And hereafter in the employment of Indian police, or any other employees in the public service among any of the Indian tribes or bands affected by this act, and where Indians can perform the duties required, those Indians who have availed themselves of the provisions of this act and become citizens of the United States shall be preferred.

SEC. 6. That upon the completion of said allotments and the patenting of the lands to said allottees, each and every member of the respective bands or tribes of Indians to whom allotments have been made shall have the benefit of and be subject to the laws, both civil and criminal, of the State or Territory in which they may reside; and no Territory shall pass or enforce any law denying any such Indian within its jurisdiction the equal protection of the law. And every Indian born within the territorial limits of the United States to whom allotments shall have been made under the provisions of this act, or under any law or treaty, and every Indian born within the territorial limits of the United States who has voluntarily taken up, within said limits, his residence separate and apart from any tribe of Indians therein, and has adopted the habits of civilized life, is hereby declared to be a citizen of the United States, and is entitled to all the rights, privileges, and immunities of such citizens, whether said Indian has been or not, by birth or otherwise, a member of any tribe of Indians within the territorial limits of the United States without in any manner affecting the right of any such Indian to tribal or other property.

SEC. 7. That in cases where the use of water for irrigation is necessary to render the lands within any Indian reservation available for agricultural purposes, the Secretary of the Interior be, and he is hereby, authorized to prescribe such rules and regulations as he may deem necessary to secure a just and equal distribution thereof among the Indians residing upon any such reservation; and no other appropriation or grant of water by any riparian proprietor shall be permitted to the damage of any other riparian proprietor.

SEC. 8. That the provisions of this act shall not extend to the territory occupied by the Cherokees, Creeks, Choctaws, Chickasaws, Seminoles, and Osage, Miamies and Peorias, and Sacs and Foxes, in the Indian Territory, nor to any of the reservations of the Seneca Nation of New York Indians in the State of New York, nor to that strip of territory in the State of Nebraska adjoining the Sioux Nation on the south added by executive order.

SEC. 9. That for the purpose of making the surveys and resurveys mentioned in section two of this act, there be, and hereby is, appropriated, out of any moneys in the Treasury not otherwise appropriated, the sum of one hundred thousand dollars, to be repaid proportionately out of the proceeds of the sales of such land as may be acquired from the Indians under the provisions of this act.

SEC. 10. That nothing in this act contained shall be so construed to affect the right and power of Congress to grant the right of way through any lands granted to an Indian, or a tribe of Indians, for railroads or other highways, or telegraph lines, for the public use, or condemn such lands to public uses, upon making just compensation.

SEC. 11. That nothing in this act shall be so construed as to prevent the removal of the Southern Ute Indians from their present reservation in Southwestern Colorado to a new reservation by and with consent of a majority of the adult male members of said tribe.

Eighteenth and Twenty-first Amendments to the U.S. Constitution (1919, 1933)

In 1919 the increasing momentum of the temperance movement (organized to ban the consumption of alcoholic beverages) stimulated the ratification of the Eighteenth Amendment to the Constitution, prohibiting "the manufacture, sale, or transportation of intoxicating liquors" in the United States.

The violent Prohibition era lasted from Jan. 16, 1920, until the ratification of the Twenty-first Amendment on Dec. 5, 1933, which repealed the Eighteenth Amendment. The Twenty-first Amendment has been held to mandate the preeminence of states in liquor regulation, and a resultant diversity of legislation exists among the states.

Amendment XVIII: Prohibition Of Alcoholic Beverages

Section 1. After one year from the ratification of this article the manufacture, sale, or transportation of intoxicating liquors within, the importation thereof into, or the exportation thereof from the United States and all territory subject to the jurisdiction thereof for beverage purposes is hereby prohibited.

Section 2. The Congress and the several States shall have concurrent power to enforce this article by appropriate legislation.

Section 3. This article shall be inoperative unless it shall have been ratified as an amendment to the Constitution by the legislatures of the several States, as provided in the Constitution, within seven years from the date of the submission hereof to the States by the Congress. (Ratified January, 1919.)

Amendment XXI: Repeal Of Alcohol Prohibition

Section 1. The eighteenth article of amendment to the Constitution of the United States is hereby repealed.

Section 2. The transportation or importation into any State, Territory, or possession of the United States for delivery or use therein of intoxicating liquors, in violation of the laws thereof, is hereby prohibited.

Section 3. This article shall be inoperative unless it shall have been ratified as an amendment to the Constitution by conventions in the several States, as provided in the Constitution, within seven years from the date of the submission hereof to the States by the Congress. (Ratified December, 1933.)

Nineteenth Amendment to the U.S. Constitution (1920)

Amendment XIX: Female Suffrage

The right of citizens of the United States to vote shall not be denied or abridged by the United States or by any State on account of sex.

Congress shall have power to enforce this article by appropriate legislation. (Ratified August, 1920.)

Universal Declaration of Human Rights (1948)

In 1948 the United Nations Commission on Human Rights completed a Universal Declaration of Human Rights, prepared under the chairmanship of former U.S. First Lady Eleanor Roosevelt. The document was passed unanimously by the UN General Assembly (resolution 217 A (III))on December 10, 1948. The Declaration begins this way:

Preamble

Whereas recognition of the inherent dignity and of the equal and inalienable rights of all members of the human family is the foundation of freedom, justice and peace in the world,

Whereas disregard and contempt for human rights have resulted in barbarous acts which have outraged the conscience of mankind, and the advent of a world in which human beings shall enjoy freedom of speech and belief and freedom from fear and want has been proclaimed as the highest aspiration of the common people,

Whereas it is essential, if man is not to be compelled to have recourse, as a last resort, to rebellion against tyranny and oppression, that human rights should be protected by the rule of law,

Whereas it is essential to promote the development of friendly relations between nations,

Whereas the peoples of the United Nations have in the Charter reaffirmed their faith in fundamental human rights, in the dignity and worth of the human person and in the equal rights of men and women and have determined to promote social progress and better standards of life in larger freedom,

Whereas Member States have pledged themselves to achieve, in cooperation with the United Nations, the promotion of universal respect for and observance of human rights and fundamental freedoms,

Whereas a common understanding of these rights and freedoms is of the greatest importance for the full realization of this pledge,

Now, therefore,

The General Assembly,

Proclaims this Universal Declaration of Human Rights as a common standard of achievement for all peoples and all nations, to the end that every individual and every organ of society, keeping this Declaration constantly in mind, shall strive by teaching and education to promote respect for these rights and freedoms and by progressive measures, national and international, to secure their universal and effective recognition and observance, both among the peoples of Member States themselves and among the peoples of territories under their jurisdiction.

Article I

All human beings are born free and equal in dignity and rights. They are endowed with reason and conscience and should act towards one another in a spirit of brotherhood.

Article 2

Everyone is entitled to all the rights and freedoms set forth in this Declaration, without distinction of any kind, such as race, colour, sex, language, religion, political or other opinion, national or social origin, property, birth or other status.

Furthermore, no distinction shall be made on the basis of the political, jurisdictional or international status of the country or territory to which a person belongs, whether it be independent, trust, non-self-governing or under any other limitation of sovereignty.

Article 3

Everyone has the right to life, liberty and security of person.

Article 4

No one shall be held in slavery or servitude; slavery and the slave trade shall be prohibited in all their forms.

Article 5

No one shall be subjected to torture or to cruel, inhuman or degrading treatment or punishment.

Article 6

Everyone has the right to recognition everywhere as a person before the law.

Article 7

All are equal before the law and are entitled without any discrimination to equal protection of the law. All are entitled to equal protection against any discrimination in violation of this Declaration and against any incitement to such discrimination.

Article 8

Everyone has the right to an effective remedy by the competent national tribunals for acts violating the fundamental rights granted him by the constitution or by law.

Article 9

No one shall be subjected to arbitrary arrest, detention or exile.

Article 10

Everyone is entitled in full equality to a fair and public hearing by an independent and impartial tribunal, in the determination of his rights and obligations and of any criminal charge against him.

Article 11

1. Everyone charged with a penal offence has the right to be presumed innocent until proved guilty according to law in a public trial at which he has had all the guarantees necessary for his defence.
2. No one shall be held guilty of any penal offence on account of any act or omission which did not constitute a penal offence, under national or international law, at the time when it was committed. Nor shall a heavier penalty be imposed than the one that was applicable at the time the penal offence was committed.

Article 12

No one shall be subjected to arbitrary interference with his privacy, family, home or correspondence, nor to attacks upon his honour and reputation. Everyone has the right to the protection of the law against such interference or attacks.

Article 13

1. Everyone has the right to freedom of movement and residence within the borders of each State.
2. Everyone has the right to leave any country, including his own, and to return to his country.

Article 14

1. Everyone has the right to seek and to enjoy in other countries asylum from persecution.
2. This right may not be invoked in the case of prosecutions genuinely arising from non-political crimes or from acts contrary to the purposes and principles of the United Nations.

Article 15

1. Everyone has the right to a nationality.
2. No one shall be arbitrarily deprived of his nationality nor denied the right to change his nationality.

Article 16

1. Men and women of full age, without any limitation due to race, nationality or religion, have the right to marry and to found a family. They are entitled to equal rights as to marriage, during marriage and at its dissolution.
2. Marriage shall be entered into only with the free and full consent of the intending spouses.
3. The family is the natural and fundamental group unit of society and is entitled to protection by society and the State.

Article 17

    1. Everyone has the right to own property alone as well as in association with others.

    2. No one shall be arbitrarily deprived of his property.

Article 18

Everyone has the right to freedom of thought, conscience and religion; this right includes freedom to change his religion or belief, and freedom, either alone or in community with others and in public or private, to manifest his religion or belief in teaching, practice, worship and observance.

Article 19

Everyone has the right to freedom of opinion and expression; this right includes freedom to hold opinions without interference and to seek, receive and impart information and ideas through any media and regardless of frontiers.

Article 20

    1. Everyone has the right to freedom of peaceful assembly and association.

    2. No one may be compelled to belong to an association.

Article 21

    1. Everyone has the right to take part in the government of his country, directly or through freely chosen representatives.

    2. Everyone has the right to equal access to public service in his country.

    3. The will of the people shall be the basis of the authority of government; this will shall be expressed in periodic and genuine elections which shall be by universal and equal suffrage and shall be held by secret vote or by equivalent free voting procedures.

Article 22

Everyone, as a member of society, has the right to social security and is entitled to realization, through national effort and international co-operation and in accordance with the organization and resources of each State, of the economic, social and cultural rights indispensable for his dignity and the free development of his personality.

Article 23

    1. Everyone has the right to work, to free choice of employment, to just and favourable conditions of work and to protection against unemployment.

    2. Everyone, without any discrimination, has the right to equal pay for equal work.

    3. Everyone who works has the right to just and favourable remuneration ensuring for himself and his family an existence worthy of human dignity, and supplemented, if necessary, by other means of social protection.

4. Everyone has the right to form and to join trade unions for the protection of his interests.

Article 24

Everyone has the right to rest and leisure, including reasonable limitation of working hours and periodic holidays with pay.

Article 25

3. Everyone has the right to a standard of living adequate for the health and well-being of himself and of his family, including food, clothing, housing and medical care and necessary social services, and the right to security in the event of unemployment, sickness, disability, widowhood, old age or other lack of livelihood in circumstances beyond his control.
4. Motherhood and childhood are entitled to special care and assistance. All children, whether born in or out of wedlock, shall enjoy the same social protection.

Article 26

3. Everyone has the right to education. Education shall be free, at least in the elementary and fundamental stages. Elementary education shall be compulsory. Technical and professional education shall be made generally available and higher education shall be equally accessible to all on the basis of merit.
4. Education shall be directed to the full development of the human personality and to the strengthening of respect for human rights and fundamental freedoms. It shall promote understanding, tolerance and friendship among all nations, racial or religious groups, and shall further the activities of the United Nations for the maintenance of peace.
5. Parents have a prior right to choose the kind of education that shall be given to their children.

Article 27

3. Everyone has the right freely to participate in the cultural life of the community, to enjoy the arts and to share in scientific advancement and its benefits.
4. Everyone has the right to the protection of the moral and material interests resulting from any scientific, literary or artistic production of which he is the author.

Article 28

Everyone is entitled to a social and international order in which the rights and freedoms set forth in this Declaration can be fully realized.

Article 29

   3. Everyone has duties to the community in which alone the free and full development of his personality is possible.

   4. In the exercise of his rights and freedoms, everyone shall be subject only to such limitations as are determined by law solely for the purpose of securing due recognition and respect for the rights and freedoms of others and of meeting the just requirements of morality, public order and the general welfare in a democratic society.

   5. These rights and freedoms may in no case be exercised contrary to the purposes and principles of the United Nations.

Article 30

Nothing in this Declaration may be interpreted as implying for any State, group or person any right to engage in any activity or to perform any act aimed at the destruction of any of the rights and freedoms set forth herein.

Civil Rights Act (1964)

The Civil Rights act of 1964, including provisions regarding access to public accommodations, use of federal funds without discrimination, and equal employment opportunity, was signed into law (July 2, 1964) during the early months of President Lyndon B. Johnson's administration. It was the most far-reaching civil rights legislation since 1875.

Title II (portions of which are reprinted below) is the centerpiece of the law, declaring discrimination in public accommodation illegal.

Title VI (also reprinted below), which prohibited discrimination in any federally assisted programs, was to prove instrumental in accelerating school desegregation during the Johnson administration.

Title II

Sec. 201. (a) All persons shall be entitled to the full and equal enjoyment of the goods, services, facilities, privileges, advantages, and accommodations of any place of public accommodation, as defined in this section, without discrimination or segregation on the ground of race, color, religion, or national origin.

(b) Each of the following establishments which serves the public is a place of public accommodation within the meaning of this title if its operations affect commerce, or if discrimination or segregation by it is supported by State action:

(1) any inn, hotel, motel, or other establishment which provides lodging to transient guests, other than an establishment located within a building which contains not more than five rooms for rent or hire and which is actually occupied by the proprietor of such establishment as his residence;

(2) any restaurant, cafeteria, lunchroom, lunch counter, soda fountain, or other facility principally engaged in selling food for consumption on the premises, includ-

ing, but not limited to, any such facility located on the premises of any retail establishment; or any gasoline station;

(3) any motion picture house, theater, concert hall, sports arena, stadium or other place of exhibition or entertainment; and

(4) any establishment (A)(i) which is physically located within the premises of any establishment otherwise covered by this subsection, or (ii) within the premises of which is physically located any such covered establishment, and (b) which holds itself out as serving patrons of such covered establishment.

(c) The operations of an establishment affect commerce within the meaning of this title if

(1) it is one of the establishments described in paragraph (1) of subsection (b); (2) in the case of an establishment described in paragraph (2) of subsection (b), it serves or offers to serve interstate travelers or a substantial portion of the food which it serves, or gasoline or other products which it sells, has moved in commerce; (3) in the case of an establishment described in paragraph (3) of subsection (b), it customarily presents films, performances, athletic teams, exhibitions, or other sources of entertainment which move in commerce; and (4) in the case of an establishment described in paragraph (4) of subsection (b), it is physically located within the premises of, or there is physically located within its premises, an establishment the operations of which affect commerce within the meaning of this subsection. For purposes of this section, "commerce" means travel, trade, traffic, commerce, transportation, or communication among the several States, or between the District of Columbia and any State, or between any foreign country or any territory or possession and any State or the District of Columbia, or between points in the same State but through any other State or the District of Columbia or a foreign country.

(d) Discrimination or segregation by an establishment is supported by State action within the meaning of this title if such discrimination or segregation (1) is carried on under color of any law, statute, ordinance, or regulation; or (2) is carried on under color of any custom or usage required or enforced by officials of the State or political subdivision thereof; or (3) is required by action of the State or political subdivision thereof...

(e) The provisions of this title shall not apply to a private club or other establishment not in fact open to the public, except to the extent that the facilities of such establishment are made available to the customers or patrons of an establishment within the scope of subsection (b).

Sec 202. All persons shall be entitled to be free, at any establishment or place, from discrimination or segregation of any kind on the ground of race, color, religion, or national origin, if such discrimination or segregation is or purports to be required by any law, statute, ordinance, regulation, rule, or order of a State or any agency or political subdivision thereof.

Sec. 203. No person shall (a) withhold, deny, or attempt to withhold or deny, or deprive or attempt to deprive, any person of any right or privilege secured by section 201 or 202, or (b) intimidate, threaten, or coerce, or attempt to intimidate, threaten, or coerce any person with purpose of interfering with any right or privilege secured by section 201 or 202, or (c) punish or attempt to punish any person for exercising or attempting to exercise any right or privilege secured by section 201 or 202.

Title VI—Nondiscrimination in Federally Assisted Programs

SEC. 601. No person in the United States shall, on the ground of race, color, or national origin, be excluded from participation in, be denied the benefits of, or be subjected to discrimination under any program or activity receiving Federal financial assistance.

SEC. 602. Each Federal department and agency which is empowered to extend Federal financial assistance to any program or activity, by way of grant, loan, or contract other than a contract of insurance or guaranty, is authorized and directed to effectuate the provisions of section 601 with respect to such program or activity by issuing rules, regulations, or orders of general applicability which shall be consistent with achievement of the objectives of the statute authorizing the financial assistance in connection with which the action is taken. No such rule, regulation, or order shall become effective unless and until approved by the President. Compliance with any requirement adopted pursuant to this section may be effected (1) by the termination of or refusal to grant or to continue assistance under such program or activity to any recipient as to whom there has been an express finding on the record, after opportunity for hearing, of a failure to comply with such requirement, but such termination or refusal shall be limited to the particular political entity, or part thereof, or other recipient as to whom such a finding has been made and, shall be limited in its effect to the particular program, or part thereof, in which such non-compliance has been so found, or (2) by any other means authorized by law: Provided, however, That no such action shall be taken until the department or agency concerned has advised the appropriate person or persons of the failure to comply with the requirement and has determined that compliance cannot be secured by voluntary means. In the case of any action terminating, or refusing to grant or continue, assistance because of failure to comply with a requirement imposed pursuant to this section, the head of the federal department or agency shall file with the committees of the House and Senate having legislative jurisdiction over the program or activity involved a full written report of the circumstances and the grounds for such action. No such action shall become effective until thirty days have elapsed after the filing of such report.

SEC. 603. Any department or agency action taken pursuant to section 602 shall be subject to such judicial review as may otherwise be provided by law for similar action taken by such department or agency on other grounds. In the case of action, not otherwise subject to judicial review, terminating or refusing to grant or to continue financial assistance upon a finding of failure to comply with any requirement imposed pursuant to section 602, any person aggrieved (including any State or political subdivision thereof and any agency of either) may obtain judicial review of such action in accordance with section 10 of the Administrative Procedure Act, and such action shall not be deemed committed to unreviewable agency discretion within the meaning of that section.

SEC. 604. Nothing contained in this title shall be construed to authorize action under this title by any department or agency with respect to any employment practice of any employer, employment agency, or labor organization except where a primary objective of the Federal financial assistance is to provide employment.

SEC. 605. Nothing in this title shall add to or detract from any existing authority with respect to any program or activity under which Federal financial assistance is extended by way of a contract of insurance or guaranty.

The complete text of the Civil Rights Act of 1964 can be found on the Department of Civil Rights Homepage (http://www.dot.gov/ost/docr/CR64LKS.HTM).

Equal Rights Amendment (1972)

The Equal Rights Amendment was written in 1921 by Alice Paul. It has been introduced in Congress every session since 1923. It passed Congress in 1972, but failed to be ratified by the necessary thirty-eight states by the July 1982 deadline. It was ratified by thirty-five states.

Section 1. Equality of Rights under the law shall not be denied or abridged by the United States or any state on account of sex.

Section 2. The Congress shall have the power to enforce, by appropriate legislation, the provisions of this article.

Section 3. This amendment shall take effect two years after the date of ratification.

Ways to Help

Citizenship is the quality of an individual's response to membership in a community. Have you ever thought about becoming involved in your community? Did the profiles of the humanitarians and social reformers in this volume inspire you? There are many ways to help. You can volunteer, you can donate money, you can raise money for a good cause. The following list of Web sites is a good way to explore the many ways that you can contribute. It feels good to help.

Civil Rights

- *The American Civil Liberties Union (ACLU)*. The ACLU is dedicated to fighting for the freedom of the individual. Its Web site has an "Act Now!" page with a list of opportunities to campaign for individual rights, and a "Freedom Network" that allows users discuss and learn more about issues ranging from criminal justice to rights in the workplace.
http://www.aclu.org/
- *AFL-CIO*. The mission of the AFL-CIO is "to improve the lives of working families and to bring economic justice to the workplace and social justice to the nation." Its "You have a voice—Make it heard!" page helps you send messages to your congressperson. You can also choose to join its National Issues Mobilization team, or find out what's on the schedule for the day in Congress.
http://www.aflcio.org
- *The American Anti-Slavery Group*. Slavery still exists in many parts of the world. This group is dedicated to eliminating slavery through political action. Check out its "What You Can Do" page for information on donations and volunteering.
http://www.anti-slavery.org/
- *Anti-Defamation League*. For 85 years the goals of the ADL have been "to stop the defamation of the Jewish people and to secure justice and fair treatment to all people alike." The site offers a "Tools for Teachers" section, and a "Legislative Action" page that lets you e-mail members of Congress on issues like school vouchers, anti-Semitism in Russia, and the Hate Crimes Prevention Act.
http://www.adl.org/
- *NAACP Online: Youth and College Division*. This division of the NAACP is organized "to develop an intelligent and militant Youth leadership through devising, working out and pursuing local programs." Young people may become involved with several different outreach programs including Supreme Court Phone/Fax Protest, Vote for Me, Challenging a Campus for Conscience, and National Day of Nonviolence.
http://www.naacp.org/youth-college/

- *The Milarepa Fund.* This organization is "dedicated to the promotion of universal compassion and nonviolence that supports (the) Tibetan struggle for freedom." On its action page you can explore opportunities to bring about political and economic change through nonviolent protest and political activism.
http://www.milarepa.org/

- *The National Urban League.* Founded in 1910, the League strives to "assist African Americans in the achievement of social and economic equality." The League's Resources and Programs page offers a number of educational and community leadership opportunities.
http://www.nul.org/

Human Rights

- *American Red Cross.* The International Red Cross is a humanitarian organization led by volunteers and provides relief to victims of disasters. It also helps people prevent, prepare for, and respond to emergencies. You can volunteer or make a financial donation to help disaster victims by contributing to the American branch of the Red Cross.
http://www.redcross.org/donate/

- *Asian Human Rights Commission.* This organization "seeks to promote greater awareness and realization of human rights in the Asian region, and to mobilize Asian and international public opinion to obtain relief and redress for the victims of human rights violations."
http://is7.pacific.net.hk/~ahrchk/

- *The B'nai B'rith Center for Community Action.* This Web site describes several opportunities to contribute including disaster relief, care for kids, cancer awareness, and community projects.
http://bnaibrith.org/cca/

- *Catholic Relief Services.* This organization was founded in 1943 by the Catholic Bishops of the United States to assist the poor and disadvantaged outside the country. It provides assistance for victims of man-made and natural disasters throughout the world.
http://www.catholicrelief.org/howtohelp/

- *Amnesty International.* This group is dedicated to fighting for human rights worldwide. In particular, it stresses gaining the freedom of all political prisoners, or "prisoners of conscience," ensuring fair trials, and abolishing the death penalty. Its "Act Now" page offers a host of options for taking immediate action on behalf of those in need all over the world.
http://www.amnesty.org/

Women's Rights

- *National Organization for Women.* One of the first organizations to emerge from the women's movement, NOW is a legendary champion of women's rights. Volunteer opportunities include internships and the chance to travel with the Lilith Fair music festival as a NOW representative.
http://www.now.org/

• *Boston Women's Web.* For women in the Boston area, this Web site has a calendar of women's events and a list of available internships, volunteer opportunities, and jobs.
http://www.bostonwomen.com/

• *Webgrrls International.* Mission Statement: "Webgrrls International provides a forum for women in or interested in new media and technology to network, exchange job and business leads, form strategic alliances, mentor and teach, intern and learn the skills to help women succeed in an increasingly technical workplace and world."
http://www.webgrrls.com/participate

• *Sawnet (South Asian Women's NETwork).* "A forum for those interested in South Asian women's issues." Click on "South Asian Women's Organizations" for a list of international as well as American organizations that focus on issues affecting South Asian women.
http://www.umiacs.umd.edu/users/sawweb/sawnet/

• *Sisterhood Is Global Institute.* This site "seeks to deepen the understanding of women's human rights at the local, national, regional and global levels, and to strengthen the capacity of women to exercise their rights." It offers opportunities for an internship with its Maryland office as well as "Action Alerts" that periodically spotlight different events (like the car bomb that killed a Northern Ireland human rights lawyer) and policymakers to contact regarding the event.
http://www.sigi.org/

• *American Association of University Women.* "A national organization that promotes education and equity for all women and girls." The "Getting Involved" page lists a host of activist opportunities.
http://www.aauw.org/

• *Third Wave.* An organization designed to give young women "a national voice and greater visibility."
http://www.feminist.com/3wave.htm

• *American Civil Liberties Union: Women's Rights.* Web site for the women's rights section of the famous civil rights organization contains many "Action Alerts" along with links to the people in a position to make changes that will benefit all women.
http://www.aclu.org/issues/women/hmwo.html

Saving the Environment

• *Earth Day Network.* The Earth Day Network is a network of volunteers dedicated to increasing awareness and responsibility about the condition of the planet and to inspiring "action towards a clean, healthy environment for all living things using Earth Day as a catalyst." Its "What You Can Do" page offers many suggestions on the way individuals and businesses can help the earth. You can also get involved with the planning of Earth Day 2000.
http://www.sdearthtimes.com/edn/

- *Environmental Defense Fund.* The main goal of this organization is to "stabilize the Earth's climate, safeguard the world's oceans, protect human health, and defend and restore biodiversity."
http://www.edf.org/
- *Friends of the Earth.* "A national, non-profit advocacy organization dedicated to protecting the planet from environmental degradation; preserving biological, cultural, and ethnic diversity; and empowering citizens to have an influential voice in decisions affecting the quality of their environment — and their lives." A comprehensive site for environmental issues.
http://www.foe.org/
- *Green Corps.* This group describes itself as "a field school for environmental organizing." It offers an environmental leadership training program that is divided into three parts: classroom training, campaign training, and job placement.
http://www.greencorps.org/index.htm
- *Greenpeace.* This organization is famous for its radical agenda for protecting the earth's resources. On its "Inter@ct" page you can become a "cyber-activist" or join one of its many mailing lists for more information.
http://www.greenpeace.org/
- *Sierra Club.* "A nonprofit, member-supported public interest organization that promotes conservation of the natural environment by influencing public policy decisions: legislative, administrative, legal, and electoral." It has an "Activism" page that gives tips on "everyday activism," updates current situations, and helps you e-mail the president in support of environmental causes.
http://www.sierraclub.org/
- *The National Wildlife Federation.* NWF is "the nation's largest member-supported conservation group, uniting individuals, organizations, businesses and government to protect wildlife, wild places, and the environment." There are numerous action possibilities on the group's home page.
http://www.nwf.org/nwf/index.html
- *The Rainforest Action Network.* Working to preserve the world's rain forests, RAN's "Action Alert" and "What You Can Do" pages describe different areas of the globe that are in need. It also includes information on how to start your own rain forest group and on how to volunteer and intern at RAN.
http://www.ran.org/
- *The TAKE ACTION Page.* This page is "your link to actions you can take to help create a healthy environment and a safe world. Each of our programs suggest what you can do to make a difference."
http://www.ucsusa.org/action/act-home.html

Working with Children

- *Big Brothers/Big Sisters of America.* BBBSA is the oldest mentoring group in the country. Founded in 1904, it currently serves over 100,000 children from 500 offices.

Its national Web site lets you search for the office nearest you and gives you more information on becoming a Big Brother or Big Sister.
http://www.bbbsa.org/

• *Covenant House.* "The largest privately funded childcare agency in the United States providing shelter and service to homeless and runaway youth." To find out how to become a volunteer, mentor, or tutor at one of Covenant House's eleven different locations in the United States go to its Web site.
http://www.covenanthouse.org

• *Ronald McDonald House Charities.* Ronald McDonald House Charities provide comfort and care to children and their families by supporting Ronald McDonald Houses in communities around the world and by making grants to other not-for-profit organizations whose programs help children in need. You can help children and families by getting involved with the Ronald McDonald House in your area.
http://www.rmhc.com/

• *Special Olympics* states that "as a movement [we rely] on dedicated volunteers to provide year-round sports training and athletic competition in a variety of Olympic-type sports for people eight years of age and older with mental handicaps." Go to their Web site to find out more about becoming one of these volunteers.
http://www.specialolympics.org/

• *The Hole in the Wall Gang.* An organization started by actor/philanthropist Paul Newman that provides a summer camp in Connecticut for children suffering from cancer and other life-threatening diseases. Volunteers serve as counselors and assistants in camp activities like arts and crafts and boating and fishing. The organization also accepts off-season volunteers to help with its administrative and fund-raising needs.
http://www.holeinthewallgang.org/vol-program.html

• *The Make a Wish Foundation.* In 1980 Arizona State troopers granted a seven-year-old boy's lifelong wish to become a policeman and swore him in as an "honorary state trooper." Days later he died of leukemia. The Foundation grew out of the media coverage generated by the granting of the wish and it has been going strong ever since. To find out how to get involved, visit its Web site.
http://www.wish.org/

• *The National Mentoring Program.* This excellent site shows you how to become a mentor to children and lists many different offices around the country that offer mentoring opportunities.
http://www.mentoring.org/

Fighting AIDS and Discrimination

• *Community Research Initiative on AIDS (CRIA).* Located in midtown Manhattan (230 West 38th Street, 17th Fl. NYC 10018), CRIA is "an independent, non-profit community-based AIDS research & treatment education center which studies new treatments for HIV-related diseases. CRIA's goal is to rapidly improve

the length and quality of life for people with HIV/AIDS through clinical research and treatment education."
http://www.aidsinfonyc.org/cria/

• *Gay Men's Health Crisis (GMHC).* This organization is famous for sponsoring events like AIDS Walk/NY, the AIDS Dance Marathon, and AIDS bike rides among others. There are many volunteer opportunities on the "What Can You Do?" page. http://www.gmhc.org/

• *The NAMES Project Foundation: The AIDS Memorial Quilt.* The AIDS Memorial Quilt consists of over 41,000 handmade panels memorializing the life of someone who died of AIDS. Volunteer for the project, become an intern, or find out how to bring the Quilt to your town.
http://www.aidsquilt.org/

Suggested Reading

General Sources

Books

Aeseng, Nathan. *The Peace Seekers: The Nobel Peace Prize*. Lerner Publications, 1987.

Archer, Jules. *They Had a Dream: The Civil Rights Struggle from Frederick Douglass to Marcus Garvey to Martin Luther King, Jr. and Malcolm X*. Viking, 1993.

Archer, Jules. *To Save the Earth: The American Environmental Movement*. Viking, 1998.

Berlin, Ira. *Many Thousands Gone: The First Two Centuries of Slavery in North America*. Harvard University Press, 1998.

Bradley, David, ed. *Encyclopedia of Civil Rights in America*. M. E. Sharpe, 1998.

Cullen-Du Pont, Kathryn. *The Encyclopedia of Women's History in America*. Da Capo Press, 1998.

DiCanio, Margaret. *Encyclopedia of American Activism*. ABC-CLIO, 1998.

Franklin, John Hope. *From Slavery to Freedom: A History of Negro Americans*. New York: Alfred A. Knopf, 1988.

Foner, Eric. *The Story of American Freedom*. W. W. Norton, 1998.

Gay, Kathlyn. *Heroes of Conscience: A Biographical Dictionary*. ABC-CLIO, 1996.

Helmer, Diana Star. *Women Suffragists*. Facts on File, 1998.

Johnson, Michael. *The Macmillan Encyclopedia of Native American Tribes*. Macmillan Library Reference, 1999.

Keene, Ann. *Peacemakers: The Winners of the Nobel Peace Prize*. Oxford University Press, 1998.

Kellert, Stephen R. *The Macmillan Encyclopedia of the Environment*. Macmillan Library Reference, 1998.

Lawson, Edward, ed. *Encyclopedia of Human Rights*. Taylor & Francis, 1996.

McPherson, James M. *The Abolitionist Legacy: From Reconstruction to the NAACP*. Princeton University Press, 1995.

Martin, Waldo E. *Civil Rights in the United States*. Macmillan Reference, 1999.

Murdoch, David. *The North American Indian*. Alfred A. Knopf, 1995.

Murray, Paul T. *The Civil Rights Movement: References and Resources*. G.K. Hall, 1993.

Olson, James. *The Encyclopedia of American Indian Civil Rights*. Greenwood Publishing, 1997.

Peika, Fred. *The ABC-CLIO Companion to the Disability Rights Movement*. ABC-CLIO, 1997.

Redman, Nina E. *Human Rights,* Second Edition. ABC-CLIO, 1998.

Stanton, Elizabeth Cady. *The History of Woman Suffrage.* 1881–1922. Reissue, Arno Press, 1969.

Weber, Michael. *The African-American Civil Rights Movemement: Causes and Consequences.* Raintree/Steck Vaughn, 1998.

Weatherford, Doris. *A History of the American Suffragist Movement.* ABC-CLIO, 1998. See companion Web site below.

Videorecordings

Eyes on the Prize. A documentary history of the black struggle for equality from 1965 to the 1980s. PBS Video, 1990.

Web Sites

African-American Perspectives Website. Part of the Library of Congress American Memory site. http://memory.loc.gov/ammem/aap/

Latino Issues Forum: http://www.lif.org/

The League of Women Voters: http://www.lwv.org/

The Nobel Prize Internet Archive. http://nobelprizes.com/nobel/nobel.html

The Nobel Foundation. Official Web site for the Nobel Foundation. http://www.nobel.se/

National Association for the Advancement of Colored People (NAACP): http://www.naacp.org/

National Council of Native Americans: http://www.ncai.org/

National Council of Negro Women: http://www.usbol.com/ncnw/

National Council of La Raza: http://www.nclr.org/

National Organization for Women: http://www.now.org/

Native American Rights Fund: http://www.narf.org/

Suffragist.com. Companion Web site for *A History of the American Suffragist Movement:* http://www.suffragist.com/

United Nations High Commissioner for Human Rights. Official UN Web site. http://www.unhchr.ch/

Sources on Individual Humanitarians and Reformers

Ralph Abernathy

Abernathy, Ralph. *And the walls came tumbling down: an autobiography.* Harper & Row, 1989.

Abernathy, Donzaleigh, and Robert F. Kennedy Jr. *Partners to History: Martin Luther King, Jr., Ralph Abernathy and the Civil Rights Movement.* General Publishing Group.

http://www.us.net/upa/guides/sclc4.htm

http://www.unbrokencircle.org/scripts09.htm

Jane Addams

Addams, Jane. *Twenty Years at Hull-House*. 1910. Reissue, Signet Classic, 1999.

Harvey, Bonnie C. *Jane Addams*. Enslow Publishers, 1999.

Stebner, Eleanor J. *The Women of Hull House*. State University of New York Press, 1997.

http://www.greatwomen.org/addams.htm

Susan B. Anthony

Davis, Lucille. *Susan B. Anthony: A Photo-Illustrated Biography*. Bridgestone Books, 1998.

Parker, Barbara Keevil. *Susan B. Anthony: Daring to Vote*. Millbrook Press, 1998.

Sherr, Lynn. *Failure Is Impossible: Susan B. Anthony in Her Own Words*. Times Books, 1995.

Ward, Geoffrey C. *Stanton & Anthony: The Struggle for Women's Rights*. Alfred A. Knopf, 1999.

Weisberg, Barbara. *Susan B. Anthony*. Chelsea House Publishers, 1988.

http://www.gis.net/~mtf/sba.htm

http://www.graceproducts.com/text_only/anthony/

Oscar Arias Sánchez

Peduzzi, Kelli. *Oscar Arias: Peacemaker and Leader Among Nations*. G. Stevens Children's Books, 1991.

Rolbein, Seth. *Nobel Costa Rica: A Timely Report on Our Peaceful Pro-Yankee, Central American Neighbor*. St. Martin's Press, 1989.

http://www.peacecouncil.org/arias.html

Aung San Suu Kyi

Aung San Suu Kyi. *The Voice of Hope*. Seven Stories Press, 1997.

Aung San Suu Kyi. *Freedom from Fear and Other Writings*. Penguin Books, 1995.

Ling, Bettina. *Aung San Suu Kyi: Standing for Democracy in Burma*. Feminist Press at the City University of New York, 1999.

Victor, Barbara. *The Lady: Aung San Suu Kyi, Nobel Laureate and Burma's Prisoner*. Faber & Faber, 1998.

http://danenet.wicip.org/fbc/dassk

http://falcon.cc.ukans.edu/~jrchien/politics/assk-statement.html

Ella Baker

Dallard, Shyrlee. *Ella Baker: A Leader Behind the Scenes*. Silver Burdett Press, 1990.

Grant, Joanne. *Ella Baker: Freedom Bound*. Wiley, 1998.

http://www.primenet.com/~bobwason/Biography/Wason/ElBa1862.html

http://www.greatwomen.org/baker.htm

James Baldwin

Baldwin, James. *The Fire Next Time*. Franklin Watts, 1963.

Campbell, James. *Talking at the Gates: A Life of James Baldwin*. Viking, 1991

Gottfried, Ted. *James Baldwin: Voice from Harlem*. Franklin Watts, 1997.

Leeming, David Adams. *James Baldwin: A Biography*. Henry Holt, 1995.

http://www.panafrikanedge.com/baldwin.html

Carlos Ximenes Belo and José Ramos-Horta

Ramos-Horta, José. *Funu: The Unfinished Saga of East Timor*. Red Sea Press, 1987.

Kohen, Arnold. *From the Place of the Dead: The Epic Struggles of Bishop Belo of East Timor*. St. Martin's Press, 1999.

http://www.pactok.net.au/docs/et/bcbelo.html

Mary McLeod Bethune

Anderson, LaVere. *Mary McLeod Bethune: Teacher with a Dream*. Garrard Publishing, 1976.

Kelso, Richard. *Building a Dream: Mary Bethune's School*. Raintree/Steck Vaughn, 1993.

Poole, Bernice Anderson. *Mary McLeod Bethune*. Melrose Square Publishing Company, 1994.

http://www.isc.rit.edu/~kecncp/famouslist.htm

Annie Ellicott Kennedy Bidwell

Bidwell, Annie E. Kennedy. *Rancho Chico Indians*. Bidwell Mansion Cooperating Association, 1980.

Hill, Dorothy J. *The Indians of Chico Rancheria*. State of California, Resources Agency, Dept. of Parks & Recreation, 1978.

Potts, Marie. *The Northern Maidu*. Naturegraph Publishers, 1977.

Rawlings, Linda, ed. *Dear General: The Private letters of Annie E. Kennedy and John Bidwell, 1866–1868*. California Dept. of Parks & Recreation, 1993.

http://www.chs.chico.k12.ca.us/libr/Bidwell/bidman

Stephen Biko

Biko, Steve. *Steve Biko: Black Consciousness in South Africa*. Random House, 1978.

Woods, Donald. *Biko*. Henry Holt, 1987.

Julian Bond

Ball, Thomas E. *Headlines— Julian Bond vs John Lewis: On the Campaign Trail with John Lewis & Julian Bond*. W. H. Wolfe Associates, 1988.

Bond, Julian. *The Time to Speak and the Time to Act: The Movement in Politics*. Simon & Schuster, 1972.

McGuire, William, ed. *American Social Leaders.* "Julian Bond" by Amy Lewis. ABC-CLIO, 1993.

Thornton, Jeannye. "Bond Rallies." *US News and World Report*, July 27, 1998.

Hurd, Hilary L. "A Bonding Force." *Emerge*, May 1998.

White, Jack E. "It's Still a White Supremacy." *Time*, July 27, 1998.

Tony Bonilla

http://www.latnn.com/

Gertrude Simmons Bonnin

Bonnin, Gertrude Simmons (Zitkala-Sa). *American Indian Stories.* 1921. Reprint, 1976.

France, Steve A. "A Constitutional Seesaw." *ABA Journal*, July 1998.

Johnson, David L., and Raymond Wilson. "Gertrude Simmons Bonnin, 1876–1938." *American Indian Quarterly* 12, 1988.

Rappaport, Doreen. *The Flight of Redbird: The Life of Zitkala-Sa.* Dial Books, 1997.

Willard, William. "Gertrude Bonnin and Indian Policy Reform, 1911–1938." In *Indian Leadership*, edited by Walter Williams. University of Kansas Press, 1984.

Hubert "H. Rap" Brown

Brown, H. Rap. *Die Nigger, Die!* Dial Press, 1969.

Puttmaker, Charles. "My Brush with History —What Might Have Happened." *American Heritage*, October 1991.

Van Deburg, William. *A New Day in Babylon: The Black Power Movement and American Culture, 1965–1975.* University of Chicago Press, 1992.

"Return of H. Rap Brown." Television program transcript: *Like It Is.* WABC-TV, Feb. 23, 1992, Program no. 845.

http://www.swt.edu/studentorg/kammaasi/sixties.html

John Brown

Du Bois, W. E. B. *John Brown: A Biography.* M. E. Sharpe, 1997.

Everett, Gwen. *John Brown: One Man Against Slavery.* Rizzoli, 1993.

Rossbach, Jeffrey. *Ambivalent Conspirators: John Brown, The Secret Six, and a Theory of Slave Violence.* University of Pennsylvania Press, 1982.

Finkelman, Paul. *His Soul Goes Marching On.* University Press of Virginia.

Ralph Bunche

Bunche, Ralph J. *An African American in South Africa: The Travel Notes of Ralph J. Bunche, 28 September 1937–1 January 1938.* Edited by Robert R. Edgar. Ohio University Press, 1992.

Cornell, Jean Gay. *Ralph Bunche: Champion of Peace.* Garrard Publishing, 1976.

Rivlin, Benjamin, ed. *Ralph Bunche, The Man and His Times.* Holmes & Meier, 1990.

Urquhart, Brian. *Ralph Bunche: An American Life.* W. W. Norton, 1993.

Stokely Carmichael

Carmichael, Stokely. *Black Power: The Politics of Liberation in America.* 1967. Reissue, Vintage Books, 1992.

Carmichael, Stokely. *Stokely Speaks: Black Power to Pan-Africanism.* Random House, 1971.

Cwiklik, Robert. *Stokely Carmichael and Black Power.* Millbrook Press, 1994.

Johnson, Jacqueline. *Stokely Carmichael: The Story of Black Power.* Silver Burdett Press, 1990.

http://www.sonarchy.org/archives/carmichael.html

http://www.theblackscholar.org

Andrew Carnegie

Bowman, John. *Andrew Carnegie: Steel Tycoon.* Silver Burdett Press, 1989.

Carnegie, Andrew. *The Autobiography of Andrew Carnegie.* 1948. Reissue, Northeastern University Press, 1986.

MacKay, James A. *Andrew Carnegie: His Life and Times.* Wiley, 2000.

http://www.carnegie.org

http://www.carnegie.lib.oh.us/andrewcarnegie.htm

Jimmy Carter

Brinkley, Douglas. *The Unfinished Presidency: Jimmy Carter's Journey Beyond the White House.* Viking, 1998.

Carter, Jimmy. *Keeping Faith: Memoirs of a President.* University of Arkansas Press, 1995.

Carter, Jimmy, and Gary Gunderson. *Deeply Woven Roots: Improving the Quality of Life in Your Community.* Fortress Press, 1997.

Glad, Betty. *Jimmy Carter: In Search of the Great White House.* W. W. Norton, 1980.

Malcolm, Teresa. "Eliminate Weapons, Leaders Say." *National Catholic Reporter,* August 28, 1998.

Morris, Kenneth Earl. *Jimmy Carter: American Moralist.* University of Georgia Press, 1996.

Muravchik, Joshua. *The Uncertain Crusade: Jimmy Carter and the Dilemmas of Human Rights Policy.* Hamilton Press, 1986.

Lazo, Caroline. *Jimmy Carter: On the Road to Peace.* Silver Burdett Press, 1996.

Schraff, Anne. *Jimmy Carter.* Enslow Publishers, 1998.

http://www.habitat.org

http://www.CarterCenter.org

René-Samuel Cassin

http://www.stthomasu.ca./research/AHRC/ORIGINS.HTM

Carrie Chapman Catt

Van Voris, Jacqueline. *Carrie Chapman Catt: A Public Life*. Feminist Press at the City University of New York, 1987.

Fowler, Robert Booth. *Carrie Catt: Feminist Politician*. Northeastern University Press, 1986.

Peck, Mary Gray. *Carrie Chapman Catt: A Biography*. Hyperion Press, 1976.

James Chaney

Cagin, Seth. *We Are Not Afraid: The Story of Goodman, Schwerner, and Chaney, and the Civil Rights Campaign for Mississippi*. Bantam Books, 1991.

César Chávez

Abbott, Cathryn. *César Chávez — Labor Leader*. Vantage Press, 1997.

Altman, Linda Jacobs. *César Chávez*. Lucent Books, 1996.

Cedeño, Maria E. *César Chávez: Labor Leader*. Millbrook Press, 1993.

Ferriss, Susan. *The Fight in the Fields: César Chávez and the Farmworkers Movement*. Edited by Diana Hembree. Harcourt Brace, 1997.

Griswold del Castillo, Richard. *César Chávez: A Triumph of Spirit*. University of Oklahoma Press, 1995.

Holmes, Burnham. *César Chávez: Farmworker Activist*. Raintree/Steck Vaughn, 1994.

http://www.ufw.org/

Benjamin Franklin (Muhammad) Chavis Jr.

Thomas, Larry Reni. *The True Story Behind the Wilmington Ten*. U.B. & U.S. Communications Systems, 1993.

Myerson, Michael. *Nothing Could Be Finer*. International Publishers, 1978.

Noel, Peter. "Another City, Not My Own." *Village Voice*, December 2, 1997.

Mercadante, Linda A. "Questioning Chavis Muhammad." *Christian Century*, June 4–11, 1997.

Septima Clark

Clark, Septima Poinsette. *Ready From Within: Septima Clark and the Civil Rights Movement*. Wild Trees Press, 1986.

Various Authors. *Women of Hope: African Americans Who Made a Difference: Septima P. Clark*. Knowledge Unlimited, 1994.

http://www.us.net/upa/guides/sclc4.htm

Eldridge Cleaver

Cleaver, Eldridge. *Soul on Ice*. 1967. Reissue, Laurel Publishing, 1992.

Cleaver, Eldridge. *Soul on Fire*. Word Books, 1978.

Rout, Kathleen. *Eldridge Cleaver*. Twayne Publishers, 1991.

http://www.pbs.org/wgbh/pages/frontline/shows/race/

Mairead Corrigan and Betty Williams

O'Donnell, Dalry. *The Peace People of Northern Ireland* .

Deutsch, Richard. *Mairead Corrigan and Betty Williams*. Barron's, 1977.

http://www.peacepeople.com/

http://nobelprizes.com/nobel/peace/1976b.html

Bill Cosby

Cosby, Bill. *Time Flies*. ABC-CLIO, 1987.

Solomon, Herbert J. *Bill Cosby*. Chelsea House Publishers, 1992.

Smith, Ronald L. *Cosby: The Life of a Comedy Legend*. Prometheus Books, 1997.

http://www.rpu.com/cosby.htm

Dalai Lama

Dalai Lama XIV. *My Land and My People: The Original Autobiography of His Holiness the Dalai Lama of Tibet*. Warner Books, 1997.

Demi. *The Dalai Lama: A Biography of the Tibetan Spiritual and Political Leader*. Henry Holt, 1998.

Farrer-Halls, Gill. *The World of the Dalai Lama: An Inside Look at His Life, His People, and His Vision*. Theosophical Publishing House, 1998.

http://www.tibet.com/DL/nobelaccept.html

http://www.tibet-society.org.uk/tibet.html

Angela Davis

Davis, Angela. *Blues Legacy and Black Feminism*. Pantheon Books, 1998.

Davis, Angela. *Angela Davis—An Autobiography*. International Publishers, 1988.

Aptheker, Bettina. *The Morning Breaks: The Trial of Angela Davis*. Cornell University Press, 1999.

http://www.vida.com/speakout/People/AngelaDavis.html

http://www.proactivist.com/links_peo/Angela_Davis/

Frederik W. de Klerk

F. W. de Klerk. *The Last Trek*. St. Martin's Press, 1999.

Ottaway, David. *Chained Together: Mandela, de Klerk, and the Struggle to Remake South Africa.* Times Books, 1997.

De Klerk, Willem. *F. W. de Klerk: The Man in His Time.* J. Ball: Thorold's Africana Books (distributor), 1991.

http://nobel.sdsc.edu/laureates/peace-1993-2-bio.html

http://www.almaz.com/nobel/peace/1993b.html

John Dewey

Dewey, John. *Experience and Education.* Macmillan Publishing Company, 1997.

Berube, Maurice R. *Eminent Educators: Studies in Intellectual Influence.* Greenwood Press, 2000.

Simpson, Douglas J. *Educational Reform: A Deweyan Perspective.* Garland Publishing, 1997.

http://www.cisnet.com/teacher-ed/dewey.html

Diana, Princess of Wales

Adler, Bill, ed. *Diana: A Portrait in Her Own Words.* William Morrow, 1999.

Cerasini, Marc A. *Diana: Queen of Hearts.* Random House, 1997.

Davies, Nicholas. *Diana: The Lonely Princess.* Carol Publishing, 1996.

Graham, Tim. *Diana, Princess of Wales.* Welcome Rain, 1997.

Morton, Andrew. *Diana: Her True Story in Her Own Words.* Simon & Schuster, 1977.

Frederick Douglass

Barksdale, Richard, and Kenneth Kinnamon. *Black Writers of America: A Comprehensive Anthology.* Prentice Hall Humanities/Social Science, 1997.

Douglass, Frederick. *The Narrative Life of Frederick Douglass: An American Slave.* Signet, 1845. Reissue, 1997.

Douglass, Frederick. *The Life and Times of Frederick Douglass: Written by Himself.* 1892. Reprint, National Textbook Company, 1998.

McCurdy, Michael, ed. *Escape from Slavery: The Boyhood of Frederick Douglass in His Own Words.* Alfred A. Knopf, 1994.

McFeely, William S. *Frederick Douglass.* W. W. Norton, 1995.

Washington, Booker T. *Frederick Douglass.* 1907. Reissue, 1970. Greenwood Publishing.

"Exile as Emergence: Frederick Douglass in Great Britain, 1845–1847." *Quarterly Journal of Speech* 60 (1974): 69–82.

Douglass: An Electronic Archive of American Oratory and Related Documents. douglass.speech.nwu.edu/

Frederick Douglass's Papers: www.iupui.edu/~douglass/

W. E. B. Du Bois

Du Bois, W. E. B. *The Souls of Black Folk.* Bantam Classics. Reissue, 1989.

Du Bois, W. E. B. *The Correspondence of W. E. B. Du Bois.* Edited by Herbert Aptheker. University of Massachusetts Press, 1997.

Lewis, David Levering, *W. E. B. Du Bois: A Biography of Race 1869–1919.* Henry Holt & Co., 1993.

Rowh, Mark. *W. E. B. Du Bois: Champion of Civil Rights.* Enslow Publishers, 1999.

Stafford, Mark. *W. E. B. Du Bois.* Chelsea House, 1989.

Stull, Bradford T. *Amid the Fall, Dreaming of Eden: Du Bois, King, Malcolm X, and Emancipatory Composition.* Southern Illinois University Press, 1999.

Sundquist, Eric J. *The Oxford W. E. B. Du Bois Reader.* Oxford University Press, 1996.

http://www.usia.gov/usa/blackhis/web.htm

http://rs6.loc.gov/ammem/aap/dubois.html

Abigail Scott Duniway

Moynihan, Ruth Barnes. *Rebel for Rights, Abigail Scott Duniway.* Yale University Press, 1983.

Smith, Helen K. *Presumptuous Dreamers: A Sociological History of the Life & Times of Abigail Scott Duniway, 1834–1871.* Smith Smith & Smith Publishing Co., 1974.

http://libweb.uoregon.edu/exhibits/feminist-voices/

Charles Alexander Eastman

Eastman, Charles Alexander. *Indian Boyhood.* Time-Life Books, 1993.

Eastman, Charles Alexander. *From the Deep Woods to Civilization: Chapters in the Autobiography of an Indian.* 1916. Reissue, University of Nebraska Press, 1977.

Wilson, Raymond. *Ohiyesa: Charles Eastman, Santee Sioux.* University of Illinois Press, 1983.

http://www.bluecloud.org/dakota.html

http://santeedakota.org/normal.htm

Marian Wright Edelman

Edelman, Marian Wright. *Guide My Feet: Prayers and Meditations on Loving and Working for Children.* Harperperennial Library, 1996.

Edelman, Marian Wright. *The Measure of Our Success: A Letter to My Children and Yours.* Beacon Press, 1994.

Edelman, Marian Wright, and Adrienne Yorinks, illus. *Stand for Children.* Hyperion Press, 1998.

Old, Wendie C. *Marian Wright Edelman: Fighting for Children's Rights.* Enslow Publishers, 1995.

Siegel, Beatrice. *Marian Wright Edelman: The Making of a Crusader.* Simon & Schuster, 1995.

http://www.childrensdefense.org/cwatch092397.html

http://www.ibb.gov/childsurvival/wright.htm

James Farmer

Farmer, James. *Lay Bare the Heart: An Autobiography of the Civil Rights Movement.* Arbour House Press, 1985.

Jakoubek, Robert E. *James Farmer and the Freedom Rides.* Millbrook Press, 1994.

Sklansy, Jeff. *James Farmer.* Chelsea House Publishers, 1992.

http://www.greensboro.com/sitins/activists.htm

Louis Farrakhan

Alexander, Amy, ed. *The Farrakahn Factor: African-Americans on Leadership, Nationhood, and Minister Louis Farrakhan.* Grove Press, 1998.

De Angelis, Therese. *Louis Farrakhan.* Chelsea House Publishers, 1998.

Haskins, James. *Louis Farrakhan and the Nation of Islam.* Walker & Co., 1996.

Levinsohn, Florence Hamlish. *Looking for Farrakhan.* Ivan R. Dee, 1997.

Mary Fisher

Fisher, Mary. *Sleep with the Angels: A Mother Challenges AIDS.* Moyer Bell Ltd., 1994.

Fisher, Mary. *I'll Not Go Quietly.* Scribner, 1995.

Hanson, Cynthia, and Kathryn Casey. "Acts of Courage." *Ladies Home Journal* 115, no. 11 (November 1998): 40 (4)

http://maryfisher.com/

http://digitaljournalist.org/issue9712/hero13.htm

http://www.familyaidsnet.org

Alice Cunningham Fletcher

Fletcher, Alice Cunningham. *The Omaha Tribe.* University of Nebraska Press, 1992.

Gay, E. Jane. *With the Nez Percés: Alice Fletcher in the Field, 1889–1892.* University of Nebraska Press, 1987.

www.cas.usf.edu/anthropology/women/fletcher/fletcher.htm

www.magicnet.net/~itms/indianFL2.html

James Forman

Carson, Clayborne. *In Struggle: SNCC and the Black Awakening of the 1960s.* Harvard University Press, 1981.

Forman, James. *The Making of Black Revolutionaries.* 1972. Reissue, University of Washington Press, 1997.

Rogers, Michael. "The Making of Black Revolutionaries." *Library Journal,* December 1997.

Valentine, Victoria. "In the Force of the Movement." *Emerge,* April 1996.

www.thekingcenter.com/library.html

James Forten

Aptheker, Herbert, ed. *A Documentary History of the Negro People in the United States.* Carol Publishing, 1951.

Johnston, Brenda A. *Between the Devil and the Sea: The Life of James Forten.* Harcourt Brace Jovanovich, 1974.

Myers, Walter Dean. *Amistad: A Long Road to Freedom.* Dreamworks, 1998.

http://sisnet.ssku.k12.ca.us/users/scotrftp/public_html/afrbios.htm

http://casenet.thomson.com/gale/bhm/fortenja.html

Timothy Thomas Fortune

Fortune, Timothy Thomas. *Black and White: Land, Labor, and Politics in the South.* 1884. Reissue, Johnson Publishing Co., 1970.

Thornbrough, Emma Lou. *T. Thomas Fortune: Militant Journalist.* University of Chicago Press, 1972.

http://www.africanhistory.com/booker.htm

www.alcyone.com/max/lit/slavery/xvii.html

Betty Friedan

Adler Hennessee, Judith. *Betty Friedan: Her Life.* Random House, 1999.

Blau, Justine. *Betty Friedan.* Chelsea House Publishers, 1990.

Friedan, Betty. *The Feminine Mystique.* Dell Publishing Co., 1984.

Henry, Sondra. *Betty Friedan: Fighter for Women's Rights.* Enslow Publishers, 1990.

http://greatwomen.org/frdan.htm

Mohandas Gandhi

Fischer, Louis. *The Life of Mahatma Gandhi.* 1950. Reissue, Harper & Row, 1983.

Gandhi, Mohandas. *An Autobiography. The Story of My Experiments with Truth.* Beacon Press, 1993.

Gandhi, Mohandas. *Gandhi on Non-Violence.* Edited by Tomas Merton. W. W. Norton, 1965.

Severance, John B. *Gandhi, Great Soul.* Clarion Books, 1997.

Payne, Robert. *The Life and Death of Mahatma Gandhi.* Dutton, 1969.

http://www.norfacad.pvt.k12.va.us/project/gandhi/gandhi.htm

http://cgi.pathfinder.com/time/time100/leaders/profile/gandhi.html

Alfonso García Robles

Shirley, John. "A Latin Diplomat of Peace." *Guardian,* September 9, 1991.

nobelprizes.com/nobel/peace/1982b.html

William Lloyd Garrison

Cain, William. *William Lloyd Garrison and the Fight Against Slavery*. St. Martin's Press, 1997.

Faber, Doris. *I Will Be Heard: The Life of William Lloyd Garrison*. Lothrop, Lee and Shepard, 1970.

Grimke, Archibald. *William Lloyd Garrison*. AMS Press, 1991.

Mayer, Henry. *All on Fire: William Lloyd Garrison and the Abolition of Slavery*. St. Martin's Press, 1998.

Thomas, John. *The Liberator: William Lloyd Garrison*. Little Brown, 1963.

http://192.204.74.15/community/amilobook/12Garrison.html

http://www.nps.gov/boaf/garris%7e1.htm

Marcus Garvey

Clarke, John Henrik. *Marcus Garvey and the Vision of Africa*. Random House, 1974.

Garvey, Marcus. *The Philosophy and Opinions of Marcus Garvey, Or, Africa for the Africans*. Majority Press, 1986.

Cronon, Edmund David, and John Hope Franklin. *Black Moses: The Story of Marcus Garvey and the Universal Negro Improvement Association*. University of Wisconsin Press, 1969.

Lawler, Mary. *Marcus Garvey*. Melrose Square Publishing, 1990.

http://www.ritesofpassage.org/g-dubois.htm

Mikhail Gorbachev

Beschloss, Michael R. *At the Highest Level: The Inside Story of the End of the Cold War*. Little Brown, 1993.

Doder, Dusko. *Gorbachev: The Heretic in the Kremlin*. Viking, 1990.

Gorbachev, Mikhail. *Memoirs*. Doubleday, 1996.

Gorbachev, Mikhail. *Gorbachev*. Columbia University Press, 1999.

Galeotti, Mark. *Gorbachev and His Revolution*. St. Martin's Press, 1997.

Malcolm, Teresa. "Eliminate Weapons, Leaders Say." *National Catholic Reporter*, August 28, 1998.

Sheehy, Gail. *The Man Who Changed the World: The Lives of Mikhail S. Gorbachev*. HarperCollins, 1990.

http://www.dismantle.org/gorby.htm

http://www4.gve.ch/gci/GreenCrossFamily/gorby/gorby.html

Fannie Lou Hamer

Mills, Kay. *This Little Light of Mine: The Life of Fannie Lou Hamer*. Plume, 1994.

Lee, Chana Kai. *For Freedom's Sake: The Life of Fannie Lou Hamer*. University of Illinois Press, 1999.

Rubel, David. *Fannie Lou Hamer: From Sharecropping to Politics.* Silver Burdett Press, 1990.

http://www.beejae.com/hamer.htm

http://www.greatwomen.org/hamer.htm

Antonia Hernández

Gorr, Yolanda. "Women of Hope." *Hispanic*, January 1996.

Gross, Liza. "Antonia Hernández." *Hispanic*, December 1990.

Estrada, Alfredo. "A Nation of Immigrants." *Harvard Journal of Hispanic Policy*, 1993.

www.hisp.com/nov97/20hernandez.html

www.latinolink.com/

Dolores Huerta

Perez, Frank. *Dolores Huerta.* Raintree/Steck Vaughn, 1996.

De Ruiz, Dana Catharine. *La Causa: The Migrant Farmworker's Story.* Raintree/Steck Vaughn, 1993.

www.ufw.org/ufw/dh.htm

www3.pbs.org/chicano/bios/huerta.html

John Hume and David Trimble

Hume, John. *A New Ireland: Politics, Peace and Reconciliation.* Roberts Rinehart Publishers, 1997.

http://www.irishnews.com/k_archive/021198/politics4.html

http://cain.ulster.ac.uk/events/peace/docs/nobeljh.htm

http://www.pbs.org/newshour/bb/europe/july-dec98/hume_10-16.html

Helen Hunt Jackson

Banning, Evelyn I. *Helen Hunt Jackson.* Vanguard Press, 1973.

Jackson, Helen Hunt. *A Century of Dishonor: The Early Crusade for Indian Reform.* Harper & Row, 1963.

Mathes, Valerie Sherer. *Helen Hunt Jackson and Her Indian Reform Legacy.* University of Texas Press, 1990.

Jesse Jackson

Chaplik, Dorothy. *Up With Hope: A Biography of Jesse Jackson.* Dillon Press, 1990.

Frady, Marshall. *Jesse Jackson: A Biography.* Random House, 1996.

Jackson, Jesse. *Jesse Jackson: Still Fighting for the Dream.* Silver Burdett Press, 1990.

http://www.pbs.org/wgbh/pages/frontline/shows/race/interviews

http://www.jessejacksonjr.org

http://www.rainbowpush.org/

Wei Jingsheng

Chen, Jinsong. *Biography of Wei Jingsheng.* Pacific International Publishing Co., Inc., 1998.

Jingsheng, Wei. *The Courage to Stand Alone: Letters from Prison and Other Writings.* Penguin USA, 1998.

http://www.rjgeib.com/thoughts/china/what-to-do-about-china.html

http://www.bbc.co.uk/worldservice/eastasiatoday/weipage.htm

James Weldon Johnson

Johnson, James Weldon. *The Books of American Negro Spirituals: Including the Book of American Negro Spirituals and the Second Book of Negro Spirituals.* Da Capo Press, 1988.

Johnson, James Weldon. *The Autobiography of an Ex-Colored Man.* X-Press, 1997.

http://www.cviog.uga.edu/Projects/gainfo/jwjohnson.htm

Barbara Jordan

Jeffrey, Laura S. *Barbara Jordan: Congresswoman, Lawyer, Educator.* Enslow Publishers, 1997.

Jordan, Barbara. *Selected Speeches.* Howard University Press, 1999.

Johnson, Linda Carlson. *Barbara Jordan: Congresswoman.* Blackbirch Marketing, 1997.

Patrick-Wexler, Diane. *Barbara Jordan.* Raintree/Steck Vaughn, 1995.

Rogers, Mary Beth. *Barbara Jordan: American Hero.* Bantam Doubleday Dell Publishers, 1998.

http://uts.cc.utexas.edu/~lpaj254/forum/BJ.html

Martin Luther King Jr.

Branch, Taylor. *Parting the Waters: America in the King Years, 1954–63.* Simon & Schuster, 1988.

Jakoubek, Robert E. *Martin Luther King, Jr.* Chesea House Publishers, 1989.

Posner, Gerald L. *Killing the Dream: James Earl Ray and the Assassination of Martin Luther King, Jr.* Random House, 1998.

Stull, Bradford T. *Amid the Fall, Dreaming of Eden: Du Bois, King, Malcolm X, and Emancipatory Composition.* Southern Illinois University Press, 1999.

King, Martin Luther, Jr., *The Martin Luther King, Jr. Companion: Quotations from the Speeches, Essays, and Books of Martin Luther King, Jr.* St. Martin's Press, 1999.

King, Martin Luther, Jr. *The Autobiography of Martin Luther King, Jr.* Edited by Clayborne Carson. Warner Books, 1998.

Lewis, David Levering. *King: A Biography.* University of Illinois Press, 1978.

http://www.geocities.com/Athens/Forum/9061/afro/mlk.html

http://www.mecca.org/~crights/mlk.html

http://www.pipeline.com/~juel/mlk.html

John Lewis

Garrow, David. *Bearing the Cross: Martin Luther King, Jr. and the Southern Christian Leadership Conference*. Morrow, 1986.

Pauley, G. E. "John Lewis's 'Serious Revolution': Rhetoric, Resistance, and Revision at the March on Washington." *Quarterly Journal of Speech*, 1998.

http://www.house.gov/democrats/bio_john_lewis.html

James Russell Lowell

Scudder, Horace E. *James Russell Lowell: Biography*. AMS Press, 2001.

Lowell, James Russell. *Letters of James R. Lowell*. AMS Press, 1990.

http://xroads.virginia.edu/~JOURNAL/JAF/spring2.html

http://www.lib.rochester.edu/camelot/auth/lowell.htm

Albert John Lutuli

Gordimer, Nadine. "Chief Luthuli." *Atlantic Monthly* 203, no. 4 (1959): 34–39.

Lutuli, Albert John. *Let My People Go*. McGraw-Hill, 1962.

Okakpu, Amatullah S. "President Oliver R. Tambo of the ANC Returns Home to South Africa." *American Muslim Journal*, January 11, 1991.

http://www.anc.org.za/ancdocs/history/lutuli/index.html

http://www.sacp.org.za/docs/history/fifty5.html

Seán MacBride

Adams, Gerry. *Free Ireland: Towards a Lasting Peace*. Roberts Rinehart Publishers, 1994.

Sands, Bobby, Seán MacBride, and Gerry Adams. *Bobby Sands: Writings from Prison*. Roberts Rinehart Publishers, 1997.

Stivers, Robert L. "Northern Ireland and the MacBride Principles." *Christian Century*, February 17, 1988.

http://www.gn.apc.org/wcp/inf13.htm

http://www.ipb.org/prizes/aboutsean.html

Malcolm X

Barr, Roger. *Malcolm X*. Lucent Books, 1994.

Carson, Clayborne. *Malcolm X: The FBI File*. Carroll & Graf Publishers, 1991.

Haley, Alex, and Malcolm X. *The Autobiography of Malcolm X*. African American Images, 1989.

Malcolm X. *By Any Means Necessary*. Pathfinders Press, 1992.

Stull, Bradford T. *Amid the Fall, Dreaming of Eden: Du Bois, King, Malcolm X, and Emancipatory Composition*. Southern Illinois University Press, 1999.

Perry, Bruce. *Malcolm X: The Life of a Man Who Changed Black America*. Station Hill, 1990.

http://www.webcorp.com/civilrights/malcolm.htm

Nelson Mandela

Hoobler, Dorothy, and Thomas Hoobler. *Mandela*. Franklin Watts, 1992.

Hughes, Libby. *Nelson Mandela*. Dillon Press, 1992.

Mandela, Nelson. *Long Walk to Freedom: The Autobiography of Nelson Mandela*. Little Brown, 1995.

Meredith, Martin. *Nelson Mandela: A Biography*. Griffin Trade Paperback, 1999.

http://www.anc.org.za/ancdocs/history/mandela/index.html

Horace Mann

Mann, Horace. *On the Art of Teaching*. Applewood Books, 1990.

http://jne.law.howard.edu/generalinfo.html

Thurgood Marshall

Rowan, Carl T. *Dream Makers, Dream Breakers: The World of Justice Thurgood Marshall*. Little Brown, 1994.

Williams, Juan. *Thurgood Marshall: American Revolutionary*. Times Books, 1998.

http://www.thurgoodmarshall.com/speeches/constitutional_speech.htm

http://www.thurgoodmarshall.com/

Rigoberta Menchú-Tum

Heptig, Vince. *A Mayan Struggle: Portrait of a Guatemalan People in Danger*. Maya Media, 1997.

When the Mountains Tremble. Skylight Pictures/New Yorker Video. This documentary charts the struggles of the largely Indian Guatemalan peasantry against a long heritage of state and foreign oppression. It is based on the experiences of Rigoberta Menchú Tum.

http://gos.sbc.edu/m/menchunobel.html

http://www.unesco.org/opi/eng/3may98/menchu.htm

Kweisi Mfume

Mfume, Kweisi. *No Free Ride: From the Mean Streets to the Mainstream*. Ballantine Books, 1997.

http://www.horizonmag.com/2/mfume.htm

http://www.naacp.org/

Clarence Mitchell Jr.

Watson, Denton L. *Lion in the Lobby: Clarence Mitchell, Jr.'s Struggle for the Passage of Civil Rights Laws*. Morrow, 1990.

http://www.booknotes.org/transcripts/50121.htm

http://www.naswdc.org/prac/blckmon2.htm

Carlos Montezuma

Iverson, Peter. *Carlos Montezuma and the Changing World of American Indians.* University of New Mexico Press, 1982.

http://home.epix.net/~landis/

Luisa Moreno

Ruiz, Vicki L. *Cannery Women, Cannery Lives: Mexican Women, Unionization and the California Food Processing Industry, 1930–1950.* Albuquerque, NM, 1987.

http://www.pbs.org/chicano/19411960.html

http://www.notredamehighschool.org/hispanic6.html

Robert P. Moses

Belfrage, Sally, and Robert P. Moses. *Freedom Summer.* University Press of Virginia, 1990.

Burner, Eric. *And Gently He Shall Lead Them: Robert Parris Moses and Civil Rights in Mississippi.* New York University Press, 1994.

http://www.sirius.com/~casha/over.html

Mother Teresa

Mother Teresa, Becky Benenate, and Marianne Williamson. *In the Heart of the World: Thoughts, Stories, & Prayers.* New World Library, 1997.

Mother Teresa and Lucinda Vardy. *Meditations from a Simple Path.* Ballentine Books, 1996.

Wellman, Sam. *Mother Teresa: Missionary of Charity.* Barbour Publishing, 1997.

Woodworth, Deborah. *Faith: The Story of Mother Teresa.* Child's World, 1999.

http://www.nando.net/newsroom/nt/moreteresa.html

Lucretia Mott

Bryant, Jennifer Fisher. *Lucretia Mott: A Guiding Light.* Wm. B. Eerdmans Publishing Company, 1995.

Faber, Doris. *Lucretia Mott, Foe of Slavery.* Garrard Publishing, 1971.

Audiocassette: *Great American Women's Speeches: Lucretia Mott/Sojourner Truth/Ernestine Rose/Lucy Stone/Susan B. Anthony/Elizabteh Cady Stanton/Carrie Chapman Catt.* Harper Audio, 1995.

http://www.mott.pomona.edu/

http://www.greatwomen.org/mott.htm

Elijah Muhammad

Clegg, Claude Andrew. *An Original Man: The Life and Times of Elijah Muhammad.* St. Martin's Press, 1997.

Halasa, Malu. *Elijah Muhammad*. Chelsea House Publishers, 1990.

Lincoln, C. Eric. *The Black Muslims in America*. 1961. Reissue, Africa World Press, 1994.

http://www.nhc.rtp.nc.us:8080/tserve/twenty/tkeyinfo/islam.htm

John Muir

Ito, Tom. *John Muir*. Lucent Books, 1996.

Fox, Stephen. *John Muir and His Legacy: The American Conservation Movement*. Little Brown, 1981.

Tolan, Sally. *John Muir*. Morehouse Publishing Company, 1990.

Muir, John. *John Muir: His Life and Letters and Other Writings*. Mountaineers Books, 1996.

Muir, John. *Nature Writings: The Story of My Boyhood and Youth, My First Summer in the Sierra, the Mountains of California*. Library of America/Penguin, 1997.

Wadsworth, Ginger. *John Muir, Wilderness Protector*. Lerner Publications, 1992.

http://www.sierraclub.org/john_muir_exhibit/

http://www.terraquest.com/highsights/valley/muir.html

Alva Myrdal

Bok, Sissela. *Alva Myrdal: A Daughter's Memoir*. Addison Wesley, 1992.

Myrdal, Alva. *The Game of Disarmament: How the United States and Russia Run the Arms Race*. Pantheon Books, 1976.

http://www.rit.edu/~arepph/women/myrdal.html

Ralph Nader

Celsi, Teresa. *Ralph Nader: The Consumer Revolution*. Millbrook Press, 1991.

Isaac, Katherine, and Ralph Nader. *Ralph Nader's Practicing Democracy 1997: A Guide to Student Action*. St. Martin's Press, 1997.

Nader, Ralph. *No Contest: Corporate Lawyers and the Perversion of Justice in America*. Random House, 1996.

Nader, Ralph. *Unsafe at Any Speed: The Designed-In Dangers of the American Automobile*. Grossman, 1972.

http://www.sfbg.com/nader/50.html

http://www.emagazine.com/september-october_1996/0996conv.html

Carry Amelia Moore Nation

Asbury, Herbert. *Carry Nation: The Woman with the Hatchet*. New York, 1929.

Kobler, John. *Ardent Spirits: The Rise and Fall of Prohibition*. Putnam, 1973.

Taylor, Robert Lewis. *Vessel of Wrath: The Life and Times of Carry Nation*. New American Library, 1966.

Paul Newman

Larned, Marianne, and Paul Newman. *Stone Soup for the World: Life-Changing Stories of Kindness & Courageous Acts of Service*. Conari Press, 1998.

Lax, Eric. *Paul Newman: A Biography*. Turner Publishing, 1996.

Oumano, Elena. *Paul Newman*. St. Martin's Press, 1989.

http://www.npr.org/programs/watc/pnewman.html

Huey Newton

Newton, Michael. *Bitter Grain: Huey Newton and the Black Panther Party*. Holloway House Publishers, 1991.

Newton, Huey P. *To Die for the People: The Writings of Huey P. Newton*. Edited by Toni Morrison. Writers & Readers, 1995.

Pearson, Hugh. *The Shadow of the Panther: Huey Newton and the Price of Black Power in America*. Addison Wesley, 1994.

Seale, Bobby. *Seize the Time: The Story of the Black Panther Party and Huey Newton*. Black Classic Press, 1997.

http://www.blackpanther.org

Philip Noel-Baker

Noel-Baker, Philip. *The Arms Race: A Programme for World Disarmament*. Atlantic Books, 1958.

http://www.quaker.org

Emmeline Pankhurst

Pankhurst, E. G. *My Own Story*. Greenwood Publishing, 1985.

Rosa Parks

Celsi, Teresa. *Rosa Parks and the Montgomery Bus Boycott*. Demco Media, 1994.

Friese, Kai Jabir. *Rosa Parks: The Movement Organizes*. Silver Burdett Press, 1990.

Greenfield, Eloise. *Rosa Parks*. Harpercrest, 1996.

Hull, Mary. *Rosa Parks*. Chelsea House Publishers, 1994.

Parks, Rosa, and Jim Haskins. *Rosa Parks: Mother to a Movement*. Dial Press for Young Readers, 1992.

Parks, Rosa. *Dear Mrs. Parks: A Dialogue with Today's Youth*. Demco Media, 1997.

Parks, Rosa. *Rosa Parks: My Story*. Puffin, 1999.

http://www.greatwomen.org/parks.htm

Alice Paul

Lunardini, Christine A. *From Equal Suffrage to Equal Rights: Alice Paul and the National Woman's Party, 1910–1928*. New York University Press, 1986.

http://www.apnow.org/alicepaulbio.html

http://www.greatwomen.org/paul.htm

Linus Pauling

Goertzel, Ted George. *Linus Pauling: A Life in Science and Politics*. Basic Books, 1995.

Hager, Thomas. *Force of Nature: The Life of Linus Pauling*. Simon & Schuster, 1995.

Pauling, Linus. *Linus Pauling: In His Own Words: Selected Writings, Speeches, and Interviews*. Simon & Schuster, 1995.

Sarafini, Anthony. *Linus Pauling: A Man and His Science*. Paragon House, 1989.

Adolfo Pérez Esquivel

Adolfo Pérez Esquivel. *Christ in a Poncho: Testimonials of the Nonviolent Struggles in Latin America*.

http://www.igc.org/napf/peace_heroes.html

http://nobelprizes.com/nobel/peace/1980a.html

http://www.unesco.org/drg/human-rights/Pages/English/EsquivE.html

Wendell Phillips

Bartlett, Irving H. *Wendell and Ann Phillips: The Community of Reform, 1840–1880*. W. W. Norton, 1981.

Sherwin, Oscar. *Prophet of Liberty: The Life and Times of Wendell Phillips*. Bookman Association Publishing, 1958.

Stewart, James Brewer. *Wendell Phillips, Liberty's Hero*. Louisiana State University Press, 1986.

http://www.uark.edu/depts/comminfo/oxford/lovejoy.html

Susan LaFlesche Picotte

Ferris, Jeri. *Native American Doctor: The Story of Susan LaFlesche Picotte*. Carolrhoda Books, 1991.

Tong, Benson. *Susan LaFlesche Picotte, M.D.: Omaha Indian Leader and Reformer*. University of Oklahoma Press, 1999.

http://www.nde.state.ne.us/SS/notables/picotte.html

Robert Purvis

Barksdale, Richard, and Keneth Kinnamon. *Black Writers of America: A Comprehensive Anthology*. Prentice Hall Humanities/Social Science, 1997.

"Encountering Angelina Grimké: Violence, Identity, and the Creation of Radical Community." *Quarterly Journal of Speech* 82 (1996): 38–54.

http://www.usia.gov/abtusia/posts/SF1/wwwhbhmc.html

A. Philip Randolph

Anderson, Jervis. *A. Philip Randolph: A Biographical Portrait.* Harcourt Brace Jovanovich, 1973.

Hanley, Sally. *A. Phillip Randolph.* Chelsea House Publishers, 1989.

Neyland, James. *A. Philip Randolph.* Melrose Square Publishing, 1994.

Patterson, Lillie. *A. Philip Randolph: Messenger for the Masses.* Facts on File, 1996.

Pfeffer, Paula F. *A. Philip Randolph: Pioneer of the Civil Rights Movement.* Louisiana State University Press, 1990.

http://www2.pbs.org/weta/apr/aprsites.html

Jeannette Rankin

Davidson, Sue. *Jeannette Rankin and Patsy Takemoto Mink: A Heart in Politics.* Seal Press, 1994.

O'Brien, Mary Barmeyer. *Jeannette Rankin, 1880–1973: Bright Star in the Big Sky.* Falcon Press, 1995.

White, Florence. *First Woman in Congress, Jeannette Rankin.* J. Messner, 1980.

http://www.igc.org/napf/peace_heroes.html

Christopher Reeve

Oleksy, Walter G. *Christopher Reeve.* Lucent, 2000.

Rosenblatt, Roger. "New Hopes, New Dreams." *Time* 148, no. 10 (August 26, 1996): 40 (13).

Reeve, Christopher. *Still Me.* Random House, 1998.

http://paralysis.apacure.org/crf/ww/index.html

John D. Rockefeller

Chernow, Ron. *Titan: The Life of John D. Rockefeller, Sr.* Random House, 1998.

Coffey, Ellen G. *John D. Rockefeller: Empire Builder.* Silver Burdett Press, 1989.

Harr, John E., and P. J. Johnson. *The Rockefeller Century.* Scribner, 1988.

Hawke, David Freeman. *John D.: The Founding Father of the Rockefellers.* Harper & Row, 1980.

Nevins, Allan. *Study in Power: John D. Rockefeller, Industrialist and Philanthropist.* Scribner, 1953.

Rockefeller, John D. *Dear Father/Dear Son: Correspondence of John D. Rockefeller and John D. Rockefeller, Jr.* Fordham University Press in cooperation with the Rockefeller Archive Center, 1994.

Eleanor Roosevelt

Cook, Blanche Wiesen. *Eleanor Roosevelt.* Viking, 1992.

Freedman, Russell. *Eleanor Roosevelt: A Life of Discovery*. Clarion Books, 1993.

Goodwin, Doris Kearns. *No Ordinary Time: Franklin and Eleanor Roosevelt: The Home Front in World War II*. Touchstone Books, 1995.

Gottfried, Ted. *Eleanor Roosevelt: First Lady of the Twentieth Century*. Franklin Watts, 1997.

McAuley, Karen. *Eleanor Roosevelt*. Chelsea House Publishers, 1987.

Roosevelt, Eleanor. *Tomorrow Is Now*. Harper & Row, 1963.

Roosevelt, Eleanor. *This Is My Story*. Harper, 1937.

Winget, Mary. *Eleanor Roosevelt*. Lerner Publications, 2000.

http://newdeal.feri.org/feri/

Theodore Roosevelt

Brands, H. W. *T.R.: The Last Romantic*. Basic Books, 1997.

Fritz, Jean. *Bully for You, Teddy Roosevelt!* Putnam, 1991.

McCullough, David G. *Mornings on Horseback: The Story of an Extraordinary Family, a Vanished Way of Life, and the Unique Child Who Became Theodore Roosevelt*. Simon & Schuster, 1981.

Meltzer, Milton. *Theodore Roosevelt and His America*. Franklin Watts, 1994.

Roosevelt, Theodore. *The Rough Riders*. Modern Library, 1999.

Morris, Edmund. *The Rise of Theodore Roosevelt*. Ballentine Books, 1988.

Welsbacher, Anne. *Theodore Roosevelt*. Abdo & Daughters, 1998.

http://cgi.pathfinder.com/time/time100/leaders/profile/troosevelt.html

Bayard Rustin

O'Reilly, Kenneth. *Black Americans: The FBI Files*. Edited by David Gallen. Carroll & Graf Publishers, 1994.

Rustin, Bayard. *Down the Line: Collected Writings of Bayard Rustin*. Quadrangle Books, 1971.

Rustin, Bayard. *Strategies for Freedom: The Changing Patterns of Black Protest*. Columbia University Press, 1976.

http://www.idsonline.com/sdusa/brindex.html

Andrei Sakharov

Bonner, Elena. *Alone Together*. Alfred A. Knopf, 1986.

Sakharov, Andrei. *Moscow and Beyond, 1986 to 1989*. Vintage Books, 1992.

Sakharov, Andrei. *Memoirs*. Alfred A. Knopf, 1990.

Sakharav, Andrei. *Andrei Sakharov and Peace*. Edited by Edward D. Lozansky. Avon, 1985.

http://www.wdn.com/asf/index.html

Albert Schweitzer

Cousins, Norman. *The Words of Albert Schwietzer*. Newmarket Press, 1990.

Greene, Carol. *Albert Schweitzer: Friend of All Life*. Children's Press, 1993.

Schweitzer, Albert. *Out of My Life and Thought: An Autobiography*. Johns Hopkins University Press in association with the Albert Schweitzer Institute for the Humanities, 1998.

Schweitzer, Albert. *Reverence for Life*. Irvington Publishing, 1993.

http://www.pcisys.net/~jnf/

Bobby Seale

Freed, Donald. *Agony in New Haven: The Trial of Bobby Seale*. Simon & Schuster, 1973.

Seale, Bobby. *A Lonely Rage:The Autobiography of Bobby Seale*. Times Books, 1978.

Seale, Bobby. *Seize the Time: The Story of the Black Panther Party and Huey P. Newton*. Black Classic Press, 1997.

http://http://www.bobbyseale.com

Elizabeth Cady Stanton

Gleiter, Jan, and Kathleen Thompson. *Elizabeth Cady Stanton*. Raintree, 1988.

Griffith, Elisabeth. *In Her Own Right: The Life of Elizabeth Cady Stanton*. Oxford University Press, 1985.

Stansell, Christine. "The Road from Seneca Falls: The Feminism of the Mothers, The Feminism of the Daughters, The Feminism of the Girls." *The New Republic* 219, no. 6 (August 1998): 26 (12).

Stanton, Elizabeth Cady, and Ellen Carol Du Bois. *Eighty Years and More: Reminiscences 1815–1897*. Reissue, Northeastern University Press, 1992.

Audiocassette: *Great American Women's Speeches: Lucretia Mott/Sojourner Truth/Ernestine Rose/Lucy Stone/Susan B. Anthony/Elizabeth Cady Stanton/Carrie Chapman Catt*. Harper Audio, 1995.

http://www.nps.gov/htdocs1/boaf/stanto~1.htm

Gloria Steinem

Heilbrun, Carolyn G. *The Education of a Woman: A Life of Gloria Steinem*. Dial Press, 1995.

Hoff, Mark. *Gloria Steinem and the Women's Movement*. Millbrook Press, 1991.

Stern, Sydney Ladensohn. *Gloria Steinem: Her Passions, Politics, and Mystique*. Carol Publishing Group, 1997.

Steinem, Gloria. *Revolution from Within*. Little Brown, 1992.

Gloria Seinem on A&E's Biography, Videorecording, A&E Home Video, 1995.

http://www.greatwomen.org/stnem.htm

Lucy Stone

Kerr, Andrea Moore. *Lucy Stone: Speaking Out for Equality*. Rutgers University Press, 1992.

http://www.undergroundrailroad.com/history/lucy_stone.html

Mary Church Terrell

Swain, Gwenyth. *Civil Rights Pioneer: A Story about Mary Church Terrell*. Carolrhoda Books, 1999.

Terrell, Mary Church. *A Colored Woman in a White World*. G.K. Hall [1996], orig. pub. 1940.

http://lcweb2.loc.gov/ammem/aaohtml/aopart7.html

Susette LaFlesche Tibbles

http://www.nde.state.ne.us/SS/notables/tibbles.html

Sojourner Truth

Spinale, Laura. *Sojourner Truth*. Child's World, 1999.

Gilbert, Olive. *Narrative of Sojourner Truth: A Bondswoman of Olden Time, with a History of Her Labors and Correspondence Drawn from Her Book of Life*. Also, a memorial chapter. Penguin Books, 1998.

Audio Cassette: *Great American Women's Speeches: Lucretia Mott/Sojourner Truth/Ernestine Rose/Lucy Stone/Susan B. Anthony/Elizabeth Cady Stanton/Carrie Chapman Catt*. Harper Audio, 1995.

The famous "Ain't I a Woman?" speech at: www.ugrr.org/learn/soj-spch.htm

http://www.sojournertruth.org/Default.htm

Desmond Tutu

Bentley, Judith. *Archbishop Tutu of South Africa*. Enslow Publishers, 1988.

Du Boulay, Shirley. *Tutu: Voice of the Voiceless*. Wm. B. Eerdmans Publishing Company, 1988.

Lantier-Sampon, Patricia. *Desmond Tutu: Religious Leader Devoted to Freedom*. G. Stevens Children's Books, 1991.

Tutu, Desmond. *Hope and Suffering: Sermons and Speeches*. Wm. B. Eerdmans Publishing Company, 1984.

Tutu, Desmond. *The Rainbow People of God: The Making of a Peaceful Revolution*. Doubleday, 1994.

Tutu, Desmond. *The Essential Desmond Tutu*. D. Philip Publishers, 1997.

http://www.igc.org/napf/desmond_tutu.html

http://www.pbs.org/whatson/1999/04/descriptions/BMDT.html

Lech Wałesa

Craig, Mary. *Lech Wałesa and His Poland.* Continuum, 1987.

Vnenchak, Dennis. *Lech Wałesa and Poland.* Dillon Press, 1994.

Wałesa, Lech. A Way of Hope: An Autobiography. Henry Holt, 1987.

Wałesa, Lech. *The Struggle and The Triumph: An Autobiography.* Arcade Publishers, 1992.

Weschler, Lawrence. *Solidarity: Poland in the Season of Its Passion.* Simon & Schuster, 1981.

Booker T. Washington

Harlan, Louis R. *Booker T. Washington Papers.* University of Illinois Press, 1989.

Harris, Thomas E. *Analysis of the Clash over the Issues Between Booker T. Washington and W. E. B. Du Bois.* Garland Publishers. 1993.

Harlan, Louis R. *Booker T. Washington: Wizard of Tuskegee, 1901–1915.* Oxford University Press, 1983.

Neyland, James. *Booker T. Washington, Educator.* Holloway House, 1993.

Pryor, T. M. (Theodore M.). *Wealth Building Lessons of Booker T. Washington for a New Black America.* Duncan & Duncan, 1995.

Washington, Booker T. *Up from Slavery: An Autobiography.* Modern Library, 1901. Reissue, 1999.

Electronic text version of *Up From Slavery: An Autobiography by Booker T. Washington.* On the Web site documenting the American South, hosted by the University of North Carolina Library Web server—http://metalab.unc.edu /docsouth/washington/menu.html

Theodore Weld

Barnes, Gilbert. *Letters of Theodore Dwight Weld, Angelina Grimké Weld, and Sarah Grimké, 1822–1844.* 1934. Reissue, Da Capo Press, 1970.

" 'Like Gory Spectres': Representing Evil in Theodore Weld's American Slavery As It Is." *Quarterly Journal of Speech* 80 (1994): 277–92.

Uncle Tom's Cabin & American Culture: A Multimedia Archive. Hosted on the University of Virginia Web site. http://jefferson.village.virginia.edu/utc/

Weld, Theodore. *American Slavery As It Is: A Testimony of a Thousand Witnesses.* Ayer, 1968.

Ida B. Wells-Barnett

McMurray, Linda. *To Keep the Waters Troubled: The Life of Ida B. Wells.* Oxford University Press, 1999.

Wells-Barnett, Ida B. *The Crusade for Justice: The Autobiography of Ida B. Wells-Barnett.* University of Chicago Press, 1991.

Wells-Barnett, Ida B. *On Lynching: Southern Horrors, a Red Record Mob Rule in New Orleans.* Ayer, 1990.

Walter Francis White

McPherson, James, ed. *The Abolitionist Legacy: From Reconstruction to the NAACP.* Princeton University Press, 1995.

Sigler, Jay A. *Civil Rights in America: 1500 to the Present.* Gale Research, 1998.

White, Walter. *A Man Called White: The Autobiography of Walter White.* University of Georgia Press, 1995.

Elie Wiesel

Abramson, Irving, ed. *Against Silence: The Voice and Vision of Elie Wiesel.* Schocken Books, 1987.

Lazo, Caroline. *Elie Wiesel.* Dillon Press, 1994.

Mitterand, Francois. *A Memoir in Two Voices.* Arcade Publishers, 1997. A dialogue between Mitterand, the late president of France and Nobel Laureate Elie Wiesel on such topics as wide-ranging as childhood, faith, war, and literature.

Wiesel, Elie. *The Night Trilogy: Night, Dawn, The Accident.* Hill & Wang, 1987.

Wiesel, Elie. *The Fifth Son.* Warner, 1986.

Wiesel, Elie. *All Rivers Run to the Sea: Memoirs.* Alfred A. Knopf, 1995.

Profile from the American Academy of Achievement Web site. http://www.achievement.org/autodoc/page/wie0bio-1

Roy Wilkins

Wilkins, Roy. *Standing Fast: The Autobiography of Roy Wilkins.* Viking Press, 1982.

Wilson, Sandra. *In Search of Democracy: The NAACP Writings of James Weldon Johnson, Walter White and Roy Wilkins (1920–1977).* Oxford University Press, 1999.

Roy Wilkins videorecording. *The Right to Dignity.* Carousel Films, 1989.

The Roy Wilkins Memorial. A virtual tour of this unique memorial to civil rights leader and Minnesota native Roy Wilkins. http://www.tccom.com/wilkins/

Jody Williams

Bellafonte, Ginia. "Kudos for a Crusader." *Time,* October 20, 1997.

Cameron, Maxwell, ed. *To Walk Without Fear: The Global Movement to Ban Landmines.* Oxford University Press, 1999.

Human Rights Watch Staff. *Landmines: A Deadly Legacy.* Human Rights Watch, 1999.

Roberts, Sean, and Jody Williams. *After the Guns Fall Silent: The Enduring Legacy of Landmines.* Stylus Publishing Llc., 1995.

"Grassroots Activist Receives Nobel Peace Prize for Landmine Campaign." *International Journal for World Peace,* December 1997.

"Beyond Land Mines." *The Nation,* November 3, 1997.

Jody Williams Nobel Laureate Speech, December 3, 1997, from Gifts of Speech: The International Campaign to Ban Land Mines Web site. http://www.icbl.org/

Human Rights Watch Campaign to Ban Land Mines. http://www.hrw.org/hrw/campaigns/mines/1999/

Physicians for Human Rights. http://www.phrusa.org/

Sarah Winnemucca

Bataille, Gretchen, ed. *Native American Women—A Biographical Dictionary*. Garland Publishing, 1993.

Hopkins, Sarah Winnemucca. *Life Among the Paiutes: Their Wrongs and Claims*. University of Nevada Press, 1994.

Morrow, Mary F. *Sarah Winnemucca, Paiute*. Raintree/Steck Vaughn, 1996.

Scordato, Ellen. *Sarah Winnemucca: Northern Paiute Writer and Diplomat*. Chelsea House Publishers, 1992.

Tocmetone (Sarah Winnemucca). From Women Spirit, a Web site hosted on Powersource Gallery Website. http://www.neosoft.com/~sestrapp/gallery/womansp/paiute.html

Victoria Woodhull

Gabriel, Mary. *Notorious Victoria: The Life of Victoria Woodhull Uncensored*. Algonquin Books, 1998.

Goldsmith, Barbara. *Other Powers: The Age of Suffrage, Spiritualism and the Scandalous Victoria Woodhull*. Alfred A. Knopf, 1998.

Goldsmith, Barbara. "The Woman Who Set America On Its Ear." *Parade*, March 8, 1998.

Guinn, Jeff. "More Than 100 Years Ago, a Woman Ran for President and Preached Free Love." Knight-Ridder, March 11, 1998.

Meade, Marrion. *Free Woman: The Life and Times of Victoria Woodhull*. Alfred A. Knopf, 1976.

Victoria Woodhull. University of Maryland. Online. http://www.glue.umd.edu/~cliswp/Bios/vwbio.html

Harry Wu

Wu, Hongda Harry. *Laogai—The Chinese Gulag*. Westview Press, 1992.

Wu, Hongda Harry. *Bitter Winds: A Memoir of My Years in China's Gulag*. Wiley, 1994.

Wu, Hongda Harry. *Troublemaker: One Man's Struggle Against China's Cruelty*. Times Books, 1998.

Andrew Young

Haskins, James. *Andrew Young: A Man with a Mission*. Lothrop, Lee & Shepard Co., 1979.

Westman, Paul. *Andrew Young: Champion of the Poor*. Dillon Press, 1986.

Young, Andrew. *An Easy Burden: The Civil Rights Movement and the Transformation of America*. HarperCollins, 1996.

Raul Yzaguirre

Jones-Correa, Michael. "The Role of Hispanics in the 1996 Elections." *Harvard Journal of Hispanic Policy* 9 (1995–96).

Schnaiberg, Lynn. "Chairman's Resignation Latest Upset for Hispanic Panel." *Education Week*, April 24, 1996.

Torre, Joe. "Latinos Toe the Party Line on Clinton." *Hispanic*, October 1998.

National Council of La Raza (NCLR), a nonpartisan organization established in 1968 to reduce poverty and discrimination, and improve life opportunities for Hispanic Americans. It is the largest advocacy group for Latinos in the United States. http://www.nclr.org/

Hispanic Online: the leading online forum for Latinos living in the United States. A short biography of Raul Yzaguirre can be found by searching the site. http://www.hisp.com/

Glossary

abolitionism (ăb′ə-lĭsh′ə-nĭz′əm)   Most commonly used to refer to the political or philosophical policy supporting the abolition of slavery in the southern states prior to the Civil War.

accolade (ăk′ə-lād′, -läd ′)   A special acknowledgement or expression of approval.

acculturation (ə-kŭl′chə-rā′shən)   The changes brought to the culture of a group or individual as the result of contact with a different culture.

acquit (ə-kwĭt′)   In law, to find not guilty or clear of a charge or accusation.

acronym (ăk′rə-nĭm′)   A word formed from the initials or first letters of a name, phrase, or expression, such as "scuba" or "posh."

activism (ăk′tə-vĭz′əm)   In political terms, the philosophy or practice of assertive action.

activist (ăk′tə-vĭst)   A person involved, or "active," in political actions, such as protests or demonstrations, designed to bring about change.

ad hoc (ăd h ŏk′, h ōk′)   A Latin phrase meaning only for the specific case or situation at hand. It is also used to mean impromptu, or improvised.

administration (ăd-mĭn′ĭ-strā′shən)   In politics, a general term for a president's time in office, and for the people in positions of power during that time.

advisory committee (ăd-vī′zə-rē kə-mĭt′ē)   A group, often consisting of persons with specialized knowledge or influence, brought together to provide advice or guidance on a particular issue.

advocacy group (ăd′və-kə-sē gro͞op)   An organization concerned with promoting the interests of a specific cause or group.

affiliation (ə-fĭl′ē-ā′shən)   A close connection to or association with a particular group or person.

affirmative action (ə-fûr′mə-tĭv ăk′shən)   The collective term for government policies in the United States intended to promote opportunities for minorities by setting specific goals or quotas.

agitation (ăj′ĭ-tā′shən)   In politics, especially political activism, the stirring up of public interest or emotion in a matter of controversy or debate.

agrarian (ə-grâr′ē-ən)   A sociological term used to refer to cultures or economies that are based on or derive their primary economic means from uses of the land, such as farming.

alarmist (ə-lär′mĭst)   Most often used to refer to a person who attempts to frighten or worry others by spreading false or exaggerated rumors, focusing on very negative or narrow interpretations, or otherwise arousing concern, often for political gain.

alienation (āl′yə-nā′shən)   In psychological terms, an estrangement between one's self and the rest of the world; a feeling of not belonging.

ally (ə-lī′, ă l′ī)   A friend or friendly association. In global international relations, most often used to refer to a nation with which one has mutually supportive treaties or common political interests.

amateur (ăm′ə-tûr′)   In athletics, a person involved in a sport or activity as a pastime rather than as a profession; an athlete who is not paid for his or her participation in a sport.

ambassador (ăm-băs′ə-dər, -dôr ′)   The formal representative of one country or nation to another.

amnesty (ăm′nĭ-stē)   A general pardon, often granted for political offenses.

annexation (ə-nĕks′āshən)   The process of adding onto or joining various elements into a larger single unit.

anti-Semitism (ăn′tē-sĕm′ĭ-tĭz′əm, ă n′tī-)   The hostility, hatred, or practice of discrimination against Jews.

apartheid (ə-pärt′hīt′, -h āt′)   A policy of racial segregation formerly followed in the Republic of South Africa, meaning "separation" in the Afrikaans language. Introduced in 1948 and maintained until the early 1990s, the system maintained strict political, social, and economic divisions between the governing white minority population and the nonwhite majority. Under apartheid, people were classified according to their ethnic or racial group, and the laws determined where members of each group could live, what type of jobs they could hold, and what education they could receive.

apologist (ə-pŏl′ə-jĭst)   A person who writes or speaks in defense of someone or something. The term is often used to refer to a person who seeks to justify the actions of another, or to reconcile behavior or beliefs with established principles.

appeal (ə-pēl′)   In legal terms, the process of transferring a case from a lower court to a higher for the purpose of a new hearing. The term also refers to the case itself.

appellation (ăp′ə-lā′shən)   A term often used in a formal sense, meaning a name, title, or designation.

apprentice (ə-prĕn′tĭs)   In modern terms, one who studies or learns a trade or skill under the supervision of a recognized or accredited master.

archaeology (är′kē-ŏl′ə-jē)   The science and study of past human life and culture by means of recovered artifacts and other material evidence.

archipelago (är′kə-pĕl′ə-gō′)   A large group or chain of islands.

architect (är′kĭ-tĕkt′)   Literally, a person who designs or supervises the construction of buildings, the term is often used to refer to someone who plans or devises a group or action.

aristocracy (ăr′ĭ-stŏk′rə-sē)   From the Greek words *aristos*, meaning "best," and *kratos*, meaning "power," a term used either for a form of government ruled by an elite class or group, or to refer to the members of such a group.

armistice (är′mĭ-stĭs)   A truce or other temporary stop in fighting by the mutual agreement of the warring parties.

arsenal (är′sə-nəl)   A stockpile of weapons. The term also refers to a structure used for the storage, testing, manufacture, and repair of weapons and ammunition.

arson (är′sən)   A legal term for the crime of deliberately setting fire to a building or other property.

assassinate (ə-săs′ə-nāt′)   To murder. The term is most often used to refer to the killing of an important person, often for political reasons.

assimilation (ə-sĭm′ə-lā′shən)   A sociological term referring to the process by which individuals or groups are brought and absorbed into a new and dominant culture.

authoritarian (ə-thôr′ĭ-târ′ē-ən)   A person or political system that enforces absolute obedience to authority.

autonomy (ô-tŏn′ə-mē)   From the Greek word *autonomos*, meaning self-ruling, a person, group, or nation not controlled by others, or self-governing.

ballot (băl′ət)   From the term for a sheet of paper used to cast a vote, a term often used for the process of casting votes, or for a list of candidates.

Baptist (băp′tĭst)   A member of an evangelical Protestant denomination characterized by belief in individual freedom, the separation of church and state, and the baptism, or acceptance into the body of the church of only voluntary, conscious believers.

bar (bär)   A legal term used to describe the profession of law or attorneys that are considered to be part of a group.

bigotry (bĭg′ə-trē)   The attitude or behavior of intolerance, often on the basis of race, nationality, sex, or religion.

bill (bĭl)   In politics, the draft of a proposed law submitted to a legislative body, such as the House of Representatives, for approval. The term may also refer to the resultant law.

bisexual (bī-sĕk′shoo-əl)   Of or relating to both the male and female sex. The term is most commonly used to describe a person who has sexual interest in partners of both sexes.

black separatism (blăk sĕp′ər-ə-tĭsm)   A political principle, or movement, advocated by the Black Muslim organization under the leadership of Elijah Muhammad, to establish a separate homeland for African Americans in the United States.

blues (blooz)   In music, a term, short for "blue devils," that refers to a style that originated in the American South, evolved from black secular songs, and is usually characterized by a slow tempo and often melancholy subjects.

boarding school (bôrd ĭng skool)   An educational facility, primarily for primary- and high-school-level education, where students are in residence and provided with room and board.

Bolshevik (bōl′shə-vĭk′, b ŏl′-)   A member of the radical political party that seized power in the Russian Revolution of 1917. Bolshevism is based on the theories of Karl Marx, which were formulated or interpreted by Vladimir Ilich Lenin, who advocated an actively revolutionary party, committed to establishing a communist society at any cost.

botany (bŏt′n-ē)   The science or study of plants.

boycott (boi′kŏt′)   A form of protest in which a person or group refuses to buy products from or support companies, individuals, nations, or other groups with which they disagree. The intent of a boycott is to bring about or force change. It is used as a tool or weapon in labor disputes, by consumers, and in international affairs.

brownstone (broun′stōn′)   A type of building, often associated with urban residences, characterized by a brownish-red sandstone used in its construction or façade.

Buddhism (boo′dĭz′əm)   One of the world's major religions, Buddhism began in northeastern India and is based on the teachings of Siddhartha Gautama, known as the Buddha, or Enlightened One. Originally a monastic movement within the Brahman tradition, it developed in a distinctive direction, as the Buddha rejected significant aspects of the Hindu philosophy and structure. In its present form, it consists of two major branches known as Theraveda, the Way of the Elders, and Mahayana, the Great Vehicle. Buddhism has great force and significance not only in India, but throughout much of southeast Asia.

burlesque (bər-lĕsk′)   A type of vaudeville entertainment or comic art characterized by ridiculous exaggeration, racy humor, and displays of nudity.

by-election (bī-ĭ-lĕk′shən)   An election held at other than the normally scheduled time, usually to fill a vacancy that has arisen since the last scheduled election.

cabinet (kăb′ə-nĭt)   In politics, the group of highest-ranking ministers of state in a president's or other national leader's administration.

cadence (kād′ns)   A balanced, rhythmic flow in music, poetry, or oratory. The term is also used to refer to a measure or beat of movement.

Calvinist (kăl′vĭ-nĭst)   A form of Christian belief or theology, a Protestant offshoot of the Catholic church, led by French reformer John Calvin (1509-64). It is characterized by belief in the absolute sovereignty of God, in predestination, and the absence of free will.

caste (kăst)   From the Spanish *casta*, meaning race, a term that most often refers to any of the subclasses, or levels, in the Hindu society structure.

caucus (kô′kəs)   Most often used to refer to a meeting of political party leaders at the local level, often to select delegates to a broader convention or to establish preferences for candidates running for office.

caulker (kôk′ər)   A person who makes an item or structure water- or airtight by use of a filling or sealing substance, commonly referred to as caulk.

cause célèbre (kōz′ s ā-lĕb′rə)   A specific issue or instance that arouses intense controversy or public debate, which becomes symbolic or representational of a larger issue or cause.

chamber (chām′bər)   In political terms, used to refer to the different parts of a governmental structure; for example, the U.S. Senate is sometimes referred to as the "upper chamber."

chapbook (chăp′book′)   A small book or pamphlet. The inexpensive format is often used by small or independent presses to produce volumes of limited or specialized appeal, such as poetry or political or religious tracts.

chargé d'affairs (shär-zhā′ d ə-fâr′, dä-)   A lower-level diplomat who in a particular case or period of time is required to substitute for an ambassador or high-ranking minister of state.

charisma (kə-rĭz′mə)   An indefinable personal quality sometimes found in leaders that inspires devotion and enthusiasm in others.

Chicano (chĭ-kä′nō)   A term used to describe someone of Mexican-American descent.

civil liberties (sĭv′əl lĭb′ər-tēz)   A general term used to refer to the rights, protections, and privileges granted to U.S. citizens under the Constitution.

civil rights movement (also **civil rights**)   The overall name given to the political, legal, and social struggle by African Americans to challenge and bring an end to segregation and segregation laws, and to establish full citizenship rights and racial equality.

class conflict (klăs kŏn′flĭkt′)   Differences or confrontation between members of different ethnic groups.

clause (klôz)   A subordinate detail or condition often associated with or part of a contract or law. Clauses often clarify or amend provisions set forth in the main body of the text.

clergyman (klûr′jē-mən)   A person who is a recognized member of the clergy, or ordained ministry, of a religion.

coalition (kō′ə-lĭsh′ən)   An alliance or union of two or more parties, usually temporary, established for the purpose of attaining goals favorable to those involved. The term is most often used to refer to political alliances.

coeducational (kōĕj′ə-kā′shə-nəl)   An institution of learning, such as a college or university, that is open to both men and women.

collective psyche (kə-lĕk′tĭv sī′kē)   A sociological or cultural term used to refer to the overall mood or feeling of a group of people.

colonialism (kə-lō′nē-ə-lĭz′əm)   A political philosophy or policy by which a governing nation maintains control over its foreign colonies. The term is also used to refer to an attitude in which a citizen of the ruling country may view citizens of a subject nation with a certain disdain or sense of superiority.

commandant (kŏm′ən-dănt′, -dänt ′)   One of several different terms used interchangeably to refer to the commanding officer in a military organization.

commission (kə-mĭsh′ən)   A group or body, similar to a committee, assembled for the purpose of dealing with specific duties, tasks, or issues.

communism (kŏm′yə-nĭz′əm)   A political theory and model for a government system in which all resources, businesses, and means of production are jointly owned by all members of the community.

comptroller (kən-trō′lər)   A variant of the word "controller," most often used to refer to the position or person responsible for auditing and/or supervising the financial affairs of a corporation or government body.

conduit (kŏn′dōo-ĭt, -d ĭt)   Literally a channel, such as a pipe, for conveying liquids, the term often refers to a source through which information or materiel is conveyed.

congregation (kŏng′grĭ-gā′shən)   The members of a specific religion who regularly worship together at a church or synagogue.

Congress (kŏng′grĭs)   A branch of the United States government, consisting of both the Senate and the House of Representatives, that represents the citizens from its members' state of origin. Congress acts to pass laws and make decisions on behalf of the citizens within the home state district.

Congress of Racial Equality (CORE)   A civil rights organization founded in 1942 by James Leonard Farmer to protect the rights of black Americans and seek equal opportunity in jobs, housing, and education for them. CORE advocates a policy of nonviolent, direct action, including sit-ins, voter registration drives, and large public demonstrations.

conscientious objector (kŏn′shē-ĕn′shəs ŏb′jĭktər)   The legal or political term for a person who, for reasons of conscience or belief, refuses to use weapons or serve in the armed forces.

consecrated (kŏn′sĭ-krāt′ ĭd)   Made holy or sacred.

conservationist (kŏn′sûr-vā′shə-nĭst)   Someone who advocates the preservation and protection of the environment.

conservative (kən-sûr′və-tĭv)   A term used to describe someone who is traditional in his or her views and values, and tends to oppose change merely for the sake of change.

conservatory (kən-sûr′və-tôr′ē, -t ōr′ē)   Most often used to refer to a school for music or drama.

consortium (kən-sôr′tē-əm, -sh ē-əm)   An association or combination of businesses, organizations, or individuals in a cooperative organization intended to achieve specific goals or objectives.

conspiracy (kən-spîr′ə-sē)   An agreement or plan between two or more individuals or organizations to perform an illegal or subversive act.

constituency (kən-stĭch′o͞o-ən-sē)   The voters or district represented by an elected legislator.

constitutional amendment (kŏn′stĭ-to͞o′shə-nəl ə-mĕnd′mənt)   The process by which changes are made, or new legislation is added, to the Constitution of the United States. Because the U.S. Congress does not have the authority to alter the Constitution itself, provision was made in Article V, which states that an amendment passes after a two-thirds vote of both houses of Congress or after the petition of two-thirds of the state legislatures. An amendment must then be ratified by the legislatures of three-fourths of the states or by "constitutional conventions" in three-fourths of the states. There are currently twenty-seven amendments to the Constitution, of which the first ten, added immediately after the ratification of the Constitution itself, are referred to as the Bill of Rights.

constitutionalist (kŏn′stĭ-to͞o′shə-nəlĭst)   A person who believes in or advocates the interpretation of rights or laws as specifically outlined in the U.S. Constitution.

convalescence (kŏn′və-lĕs′əns)   The period of time needed to return to health after an illness.

corecipient (kō- rĭ-sĭp′ē-ənt)   A person who receives something, such as an award or prize, in conjunction with or at the same time as another person.

counterculture (koun′tər kŭl′chər)   A sub- or alternate culture or aesthetic that exists along with and in contrast to the dominant culture.

counterrevolutionary (koun′tər rĕv′ə-lōō′shə-nĕr′ē)   A revolutionary whose goals or objectives are to depose or undo the administration or effects of a previous revolution.

creed (krēd)   A belief, usually referring to religion or faith.

Creole (krē′ōl′)   Most often used to refer to a person descended from the original French settlers of Louisiana, the term also describes the French dialect or culture of these people, or a person of mixed black and European descent.

crusade (krōō-sād′)   Originally referring to any of the military expeditions undertaken by the Christian leaders of Europe in the Middle Ages to recover the Holy Land from the Moslems, now commonly used to describe an organized, passionate campaign or movement for a specific cause. Its use is often meant to imply religious or spiritual overtones.

cum laude (kōōm lou ′də)   A Latin term, literally translated as *with praise*, that is used to express academic distinction. The term is often used as a classification during graduation of the students receiving top honors.

curriculum (kə-rĭk′yə-ləm)   All the courses of study offered at an educational institution, or the related courses of one specific field of study.

dean (dēn)   In the academic community, the term refers to an administrative officer who is in charge of a specific faculty, college, or division within the university.

debilitated (dĭ-bĭl′ĭ-tā′tĭd)   Someone or something that shows an impairment of energy or strength.

Declaration of Independence   The document, written by Thomas Jefferson and adopted by the Second Continental Congress on July 4, 1776, that outlined the complaints of the American colonies against the king of England, and declared them in revolt from Great Britain, and a free and independent nation.

defrock (dē-frŏk′)   A religious term referring to stripping someone of his privileges and functions within the church.

delegation (dĕl′ĭ-gā′shən)   A group of representatives from a specific group or organization that speaks for the whole in matters dealing with outside groups.

demilitarization (dē-mĭl′ĭ-tə-rīz′ ā′shən)   The process of eliminating or removing the military force from an area.

democracy (dĭ-mŏk′rə-sē)   A form of government in which the political and social units are ruled or decided by the citizens, or through their elected representatives.

democrat (dĕm′ə-krăt′)   A member of a political party of the United States, or a general term used to describe someone who is an advocate of the political system of democracy.

democratization (dĭ-mŏk′rətĭ-zā′shən)   To place under the system of democracy, in which a country is ruled by its citizens, or representatives of the citizens, rather than by a monarchy or other nonelective system.

demographic (dĕm′ə-grăf′ĭk)   A classification based on the characteristics of human populations. The classifications can include population, race, growth, and vital statistics.

demonstration (dĕm′ən-strā′shən)   An organized form of protest, often political in nature, in which a public display of opposition is made.

desegregation (dē-sĕg′rĭ-gāt′ shən)   The opposite of segregation, which separates one group from another, desegregation refers to the end of the separation. Most often used in reference to the civil rights struggles of the 1960s, which sought to end the forced segregation of blacks and whites.

détente   A policy or state of relaxing or relaxed tensions between two nations.

diplomat (dĭp′lə-măt′)   A person who is skilled in the practice of conducting international business or relations.

disarmament (dĭs-är′mə-mənt)   The act of removing or laying down arms, often referring to a defeated military force.

discrimination (dĭ-skrĭm′ə-nā′shən)   An action or situation in which an individual or group is treated differently from another based on factors other than individual or personal reasons, usually because of his or her membership in a social or racial group or category. The term is most often used to refer to the preferential treatment given to white Americans as opposed to black Americans on the basis of race, or to men as opposed to women.

disfranchise (dĭs-frăn′chīz′)   In general, meaning to deprive of any of the rights and privileges of citizenship, but used most often to refer specifically to taking away the right to vote.

dissent (dĭ-sĕnt′)   To disagree or differ in feeling or opinion.

dissertation (dĭs′ər-tā′shən)   A lengthy, formal treatise or thesis, most often one written by a candidate for the doctoral degree at a university.

district (dĭs′trĭkt)   A division of an area such as a city or state, for administrative or political purposes.

divinity (dĭ-vĭn′ĭ-tē)   A term referring to possessing the quality or state of being divine or godlike.

doctrine (dŏk′trĭn)   The collective term for the body of principles, or beliefs, accepted by a religious, political, or philosophical group.

doctrine of popular sovereignty   In 19th-century United States, the right of the inhabitants of a territory, when applying or being considered for statehood, to determine whether their state would sanction or disallow slavery.

domestic (də-mĕs′tĭk)   A term referring to the internal affairs of a country. The term also refers to affairs relating to a family or household.

draft (drăft)   A governmental order of nonvoluntary enrollment in the armed forces, most often during a time of war.

dysentery (dĭs′ən-tĕr′ē)   An inflammatory disorder of the lower intestinal tract, usually caused by a bacterial or parasitic infection and resulting in pain, fever, and severe diarrhea, often accompanied by the passage of blood and mucus.

eclecticism (ĭ-klĕk′tə-sĭz′əm)   The grouping of objects that have no relation to one another.

ecology (ĭ-kŏl′ə-jē)   The science or study of the relationships between living things and their environment.

ecosystem (ĕk′ō-sĭs′təm)   The collective term for all living things and the environment of a particular area, most often identified by the interlocking relationships of the various parts.

edict (ē′dĭkt′)   A proclamation, which has the force of a law, that is issued by an authority.

egalitarian (ĭ-găl′ĭ-târ′ē-ən)   The affirmation of one who professes political, economic, and social equality for all people.

Electoral College (ĭ-lĕk′tər-əl kŏl′ĭj)   The collective name for the representatives, or electors, who choose the president and vice president of the United States. Each state is entitled to a certain number of electors based on the total number of senators and representatives it has in the U.S. Congress, and the District of Columbia has three. The process by which the Electoral College selects the president and vice president is detailed in the U.S. Constitution, and was later modified by the 12th and 23rd Amendments.

elephantiasis (ĕl′ə-fən-tī′ə-sĭs)   A chronic, often extreme enlargement and hardening of tissue, especially of the legs and external genitals, resulting from lymphatic obstruction and usually caused by infestation of the lymph glands and vessels with a parasitic worm.

emancipation (ĭ-măn′sə-pā′shən)   Literally meaning to free from bondage, oppression, or restraint, most often used to refer to freedom from slavery, as in the Emancipation Proclamation.

Emancipation Proclamation (ĭ-măn′sə-pā′shən prŏk′lə-mā′shən)   Proclamation issued by U.S. president Abraham Lincoln on January 1, 1863, effectively ending slavery in the United States. Although excluding some slaves in areas of the Confederacy held by Union armies, the Emancipation Proclamation was instrumental in leading to the enactment of the 13th Amendment to the Constitution in 1865, by which slavery was wholly abolished.

embassy (ĕm′bə-sē)   A building containing the offices of an ambassador and staff from a foreign country.

emeritus (ĭ-mĕr′ĭ-təs)   A retired person who retains an honorary title corresponding to the position he or she held immediately before retirement.

Emmy (ĕm′ē)   The commonly used name for the awards, presented annually by the Academy of Television Arts and Sciences, for outstanding achievement in television.

enclave (ĕn′klāv′, ŏ n′-)   Most often used to refer to a clearly marked or defined area contained within another, most often defined by ethnicity or race.

endorsement (ĕn-dôrs′mənt)   Used mostly as an advertising or public relations tool, an endorsement is a public statement of approval or support by an individual for a specific product.

Enlightenment (ĕn-līt′n-mənt)   A philosophical movement of the 18th century that emphasized the use of reason to question previously accepted practices.

entourage (ŏn′tŏŏ-räzh′)   A group of attendants or servants, often surrounding and supporting a person of power or influence.

entrepreneur (ŏn′trə-prə-nûr′, -n ŏŏr′)   A person who organizes and operates a business venture, commonly used to refer to people who seek business opportunities on their own rather than as part of an organization or corporation.

equality (ĭ-kwŏl′ĭ-tē)   In a political and social sense, the right of each individual to the same opportunities and legal protections as any other, without regard to race, religion, or other differences.

eschatological (ĭ-skăt′l-ŏj′ĭ-kəl)   The branch of theology that is concerned with the end of the world or of humankind.

eschew (ĕs-chŏŏ′)   To avoid or shun.

espionage (ĕs′pē-ə-näzh′, -n ĭj)   Spying.

ethnic slur (ĕth′nĭk slûr)   An insulting or derogatory comment that includes specific reference to ethnicity or race.

ethnicity (ĕth-nĭs′ĭ-tē)   A sociological classification referring to a person's ethnic character, background, or affiliation.

ethnocentric (ĕth′nō-sĕn′trĭk)   The belief or philosophy that one's ethnic or racial heritage is superior to another's.

ethnology (ĕth-nŏl′ə-jē)   A subdivision of anthropology concerned with the study of cultures in their traditional form, and their adaptation to modern influences.

eulogy (yŏŏ′lə-jē)   A spoken or written tribute, most often given when a person has died.

evangelism (ĭ-văn′jə-lĭz′əm)   The preaching or spreading of a religion, as with missionary work. The term is often used to refer to the preaching of a type of minister who attempts to bring conversion to large masses of people, and carries connotations of showmanship and personality.

exclusionary (ĭk-sklŏŏzhə-nĕr′ē)   A type of act or practice that by design excludes or removes something or someone from its effects.

expatriate (ĕk-spā′trē-āt′)   A person who has left his or her native country, usually through banishment or exile, to live in another country.

expostulate (ĭk-spŏs′chə-lāt′)   A term meaning to reason earnestly with someone in an effort to dissuade or correct.

expropriation (ĕk-sprō′prē-ā′shən)   The taking or acquiring of property belonging to another. The term often refers to the taking of private property, such as land, by the government for public use.

extortion (ĭk-stôr′shən)   To obtain something, often money or other material goods, by the use of force, coercion, or intimidation.

fakir (fə-kîr)   A Hindu beggar, supported by the church, who performs feats of magic or endurance.

fascism (făsh′ĭz′əm)   A system of government that follows the principles of a centralized authority under a dictator, strict economic controls, censorship, and the use of terror to suppress opposition.

fasting (făst′ĭng)   The act of abstaining from food, often for religious reasons or in protest.

Federal Bureau of Investigation (FBI)   An agency of the United States Department of Justice, established in 1908 as the principal domestic investigative agency of the U.S. government. Its jurisdiction extends to a variety of matters of federal law, including bank robbery, racketeering, kidnapping, and drug enforcement.

fellowship (fĕl′ō-shĭp′)   The condition of sharing similar interests, ideals, or experiences, as by reason of profession, religion, or nationality. The term can also refer to a reward or grant given for outstanding academic achievements.

feminist (fĕm′ə-nĭst) (also **feminism** [fĕm′ə-nĭz′əm])   A person who believes in the social, political, and economic equality of both sexes, and the political or philosophical belief that people of both sexes should be treated equally socially and under the law.

field research (fēld rĭ-sûrch′)   Scholarly research that is conducted on-site or at the source of the object being studied.

fieldwork (fēld′wûrk′)   Most commonly used to refer to scientific work that is done firsthand outside of the laboratory or office, that is, in the field.

fiscal (fĭs′kəl)   A term referring to finances and financial information, often relating to government spending, revenues, and debt.

folklore (fōk′lôr′, -l ōr′)   The overall name for the traditions, beliefs, legends, and practices of a people or ethnic group, most often passed from generation to generation through the oral tradition.

formative (fôr′mə-tĭv)   A term referring to someone who is susceptible to transformation by growth and development.

forum (fôr′əm, f ōr′-)   A public meeting or open discussion used to voice ideas, often via television, radio, or newspaper.

foundation (foun-dā′shən)   An institution founded and supported by an endowment.

fraternal (frə-tûr′nəl)   Of or relating to brotherhood. The term is often used to refer to the relationship between members of a guild or union, or to members of a college fraternity.

fraternity (frə-tûr′nĭ-tē)   Most often used to refer to one of the organizations of male college students, the term also describes a group associated by similar backgrounds, interests, or occupations, such as a club or guild.

free state (frē stāt)   In the pre–Civil War United States, one of the states that did not sanction slavery.

frugality (frōō-găl′ĭ-tē)   A term referring to someone who is conservative in the expenditure of money or the use of material resources.

fundamentalism (fŭn′də-mĕn′tl-ĭz′əm)   A social movement, or point of view, characterized by the rigid belief in the basic principles of one's society.

G.I. Bill   Also known as the Serviceman's Readjustment Act of 1944, or the G.I. Bill of Rights, the federal legislation that provided unemployment allowances, education support, and home, farm, and business loans for veterans. It is most commonly used to refer to its provisions for educational assistance.

Garveyites   Followers of black political leader Marcus Garvey (1887–1940), who in 1914 founded the Universal Negro Improvement Association and the African Communities League.

General Assembly (jĕn′ər-əl ə-sĕm′blē)   The main deliberative body of the United Nations, comprising one representative of each member nation.

geology (jē-ŏl′ə-jē)   The scientific study of the origin, history, and structure of the earth.

ghetto (gĕt′ō)   An Italian term used originally to refer to a specific area of a city where Jews were required by law to reside, it has come to mean any section of a city, often depressed, occupied primarily by one or more minority groups, who live there because of social, economic, or legal pressure.

glaciology (glā′shē-ŏl′ə-jē)   The scientific study of glaciers and their effects on the landscape.

gospel (gŏs′pəl)   A style of music, usually religious in lyrical content, sung by a choir or group of people.

gradualist (grăj′o͞o-ə-lĭst)   Someone who practices a belief in or the policy of gradually advancing toward a goal, often in slow stages.

graft (grăft)   To unite a shoot or bud of a plant with a growing plant by placing them in close contact with each other. The term can also refer to money or an advantage gained by unscrupulous or illegal means.

Grammy Awards (grăm′ē ə-wôrd′s)   A service mark used for any of the statuettes awarded by the National Academy of Recording Arts and Sciences for excellence in the recording industry.

grassroots (grăs′ro͞ots′, -r o͞ots′)   A term used to describe people or a society living at a common, local level. In politics, a "grassroots campaign" is one that takes place at a basic level, dealing directly with individuals and communities, and gains power and influence through word of mouth.

Great Depression (grāt dĭ-prĕsh′ən)   The worst and longest economic collapse in modern industrial society, the Great Depression in the United States began in late 1929 and lasted through the early 1940s, spreading to most of the world's other industrial countries.

groundswell (ground′swĕl′)   A sudden gathering of force, often associated with that of public opinion.

guerrilla (gə-rĭl′ə)   From the Spanish word *guerra*, meaning war, a term used to refer to a soldier who is a member of a small, irregular military force that operates in small bands in hostile or occupied territory, harassing and working to undermine and disrupt the enemy. "Guerrilla warfare" refers to an organized campaign along these lines.

guru (go͞or′o͞o, g o͞o-ro͞o′)   From the Sanskrit *guruh*, meaning heavy or venerable, a term often used to refer to a spiritual or philosophical teacher or guide.

hallmark (hôl′märk′)   A mark of quality or excellence.

Hasidic (ᴋʜä′sĭdĭk)   Someone who is a member of a Jewish movement based on mysticism that was founded in eastern Europe in the 18th century.

hate crime (hāt krīm)   A phrase that refers to a crime or act of violence committed for reasons of bias or prejudice, usually against an ethnic minority.

hegemony (hǐ-jěm′ə-nē, h ěj′ə-mō′nē)   The predominant influence of one state over another.

heir apparent (âr ə-păr′ənt)   A legal term referring to an heir whose right to inheritance cannot be changed by law provided he or she survives an ancestor.

heroism (hěr′ō-ĭz′əm)   Behavior that is gallant and brave in nature or possesses the characteristics or qualities associated with a courageous or selfless act.

heterogeneous (hět′ər-ə-jē′nē-əs, -j ēn′yəs)   Something composed of a number of different or varied parts. The term is often used to refer to the ethnic or racial mix of an area or neighborhood.

heterosexual (hět′ə-rō-sěk′shoō-əl)   A term referring to someone who is sexually attracted to a person of the opposite sex.

hierarchy (hī′ə-rär′kē)   Most often used to refer to the structure of authority in a group or organization, ranked by authority or ability.

homophobia (hō′mə-fō′bē-ə)   An aversion to gay or homosexual people or their lifestyle or culture.

homosexual (hō′mə-sěk′shoō-əl)   A term referring to someone attracted to a person of the same sex.

hospice (hŏs′pĭs)   A shelter or lodging for travelers, pilgrims, or the destitute that is often maintained by a monastic order.

house arrest (hous ə-rěst′)   A term referring to a confinement to one's quarters or house as opposed to prison.

housing project (hou′zĭng prŏj′ěkt)   A publicly funded housing development for low-income families.

humanism (hyoō′mə-nĭz′əm)   A philosophy or belief that emphasizes the dignity and worth of individual human beings.

humanitarian (hyoō-măn′ĭ-târ′ē-ən)   Someone who is devoted to the promotion of the well-being of humans.

iconoclastic (ī-kŏn′ə-klăst′ ĭk)   A term used to describe an attack made as an attempt to overthrow traditional or popular ideas or institutions.

idealism (ī-dē′ə-lĭz′əm)   The philosophy or practice of envisioning things in an ideal form. The term is often used to describe the subject of a piece of artwork or literature.

ideology (ī′dē-ŏl′ə-jē, ĭ d′ē-)   The collective term for the body of ideas and principles reflecting the social needs and aspirations of an individual, group, or culture.

immigration (ĭm′ĭ-grā′shən) (also **immigrant** [ĭm′ĭ-grənt])   The process of entering and settling into a country or region that is not one's native land.

imperialism (ĭm-pîr′ē-ə-lĭz′əm)   In politics, a policy of extending a nation's rule by acquiring new territories or imposing economic and/or political control over other nations.

in absentia (ĭn ă b-sěn′shə, -sh ē-ə)   A Latin term meaning absent or not present.

inaugurate (ĭn-ô′gyə-rāt′)   To induct a person, often a member of government, into office by a formal ceremony.

incarcerate (ĭn-kär′sə-rāt′)   To imprison someone, or confine a person to jail.

incumbent (ĭn-kŭm′bənt)   A term used to refer to the person currently holding a political office.

indigenous (ĭn-dĭj′ə-nəs)   A person or object originating and living in an area or environment.

inductee (ĭn′dŭk-tē′)   A term often referring to military service for someone who is newly admitted to a group or organization.

infidelity (ĭn′fĭ-dĕl′ĭ-tē)   Unfaithfulness to a sexual partner, especially a spouse.

injunction (ĭn-jŭngk′shən)   A command, directive, or order. The term is also used in law to refer to a court order prohibiting a person or group from a specific course of action.

integration (ĭn′tĭ-grā′shən)   The incorporation of diverse ethnic or social groups into a unified society. The term is most often used to refer to the process of racial integration, by which black Americans and other ethnic minorities are afforded the same rights, status, and opportunities as whites. True integration implies that an individual's ability to enjoy any benefits of society is not denied or restricted by reason of race, religion, or national origin.

intelligentsia (ĭn-tĕl′ə-jənsē′ə)   The intellectual elite.

interracial (ĭn′tər-rā′shəl)   Of or pertaining to relations and interaction between different ethic races and social groups.

Islam (ĭs-läm′)   A religion based on a single deity that is characterized by the acceptance of the doctrine of submission to God, and to Mohammed as the chief and last prophet of God. The term is also used to refer to the people or nations who practice the religion.

Jamesian (jām′zē-ən)   A term referring to the philosophy and teachings of William James, an American psychologist and philosopher who based his studies in pragmatism and functionalism.

Jesuit (jĕzh′ōō-ĭt, j ĕz′ōō-, -y ōō-)   A member of the Society of Jesus, an order founded by Saint Ignatius of Loyola in 1534.

Jim Crow laws   A slang term describing the group of laws that enforced the segregation of blacks in the U.S. South.

journalism (jûr′nə-lĭz′əm)   The collecting, writing, editing, and presentation of news or news articles in newspapers and magazines, as well as radio and television broadcasts.

keynote speech (kē′nōt′ spēch)   An opening address, often delivered at a political convention, that outlines the issues being considered.

Koran (kə-răn′)   The sacred text of Islam, considered by Moslems to contain the revelations of God (Allah) to the prophet Mohammed.

Ku Klux Klan   A social group characterized as being white supremacists, who adhere to the belief that the white, Aryan race is superior, and that blacks and Jews, among others, are inferior and unequal.

land mine (lănd mīn)   An explosive device usually buried just below the surface of the ground.

laureate (lôr′ē-ĭt, l ôr′-)   A term used to describe someone who is worthy of the greatest honor or distinction in his or her field of expertise. The term often refers to literary masters.

lay (lā)   A term referring to people who are not members of a specific profession or specialized field. The term is often used to describe church members who are involved in the church's functions but are not ordained ministers or priests.

leftist (lĕf′tĭst)   A term used to describe someone who follows the belief in a centralized government to control many aspects of citizens' lives, including welfare, health benefits, and education. Socialists and communists are on the leftist end of the political spectrum.

legacy (lĕg′ə-sē)   Something that is handed down from an ancestor or predecessor. The term also refers to money or property that is given in a will.

legislation (lĕj′ĭ-slā′shən)   The process of debating, amending, and passing laws, or the law or laws themselves.

leprosy (lĕp′rə-sē)   A chronic, mildly contagious disease most often found in tropical and subtropical regions, which is caused by bacteria and characterized by ulcers of the skin, bone, and soft tissue ultimately resulting in deformity, paralysis, and loss of sensation.

libel (lī′bəl)   The legal term for a written, published, or pictorial statement that maliciously damages another person's reputation.

literacy (lĭt′ər-ə-sē)   The condition or quality of being able to read and write.

litigation (lĭt′ĭ-gā shən′)   Legal proceedings, such as the bringing of charges, or a trial.

lobby (lŏb′ē)   A political term referring to a group of people whose goal is to influence legislators to favor a specific cause.

lobbyist (lŏb′ēĭst)   A person, often a hired professional, who lobbies for and represents the interests of an organization, group, or individual.

lyceum (lī-sē′əm)   A Latin term for a hall where public lectures and concerts are presented.

lynching (lĭnch′ĭng)   The execution, usually by hanging, of a person without a legal trial.

magna cum laude (mäg′nə k o͞om lou ′də)   A scholastic honor given to a student who has achieved high academic distinction.

magnate (măg′nāt′)   A powerful or influential person. The term is often used to refer to business or industry leaders.

mainstream (mān′strēm′)   A social term referring to the prevailing thoughts, influences, or activities of a specific area or period.

malaria (mə-lâr′ē-ə)   An infectious disease, most often contracted from mosquitoes, which is characterized by chills and fever, and affects the operation of the liver, kidneys, and other vital organs.

manifest destiny (măn′ə-fĕst′ dĕs′tə-nē)   A policy allowing expansion within a specific location that is defended as necessary or good for the community. The term is most often associated with a 19th-century doctrine that the United States had the right and duty to expand throughout the North American continent.

Marxism (märk′sĭz′əm)   The political and economic ideas of Karl Marx and Friedrich Engels. The term specifically refers to a system of thought in which the concept of class struggle plays a primary role in analyzing Western society and in understanding its allegedly inevitable development from middle-class oppression under capitalism to a socialist society such as communism.

materialism (mə-tîr′ē-ə-lĭz′əm)   A philosophical theory or doctrine that states that physical matter is the ultimate reality, and that everything else, including human consciousness, can be explained in physical terms.

maternal (mə-tûr′nəl)   A term referring to characteristics most often associated with a mother or motherhood.

mediator (mē′dē-ā′tər)   Someone who acts as a neutral party to assist others in resolving a dispute.

menial (mē′nē-əl)   A job or task that is considered low, base, or fitting a servant. The term is also used to describe someone who works as a domestic servant.

mentor (mĕn′tôr′)   A trusted counselor or teacher. The term is most often used to describe the teacher who has had significant impact or provided great guidance in the shaping of a career or lifestyle.

Methodism (mĕth′ə-dĭz′əm) (also **Methodist** [mĕth′ə-dĭst])   A Protestant religious movement that began in Oxford, England, in 1729. The name refers to the methodical manner in which the first members carried out their religious duties and rituals. Among the founders of Methodism were John and Charles Wesley. Among its primary tenets are a belief in free will, Christian perfection, and personal salvation through faith.

migrant farmworkers   Transient, unskilled manual laborers, often illegal immigrants, forced to travel from place to place following employment opportunities in farmland and orchards.

migration (mī-grā′shən)   The act of moving from one place to another as a group.

milestone (mīl′stōn′)   An important event or turning point in a person's life, a nation's history, or the advancement of a field of study.

militant (mĭl′ĭ-tənt)   A person, political party, or course of action that is combative or aggressive, usually for a cause or to achieve a specific objective.

militarist (mĭl′ĭ-tə-rĭst)   A person who actively promotes or glories in the ideals and traditions of the professional military class, or a person who believes that armed force is the solution to a great variety of international conflicts.

militia (mə-lĭsh′ə)   The term used to describe an army made up of ordinary citizens rather than professional or career soldiers. A militia would be intended to function as a reserve or contingent force, available to be called on in case of emergency.

millinery (mĭl′ə-nĕr′ē)   Articles, chiefly hats, that are produced by a milliner who is responsible for designing, making, trimming, and selling.

minority (mə-nôr′ĭ-tē, -n ŏr′-, m ī-)   A racial, religious, political, national, or other group fewer in number than the larger group of which it is part.

missionary (mĭsh′ə-nĕr′ē)   A member of a particular religious organization whose tradition is to "witness" by word and deed to the beliefs of their religion, so that others may come to know and understand it.

monk (mŭngk)   A Christian brother, living in a monastery, following a life devoted to rituals and disciplines defined by his "order."

monopoly (mə-nŏp′ə-lē)   An economic situation in which only a single company sells or produces an item or service, allowing it to control availability and pricing.

mosque (mŏsk)   A house of worship in the Moslem faith.

muckraker (mŭk′rāk′ ər)   One who searches for and exposes the misconduct of those in public or political life.

mulatto (moō-lăt′ō, -lä ′tō, my oō-)   A term used to describe someone with one white parent and one black parent.

multiculturalism (mŭl′tē-kŭl′chər-əlĭz′əm)   The belief or practice of combining influences from a variety of different cultures and ethnic influences in a single society.

multilateral (mŭl′tĭ-lăt′ər-əl)   Literally meaning "having many sides," the term is most often used in politics to describe an agreement or treaty that involves or is agreed to by two or more nations or sides.

municipal (myoō-nĭs′ə-pəl)   A term referring to an area that is locally self-governed, rather than reliant on another city or town for government rule.

mural (myoōr′əl)   Most often used to describe a type of large painting applied directly to a wall or ceiling.

mysticism (mĭs′tĭ-sĭz′əm)   A belief in or consciousness of a transcendent or higher reality, such as God or spirits.

NAACP   An acronym for the National Association for the Advancement of Colored People, an organization founded in 1909 to protect the rights and improve the living and working conditions of black Americans.

nationalism (năsh′ə-nə-lĭz′əm)   The devotion to the beliefs and interests of a specific nation.

Native American   A term used to describe the inhabitants of the American continents prior to the arrival of the European settlers.

New Deal   The collective name given to a large-scale program of domestic government policies enacted under President Franklin D. Roosevelt, especially those intended to counteract the effects of the Great Depression, between 1933 and 1938. Programs ranged from the creation of new organizations such as the Federal Deposit Insurance Corporation (FDIC) to regulate banking and provide protection for depositors, to government subsidies and public relief efforts such as the Work Projects Administration, which put unemployed people to work on public projects.

Nobel Peace Prize (nō-bĕl′ pēs prīz)   An annual award granted to the person or persons, not more than three, who "shall have done the most or the best work for fraternity between nations, for the abolition or reduction of standing armies and for the holding and promoting of peace congresses." Established in the will of Swedish chemist, inventor, and philanthropist Alfred Bernhard Nobel, the winner(s) receives a cash award and a diploma bearing his or her name and field of achievement.

obstetrician (ŏb′stĭ-trĭsh′ən)   A doctor who deals specifically with matters relating to the care of women during pregnancy and childbirth and the period that follows delivery.

occupation (ŏk′yə-pā′shən)   In military terms, a state in which a foreign country is under the rule of and occupied by troops of another country.

opportunism (ŏp′ər-tōō′nĭzm)   The practice or trait of taking advantage of opportunities that present themselves, sometimes without regard for principles or consequences, in order to achieve a specific end.

oppression (ə-prĕsh′ən)   To be kept down or denied rights through an unjust use of force or authority. The term is often used to refer to social and legal discrimination against certain ethic groups.

oral tradition (ôr′əl trə-dĭsh′ən)   The term used to refer to the preservation of personal or cultural history by word of mouth, without written documents, usually in the form of epic songs, stories, or poetry.

oratory (ôr′ə-tôr′ē)   The art of speaking or speechmaking, especially speeches designed to influence the judgments or feelings of those listening.

ordained (ôr-dān′d)   In religious orders, one who has been formally invested with ministerial or priestly authority.

orthodoxy (ôr′thə-dŏk′sē)   An accepted or established doctrine or creed, and the adherence to it. The term "orthodox" is also often used to refer to the most conservative or traditional element, especially of a religion.

ostracize (ŏs′trə-sīz′)   To banish or otherwise exclude from a group or organization.

pacifism (păs′ə-fĭz′əm)   An ideology or belief that opposes war and other violence as a means of political gain. The goals of pacifism are to maintain a state of peace, eliminate the potential causes of conflict, to settle disagreements through an outside party, and to ensure that the conflict resolutions are followed by those involved.

pamphlet (păm′flĭt)   A small, informal publication, often political in nature, used to express a specific viewpoint or opinion.

Pan-Africanism (păn- ăf′rĭ-kə-nĭz′əm)   A movement that seeks to unite and promote the welfare and unity of all people of African descent or race. Among its early adherents was civil rights leader W. E. B. Du Bois (1868–1963), who maintained a cultural and political interest in Africa throughout his life, and was called the "father of Pan-Africanism."

paralegal (păr′ə-lē′gəl)   A person who has been specially trained to assist an attorney.

paramilitary (păr′ə-mĭl′ĭ-tĕr′ē)   A group of civilians who are organized in a military fashion.

parliament (pär′lə-mənt)   In some countries, a branch of government, similar to the U.S. Congress, that is responsible for enacting laws, levying taxes, and serving as the highest court of appeal.

parole (pə-rōl′)   The release of a prisoner who has not yet served his or her entire sentence on the condition of good behavior. The criminal is monitored while on parole, and any criminal activity he or she is involved in will result in being returned to jail.

partisan (pär′tĭ-zən)   Someone who is a strong supporter of a party, cause, idea, or person.

pastor (păs′tər)   Most commonly used to refer to a Christian minister of a Protestant order, with spiritual charge over a specific group or congregation.

patriarchal (pā′trē-är′kəl)   A type of social system in which the father is the head of the household, and ancestry is determined through the paternal, or father's, line.

patrilineal (păt′rə-lĭn′ē-əl) (also **paternal** [pə-tûr′nəl])   The determination or account of ancestry or lineage through the paternal (male) line.

penitentiary (pĕn′ĭ-tĕn′shə-rē)   A prison for those who have committed major crimes, such as murder.

pesticide (pĕs′tĭ-sīd′)   Any one of a group of chemicals that are used to kill insects or other pests.

petition (pə-tĭsh′ən)   A request or entreaty, often in written form, submitted to a higher authority by an individual or a group.

peyote (pā-ō′tē)   The button-like tubercles, or small protrusions, of a type of cactus native to Mexico and the American southwest, sometimes chewed as a narcotic drug, and used in religious or spiritual rituals by certain Native American peoples. Also known as mescaline.

philanthropy (fĭ-lăn′thrə-pē)   In business, a term used to describe the ongoing practice or philosophy, usually of an individual, of giving to or establishing charitable or humanistic causes or foundations.

philosophy (fĭ-lŏs′ə-fē)   In general terms, a speculative inquiry into the source and nature of human knowledge, or the system and ideas based on such thinking.

pickaninny (pĭk′ə-nĭn′ē)   A slang or derogative term for a young black child.

picketing (pĭk′ĭtĭng)   A form of protest or demonstration, often set up during a strike, in the form of a line intended to block or discourage nonstriking employees from entering a place of business.

plantation (plăn-tā′shən)   A term originating in colonial times, a plantation is a settlement or piece of land used to grow crops and house the workers who tend the crops. The land was independently owned and self-contained, often housing the owner of the land as well.

plaudit (plô′dĭt)   An enthusiastic expression of praise or approval.

Politburo (pŏl′ĭt-byōor′ō, p ə-lĭt′-) The chief political and executive committee of a communist party.

political asylum (pə-lĭt′ĭ-kəl ə-sī′ləm) In political terms, a type of protection extended by one nation to the citizen of another who has fled his or her native land out of fear of persecution for political beliefs.

popular vote (pŏp′yə-lər vōt) Most often used to refer to the count, in U.S. presidential elections, of the votes cast by citizens, as opposed to the electoral vote.

populism (pŏp′yə-lĭz′əm) A political belief that governmental power should be in the hands of the people, or population, rather than corporations or the rich.

posse (pŏs′ē) A group of people summoned by a sheriff or other law officer to aid in law enforcement.

poverty (pŏv′ər-tē) An economic condition in which people lack the income to obtain the minimal levels of such essentials as food, clothing, medical services, and housing necessary to maintain an adequate standard of living. In a strict sense, the "poverty line" is defined as those households earning a certain percentage below the average family income.

pragmatism (prăg′mə-tĭz′əm) The belief that the purpose of thoughts is to guide action, and that the effect of an idea is more important than its origin.

preparatory school (prĭ-păr′ə-tôr′ē skōol) Commonly called "prep school," a private educational establishment that serves to prepare students for college.

preservationism (prĕz′ər-vā′shə-nĭzm) A social movement that focuses and advocates the preservation of natural areas, historical sites, and endangered species.

primary (prī′mĕr′ē, -m ə-rē) In politics, the process prior to an election in which candidates of the same political party compete in a vote or series of votes, in order to choose a candidate.

probation (prō-bā′shən) Similar to parole, in which a convict is released from prison on the basis of good behavior.

progressive (prə-grĕs′ĭv) A social term referring to the belief in advancement or proceeding in steps.

Prohibition (prō′ə-bĭsh′ən) The legal ban on the production and sale of alcoholic beverages. The Prohibition Act, also referred to as the Volstead Act, went into effect on January 16, 1919, and was repealed on December 5, 1933.

protégé (prō′tə-zhā′, pr ō′tə-zhā′) A person who is provided for, and trained in a specific career by an influential person within that field.

pulpiteer (pōol′pĭt, p ŭl′tîr) A common or slang term for an orator or minister known for eloquent or emphatic public speaking from a pulpit or other forum.

Quaker (kwā′kər) A member of the Society of Friends, a Christian denomination of the mid-17th century that rejected formal sacraments, creeds, priesthood, and violence.

quota (kwō′tə) In legal or political terms, a predetermined number or percentage of a business's new hires that must be members of a minority.

racial separatism (rā′shəl sĕp′ər-ə-tĭzm)   A political or philosophical belief that advocates the separation of human groups into distinct physical and political entities along racial lines.

racist (also **racism** [rā′sĭz′əm])   The belief that a racial or ethnic group is inferior because of its race or nationality.

radical (răd′ĭ-kəl)   A political term used to describe those who believe in extreme and revolutionary changes within a society or government.

radicalism (răd′ĭ-kə-lĭz′əm)   A term that refers collectively to the actions or philosophies of radicals.

ratification (răt′ə-fĭ-kā′shən)   The formal process of accepting, often by means of a vote or other consensus.

realism (rē′ə-lĭz′əm)   A philosophical discipline inclined toward truth and pragmatism. In art, the representation of objects as they actually appear.

Reconstruction (rē′kən-strŭk′shən)   The term used for the rebuilding plan established for the southern, formerly Confederate states following the American Civil War.

Red Guard (rĕd gärd)   A youth organization, mobilized in communist China by Mao Zedong following the failure of a number of political programs in the 1950s, to attack his political rivals and establish "Chairman Mao" as the uncontested, almost "godlike" ruler of China.

redistricting (rē-dĭs′trĭktĭng)   Also called "gerrymandering," after Governor Eldridge Gerry of Massachusetts, the calculated restructuring of electoral or congressional districts to give the ruling party an unfair advantage in getting its candidates elected. It often involved altering the physical limits of a district into strange shapes in order to include a particular area inhabited by enough members of the party to give it a majority.

referendum (rĕf′ə-rĕn′dəm)   The submission of a proposed measure for direct public vote. The term also refers to the vote itself.

reformer (rĭ-fôrm′ər)   In political terms, a person who seeks to bring about change, often in laws and government policies, by means of the established political systems.

regime (rə-zhēm′, rĭ-)   A government or administration in power.

regiment (rĕj′ə-mənt)   A military unit made up of ground troops, consisting of at least two battalions.

reincarnation (rē′ĭn-kär-nāshən)   The rebirth of a soul or personality into another body. Reincarnation in one form or another is part of many major religions.

repatriation (rē-pā′trē-ā′shən)   The process of returning someone to his or her native country.

repression (rĭ-prĕsh′ən)   In social or sociological terms, the deliberate denial of equal rights, usually to members of a minority.

republican (rĭ-pŭb′lĭ-kən)   A member of a political party of the United States, or one who advocates a republican form of government, that is, a government in which the supreme power resides in a body of citizens entitled to vote and is exercised by representatives elected by and responsible to them and governing according to law.

reservation (rĕz′ər-vā′shən)   Land set aside by a government that provides a place for a specific group of people to live. This land is "reserved" for them to use. Most often used to refer to the areas set aside for the forced relocation of Native Americans during the settlement of the American west.

rhetoric (rĕt′ər-ĭk)   The study or art of the use of language and persuasion.

rheumatism (rōō′mə-tĭz′əm)   A general, collective term used to describe individually or collectively any of a number of physical ailments resulting in stiffness, pain, or soreness of the joints and muscles. Rheumatism is not a specific disease, and is no longer in current medical usage.

rural (rōŏr′əl)   A term used to characterize people or life of or from the country.

sabotage (săb′ə-täzh′)   A destructive action taken by an enemy intended to force its opponent to surrender.

sanatorium (săn′ə-tôr′ē-əm, -t ōr′-) (also **sanitarium** [-târ′ē-əm])   Most commonly used to refer to a medical institution for the treatment of chronic diseases, mental disorders, or recuperation that requires medical attention.

sanctions (săngk′shəns)   In political terms, restrictions or prohibitions, usually economic, against dealings or interactions with other countries.

schism (sĭz′əm, sk ĭz′-)   A separation or discord.

scholarship (skŏl′ər-shĭp′)   A grant or gift that pays in part or in full for education costs.

secede (sĭ-sēd′)   To formally withdraw from a union or branch.

segregation (sĕg′rĭ-gā′shən)   To be separated, usually through force, from the mainstream for reasons of race or creed. The term is most often used to refer to the forced separation of blacks and whites, most notably in the southern United States.

segregationist (sĕg′rĭ-gā′shə-nĭst)   A person or political philosophy that believes in or advocates the principle of separation between races.

seminary (sĕm′ə-nĕr′ē)   A school with the focus of training religious leaders such as priests, ministers, or rabbis.

sentry (sĕn′trē)   A guard or soldier posted at a particular spot to prevent the passage of unauthorized persons.

separatist (sĕp′ər-ə-tĭst, s ĕp′rə-, s ĕp′ə-ră′-)   A term used to describe someone who advocates secession from a group or organization.

sexism (sĕk′sĭz′əm)   A term used to describe discrimination based on gender. The term most often refers to discrimination against women.

sharecropper (shâr′krŏp′ər)   A person who is placed in a position of servitude by which he or she provides labor for the landowner in return for a share of the profits of the merchandise, usually an agricultural crop. The landowner not only provides the land to be tended, but also the equipment, animals and seed, and housing to the sharecropper.

signatory (sĭg′nə-tôr′ē, -t ōr′ē)   A person or nation that has signed a particular agreement. Also used to refer to the condition of being bound by an agreement.

sit-in (sĭt-ĭn)   A nonviolent protest during which the protesters literally sit as a means of reaching their goal. By the protesters physically being in place, the normal process of events is interrupted, therefore creating the obstacle that in turn gets results.

slavery (slā′və-rē, sl āv′rē)   A social institution that is considered to be the most involuntary form of human servitude. The people, or slaves, are obtained by force, are property of an owner, and are subject to perform whatever work the owner demands.

socialism (sō′shə-lĭz′əm)   A governmental system that maintains the belief that all goods are owned equally and political power is shared by the whole community but controlled and administered by a strong central government.

sociology (sō′sē-ŏl′ə-jē, -sh ē-)   The science or study of human social relations or group life and interaction. It examines the ways in which social structures, institutions, and social problems influence society. It is considered one of the social sciences, along with such studies and sciences as psychology, economics, and anthropology.

sovereignty (sŏv′ər-ĭn-tē, s ŏv′rĭn-)   A supreme political power free from external control.

status quo (stă′təs kwō)   The state of affairs as they exist.

stereotype (stĕr′ē-ə-tīp′, stîr ′-)   A simplified or representative image of a type of person, place, or thing.

strike (strīk)   An organized work stoppage carried out by a group of employees, usually as a tactic to enforce demands or protest unfair labor conditions. Strikes are most frequently conducted by workers organized into trade unions, and are often used as a bargaining tool during contract negotiations.

subsistence (səb-sĭs′təns)   Most commonly used to refer to the level of living or survival that is barely sufficient to sustain life.

subversive (səb-vûr′sĭv, -z ĭv)   Policies or actions that are intended to undermine, or subvert, established systems. The term is most often used to refer to oppositional or confrontational political activity.

suffrage (sŭf′rĭj)   The right or privilege to vote.

suffragette (sŭf′rə-jĕt′)   A person who advocates the right of an individual to exercise his or her voting rights. The term is most often used to refer to those active or sympathetic during the drive to establish voting rights for women.

summa cum laude (so͞om′ə k o͞om lou ′də, -d ā, -d ē)   A Latin term, literally meaning with highest praise, of academic distinction, used to indicate the graduate with highest honors.

Sunni (so͞on′ē)   A branch of the Islamic religion, characterized by the acceptance of the first four caliphs, or Moslem political leaders, as the rightful successors of Mohammed.

superpower (sōo′pər-pou′ər)   The distinction given to the United States and the Soviet Union, during the Cold War period, signifying global dominance.

Supreme Court (soo-prēm′ kôrt)   One of the three branches of the United States government, charged with the upholding and interpretation of the laws and Constitution. It consists of nine justices who jointly review accepted cases, and render judgements on a majority basis.

syndicate (sĭn′dĭ-kĭt)   Literally meaning an organization brought together to do business, a common term for organized crime "families" or organizations.

taboo (tə-boo′, t ă-)   A type of social ban, often resulting from strong custom or religious practice.

temperance (tĕm′pər-əns, t ĕm′prəns)   A term used to refer to the abstinence from alcoholic beverages.

theology (thē-ŏl′ə-jē)   A discipline that attempts to express the content of a religious expression in words that are contained in faith.

thesis (thē′sĭs)   Most commonly used to refer to a scholarly paper or dissertation advancing or defending a particular point of view by means of arguments supported by research and argument. It is often among the requirements for an advanced degree.

totalitarian (tō-tăl′ĭ-târ′ē-ən)   A government based on the belief that political authority exercises complete and absolute control over all aspects of the citizens' lives.

transcendentalism (trăn′sĕn-dĕn′tl-ĭz′əm)   A belief or philosophy that asserts the existence of a higher spiritual reality apart from the physical world.

transracial (trăns rā′shəl)   A term usually associated with adoption, in which parents of one culture or race adopt a child from a different culture or race. In society, the children are often not accepted in the cultural circles of their parents due to their racial differences.

treason (trē′zən)   The violation of allegiance toward one's own country or ruler.

tuberculosis (too-bûr′kyə-lō′sĭs, ty oo-)   A infectious disease, characterized by the formation of small lumps within the body, most often the lungs.

tyrant (tī′rənt)   An absolute ruler. The term is most often used to refer to a cruel or oppressive dictator.

Underground Railroad   A network of antislavery northerners that illegally helped black southern slaves escape slavery and reach safety in free states and Canada. The refugees traveled from "station" to "station" (usually farms), aided by a "conductor" who helped them find safe places to hide during their journey.

underground (ŭn′dər-ground′)   Generally used to refer to a movement or organization that works secretly against the ruling government.

union (yoon′yən)   Also called a craft or trade union, an organization or association of workers established to improve or protect their working conditions.

United Negro College Fund   An organization established in 1944, made up of an alliance of forty-one black colleges, that raises all the funds for operating expenses including teachers' salaries, scholarships, and equipment. The organization was initially established to financially aid black institutions of higher learning during World War II, a time when wartime shortages had slowed contributions. Today, the United Negro College Fund remains the premier nongovernmental funding source for historically black colleges, providing an alternative education source for its students.

urban (ûr′bən)   A commonly used sociological classification for an area that refers to those characteristics associated with a city.

valedictorian (văl′ĭ-dĭk-tôr′ē-ən, -t ôr′-)   The term given to the student with the highest academic rank in the class. This person usually delivers the keynote student speech at graduation.

vocalist (vō′kə-lĭst)   A singer in a musical performance.

voluntarism (vŏl′ən-tə-rĭz′əm)   The belief that people should give of their time to public, or volunteer, work.

welfare (wĕl′fâr′)   A public assistance program providing at least a minimum amount of economic aid to individuals who earn less money than is needed to maintain an adequate standard of living.

Yiddish (yĭd′ĭsh)   A language, based on German, that was historically used by people of the Jewish faith who lived in central and eastern Europe.

Zionism (zī′ə-nĭz′əm)   A movement aimed at uniting the Jewish people of the exile and settling them in Palestine. Founded in the late 19th century by journalist Theodor Herzl, the organization eventually grew to settle the State of Israel in 1948. Their main goal of statehood was to defend and consolidate Israel and to justify its existence. In the 1970s and 1980s, Zionist aid was extended to Soviet Jews and today guarantees a Jewish nationality to any Jew in need of it.

Photo Credits

Photographs appearing in *Humanitarians and Reformers* are from the following sources:

Ralph Abernathy (page 1): CORBIS/Flip Schulke
Jane Addams (page 4): CORBIS/Bettman
Susan B. Anthony (page 6): Library of Congress
Aung San Suu Kyi (page 9): CORBIS/Alison Wright
James Baldwin (page 16): CORBIS/Bettmann
Mary McLeod Bethune (page 23): Library of Congress
Julian Bond (page 28): CORBIS
H. Rap Brown (page 34): CORBIS
John Brown (page 36): CORBIS/Bettmann
Stokely Carmichael (page 43): CORBIS/Flip Schulke
Andrew Carnegie (page 45): CORBIS/Bettmann
Jimmy Carter (page 46): Library of Congress
Carrie Chapman Catt (page 53): Library of Congress
César Chávez (page 57): CORBIS/Ted Streshinsky
Eldridge Cleaver (page 64): CORBIS/Bettmann
Bill Cosby (page 70): CORBIS
Angela Davis (page 78): CORBIS/Zajic Miroslav
John Dewey (page 81): CORBIS/Bettmann
Diana, Princess of Wales (page 83): CORBIS/Photo B.D.V.
Abigail Scott Duniway (page 93): Library of Congress
Marian Wright Edelman (page 97): CORBIS/Bettmann
Louis Farrakhan (page 101): CORBIS/Jacques M. Chenet
Betty Friedan (page 116): CORBIS/Shelley Gazin
William Lloyd Garrison (page 125): CORBIS/Bettmann
Mikhail Gorbachev (page 131): CORBIS/Bryn Colton; Assignments Photography
Helen Hunt Jackson (page 145): CORBIS/Bettmann
James Weldon Johnson (page 155): CORBIS
Martin Luther King Jr. (page 161): CORBIS/Bettmann
Seán MacBride (page 175): CORBIS/Bettmann
Malcolm X and Martin Luther King Jr. (page 178): CORBIS/Bettmann
Thurgood Marshall (page 187): CORBIS
Mother Teresa (page 201): CORBIS/Bettmann
Lucretia Mott (page 204): CORBIS/Bettmann
John Muir (page 208): Library of Congress
Alva Myrdal (page 211): CORBIS/Bettmann
Carry Nation (page 218): CORBIS/Bettmann
Paul Newman (page 219): CORBIS/Bettmann
Emmeline Pankhurst (page 229): CORBIS/Hulton Deutsch Collection
Alice Paul (page 234): Library of Congress
Wendell Phillips (page 241): CORBIS

Christopher Reeve (page 250): CORBIS/Wally McNamee
Eleanor Roosevelt (page 255): Library of Congress
Theodore Roosevelt (page 256): Library of Congress
Albert Schweitzer (page 271): CORBIS/Bettmann
Elizabeth Cady Stanton and Susan B. Anthony (page 277): Library of Congress
Mary Church Terrell (page 283): Library of Congress
Sojourner Truth (page 286): Library of Congress
Lech Wałesa (page 291): CORBIS/Peter Turnley
Booker T. Washington (page 296): CORBIS/Oscar White
Roy Wilkins (page 311): CORBIS
Victoria Woodhull (page 317): CORBIS/Bettmann
Raul Yzaguirre (page 325): National Council of La Raza

Article Sources

The following eighteen biographies in Macmillan Profiles: *Humanitarians and Reformers* were written exclusively for this volume:

Belo, Carlos, and José Ramos-Horta	Mark Grant
Diana, Princess of Wales	Deborah Savadge
Fisher, Mary	Deborah Savadge
Gorbachev, Mikhail	Isabel Keating
Hernández, Antonia	Karen H. Meyer
Huerta, Delores	Karen H. Meyer
Hume, John, and David Trimble	Mark Grant
Jingsheng, Wei	Karen H. Meyer
Mfume, Kweisi	Karen H. Meyer
Nader, Ralph	Karen H. Meyer
Newman, Paul	Jill Lectka
Parks, Rosa	Barbara Morrow
Reeve, Christopher	Deborah Savadge
Steinem, Gloria	Barbara Morrow
Stone, Lucy	Barbara Morrow
Williams, Jody	Mark Grant
Woodhull, Victoria	Barbara Morrow
Wu, Harry	Karen H. Meyer

The remaining biographies in Macmillan Profiles: *Humanitarians and Reformers* were extracted from the following Macmillan Library Reference publications:

Encyclopedia of Africa, Charles Scribner's Sons, 1998.
Encyclopedia of African American Culture and History, Macmillan Reference, 1996.
Encyclopedia of the American Presidency, Macmillan Reference, 1994.
Encyclopedia of American West, Macmillan Reference, 1996.
Encyclopedia of the American Presidency, Charles Scribner's Sons.
Encyclopedia of Latin American History and Culture, Charles Scribner's Sons, 1996.
Macmillan Profiles: Heroes and Pioneers, Macmillan Reference, 1998.
Macmillan Profiles: Latino Americans, Macmillan Reference, 1998.
Record of America: A Reference History of the United States, Charles Scribner's Sons, 1976.
They Made History: A Biographical Dictionary, Macmillan Reference, 1993.
The Nobel Peace Prize and the Laureates, G.K. Hall & Co., 1988.
The Presidents: A Reference History, Second Edition, Charles Scribner's Sons, 1996.

The following authors contributed articles to the sources listed above.

Article	Author
Abernathy, Ralph	Randolph Meade Walker
Arias Sánchez, Oscar	John Patrick Bell
Aung San Suu Kyi	Patricia Ohlenroth
Baker, Ella	Joanne Grant
Baldwin, James	Horace Porter
Bethune, Mary McLeod	Judith Weisenfeld
Bidwell, Annie Ellicott Kennedy	Margaret D. Jacobs
Biko, Stephen	John N. Jones
Bond, Julian	Evan Shore and Greg Robinson
Bonilla, Tony	Mark LaFlaur
Bonnin, Gertrude Simmons	Raymond Wilson
Brown, Hubert "H. Rap"	Mansur M. Naruddin and Robyn Spencer
Brown, John	Joseph Snell
Bunche, Ralph	C. Gerald Fraser
Carmichael, Stokely	William L. Van Deburg
Carter, Jimmy	Richard S. Kirkendall
Cassin, René-Samuel	Irwin Abrams
Chaney, James	Robyn Spencer
Chávez, César	Patricia Ohlenroth
Chavis, Benjamin Franklin, Jr.	Mansur M. Naruddin and Alexis Walker
Clark, Septima	Chana Kai Lee
Cleaver, Eldridge	Amritjit Singh
Corrigan, Mairead, and Betty Williams	Irwin Abrams
Cosby, Bill	Jannette L. Dates
Dalai Lama	Patricia Ohlenroth
Davis, Angela	Christine A. Lunardini
de Klerk , Frederik Willem	Denis Vener
Douglass, Frederick	Waldo E. Martin, Jr.
Du Bois, W. E. B.	Arnold Rampersad
Duniway, Abigail Scott	Lauren Kessler
Eastman, Charles Alexander	Raymond Wilson
Edelman, Marian Wright	Sabrina Fuchs
Farmer, James	Steven J. Leslie
Farrakhan, Louis	Lawrence H. Mamiya
Fletcher, Alice Cunningham	C. Elizabeth Raymond
Forman, James	Jeanne Theoharis
Forten, James	Evan A. Shore
Fortune, T. Thomas	Tami J. Friedman
García Robles, Alfonso	Irwin Abrams
Garvey, Marcus	Robert A. Hill
Hamer, Fannie Lou	Chana Kai Lee
Jackson, Helen Hunt	Valerie Sherer Mathes
Jackson, Jesse	Michael Eric Dyson
Johnson, James Weldon	George P. Cunningham
Jordan, Barbara	Christine A. Lunardini

King, Martin Luther, Jr.   Irwin Abrams
Lewis, John   Marshall Hyatt
Lutuli, Albert John   Irwin Abrams
MacBride, Seán   Irwin Abrams
Malcolm X   James H. Cone
Marshall, Thurgood   Randall Kennedy
Menchú-Tum, Rigoberta   Marilyn M. Moors
Mitchell, Clarence, Jr.   Greg Robinson
Montezuma, Carlos   R. David Edmunds
Moreno, Luisa   Vicki L. Ruiz
Moses, Robert P.   Marshall Hyatt
Mother Teresa   Patricia Ohlenroth
Muhammed, Elijah   Lawrence H. Mamiya
Muir, John   Patricia Hogan
Myrdal, Alva   Irwin Abrams
Nation, Carry Amelia Moore   David Dary
Newton, Huey   Robyn Spencer
Noel-Baker, Philip   Irwin Abrams
Pauling, Linus   Irwin Abrams
Pérez Esquivel, Adolfo   Margaret E. Crahan
Picotte, Susan LaFlesche   Peggy Pascoe
Purvis, Robert   Julie Winch
Randolph, A. Philip   Jervis Anderson
Rankin, Jeannette   Mary Murphy
Roosevelt, Eleanor   Elisabeth Israels Perry
Rustin, Bayard   Carol V. R. George
Sakharov, Andrei   Irwin Abrams
Schweitzer, Albert   Irwin Abrams
Seale, Bobby   Levi A. Nwachuku
Terrell, Mary Church   Quandra Prettyman
Tibbles, Susette LaFlesche   Peggy Pascoe
Truth, Sojourner   Margaret Washington
Tutu, Desmond   John W. De Gruchy
Wałesa, Lech   Irwin Abrams
Washington, Booker T.   Raymond W. Smock
Wells-Barnett, Ida B.   Margaret L. Dwight
White, Walter Francis   Denton L. Watson
Wiesel, Elie   Irwin Abrams
Wilkins, Roy   James A. Donaldson
Winnemucca, Sarah   Patricia Hogan
Young, Andrew   Christine A. Lunardini
Yzaguirre, Raul   Michael Levine

Index